Hirkani, a young working mother who scaled a mountain 300 years ago in order to breastfeed her baby, gets reincarnated as a doctor, veterinarian, dancer, lawyer, housekeeper, statistician, manager, caterer, WHO staff member, business director, and other professions. Impressive women from around the world surmount difficulties such as brief maternity leaves, long work hours, unsupportive colleagues, and more. This book is an inspiring lighthouse and a must read for all working mothers.

Prashant Gangal, MD
Pediatrician, India

One of the biggest barriers for women who want to breastfeed is work. The United States is a country with more than 50% of mothers with children under the age of one in the workforce. At the same time our society does little to promote what is medically proven to be the healthiest for both the mother and child—breastfeeding. This important book takes a look at what others are doing to confront this problem and promotes opportunities for women to continue to breastfeed after they return to work.

U.S. Congresswoman Carolyn B. Maloney (NY),
author of the Right to Breastfeed Act

These are the tales of mothers who recognize the importance of breastfeeding, and make it work…while they work! Like Hirkani, these mothers are driven to find ways around the barriers erected by society to discourage this most elemental of mother-child relationships. They are driven, and they are succeeding. This is an inspiring, important book that offers a hopeful look into the future of a new generation.

Ana June,
Book Editor, *Mothering* Magazine

HIRKANI'S DAUGHTERS is an empowering and heroic book that urges us to think beyond our own struggles, and gain wisdom and strength from mothers through history and around the globe. It is a thought-provoking, informative, and vibrantly human collection of stories that offer us perspective, hope, and inspiration.

Lu Hanessian,
Discovery Health Channel host and author of *Let the Baby Drive*

These stories of working, breastfeeding mothers around the world from all walks of life are inspirational. The stories provide joy, wisdom, and encouragement to all families who want to provide the gift of human milk to their babies. La Leche League has put together an outstanding mother-to-mother support resource.

Karen LeBan,
Executive Director, The CORE Group

With stories collected from women around the world, HIRKANI'S DAUGHTERS provides inspiration and practical ideas. It supports the unique mother/baby relationship in a world that often lacks appreciation of how a mother's decision to breastfeed her baby benefits us all.

Marian Tompson,
Co-Founder, La Leche League International

Hirkani's Daughters

Women Who Scale Modern Mountains to Combine Breastfeeding and Working

Compiled and edited by
Jennifer Bowen Hicks

La Leche League International
Schaumburg, Illinois

First printing, February, 2006

Library of Congress Catalogue Number 2005937918

ISBN 0-976869-2-3

Printed in the United States of America

Book and Cover Design by Paul Torgus

Credits on page 346

La Leche League International
1400 N. Meacham Road
Schaumburg IL 60173-4808 USA
www.lalecheleague.org

Contents

Foreword, Miriam Labbok MD, MPH — XII
Foreword, Dr. Judith Galtry — XV
Foreword, Marta Trejos & Sarah Amin — XVIII
Introduction, Jennifer Bowen Hicks — XXI
Acknowledgements — XXV
Hirkani's Story — XXIX

PART ONE | North America

Schooling the Faculty
Nicole Austin Daleiseo, Teacher, California, USA — 3

A Pumping Queen
Mariah Boone, Social Worker, Texas, USA — 7

A Funny Thing Happened...
Tricia Shore, Stand-Up Comedian, California, USA — 12

Dr. Mom, Nursing Twins
Carrie McAdams, Post Doctoral Fellow, Massachusetts, USA — 16

The Diary of My Return to Work
Rebecca Novak Tibbitt, Senior Manager, Connecticut, USA — 21

Quiet Detours
Sophie Lesiege, Home Daycare Provider, Quebec, Canada — 28

Co-Workers Become My Support System
Judy Coughenour, Information Technology, Pennsylvania, USA — 30

Redefining Success
Ruth Tincoff, Research Associate, Massachusetts, USA — 34

Moving Across the Atlantic
Nicola Evans, Scientist, Illinois, USA — 38

No Need to Worry After All
Thia Tomasich, Dispatcher, Missouri, USA — 41

New Ways of Seeing the World
Laura Barbas-Rhoden, Professor, North Carolina, USA — 43

Averting Disaster
Cynthia Spidell, Executive Analyst, Florida, USA — 45

Bartering Allows Me to Be at Home
Terry Magalhaes, Child Care Provider, Iowa, USA — 49

Breastfeeding Road Warrior
Diane Cloutier, Business Director, Florida, USA — 53

Breastfeeding on Active Duty
Robin Roche Paull, Aircraft Mechanic, US Navy, California, USA 57

An African Lesson in Motherhood
Mona Nyandoro, Peace Corps Recruiter, California, USA 60

Finding Value in Mothering
Kymberlie Stefanski, Information Technology, Illinois, USA 62

Working the Nightshift, Nursing the Dayshift
Melissa Hulse, Pharmacist, Kansas, USA 66

Working Mother, Disabled Father, Breastfed Children
Mary Joan Jordan Vacarella, Family Lumber Business, Georgia, USA 68

Breastfeeding My Special Needs Child
Felicia Fogal, Marketing Director, Texas, USA 73

Surrendering One Dream Job for Another
Lisa Kopecky, Registered Dietitian, Nebraska, USA 76

Sudden Illness
Roswita Dressler, Teacher, British Columbia, Canada 82

Nothing but Mother's Milk
Kim Johnson, Assistant Food Service Manager, Missouri, USA 88

Driven from the Pump
Raquel Phillips, Marketing Assistant, Washington, DC, USA 91

Fighting for My Son
Tammy Miner, Casino Dealer, Connecticut, USA 93

On Tour with My Son
Carrie Nimmo, Traveling Performer, British Columbia, Canada 96

PART TWO | LATIN AMERICA

Animal Care—A Family Affair
Ada Frias de Torres, Veterinarian, Dominican Republic 101

United for a Better Life
Angela Bailon, Computer Specialist, Guatemala 103

Teaching Life Lessons
Viana Maza, Professor of Psychology, Guatemala 105

The Wisdom of Nature
Guadalupe Vega, Quality Engineer, Mexico 109

A Bicycle Ride Away
Veronica Garea, Physicist, Argentina 112

Mountain Mothering
Victoria Escobar, Agronomist, Bolivia 115

Things I Never Thought I Would Do...
Elizabeth Power, Foreign Service Officer, Mexico 118

Jungle Love
Raquel Sigüenza de Micheo, Field Biologist, Guatemala 125

A Return to My Milk
Margarita Santiago Ramirez, Live-In Maid, Mexico 128

Grounded in More Ways Than One
Ana Raquel Bueno Moraes Ribeiro,
Organizational Development Consultant, Brazil 130

Making Space for My Baby
Silvia Valderrama Sanchez,
Social Development Consultant, Peru 132

PART THREE | EUROPE

The Best of Both Worlds
Sue Low, Graphic Designer, United Kingdom 139

Museum-Bound Babies
Anne Betting, Professor, France 142

My New Swiss "Entitlement"
Linda Hooper, Statistician, Switzerland 147

Working a 24-Hour Shift
Titia Vanderwerf, Social Worker, Holland 151

The Politics of Life
Karmen Mlinar, Electrotechnical Engineer, Slovenia 153

A Father's Foresight
Marta Marina González, Music Teacher, Spain 158

Thriving on Mummy's Milk
Lisa Marrett, Mental Health Nurse, England 161

A Month-Long Absence Quickly Erased
Tamar Kaloiani, Cytologist, Georgia 165

A Home Office Helps
Julia Zantke, Financial Officer, Germany 168

Nature's Law
Monica Tornadijo Sabate, Lawyer/Publisher, Spain 171

Bulgarian Baby Boy
Silviya Zaharieva Andreeva, Operations Manager, Bulgaria 173

Breastfeeding Is Not a Barrier to My Business
Lucy Cokes, Business Owner, England 178

Nam-Nam in the Netherlands
Tanja Schulin, Physician, Netherlands 181

Perfect Nutrition in Any Language
Tatyana Zorina, Interpreter, Russia 183

Easing the Transition
Judith Montgomery-Watson, Wildlife Site Manager, Northern Ireland 185

Open Arms, Uncompromising Ideals
Catherine Mulholland, Senior Technical Officer, France 188

PART FOUR | AFRICA, MIDDLE EAST

Supporting My Extended Family
Anita Coles, International Development Relief Worker, Pakistan 197

Third Son's a Charm
Ghada Sayed, Pediatrician, Egypt 201

Hand-Expression Works
Tsviya Shir, Attorney, Israel 203

Going to "All That Trouble" for My Son
Avital Mulay, Computer Programmer, Israel 206

The Other Side of the Wall
Jennifer Moorehead, Documentation Manager, West Bank 208

Silencing the Cacophony of Advice
Victoria Kisanga, Caterer, Tanzania 210

The Nanny from Heaven
Ena du Plessis, Attorney, South Africa 213

PART FIVE | ASIA, AUSTRALIA, NEW ZEALAND

Jungle Expression
Utkarsh Naik, Actress, India 219

Exclusive Breastfeeding, a Family Effort
Chim Sophorn, Housekeeper, Cambodia 222

College, Career, and Chemotherapy
Melissa Reyes, Professor, Philippines 224

The Sound of Mother's Milk
Yuriko Inukai, IT Engineer, Japan 230

Support from Around the World
Azleena bt Wan Mohamad, Environmental Control Officer, Malaysia 232

My Greatest Accomplishment
Eunie 'Lou, Accountant, Mongolia 235

Changing Society's Collective Consciousness
Crystal Hui Man Lai, Preschool Director, Taiwan 239

Finding the Right Child Care Centre
Midori Fujita, District Nurse, Japan 243

Searching for Balance
Shubhada Chaukar, Newspaper Editor, India 245

The Value of a Happy Employee
Carolyn Rushworth, Management Accountant, Australia 248

Early Childhood Policies
Sarah E. Farquhar, Early Childhood Development Specialist, New Zealand 252

PART SIX | Breastfeeding-Friendly Employers

Pioneering a Better Workplace 259

Award-Winning Workplace—Home to Healthy Families
SAS Corporation, North Carolina, USA 263

A Prescription for Happier, Healthier Working Mothers
Mayo Clinic, Minnesota, USA 268

Mothering Mamas Enjoy a Progressive, Productive Workplace
Mothering Magazine, New Mexico. USA 271

Cost Savings Promote Health
CIGNA Corporation, Pennsylvania, USA 275

Employing Women, Improving Lives
UPAVIM, Guatemala 279

Family-Owned Company with Family-Focused Benefits
Carlson Companies, Minnesota, USA 282

A Picture of Health and Happiness
Eastman Kodak, New York, USA 285

PART SEVEN | WHAT WORKING MOTHERS NEED TO KNOW

Expressing Milk 291
Breastfeeding-Friendly Child Care 299
Taking Baby to Work 307
Cosleeping and Working Mothers 311
Taking Action 313
Helpful Resources 320

APPENDIX

Mother-to Mother 325
Contributors to This Book 339
Credits 345
Afterword 346
Index 348
About La Leche League 352

Foreword

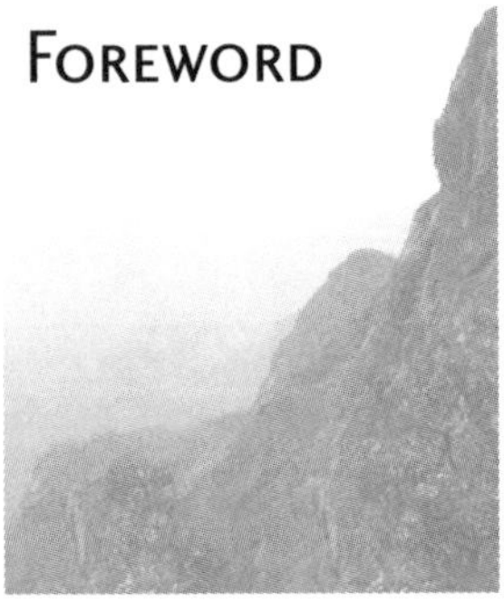

Optimal Infant Feeding

UNICEF, and its sister organization WHO, have long supported breastfeeding, and were prime organizations in support of the International Code of Marketing of Breast Milk Substitutes and related activities. We reconfirm our dedication to infant and young child feeding in our support of the 2002 Global Strategy for Infant and Young Child Feeding.

With the development of the Golden Bow symbol in concert with the launching of the Global Strategy, we reconfirm that early and exclusive breastfeeding is the "gold standard" for infant feeding in the early months, along with continued breastfeeding with complementary feeding and child spacing for optimal mother and child health. This optimal approach to infant feeding is beneficial when compared to any other pattern of feeding. Giving birth is, indeed, one of life's most important miracles, and breastfeeding is the continued miracle that only a mother can provide. The fact that scientific findings on the patterns, components, and effects of breastfeeding and human milk feeding seem to increase on nearly a daily basis simply reconfirms the miraculous nature of breastfeeding.

For optimal feeding to be considered normative behavior we must shift from discussing breastfeeding as a benefit and change to the recognition that lack of breastfeeding is a risk behavior. Babies who are not breastfed are more likely to develop allergies, have lower IQs, die of SIDS, be obese as children and as adults, and have risk factors for cardiac disease in later life. They will have an increased risk of certain cancers, as will their mothers who did not breastfeed. Perhaps, most importantly, these non-breastfed babies will have deficient immune systems, rendering them more susceptible to a wide variety of diseases and less able to fight the infectious diseases that they do experience.

Early and exclusive breastfeeding for six months carries even more protection than mixed feeding. Low birth weight babies may well have a better chance of catching up if exclusively breastfed, and breastfed children of HIV-positive mothers appear to have a lower likelihood of becoming infected. In at least one study, babies breastfed immediately after delivery are less likely to be deserted, and many studies show that early breastfeeding is associated with increased breastfeeding success. Based on many of these findings, every effort has been made to base the new growth charts under development by WHO on the growth of optimally fed children across the globe.

Lack of exclusive breastfeeding has been shown to be a drain on family resources, not only for paying the costs of the artificial milk substitutes and their preparation and storage, but also for the extra cost of illness and the lost wages due to absences associated with child illness. Some countries spend considerable international currency on the importation of the feeding substitutes, and hospitals can measure the costs associated with lack of breastfeeding. When frequent breastfeeding is practiced, exclusive breastfeeding and amenorrhea serve as markers of reduced fertility. Based on this physiology, if a mother chooses, she may use the Lactational Amenorrhea Method for reliable contraception.

Today, we are seeing increased population impacts of natural and manmade emergencies and other more chronic disasters. In these circumstances, breastfeeding is an act of hope and survival. It is always available, always the right temperature, and continues to be of adequate composition even when food or water for the mother may be temporarily suboptimal. With the increased rates of infections in these settings, exclusive breastfeeding is even more essential for child health and survival. It is essential that breastfeeding be supported from the earliest days in emergencies, to avoid the potential for greater health and relactation problems in later days and weeks.

There are two common obstacles to the choice and success of breastfeeding: workplace/societal pressures and marketing pressures.

Mothers have always worked, and breastfeeding was continued with mother's work since the beginning of the human race. Today, however, the workplace and some social settings can create obstacles to normal, healthy breastfeeding. For some workers, human milk feeding can be continued by expression and storage of milk, while others adopt a "reverse feeding" behavior, wherein the baby is breastfed when the mother is present, generally at night.

In many settings, the pressures of aggressive marketing lead women, and health care practitioners, to believe that there is little difference between breastfeeding and formula feeding. Advertising can be very powerful, especially in countries where a market economy has welcomed sophisticated advertising as an essential element of the marketplace. Newly emerging and other "naïve" markets are particularly vulnerable, and it is often in these settings that feeding human milk substitutes carries the highest risk.

Every book, every movie or TV show, every communication with honest, factual information on breastfeeding is a welcome alternative to the ads and marketing for formula brands that fill our magazines, airwaves, and far too many hospital hallways worldwide. My hope is that this book will present alternative viewpoints to this marketing, featuring the realities of breastfeeding. Such information can only help to enable mothers, families, and society to choose optimal infant and young child feeding as the normative behavior and the only logical option for their children, as well as for our future.

Miriam H. Labbok, MD, MPH, IBCLC
Senior Advisor, Infant & Young Child Feeding and Care,
UNICEF (2001-2005)
Professor of the Practice of Public Health in the
Department of Maternal and Child Health, University of
North Carolina/Chapel Hill

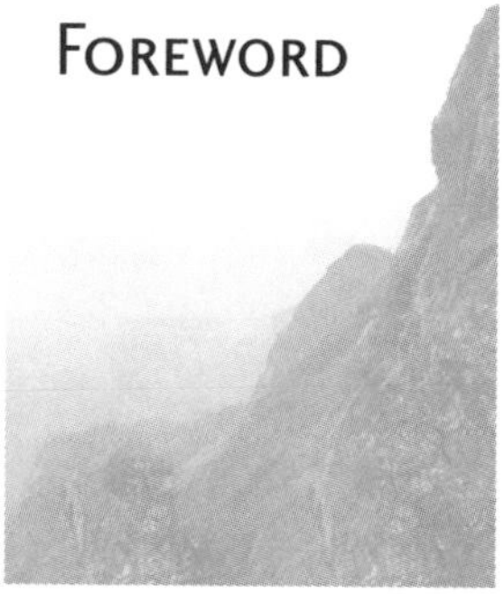

Women and Work: A Global Overview

Women have always worked. This includes income-generating activities in the recognized labour market, work in the informal sector, such as family farms and market stalls, and unpaid services in the home and community. Recent decades have nevertheless seen an unprecedented worldwide increase in women's paid work. The International Labour Organization notes that women now comprise an increasing share of the world's paid labour force, at least one-third in all regions except northern Africa and western Asia.

One of the most significant changes has been the increase in paid work–much of it outside the home–among women in their childbearing years. The USA is an example of change over time in a high-income country where the economic activity rate for women aged 25 to 29 increased from around 45 percent in the 1970s to around 80 percent at the turn of the 21st century. By contrast, relatively poor Sudan has seen women's economic activity rise from around 20 percent in the early 1970s to around 40 percent in the late 1990s.

While for most industrialized countries the economic activity rates of women in the 20 to 29 year age group is between 60 and 80 percent, there is a cluster of countries, including Canada, Denmark,

Norway, and Singapore, where the figure is around 80 percent or higher. In contrast, there are a number of countries that still have relatively low rates of women working in the officially recognized formal economy, e.g., Costa Rica (46), Mexico (47), Oman (27), Pakistan (18), and Sri Lanka (49).

Although subject to regional variations, these trends have been driven by a variety of factors, including reliance among more households on two incomes, with women often earning the higher income; an increase in both divorce and male unemployment; delayed fertility; expansion of the service sector; and the increasing "professionalization" of unpaid work. In both medium- and high-income countries, there has also been an increase in female-headed households, which is often associated with sole-earner status.

The picture is even more complex. While some of women's work is paid, recognized, counted, and therefore protected by labour contracts and legislation, women continue to be over-represented in the often unregulated, informal economy. For many women this increase in paid work has not been accompanied by a decrease in unpaid household work and the nurturing tasks of child-rearing. As a result many mothers worldwide bear the often cited "double burden" of paid and unpaid work.

However, unlike most other unpaid work, breastfeeding can be undertaken only by women. In low-income economies, women have traditionally worked in the fields and the marketplace while simultaneously caring for and breastfeeding their offspring. While this presents its own set of challenges, it has been an accepted feature of life for generations in many communities, with family support systems often in place to facilitate it. By contrast, one of the most significant contemporary challenges to the integration of women's economic activity and family responsibilities, including breastfeeding, has been the increased separation of working mothers and their children.

Despite some common features, even among high-income countries there is a great variation in maternal working patterns. There is a range of influences, including social norms and support systems resulting in different models of maternity/parental leave and child care policy. For instance, in the USA, where there is no federal provision for paid family or medical leave, women tend to resume full-time employment soon after childbirth. In contrast, in Sweden (which is generally seen as having high levels of social support for breastfeeding), most mothers take advantage of generous paid parental leave before returning to work at the time their infants qualify for subsidized child care around

12 to 18 months. Meanwhile, in Ireland, although women have traditionally left the workforce on the birth of a child, this is rapidly changing. New Zealand women tend to take several months off work following childbirth, usually returning on a part-time basis. By contrast, in many low- and middle-income countries, employers subsidize maternity leave, often resulting in its not being extended to those most in need.

For all these reasons, the integration of breastfeeding with other kinds of work requires both the strengthening of existing legislation and the development of new policies and actions to protect breastfeeding among working women. Also needed are a range of co-ordinated, multi-pronged international and national efforts, by both governments and non-governmental organizations that focus on women, children, health, employment, and human rights.

Dr. Judith Galtry
Researcher and Author
New Zealand

Foreword

Women Work and Breastfeed in Gendered Environments

WABA applauds La Leche League International for producing a book on women, breastfeeding, and work. It recognizes that all women work, whether in paid or unpaid work, and that breastfeeding is a valuable part of women's reproductive work and a huge contribution to society's welfare.

Women work and breastfeed in gendered environments. What does this mean? Whether at the workplace, in the community, or at home, these spaces are most of the time organized according to patriarchal principles, where men are generally in control of decisions and where the social system prioritizes and benefits men over women. In other words, women live and exist in conditions of gender inequality, without equal opportunities, and these conditions affect women's infant feeding decisions and practices.

The issue of work and breastfeeding provides one of the most interesting areas for gender analysis. Women have to make choices every day, some more difficult than others. The decision to breastfeed or not, especially when returning to work, is a major one and is influenced by a host of factors: conditions at work, national laws and practices on maternity benefits, family support, a woman's personal knowledge and experience about breastfeeding, her life and career values, her socio-economic conditions, her health, self-esteem, and confidence as well as how empowered she feels.

At the workplace, power imbalances between employers and employees, including gender differences, affect a woman's ability to breastfeed and work. For instance, if many supervisors are men, those in a position of power are less likely to understand and empathize with a working woman's need to pump or bring her baby to work. Consequently, gender bias and discrimination by colleagues can also negatively affect women's confidence in breastfeeding. Legal systems and policies, such as maternity protection laws, may or may not be supportive of women, and thus can create a gender-bias against women. Social and cultural norms that value male over female, and that do not value the reproductive work done by mothers, force women to choose between their careers and motherhood. Every woman has the right to do both if she chooses to. Society has the responsibility of enabling and supporting her decision. Women should not have to choose between a fulfilling career and mothering children. Child care and breastfeeding as part of women's reproductive work need to be valued—socially, economically, and culturally—and supported by society. Breastfeeding particularly should be recognized as a woman's right and entitlement, and not her duty. Maternity protection is a social responsibility. Breastfeeding and working out of the home should be made compatible.

Gender inequities and unequal power relations at home also affect women's health and well-being and, consequently, their breastfeeding outcomes. Women in many societies have low social status with respect to men and other family members, particularly their partners, their fathers and mothers-in-laws in some cultures, or even brothers in other cultures. As a result, many face violence within their homes. How can we expect breastfeeding to be successful in oppressive situations? Poor women are further challenged by insufficient food, malnutrition, poor health, illiteracy, overwork, stress, and other debilitating conditions. Many women, especially those in marginalized situations, are forced to leave the home to earn money for their basic survival and livelihood, and as such, are often not able to breastfeed. These women need strong legal, social, cultural, and community support measures so that their babies can continue to receive the best possible nutrition and women can be assured of sufficient help and protection from society for their own well-being.

In fact, a gender perspective requires that women's health and nutritional needs are also secured. Breastfeeding advocacy must appreciate and, where possible, address women's needs especially in poor socio-economic and health conditions. It should also call for the active involvement of men as equal partners in nurturing children and sharing responsibility in domestic work, thus providing breastfeeding support.

HIRKANI'S DAUGHTERS is a celebration of the achievements of women from all walks of life who have chosen to breastfeed while working, and made enormous sacrifices in order to succeed. WABA salutes these women!

We hope that, as breastfeeding advocates, we will continue to strengthen support systems for all women, and simultaneously support efforts of other movements, particularly the women's movement, to work toward gender equality worldwide so that breastfeeding can become a positive experience for every woman. An empowered woman has a greater chance of experiencing successful breastfeeding.

Marta Trejos, Costa Rica and Sarah Amin, Malaysia
WABA Gender Working Group

Introduction

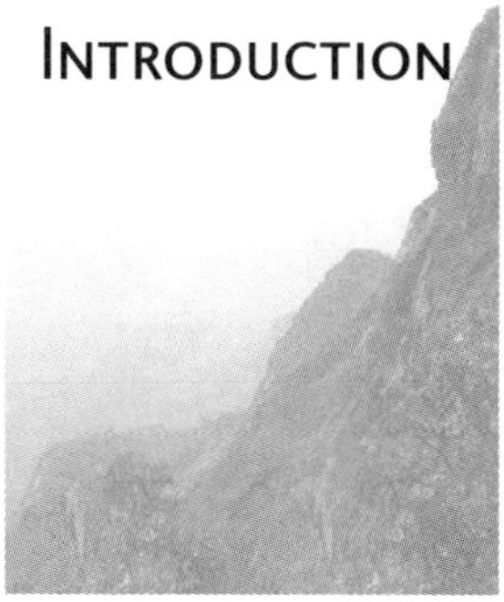

As an editor, my job was to help shape this book. As it turns out, this book has shaped me.

Hirkani's Daughters began to germinate when I was pregnant with my first son. As my belly ballooned, so did the book. I was in graduate school studying Journalism and Global Health when I contacted Rebecca Magalhães, from La Leche League International. Rebecca, a source of giving, warmth, and intelligence, had always dreamed of an anthology of breastfeeding mothers from around the world. Having worked for UNICEF, the Peace Corps, and LLLI, she knew the universalities breastfeeding mothers shared whether in Chicago or Colombia. She also knew their determination. It took little time before I saw this, too. On first visiting the LLLI office, I saw babies and toddlers playing beside their working mothers. I took note. Over five years, I worked off and on with this book in addition to other part-time commitments of teaching, writing, and editing. I breastfed one, then another son through it all and have, like so many women, felt a complicated spectrum of emotions. And like many others, I have walked tentatively across that proverbial "balance beam," trying not to tip too far in either direction. I eventually began working exclusively from home, where I remain.

When I am working from my home office, the perfect days are bliss. On those days, I feel smart and productive. But let's be honest—perfect days are rare. There are bad days. I have a deadline, a crying child who refuses to take a nap, and I accomplish very little. I feel frustrated and incompetent and I want to throw a tantrum like the ones I discourage my five-year-old from having. Like life, most days are a steady mix of both. In the end, I am exceptionally proud to be walking that balance beam, even with the occasional falls. I am not alone. By 2010, it is predicted that 80 percent of women in industrialized nations, and 70 percent of women globally, will be working. As mothers and employed women, our need for good balance is not going to change. The women in this book are no exception. Their countries and their jobs are as diverse as their ideas about breastfeeding and working. While they do not have all the answers, they offer many ideas and much inspiration.

The women who contributed stories for this book, featured or not, are a strong, inspiring, creative lot and not a day passed during the making of this book that I did not feel moved and awed by something they had done. Melissa Reyes of the Philippines breastfed her fourth son with the one breast she had left after chemotherapy and a mastectomy. Carrie Nimmo, a Canadian performer, dances around the world taking her son along, breastfeeding, and enriching him in the process. Jennifer Moorehead, the sole provider for her family, drives through an opening in a separation wall in the West Bank every day, taking her child to work so as not to be kept apart if the Wall should ever be completely closed. Nicola Evans from England found a job in the US that allowed her to breastfeed easily so she and her family moved across the Atlantic. Vedevatti Habu from India remembers nursing her daughter in between the dusty shelves of the library where she worked. Claudia Ocampo from Mexico walks to work, walks home to nurse during her lunch break, walks back to work, and then home again at the end of the day. She walks over two hours roundtrip to support her daughter financially, physically, and emotionally. This little baby, without a doubt, will someday go to great lengths for her daughters, too.

Many more stories, perhaps less dramatic but equally touching and inspiring, speak to the daily commitment of these breastfeeding, working mothers. They have each, in their own way, lived a life that is making the world a better place through the effort they are making for their children. Countless women have switched their jobs, quit their jobs, changed their employers' minds, taken their children to work, enlisted support, driven more, walked more, pumped, hurried up, slowed down, cried, and smiled for much the same reasons—their growing children. Those same children who will someday themselves be the teachers, leaders, artists, and parents of the world will do the same.

And the beat goes on.

These stories resonate with people. The universalities will be as touching as the differences are surprising. They were for me, anyway, and I read hundreds of them. After four months, stories from over 35 countries had arrived by email, fax, and snail mail; it was hard not to notice some undeniable commonalities. First, it was clear that few mothers talk about their children without starting at the Birth. Of course, for all of us mothers, this moment marks not only the arrival of our child, but the dawn of our role as Mother—a position from which we never resign. It is a natural, irresistible beginning. From there, many women energetically spoke of their child's attributes: their son's shiny black curls, their daughter's chubby hand, the joyful look of a baby nursing to sleep. In the way parents will do, they delighted in the opportunity to share their child's very existence and in the process often failed to address their jobs. While I did have to follow up a good many times to ask, "What do you do to earn income?" I never once had to say, "Can you tell me more about your child?"

And there may be no thing more universal to working, breastfeeding mothers than the comfort of reuniting with their child at day's end, especially through the connection breastfeeding provides. As a former breastfeeding mother myself, each and every homecoming story (and there were many), whether from Europe, Asia, or Africa, was familiar and moving. I vividly remember reading a story from Malaysia, followed by stories from Bolivia and the USA, where all three mothers described the joy and relief they felt at seeing, holding, and nursing their eager babies and knowing that any trouble they had endured to maintain a breastfeeding relationship while working was worth it for this moment.

Finally, there is this great shared reality: women are not doing it alone. Initially this book was going to have a section honoring the people who have provided support for these working, nursing mothers. As it turns out, it is hard to miss them, for the supporters are such a critical part of every story that without them, the stories might not exist. Fathers, grandparents, co-workers, siblings, and friends are helping.

Judy Coughenor shows us, as the first breastfeeding mother in her workplace, that co-workers can be supportive if given the chance. Meanwhile, her husband is home with their son, doing all that he can to support their family in his role as "stay-at-home dad." Thia Thomasich would have had to find another job and drop out of college if not for her employer's kind reassurance that she could bring her four-week-old baby with her to work. Berit Lewis, single and in a foreign land, had a dear friend at her side the night of her son's birth, attaching the baby to the nipple every half hour, getting that breastfeeding relationship started before work even became an issue. Chim Sophorn from Cambodia would not have had a job to return to if it had not been for family members who took on her job as a housekeeper, allowing her a maternity leave. And the grandmothers! Sylvia Sanchez Valderrama's mother and mother-in-law often accompany her on her work-related travels so that her baby can be there, and be fed her mother's milk. We see countless giving women, caring for their children's children with love and confidence, making "grandmother" the safe place while mother is at work. The support is dizzying. Husbands wash pumps, drive babies to mother's work, pack lunches, and pat backs. Co-workers (some of them) reschedule meetings, share locked-doors, and even create and decorate lactation rooms to help mothers feel comfortable. And more often than one would expect (but not as often as one would like), employers have said, "You do what needs to be done."

La Leche League, as an organization, embodies this very idea through its mother-to-mother support network, but also through its intense talent for grass roots activism. No sooner did we discern a need for this book than the request was sent through an extensive web of helping hands across the world. Like-minded friends, Leaders, members, and organizations quickly and brilliantly answered our call to action. WABA, UNICEF, WHO, IBFAN, and many, many individuals around the world spread word of this book to friends, family, and colleagues. From worldwide list-serves, to a bulletin board in Malaysia or a newspaper article in Mumbai, breastfeeding and child advocates around the world linked arms and moved quickly to make this project happen. This groundswell of support is awe-inspiring. It reinforces the importance of community and of cooperation. The collaboration it took to pull this book together, on a large scale, echoes the individual instances of help seen in each and every story between its covers.

Mothers and fathers, as you open the pages of this book, you may not agree with every parenting decision you see. Take a tip here and there, a dose of inspiration, and by all means some affirmation that combining breastfeeding with work is something that can be done. Reflect on Hirkani, the milkmaid from India. One can imagine the words echoing in her mind some four hundred years ago might have been the very words of Kaylene Proctor, a working mother today in the USA, who said, "Would I breastfeed all over again? Even with working? For this or another baby? In that first blessed heartbeat, you better believe I would."

Acknowledgements

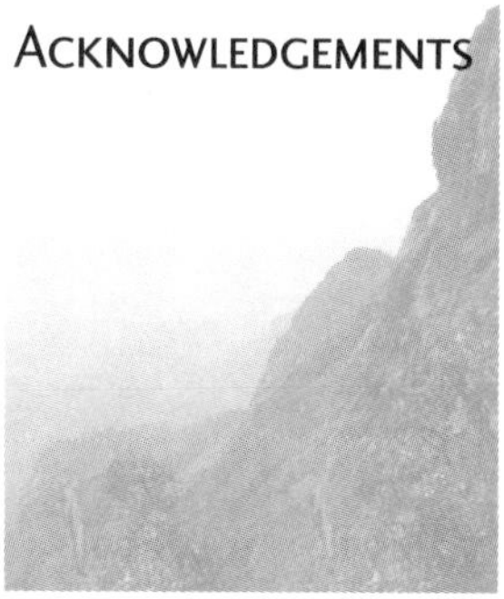

Hirkani's Daughters has truly been a worldwide effort with hundreds of people lending their expertise and time. For any who helped but are not mentioned, we thank you sincerely.

Countless numbers of people gathered and submitted stories, corresponded on behalf of breastfeeding mothers, and shared our request for stories with the world.

For Maya Sartania, Yulia Boyarkina, Iona Macnab, Melanie Wilson, Hannah Katsman, Pauline Kisanga, Paulina Allen de Smith, Kimberly Chadwick, Dr. Caroline Hilari, Priscilla Stothers, and Yanet Olivares de Saiz, and so many others around the world, this book is global because of your help.

In addition to LLL Leaders from different parts of the world, others disseminated the call for stories and provided us with important statistics for their regions. Thank you to Naomi Cassir from the International Labor Organization, Miriam Labbok from UNICEF, Sarah Amin and Anwar Fazal from WABA, Marta Trejos from Costa Rica, and Judith Galtry from New Zealand. By sharing your expertise and experience, you have all enhanced this book.

The women who contributed their personal stories have my gratitude and respect. Their willingness to talk about their fears, failings, vulnerabilities, and joys are what made this project such an intimate and special journey. I had the great good fortune of making friends around the world with smart, open, and intensely caring women. Your voices will inspire women everywhere.

Because of the global focus of the book, teams of translators were necessary. The initial call for stories was translated into several languages. Once stories arrived, many had to be translated into English so they could be reviewed. It was a taxing process, making all of the world's voices speak in one language. Our amazing translators did not hesitate to take on the work. I am so grateful for all of your talent and generosity. Thanks also to Melanie Laverman and Alicia Bartz, two former breastfeeding, working mothers who happen to be great writers. Your generosity is touching. Jennifer Esperanza, your photography is as classy as your willingness to share it. Thank you for the extra effort.

Thanks also to our featured businesses for sharing their data, employees, and photographers. I would especially like to thank Ana June at *Mothering* Magazine for going beyond the call of duty to rescue photographs and more.

It is with great enthusiasm that I thank Prashant Gangal, MD. Dr. Gangal introduced us all to Hirkani, whom we instantly loved. From his home in India, he was photographer, story solicitor, and front-row supporter. Dr. Gangal, your enthusiasm for this project kept us all upbeat and excited.

In addition, Natalia Smith Allen has been an enormous contributor. Never have I seen a more congenial, reliable jack-of-all-trades: translator, reviewer, fundraiser, and data collector. Natalia, your intelligence and vigor have been a blessing; thank you for all you have done since the book's infancy.

Thanks to my Master's committee from the University of Iowa: Dr. Claibourne Dungy, Dan Berkowitz, and especially Steve Bloom, an advisor who gave me both freedom and focus.

Thanks to the early believers who offered funds to this effort: Paulina Smith, Vania Smith, Natalia Smith, Land's End, Eastman Kodak, Judith Galtry, and Cynthia Killoran.

I offer a deep bow to our expert panel of reviewers: Chris Mulford, Natalia Smith Allen, Maryanne Stone Jiménez, Judy Torgus, and Rebecca Magalhães. Self-described as a "bleary-eyed" crew, this group of dedicated readers pored over heaping piles of stories and helped to pluck and prune the selection into a diverse and glorious garden. In addition, each of them, experts in their own fields, opened their emails, phone lines, and empathy to any issues that I needed help with. It was an honor to work with each and every one of you.

Thanks to Paul Torgus, a graphic designer who guides his mouse with both sensibility and creativity.

Judy Torgus, thank you for extending a touching trust, an impeccable eye, and years of experience to my work.

Thanks also to Sharon Barsotti, Jennifer Hopkin, Michaelene Gerster Trocola and all of the dedicated LLLI staff.

The stories in this book prove that family support is crucial to success. My story is no exception. My husband, Bill, made my own mountain easy to scale by having only one of three responses to life: "Yep," "Sure," and "Why not?" Bill, thank you for treating this as a family project. I couldn't have done this without "borrowing" a year's worth of your free time.

Elliot, my oldest son, you made this job rarely feel like work, especially when you were reading stories with me and offering editing suggestions that made me laugh.

Oliver, my second son, thank you for playing cars while I worked, and for occasionally reminding me to, "Stop working, Mama." Climbing through life with both of you is an exhilarating exercise that leaves me breathless and grateful every day.

Finally, this book exists because of Rebecca Magalhães. Not only was Hirkani's Daughters her "brainchild," but her optimism and insistence are what brought it to life. She warmly welcomed me into the plan with a trusting generosity that humbles me. In addition to being the dreamer of all things great, Rebecca is a first-rate collaborator. It is because of her that the book represents mothers from six continents, in large cities and tiny towns. Rebecca, creating this book has been a deeply rewarding, unbelievably thrilling experience. Thank you for allowing me to be a part of your dream.

Hirkani's Story

Hirkani: Ordinary Milkmaid, Extraordinary Mother

The title of this book, Hirkani's Daughters, was inspired by an ancient tale from India. Hirkani, woman, mother, and milkmaid lived in the Indian mountain ranges of Western Ghats during the 1600s. Though her story took place over four hundred years ago, Hirkani is not unlike women of today in that she embodies the same eternal mothering instinct to overcome odds for her children. It is debated whether Hirkani was real or legend. One thing is certain; her mothering instinct is real, it is biological, and most certainly, it is universal.

Hirkani's story happens during a time in Indian history when the mighty leader King Shivaji ruled from his capital on high. Within the walls of King Shivaji's royal fort began the events that place Hirkani at the heart of this book. Though she is famous in India, much of the world has never met this heroine. It is time others learn of this maternal legend who is known in her native land as a "jewel of the mountains." Here is Hirkani's story as told to us by Indian pediatrician, Dr. Prashant Gangal.

Hirkani was a milkmaid who lived in a small village at the foot of Raigad with her husband and their baby. She and her husband had a few cattle and earned money by selling the cows' milk. Her story begins during a full moon in the Hindu month of "Ashwin," a time called, "Kojagiri Poornima." This was a time for joyous celebrations and rejoicing as farmers had finally finished harvesting their crops. Naturally, the mood was upbeat during this time of plenty, especially at King Shivaji's fort. The grand occasion demanded extra supplies of milk for the palace kitchen so the milkmaids in the vicinity were instructed in advance to travel up to the fort to deliver their milk. Hirkani had never seen the capital before and the visit would give her an occasion to do so. She had heard impressive stories of magnificent palaces and buildings, a huge marketplace, and much pomp and splendor befitting a king's capital. The night before her visit, she dreamt about all she had heard. There were several obstacles, however, that would make this business trip difficult. Her husband was away on a military expedition—there was nobody to take care of her young one. In addition, she would have to manage the trip in the three to four hour interval between breastfeeding sessions. It was an exciting prospect and her family did need the money, so she made arrangements to go. The next afternoon, Hirkani breastfed the baby well, put him to sleep, and left him with family friends.

With mixed emotions, she set out on her journey. The trip involved walking a few miles to the base of the fort, and then climbing 1,250 feet up, with an additional 1,460 steps to reach the main door of the outer fort. The palace within was an additional half-mile away from the main door, and the road to it passed through the bustling marketplace. Covering this distance to and fro with the heavy cans of milk was difficult, made even more so by the fact that Hirkani felt rushed. For security reasons, the fort gates would be closed by sunset, only to open the next morning.

Hirkani was awestruck to see what she had previously only dreamt about. The milk was finally delivered to the palace and she and the other milkmaids were paid. Naturally, the area was crowded that day and Hirkani was somehow separated from her friends. She searched for them, to no avail. Finally she decided to hurry back home alone. However, with the crowd and the confusion, she could not find her way back to the main gates. Hirkani had already lost valuable time.

She soon was shocked to hear the cannons firing, indicating that the gates were about to close. With each shot that rang out, Hirkani ran faster. By the time she reached the main entrance, it was too late.

The enormous gates were locked tight. Hirkani pleaded with the guards to open them, but her pleas were in vain. The gates could now be opened only on King Shivaji's orders. The thought of her baby, now hungry in the village below, made her sob. Her blouse was wet with milk. She persisted in tears and finally the guards agreed to contact the chief officer, who in turn would go to the king for permission to open the gates.

As time passed, Hirkani became increasingly nervous. It was taking too long. The sky was now dark and the full moon reflected the worry on her face. Her motherly instinct compelled her to explore another way out, perhaps an off-beat track. She moved away from the main gate and kept walking inside the fort wall to look for an escape route. At last she found a spot where there was no reinforcement. From here she could make out the dim lights of her village in the valley far below.

It was impossible. Separating her from her village, from her baby, was a vertical cliff, rising more than 1000 feet from the depths below. Not even the best soldier in the King's army would venture down this descent, to an almost certain death. As she waited, Hirkani saw nothing but her child's face and heard nothing but his cry. Though there was a full moon, it would be of no use to her because the cliff faced away from the moon. Still, she must do it. She began to climb down; thorny shrubs and sharp stone edges pierced her skin, inflicting bruises and pain. She continued to descend with great determination until she no longer felt anything. By the time she reached the bottom, her clothes were in tatters and her legs bled. She ran to her hut and grabbed her young baby, holding him close to her chest. It was close to midnight, and bliss descended on the mother-infant pair as the gods crowded in the sky to see the earthly wonder.

In King Shivaji's fort, commotion broke out. The King had already ordered the guards to open the gates, but they could not find the desperate mother. Special torches were lit to track her. The search finally ended near the empty milk can at the tip of a cliff. The king was horribly disturbed upon hearing the news and he assumed the young mother had perished. The next morning, royal horsemen were sent down to inform the family. They arrived, instead, to hear Hirkani's tale of courage. King Shivaji was greatly impressed at this remarkable feat and honored Hirkani appropriately. The village where she lived still exists and today is called Hirkani Village in her honor.

The women in the stories you are about to read are, in so many ways, Hirkani's Daughters. In a 21st century day, they too are overcoming obstacles to work and breastfeed their babies. They too are finding their own ways around the gates people have shut before them. And they too, are excited, scared, and missing their children. Some of the stories share Hirkani's drama; others speak with a quiet calm. At their core, they are all stories of women evaluating their options through trepidation and a beating heart, and in the end, bravely taking the path that works best for their families. Hirkani, our friend from long ago, knew well the difficulty of finding that balance with each and every step that she took as she climbed slowly but certainly down the mountain

Part One

North America

UNITED STATES

Teacher

Schooling the Faculty

Nicole Austin Daleiseo, California

I chose to continue teaching after having my baby because I love what I do, but also out of financial necessity. I also admit that an important factor in choosing my profession was based on my belief that it would be a feasible career for a future mother. Teachers aren't rich, but at least, I imagined, I would somehow be able to find a way to balance work and family. With vacation time and working hours that coincide with a child's school day, teaching and being a mother seemed lifelong goals I could accomplish at the same time. Once I moved into a permanent teaching position, and had my life "settled," I planned on having children.

Getting settled was the hard part, so our dream of starting a family was put on hold for quite some time. My Brazilian husband, whom I met and married while teaching English in his country, agreed to move back to California to be near my family. I got a teaching job in my hometown, but housing prices were too high, so we resolved to move again, a little farther away, where we could afford to buy a house. After many months of a long and tedious commute, I realized that I couldn't continue what I was doing if I were to have a baby. I left my school district so that I could work closer to home. My next job, where I currently teach fourth grade, is only one mile from my house, but it wasn't easy to start all over again. Eventually I realized that there is no perfect time to have a baby, no perfect place, and no perfect situation. Motherhood is something you will never be 100 percent prepared for.

Finally, after six years of marriage, and just six months short of becoming a permanent, tenured teacher in the district, I gave birth to my daughter, Juliana. It was the proudest, happiest moment of my life, and like most parents, I wanted only the very best for my little girl. Unfortunately, although women heavily dominate the teaching career, young teacher/mothers like myself still have quite a few hurdles to overcome. I was advised to keep the good news that I was pregnant a secret for as long as possible. My upcoming maternity leave would be inconvenient for many involved. More importantly, because I was still a probationary teacher, I was told that my position would not be guaranteed, and my pending permanent status would be lost if I missed more than nine weeks of the school year. Because of this, and because I preferred to spend all of my days with the baby after she was born, I chose to work until the day I went into labor. It was also a good thing I did that because I had a cesarean. Under doctor's orders, I had to stay home for eight weeks after the birth anyway.

When it was time to go back to work, I was prepared. After stockpiling milk in my freezer, I was comfortable with the pump my sister had recommended. I had deliberately chosen a family daycare just a few blocks from my school. Although I was dreading going back to work, and worried about how I could do it all, I found that it was actually much easier than I thought. It was a happy reunion with my students, and the children's parents were more supportive than I had anticipated. I was amazed at how much I could do and how efficiently I could do it when I had to. Emotionally, I felt that my continued breastfeeding and this "cuddle" time with Juliana outside of work helped to compensate for the hours we spent apart.

My daily routine went like this: After Juliana's early morning feeding, I got up and got ready. I would give her one more feeding at daycare, before rushing off to school. At recess, or during my preparation time, I would lock up my classroom and cover my windows and pump. During my 40-minute lunch break, I would rush over to daycare for a feeding. My husband, who occasionally worked from home, would bring

California

Employers must provide a reasonable amount of break time for an employee who wishes to express human milk. If possible, the break time should run concurrent with existing break time. Any additional break time taken will be unpaid by the employer.

Employers must make reasonable efforts to provide a place nearby the work area that is not a toilet stall to express milk in private as long as it would not impose undue hardship on the operation of the employer.

her to me whenever he had a chance, and we'd all have lunch together. After school I avoided working late, and would pick her up and nurse her again before going home. At home we spent a lot of time nursing. There were some things I just couldn't get done anymore; I learned to let them go for a while. Otherwise, more important things like eating or sleeping I learned to do quite well while breastfeeding.

For the most part, things went smoothly but there were also a few awkward moments. I learned to get over them, and so did those around me. One time the school secretary unlocked my classroom door to let in a student who had forgotten a book. I crouched down in my chair in the corner so I couldn't be seen attached to a pump.

Another time, my principal, a man who was unaware of why I had put paper over my classroom door window, asked me to take it down. He wanted to be able to see inside as he walked by the class. I told him that I would be happy to leave it open during school hours, but that sometimes I needed to close it for "privacy, so I can pump." He just gave me a puzzled look, so I clarified myself, "So I can pump my milk..." I told him, "for the baby." He turned red in the face and gladly granted me my request. The next day, when he found that I had a new and improved homemade paper shade he just laughed and complimented me on my creativity. This shade was a black and white cow print. After that, people knew that if my door was locked, and the cow shade was on, it would be better not to disturb me.

People knew that if my door was locked, and the cow shade was on, it would be better not to disturb me.

Juliana often cried upon seeing me walk in to her daycare at lunch. She knew that it was lunchtime, and she was impatient to nurse. I attracted a lot of attention from one curious little girl who was fascinated and amazed when every day the crying would immediately stop the second I "cuddled" Juliana close to my body. The little girl exclaimed it was "magic," and asked what Juliana was doing. I explained that she was drinking milk, but she didn't quite understand. She returned home full of questions about where the milk came from.

For the first six months of life, I gave my baby nothing but my milk. Juliana was certainly exposed to plenty of germs from my school, her daycare, and travel during my vacation time. During my spring break we accompanied my husband to Taiwan on a business trip, and during the summer we followed him to Brazil. We had no problems on those long and crowded flights. After Juliana's baptism, we discovered many people at our party caught a very serious case of the flu, including me. Following doctor's orders, I continued to nurse Juliana, who seemed to be the only one who escaped getting sick. Amazingly, she remained in perfect health.

Today we celebrated Juliana's first birthday. My routine has gotten easier these days. Although she is eating solid food now, and my milk is gradually decreasing, she is still nursing and I have never given her formula or cow's milk. I realize that my days of nursing are numbered, and in a way, it will be a small relief when I am freed of this role. On the other hand, I will certainly miss the unique closeness I have had with my daughter through breastfeeding. In actuality, it has been just a short, sweet time in my life that has passed so quickly. I have cherished each day. Any sacrifices I made were well worth the effort. I am grateful for my ability to provide for my baby in this way and proud of my determination to make the healthiest choice for her.

Editor's Note: Writing and submitting her story had an impact on Nicole's awareness of a working woman's right to breastfeed. Here is an excerpt from a follow-up email that Nicole sent:

Any sacrifices I made were well worth the effort.

It was totally out of character for me to have a confrontation with the president of our teacher's union. I told her my story about breastfeeding and working. I told her that some changes should be made to better accommodate new breastfeeding mothers (usually the newer teachers) who have no choice but to return to work very soon after giving birth. I was totally shocked and unprepared for her answer. She told me I had no business getting pregnant when I did! This is a woman who is supposed to represent us! I wrote the union president a letter expressing my disappointment in her. Only later did I meet several other teachers who shared the exact same dilemma as me. They were all forced to return to work soon, yet insisted on continued, exclusive breastfeeding despite the sacrifices. Because of the incident with the union president, I also had an opportunity to confront my boss, the school principal, about this. I have not yet succeeded in getting anything negotiated in our contract that would directly help mothers and babies, but I hope that I have made an impression on some influential people in our district who are making decisions that affect women like me. I believe they will be more sensitive to what they say and will more seriously consider the health of new babies and their mothers in the future.

A Pumping Queen

Mariah Boone, Texas

The milk is all that matters.

That is, of course, patently untrue, but it certainly feels that way sometimes. It is so very difficult to pump enough milk for a baby who must spend much of her day away from you that a mother can get a little obsessed at times. Pumping milk starts to take up a lot more space in your mind than you ever thought it would. Getting milk for that baby becomes your primary purpose, almost.

It's exhausting. Really exhausting. It is, in a very real way, as important as it seems. That baby in daycare is your baby and she needs your milk to withstand all the germs there and to develop her wonderful brain. You have to earn a living to keep a roof over your family's heads and the only way you have to do this successfully is to leave the baby in the care of someone else while you work during the day. It breaks your heart, but you have to do it. You are determined that your baby will have your milk to keep her healthy and strong while you are away. If this describes you, then you have become a Pumping Queen. I understand, because I am one as well. This is my second reign as a Pumping Queen and I know it is worth it because I have a nine-year-old who is healthy and brilliant and kind to show for my first reign, that year of pumping long ago. It has been so long since that year that pumping for my new daughter is like starting over. It is so hard. I know, however, that all the trouble is well worth it.

My husband does not earn enough in his job as a volunteer coordinator to support even a family of very modest means. It is my job as a social worker that has provided most of our income from the start. I certainly did not plan to be our family's breadwinner, but that is the way things have worked out. I manage a division of our city government that works with troubled families. I work mostly during the day, as does my husband. Our older daughter attends elementary school and after-school care and, after my 12-week maternity leave, my infant daughter began going to a daycare center. Twelve weeks was nowhere near enough time to spend with my baby, but I know that many working mothers cannot afford to take any unpaid leave and return to work right after their babies are born. I feel blessed to have been able to save enough time and money to take the full twelve weeks of unpaid, job-protected leave that my country guarantees to most new parents.

In order to accomplish my duties as a Pumping Queen, I have a high-quality, double electric breast pump, a Medela Pump-In-Style. These are expensive, but not as expensive as a year of infant formula. Such personal pumps weren't out yet when my older daughter was a baby so I had to rent a pump that year. I only had to buy the kit of tubing, horns, and other little parts that come into contact with the milk. I was surprised to learn that if I had wanted to rent a pump, the kit alone now costs twice as much as it did when my daughter was a baby. It is still worth it, though.

On most days, my husband takes our older daughter to school before he goes to work and I take the baby to daycare before I go to work. I usually nurse the baby once or twice in the morning before leaving for work and again at daycare when I drop her off. I nurse all on one side at night and in the morning because I cannot seem to pump anywhere close to enough milk for the baby unless I save up the milk on the other side for a while.

At work, if things unfold as I wish, I pump mid-morning. I heat up some breast therapy pads and stick them in my bra to let the warmth help the milk let down. On my door I place little door-hangers that say

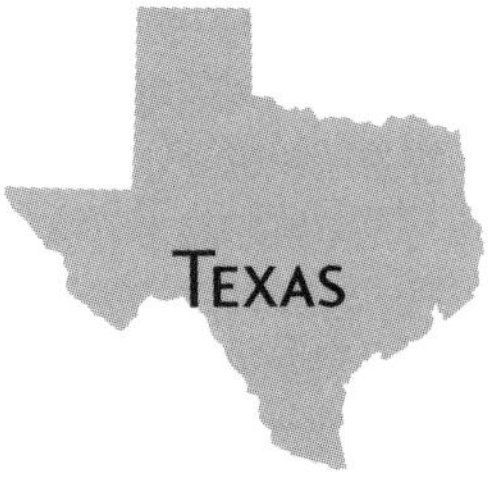

This state finds that breastfeeding a baby is an important and basic act of nurture that must be encouraged in the interest of maternal and child health and family values. The Texas legislature also recognizes breastfeeding as the best method of infant nutrition.

Businesses in Texas may use the designation "Mother-Friendly" if the business provides the following:

1 Work schedule flexibility, including scheduling breaks and work patterns which allow for expression of milk;

2 Accessible, private places for breastfeeding or expression of milk;

3 Access to a clean, safe water source and a sink for washing hands and rinsing out breast-pumping equipment;

4 Access to hygienic storage alternatives in the workplace for the mother's milk.

"Pumping In Progress—Do Not Disturb." I put the pump together and settle down with a mama-centric magazine like NEW BEGINNINGS or with a mothering discussion forum on the Internet. I relax and pump. This should take 15 to 20 minutes according to what most people say, but I can only get about half of what I need in that amount of time.

I usually end up pumping for 30 to 60 minutes and, in that amount of time, can get from seven to nine ounces on a good day. Once I even got 11 ounces (yes, I am a super hero). It took me a while to work up to these averages. The baby tends to drink from eight to ten ounces at daycare in the morning, hence the difficulty. I have tried all sorts of different timings and methods to do better, but this is the way that I get the most milk. That means that weekend morning pumping sessions are essential to provide frozen back-up milk for daycare. I also drink Mother's Milk tea and take blessed thistle and fenugreek supplements to increase my milk supply for pumping.

Obviously, I cannot take 30 to 60 minutes out of my workday to pump and still get my work done. My solution is to take the first 15 minutes to read milk-enhancing magazines or review mothering Web sites and then, once my milk has let down, I spend the rest of the time working on the computer and the telephone. I am fortunate to have a job where I am able to work and pump simultaneously. When I am finished, I pack up the pump, put the two precious little bottles of milk in the insulated pocket of my pump bag with cold packs, and open my office back up.

I certainly did not plan to be our family's breadwinner, but that is the way things have worked out.

At lunchtime, I take the two little bottles with me in my car and head to my baby's daycare center. Unfortunately, my baby's daycare center is fairly distant from where I work. Some moms are lucky enough to work near their babies' child care, but there are no centers near my job that meet my standards for the quality of care that I require for my baby. I handle this in two ways. My job often requires me to attend meetings and run errands at offices other than my own. If those locations are closer to the daycare center, I can usually arrange those trips to coincide with nursing times for the baby. That usually means that, with careful planning, I can avoid having to take too much time away. On the occasions when this does not work out, I have to make up the time. I sometimes take the baby with me to the office in the late evenings and weekends to get in a little more work while my husband is with my older daughter. This is tough, but, again, it is worth it. I am very fortunate to have a job where I can flex my hours so that I can get everything accomplished.

Once I arrive at the daycare center, I put the bottles in their refrigerator and settle down to nurse the little sweetheart that I have missed so much. I nurse and play with my baby and ask the daycare teachers about her day and theirs. I am the only mother in my baby's class of six three- to eight-month-olds who is nursing and so we are a bit of an oddity. It took a couple of months for the teachers to get used to us and for me to stop feeling a vibe of disapproval from them at the way I disrupt their routine. We like each other now, though. They know how much I love my baby and, in the end, that is what counts with them. Some days all of the babies need holding at once, so I try to help the overworked teachers as much as I can by patting fussy babies while I nurse my own.

I get to know these other delightful babies, too, because of my midday nursing sessions with my daughter. Each baby is such a fascinating individual from the very start. I enjoy them all so much. When it is time for me to go, I settle my baby down with a toy and say my goodbyes. I never like leaving.

I get to know these other delightful babies, too, because of my midday nursing sessions with my daughter.

In the afternoon, if all goes as planned, I pump at around 3:30 PM. It's the same routine as in the morning, but with less encouraging results. I usually average a more modest four ounces.

After work, I rush to the daycare like a speed-demon. I take the bottle that I pumped that afternoon and leave it in the daycare refrigerator for the next morning. If my baby has drunk only one of the morning pumping session's bottles, the second one and this afternoon bottle may be enough for the next morning in daycare (and may not be). If she has drunk both, they will almost certainly have to dip into my reserve of frozen milk for her, as well as this afternoon bottle, the next morning. I collect my daughter's things awkwardly, as I must hold her as soon as I arrive or risk her formidable baby-wrath. If I have arrived by 5:15 or earlier, I get to nurse her there as I wish. If I arrive closer to 5:30, I must get out the door with her first, so we often end up nursing squished in my older daughter's booster seat in the back of the car.

Most evenings my baby nurses fairly non-stop until she falls asleep at around 11:00 PM. I often fall asleep then, too, but try to stay up so I can get things ready for the next day. In addition to attending to my older daughter's and the baby's evening needs, I need to steam-sterilize the pump kit parts for the next day's use, put the cold packs back in the freezer to freeze them for the next day, gather the clean collection bottles and lids, and pack the pump and the baby's daycare bag and my older daughter's lunch. My husband usually does the dishes, washing and sterilizing the baby's bottles and nipples. I try to find the time to put in a little work on the writing and publishing projects that I hope will one day make me a work-at-home mom and end this crazy juggling act.

The next day, we do it all over again. The life of a Pumping Queen is exhausting. But, being able to go this far, keeping my baby healthy, secure, and growing toward her full potential, is a privilege I do not take lightly, something other Pumping Queens will understand. I am fortunate also to have a constant reminder, in my older daughter, of the difference that all of this hard work makes. Her compassion for other people, her intelligence, and her blooming vitality make it abundantly clear that being a Pumping Queen, with all its difficulties, was the right choice.

My baby is six months old now, so we have passed an important milestone. We succeeded, even amid the difficulties of full-time employment, in sustaining her solely on mother's milk for that important first half of the first year of her sweet life. Now she is starting to taste a little bit of solid food on most days, but my milk will continue to be her primary source of nourishment for the second half of her first year as well.

Keeping my baby healthy, secure, and growing toward her full potential is a privilege I do not take lightly.

Somewhere around the time of my baby's first birthday, I will probably "hang up the horns" as we Pumping Queens say, and stop pumping, as my daughter will likely be eating and drinking plenty of other things to get her through the day at daycare. I will continue to slip over there to nurse her every once in awhile and we will continue to have the wonderful re-connecting experience that nursing is when I pick her up in the evening. My daughter will probably continue to nurse when she is with me for a good while after that, until she is ready to wean herself. Then, when I look back at my reign as a Pumping Queen, there will be only sweetness. All the stresses that I feel now, the competing demands of work and pumping, will be gone and I will only feel the pride and joy of having done my very best for my baby, as I look for ways to do as well meeting her newly emerging needs as she grows and grows.

United States

Stand-up comedian

A Funny Thing Happened...

Tricia Shore, California

I was sure that six weeks would be plenty of maternity leave for me. After all, I'd been working since I was 15 years old. Most importantly, that was just the amount of time people seemed to take. I kept expecting myself to be ready to go back to work. Maybe tomorrow, I'd think, or maybe next week, I'll be ready.

Six weeks came and went and I was more than happy to get a two-week extension on my maternity benefits. I was still not ready to go back. Although my co-workers were anticipating my return, I had not yet arranged for daycare. I kept telling myself that daycare would be easy to find. And I would use a pump and bottles and leave my baby in good hands while I went back to work. After all, we'd bought our house when I was seven months pregnant under the assumption that I would continue working. We loved our house and wanted to keep it.

What I did not expect was how deeply and divinely I would fall in love with my newborn. My pediatrician, a breastfeeding advocate, explained how my baby needed my breasts, not a bottle. I read on an Internet site how breastfeeding works all 44 facial muscles, while bottle-feeding works only four. I began to see that breastfeeding was meant to keep mother and child together, as we are while the baby is in the womb. I was telling people I was planning to go back to work soon, although I was actually dreading it, and I was still avoiding the daycare issue. "Come on back and bring the baby," my employer suggested. And so I did. I relished every moment that I could be with my baby during the day, asking different eager volunteers to watch him when I had to leave my office. The other employees loved having the baby around. I only wish I had discovered the sling at that point; having a sling would have made my life so much easier. But I kept my baby in his stroller and in my lap when he wanted to nurse.

After three months back at the job, our company was feeling the repercussions of the dot-com crash; I was laid off along with half of the company. It was decided that the engineers could write proposals for themselves and they no longer needed writers, me included. Scared as I was at being unemployed with a five-month-old, I was secretly happy. Nursing and living in general were so much easier when I didn't have to worry about driving two hours each day to and from an office that I was beginning to dislike. Then again, my position had paid the most money I had ever made.

What I secretly wanted was a job in which I could work from home.

Somehow my husband, Morris, and I managed with my unemployment checks, a generous home equity loan, and credit card debt. Despite my many years of experience as a writer and teacher, I was having no luck finding a position. What I secretly wanted was a job in which I could work from home.

Seventeen months after my firstborn's birth I found myself pregnant and still nursing. While visibly pregnant, I had one job interview. The recruiter assured me it would not make a difference, but it did indeed to the hiring manager. Of course, they don't tell you that. They just say they've hired someone more qualified. I began doing stand-up comedy in the evenings. Being a pregnant comic was somewhat unique. During the day I was at home making plans for baby number two.

My obstetrician advised against nursing while pregnant. Now, from what I have seen and heard, weaning is one of the most difficult things on earth. Its closest kin must be that nebulous sleep training I've read so much about. My children's father and I chose the lazy way—no weaning and no sleep training. My pediatrician, on the other hand, assured me that many women nurse during pregnancy so I decided to continue. Then came our second son, Micah...and I learned about tandem nursing. Yes, this caused some traffic jams shortly after Micah's birth, when Caleb and Micah wanted to nurse at the same time. But nursing worked out well when I had a plugged duct in my breast. Instead of buying a pump, I simply asked my older son to nurse every hour, as his baby brother slept.

With another baby to care for, I temporarily stopped doing comedy—a hungry baby needs his mother, after all. And of course, I thought I had to leave the baby at home. When Micah was around six months old, I resumed doing comedy at night, making sure that I fed Micah before I left for a show. My husband would rock him to sleep. When I came home three or four hours later, I would find all my boys lying in bed, sound asleep.

Some time during the month of Micah's first birthday, I became pregnant with my third child. I had just turned down an offer to work full-time as a technical writer. The manager, a woman, would not consider any telecommuting and I found her decision appalling. As a writer and editor, I could easily complete assignments at home. Any company that would not realize this was not a company I wanted to work for. Meanwhile, we were sinking more deeply into debt.

I decided to continue my comedy and to continue to breastfeed.

I decided to continue my comedy and to continue to breastfeed. This time, when my doctor informed me that I should stop nursing, he added: "But you've done this before." He didn't know I was still nursing both of my sons, and he said nothing else about nursing during my pregnancy. I performed on stage throughout my pregnancy and nursed my then three-year-old and one-year-old after I returned home. I performed a showcase at the Laugh Factory in Hollywood two days before the due date of my third child.

Jadon was born four days after Caleb's fourth birthday. A wonderful lactation consultant showed me how I could nurse Micah and Jadon at the same time, alleviating much screaming and crying. While I was grateful for the position in which I could nurse two children at once, I must admit that I felt somewhat like a sow at the state fair. But at least I was now a sow with some very happy piglets.

It was my oldest son, Caleb, who encouraged me to start doing comedy right away. "But you have to do comedy. It's your job!" he told me. And four weeks after Jadon was born, we were back at Lucy's LaundryMart, a comedy venue that has been featured on the reality show "Last Comic Standing." I stood at the microphone, this time with my sleeping baby in the sling. I had performed so much comedy with him inside me that it only seemed natural to perform with him close to me on the outside.

My youngest son is now ten weeks old and I am still nursing anyone under five in our household who asks or cries. Through email lists and the Internet, I have finally found part-time editing and writing work that I am doing at home. I no longer consider jobs that would keep me away from home and place my children in daycare. I take my newborn to comedy shows with me once a week. Sometimes, Jadon nurses on stage while I perform. My husband and I are slowly but certainly digging ourselves out of debt.

At first I was afraid to bring my newborn to comedy shows, but not only have I received glowing accolades from his admirers, I have inspired women who are thinking of having children. I am realizing that somehow in our post-feminist culture, women are often afraid of motherhood and of the changes that it will bring. I realize that I have embraced those changes, not because I am especially strong or follow some particular parent-oriented philosophy, but because I am simply looking out for my infant. Allowing myself to fall in love with my firstborn helped me to see how much babies need their mothers. His brothers have benefited from my decision to nurse them exclusively, no matter what. I am finally brave enough, after child number three, to say that my newborn goes with me to work.

Allowing myself to fall in love with my firstborn helped me to see how much babies need their mothers.

Just the other day I received an email from a female comic who wrote:

> I am so glad to see you are still making the circuit with baby in tow! You are my hero . . . you set such a good example for people like me who fear that they'd lose their voice and sense of self with motherhood. Thank you for doing what you do.

And I am thankful that my babies are teaching me how to give them what they need.

United States

Post Doctoral Fellow

Dr. Mom, Nursing Twins

Carrie McAdams, Massachusetts

So far, I have nursed for 67 months of my life. (And I'm only counting the months spent nursing my twins once, despite making milk for two.) I have worked or been in a paid position as a graduate student for all but 14 of those months.

When I had my first daughter, Sage, I was in a combined degree program—a graduate student soon to be a medical student. I enjoyed my work and had no desire to give it up. So, I wrote my doctoral dissertation in the first four months of Sage's life and defended it before she was five months old. I was fortunate enough to bring her to work with me or work from home. However, we ran into a problem—she wouldn't take a bottle. Eventually, we discovered that my milk turned sour rapidly. Basically, I could pump a bottle, and it stayed fresh for only four to six hours. (See explanation later in this story.)

I was about to start back to medical school and this seemed to be a big obstacle. Fortunately, medical school involved classes that were videotaped. I brought Sage with me to watch the videos instead of going to class live a couple days of the week. Honestly, watching videos was much more efficient than attending class. There was no time wasted when professors were late or no-shows. Most importantly, when the professors said, "*That* is the one thing you need to know" —I could just rewind the tape instead of trying to find the one person who knew what *that* was among a din of students whispering, "What was *that*?"

Three days a week Sage went to daycare so I could attend labs. I pumped one side every morning while Sage nursed on the other. She would have that bottle around 10:00 AM, then I would nurse her in person around noon, and finally pick her up around 4:00 PM. I lost a lot of weight. Nursing Sage at noon meant I had little time to eat, plus I had to run about a half of a mile to and from the free parking area! I had not been that thin since high school.

After only six months of classes, I had to start working in the hospitals. Fortunately, my little one grew quickly in those six months and only wanted to nurse two or three times a day by then, and sometimes once in the middle of the night. I arranged my hospital schedules to do the easy rotations first, contrary to standard recommendations to save the easy ones for last. I was only "on call" in the hospital once a week or so at first. My husband would bring Sage to the hospital occasionally when I wouldn't be coming home, so I managed to nurse two to four times a day until she was about 15 months old. By then, it became clear that she didn't really miss nursing if I wasn't there, so we only nursed when I was around.

Sage weaned during my obstetrics and gynecology rotation. I was in the hospital every fourth night, and the breastfeeding had become more and more irregular. Soon after that we found out I was pregnant.

I was pregnant for the rest of medical school. Jade was born a month after I graduated from medical school with honors. I decided to take a year off this time. Jade became very attached to me and nursed very frequently. She didn't want anything to do with food until she could pick it up and eat it herself, and so she was exclusively nursed for at least seven or eight months. I loved having the time at home with my daughters, and worried about how Jade would do when I returned to work, now moving on to a postdoctoral fellowship.

I debated returning to work many times. It seemed crazy to have gone through eight years of post baccalaureate education to become a stay-at-home mom with an MD and a PhD. In the end, I returned to work. My mother took care of Jade, and they bonded tightly. Unfortunately, when I returned to work, I added a long commute. So

There is breastfeeding legislation in this state, but none specific to workforce protection.

Jade nursed morning, evening, and many times at night—much to my dismay. I expected her to start weaning around one-and-a-half or two years, but it just didn't happen. We did night wean around two years, but she still wanted to nurse in the morning and evening. I left her overnight several times and she did all right without me—"out of sight out of mind."

People who wean at three months or six months always seem totally shocked by those who nurse to more than a year or so, but they never reach the super easy stage where nursing is just a tiny part of the mother-child relationship. When she was three and only nursing once a day, I went to a work meeting for four nights and Jade was ready to nurse when I got back. Finally, she weaned herself at three-and-a-half years. Again, I soon discovered I was pregnant.

I loved having the time at home with my daughters, and worried about how Jade would do when I returned to work.

We took the whole family to my routine 18-week ultrasound. My daughters loved the idea of seeing the baby in my belly. My husband and I were trying to explain to our three-year-old, who really wanted a little sister, that we might be having a boy. My six-year-old daughter said "I hope we find out we're having twins." Ever the scientist, I said something to the effect of, "No we aren't having twins, I had a blood test and if it was twins it would have been abnormal…blah, blah, blah." So much for mother's intuition! I was sure that number three was another girl, and low and behold, there were two boys! That was the shock of our lives. Sage was beaming, but Jade was upset that there wasn't a little sister in there. As soon as the boys were born, Jade said "I didn't know boys could be so cute," and has become convinced that boys are much cuter than girls. Jade has always been that way, when she doesn't get what she wanted, she learns to want what she got.

Breastfeeding twins is hard, sometimes it is harder than carrying them was. But I knew it wouldn't be fair for them to be stuck with second rate nourishment. Twins have a great disadvantage starting out—they usually have to share a placenta as well as their caregivers. My boys are genetically identical, but one got less of the placenta and is still smaller. I hope that they will even out, but if not, I'll know that I tried my best. I guzzled protein drinks and bars throughout the pregnancy, trying to help them grow. Interestingly, most of the female research scientists I know are committed to breastfeeding. It only takes a little bit of research to learn the benefits of human milk.

I pretty much just nursed and tried to sleep for the first month. We dealt with thrush, a possible intolerance to cow's milk by Pierce (He had colic!), and some oversupply issues that resolved when each twin was assigned a particular side. I was very excited to discover that it was now commonly known why some women's milk soured quickly. There is an enzyme, lipase, which some women produce in excess, and it rapidly breaks down the fat in the milk. The enzyme can be deactivated by heating. So, my boys learned to take bottles of my milk that had been pumped, scalded, and cooled! That was great because I needed to go back to work.

The first task I had to accomplish was taking a medical board exam. I had decided, shortly before finding out I was pregnant, that I missed seeing patients and wanted to do a residency. My boys were kind enough to begin sleeping through the night three weeks before my exam. While studying, I was quite thrilled every time a practice exam had a question on twins or breastfeeding. The nine-hour multiple-choice exam went fine, although I didn't really have enough time to pump as much as I should have before the exam and was quite engorged by the end.

Pumping Particulars

I have found that I can always pump two to four ounces if it's been an hour since the twins last ate.

As for pumping, I have never doubted that I can make the milk. I occasionally have issues, such as, "Yikes, tomorrow is Monday and I only have six ounces!" This means I have to defrost some of my reserve supply, and pump three or four times to get ten to 14 more ounces as well as nurse the boys. I've never really built up a big freezer supply because I do once a month cooking and rarely have the freezer space. (I highly recommend dreamdinners.com for all working mothers.) I do eat oatmeal and take fenugreek, which have been found to increase milk supply for some mothers, and I have found that I can always pump two to four ounces if it's been an hour since the twins last ate.

I typically leave 20 to 24 ounces for the two boys for a seven to nine hour workday. Recently, I bought a Whisper Wear hands free pump that enables me to pump on my 45-minute commute home. It is not quite as fast as my regular pump, but when I am driving the time would be wasted anyway. I typically pump twice at work, and once on the way home with the Whisper Wear pump. Occasionally, I will pump one more time before bed or first thing in the morning if I am short on milk.

I returned to my regular job when the boys were about four months old to finish my post doctoral research. It was likely that if I didn't finish it, no one else would and my previous three years of work would have been wasted. Fortunately, my boss is comfortable with me working from home two days a week. Unfortunately, it is impossible to work from home while the boys are there, so they go to about five hours of daycare even on those days.

It only takes a little bit of research to learn the benefits of human milk.

By pumping, my boys receive the nutritional benefits of my milk. It is a hassle to keep up with their bottles at times, but I feel as though I would be cheating them to do less. It would also be a hassle if they weaned completely or I ran out of milk because I was supplementing. There is a lot of freedom in knowing I can feed them as long as I am with them. And there is that blissful joy that comes when they nurse quietly; there is the deep satisfaction of being able to console them.

I now find it peculiarly freeing to go to work. Work isn't nearly as difficult as watching the twins, for one thing. And the boys seem so happy when I come back. Of course, four months is a great age, when all they know how to do is smile and laugh! I am thrilled that they seem so happy with their other caregivers, their dad and sisters, their grandmother, a home daycare provider, and a babysitter. My other girls were very attached to me and often could not be consoled by others. With the twins, I am definitely a better mother for the time I am away from them. I feel that I have found good daytime caregivers for them and hope they will thrive knowing that other people can also meet their needs.

United States

Public Affairs Manager

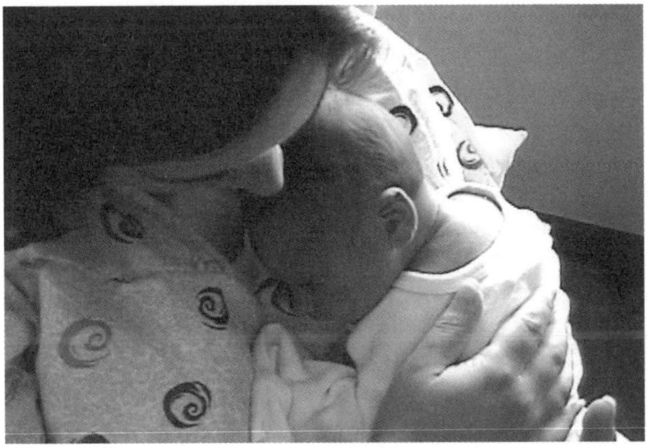

The Diary of My Return to Work

Rebecca Novak Tibbitt, Connecticut

Saturday, November 6

The weekend before my first day back at work

In the shower I start to sob—I don't want to feel sorry for myself, but I can't help it. I can't stop crying. Once driven in my career, I have no desire to leave the warm cocoon that I've built around myself and my new baby, Aidan. The elections were just held. I don't care who is president. An image enters my head. I remember visiting Cat Ba Island a few years ago in the China Sea outside of Viet Nam. In a small harbor the shrieks of a pig echoed off of a stone wall as it burrowed its feet into the sandy shore where the farmers were trying to load it onto a pickup truck (to undoubtedly meet its fate at the butcher's). I picture myself as that pig. I don't want to go, I don't want to go, I don't want to go.

CONNECTICUT

Employees can express human milk or breastfeed on the job during existing meal or break periods.

Employers must make reasonable efforts to provide a place nearby the work area that is not a toilet stall to express milk in private as long as it would not impose undue hardship on the operation of the employer.

Employers may not discriminate against, discipline, or fire a woman from her job because she has exercised her rights to express milk or breastfeed.

Monday, November 8

My first day back

1:00 AM: Aidan hasn't gotten the memo that I am going to be at work in the morning and has woken up in the middle of the night for the first time in weeks. My husband, David, is working nights so that he can watch Aidan during the day, so he's not home to help. I rock Aidan back to sleep and try to go to sleep myself.

4:00 AM: Aidan is up again. David has been home now for the past two hours and is trying to sleep. We listen to Aidan really start to cry and David gets up to console him, but forgets to turn the monitor off, so I not only hear my baby cry, but also David singing and shushing and walking for half an hour. I get up and start to scream at David—doesn't he know that tomorrow is my first day back? Doesn't he know how hard this is for me? I scream. Aidan cries even harder, and David tells me he has it under control.

5:45 AM: I get up and take a shower. My employer has let me move my hours to 8:00 AM to 4:00 PM, so I plan to get ready from 5:45 AM to 6:15 AM (shower, hair, and makeup), feed Aidan from 6:15 AM to 6:35 AM, get dressed, pack up my pumping supplies, and try to get out the door before 7:00 AM.

7:30 AM: After a sixteen-week maternity leave, I arrive early on my first day back with my Pump In Style Traveler and set up shop to pump my first bottle on the job with Purdue Pharma's Public Affairs department. Typically a "work late/get in late" environment, I don't expect to see anyone in Public Affairs for a few hours and I'm not wrong. Signs decorate my door and office that shout "Welcome Back—You Were Missed!" It's nice to feel appreciated. By 10:00 AM, I'm at a "Department Meeting," which is a ruse for my "Welcome Back" party with bagels and donuts.

Merle stops by to see how I'm doing and asks if I'm breastfeeding. I tell her "yes" and she asks to check out my pump, which I'm happy to show her. She tells me that she used a manual pump at work 25 years ago while her assistant "mooed" outside of her office.

The Public Affairs department plays as hard as it works and in moments of insanity, the team cracks jokes and comes together to get the job done. These characters are an odd bunch with the common tie of driven "type A" personalities who thrive on pressure. I used to fit right in, but now I'm not so sure. It's nice to see everyone again, and in a matter of hours I'm assigned a major press announcement scheduled for the following Monday.

Co-workers that I haven't seen in four months stop by telling me that I look good—no, actually, I look great, considering how huge I was when I left.

I enjoy showing off my brag book and telling people that it's really not so bad to be back, I'm already so busy that I can't even think, which is good. David calls me three times to report the day's events. He calls me one last time to say that Lil, our granny-for-hire, showed up as planned to cover the few hours in between our shifts.

4:00 PM: Time to go. I bolt. Traffic on I-95 is the usual nightmare, but I'm home by 4:45 and race in the door to hug my little bug. My mother and sisters call me that night to see how it went. I tell one of them that I feel guilty for not feeling more guilty.

The week flies by. David and Aidan call me on Tuesday and get my voicemail—they leave a chatty message with Aidan a-ooooing how much he misses me and can't wait to see me when I get home. I listen to it about three times a day. David tells me that Aidan seems hungry and wants to feed him more.

Saturday

Lil and I attend our Infant & Child CPR class at the hospital. I knew that Lil, at 79, was a little skeptical about taking the class, but she did great, and in the end I think she was glad that she went. She commented on how Aidan sucked his bottle right down and suggested that maybe I pump more milk. A voice in my head wants to ask her if perhaps I could pump more milk out of her, but then I laugh as she says, "Well, I guess that's easy for *me* to say!"

Monday

I've been on email this weekend checking the progress of the announcement. Last minute changes are flying around and I don't want to be caught off guard. I'm so tired; I can't believe I have to face another week. Last week was actually fun, but it's sinking in now that this is no temporary situation and I need to get used to it. Maybe it's the intensity of the day, maybe it's the first day that I stay late, knowing that Lil is covering for us, but my separation from Aidan is physical. As the afternoon flies by, I feel like an addict in need of a fix. I crave my baby; I need to hold him, smell him, taste his sweet skin.

David called this afternoon for Aidan's "coo" session, which I love.

My boss (the father of a three-week-old) walks in and I abruptly hang up the phone. I hung up on my baby. Why did I do that? Jim is a new father, maybe he would have understood. Why didn't I put him on speaker and introduce them?

I took the train today and I am waiting on the platform, heart racing. Why isn't the train here? I need to get home. It occurs to me that I'm not in DC where our spokesperson is being shepherded around by our department head. A year ago I would have made a case to be the one to go. Was I even considered? Or worse, was I considered and rejected? I said that I could go, but didn't push it. My boss said he did not want it to be a burden on my family. Standing on the platform my eyes fill with tears. Where is the train?

Tuesday

My voicemail is full and the message from Aidan and David is deleted by the system. I want to cry.

Thursday

Media is still covering this announcement like crazy. Gloria from *Investor's Business Daily* calls to request interviews with our spokespeople. I set the interviews up and ask her when she expects the article to run—she can't tell me for sure, but she promises to have a colleague follow up with me as she's going on maternity leave next week. How wonderful, I say. I'm just returning…and so begins our hour-long rap session. "Are you breastfeeding?" she asks, "How is it going?" And so on. I tell her that I'm going to my first La Leche League meeting that night, but so far so good. I pass along the best advice that an old friend gave to me—give it six weeks, I tell her. It will be hard at first, but don't give up. If you can make it six weeks, you can make it six months.

I think about pitching the idea of a working mother/breastfeeding article, but I lose the opportunity.

That night I go to my first LLL meeting—scheduled at 7:00 PM for working mothers. The group is helpful and gives me advice on switching bottles. One mother has used Evenflo Elite. My Aidan's been sucking down bottles with ease—too much ease—as he's been getting frustrated at the breast and not latching on as well lately. I call the grocery store and a baby discount store; no luck. I eventually found them online and put in my order.

Friday

I talk with Jeannette, mother of 12-year-old Janina, at work about how motherhood has changed us. I see the love in Jeannette's eyes for her daughter as she tells stories of returning to work when Janina was one. She puts words to my feelings as she says that it's not guilt that one feels—we like to work, to earn an income, to be valued outside of the home. It's more of a feeling of loss. What if I miss her first words, her first steps, her first fall? A feeling of loss that this little creature will grow up without *you*. While she reassures me that Aidan will always know who his mother is, I can tell as she talks that she still feels this loss for her little baby who is growing into a young lady.

Monday

6:00 AM: The sky has exploded in a Caribbean sunset of a sunrise on this cold November morning. Today is going to be a beautiful day, I think to myself as I snuggle up with Aidan on my lap. Normally a big sleepyhead, he's wide awake today, more interested in starting a cooing conversation than eating breakfast. I indulge him and we chat for a while. He smiles up at me and bats his chubby hand up to touch the underside of my chin. He finally settles in as we fit together like lock and key enjoying this glorious morning.

Tuesday

4:30 PM: Taking the train home I sink into a seat next to a tiny Indian woman who looks a little older than me. She gives me a tired smile and I give her one back. We start to talk, which is strange, because I never talk to people on the train. She's a babysitter who works a few days a week in Greenwich, a 50-minute train ride from New Haven, where she lives. Her husband, too, works nights so that he can stay home with their two boys during the day, so we actually have a lot in common. I'm happy to hear that she breastfed both of her children for the first year of their lives.

Thursday

2:00 PM: I'm in Purdue's lactation room, which is an exam room outside of the nurse's office outfitted with a small refrigerator, extra nursing pads, and working mother/breastfeeding literature. I can't believe that out of approximately 700 employees, there was only one other person besides myself who took advantage of this room. Maybe people didn't really know about it, I thought. Maybe I could write a little article about this in Purdue's Stamford employee e-newsletter. I wasn't sure if this would fly. While I knew the company prided itself on consistently going above and beyond, it enjoyed doing so in a tactful, discreet manner. I floated the idea by co-worker, Merle, who publishes the newsletter. She thought that it was a great idea!

10:00 PM: While preparing for my first business trip since my return—a day trip down to Baltimore—I realized that the "battery pack" that came with the Pump In Style was simply a pack that needed 8 AA batteries—not a rechargeable battery. I was exhausted and Aidan was sleeping. David was enjoying his first night out since the baby was born, playing soccer with his league and getting a few beers afterward. I called him at the bar to see if he might (please) be able to stop at the drugstore to pick up a pack of batteries on his way home. He laughed and said that he hadn't thought of me needing to pump while I was away…and that he'd literally have to tie a string around his finger to remember. He curled up to me a little after midnight and told me that he got a huge pack of batteries for me. "Remember when I used to wake you up at night to be together?" he asked and I smiled, thinking about our earlier days. "Yeah, I remember," I laughed, and went to sleep.

Friday

5:30 AM: I wake up early to have a little extra time to get ready for the trip. Aidan fed—check. Showered and dressed—check. Pump ready (with batteries)—check. Laptop, cell phone, and Blackberry—check. Makeup—will do in the car on the way to the airport.

The morning is a long one. The 9:40 AM flight to Baltimore was canceled due to "mechanical" problems, but I think that it's because Pam (who gets car sick on the train) and I are the only ones on the flight. We get pushed to 11:00 AM, which delays our meeting in Baltimore by an hour. I'm fixated on the 3:30 train that I need to be on for the return trip…if the meeting gets pushed back again I won't get to see Aidan at all tonight. I try not to panic. The turbulence on the descent was horrendous and I almost lose it when I think about how David and Aidan will manage without me if this prop plane goes down. I wonder if it's the pressure change or this thought that makes the milk in both breasts let down with a vengeance.

Miraculously, the plane lands and we're all okay. But the meeting is now so late that I know there's no way that I can excuse myself for 20 minutes to pump. We chitchat over a working lunch and I want my old self to come back, to commandeer this meeting into some kind of organized format, to make people see that I have a train to catch and a baby to feed. I insist on leaving a little early with the hopes of pumping in the Baltimore train station bathroom (yuck). One of the people we met with offers to drive me to the station, which is so nice. He comes in to show me where the train is and continues our conversation until five minutes before boarding time. Another attempt foiled, I'll need to resort to my last horrific nightmare of pumping in the Amtrak train bathroom. I tried to console myself with the fact that at least I was in business class where the bathrooms might be a little cleaner.

3:30 PM: The business car was packed, but I was able to find an aisle seat next to a heavy-set, beautiful, African-American woman dozing next to the window. She opened her eyes as I got situated and I worked up the nerve to ask her a "Huge favor…see, I'm nursing my baby…and I was away on business today…and, um, I need to pump…so, would it be okay with her if I sat by the window for about 20 minutes and then I would switch seats with her?" "Oh, honey," she said. "That's not a huge favor at all. That's a really little favor. That's so nice that you do that for your little baby." So I arranged the pump backpack on top of my laptop roller case, plugged it into the outlet strip (no batteries needed after all!), and set to work covertly pumping the left side, then the right. I held my winter coat over me like a blanket and smirked behind half-closed eyes at the business people none the wiser chattering away on cell phones or taking Amtrak power naps as the Medela clicked away, barely audible over the rattle and hum of the train. I think to myself, "We're going to be just fine…."

CANADA

Home Daycare Provider

Quiet Detours

Sophie Lesiege, Quebec

Translated from French by Lynda R. Hicks

I was a managing secretary of three driving schools during my pregnancy. After the birth of my daughter, I had to rethink my priorities and ended up changing the direction of my career. I wanted to persevere in my breastfeeding and to be a key person in Maxinne's upbringing.

When Maxinne was 11 months old, I opened a home daycare. My main tasks were to plan menus, prepare meals, and set up educational activities in an environment adaptable to multi-aged children. This adventure took roughly 65 hours per week. Though it did allow me to breastfeed on demand, it is difficult to nurse with five other babies surrounding you. Maxinne was curious and had to look around at the slightest movement and every little noise. Since I wanted to continue breastfeeding, I had to find a solution to this problem. I got the other children involved in quiet games near me so I could breastfeed in peace. It became important to make this a consistent part of their routine. Eventually, this became a special moment not only for my daughter and me but also for the other children in my group.

As time passed, feedings were spaced farther apart, and my breasts weren't demanded by her except to go to sleep or for major events such as falls and upsets. At naptime, I put the other children down first and then settled down with my little rascal for a moment of tenderness, love, and mothering—our healthy pause! I'd made the choice to be completely present for Maxinne, and these moments were the salve that made my tough week's work worthwhile.

When Maxinne was three years old, I decided to close my daycare and look for other work. I feel fortunate with her current daycare, no doubt because of my efforts in this area. Since I had always planned to return to outside work, I wanted to give her a gradual transition centered on her needs. Therefore, I instructed the new teachers that Maxinne had the habit of going to sleep at the breast and they respected our choice. They have taken the time to pat her back, caress her hair, and teach her, little by little, to manage to sleep. Certainly I have felt social pressure since few mothers in Canada nurse past two years.

I work now in a communication center with educators five days a week, about 35 hours total. I can, if necessary, bring my daughter to the workplace. I can therefore be there for her and still nurse at work when necessary.

Maxinne is now three-and-a-half years old and she wants to nurse only when saying bye-bye or going to sleep. I haven't had any disruption in milk supply, even though my body has gone through many changes. I've always believed that work and breastfeeding can be compatible, therefore, I've done all I could to reconcile them both. In this way, my work has not harmed my breastfeeding and motherhood. Certainly, I've had to make choices, but my partner, Thomas, joins with me always, encouraging me to find the solution and loving us without fail.

I believe in the blessing of stability that breastfeeding offers, and I believe it makes improvements in temperament (mildness, smoothness, sweetness). Many are surprised when they learn that Maxinne isn't yet weaned, but I explain our family choice and the benefits to the child. I explain how breastfeeding can have a positive impact on self-confidence, self-esteem, health, and autonomy. I express that our relationship is beautiful, strong, and loving. In becoming a mother, I am learning to give and to receive without limits.

In Quebec, parents are eligible to receive 55 percent of their income for 50 weeks, to a maximum of $39,000. These benefits are extended even to mothers who are self-employed. Mothers can take up to 50 weeks maternity leave and fathers can take up to 5 weeks paternity leave.

UNITED STATES

Information Technology

Co-workers Become My Support System

Judy Coughenour, Pennsylvania

When I became pregnant, there was no question in my mind that I was going to breastfeed my baby. To me, breastfeeding always seemed like a wonderfully feminine super power. It was a natural progression of my pregnancy—the next step in nurturing my baby.

My husband, Ron, and I had planned for one of us to stop working after we had a baby. We didn't have much money, but we would make up for it by living a simple lifestyle. We would be cutting our income in half, so for about a year before we started trying to conceive, we lived frugally on one of our salaries and used the other salary to pay down our debt and add to our savings. We purchased a modestly affordable home, paid off our car loans, stopped eating out, and began clipping coupons. It didn't take long for us to feel as though we were financially ready to start a family on our own terms.

When I became pregnant, it was time to decide which of us would quit our job to take care of our baby and our household. My husband had just completed his Master's degree in elementary education and was preparing for a big career change from a computer programmer to an elementary school teacher. We decided that he was in a good position to quit his job and become a stay-at-home dad. Once all of our children were in school, he could start teaching. He was so excited and we both knew he'd be great at his new job. With my husband's support at home, I would continue my career as an IT professional. When I came home, I could focus on my family.

I also needed to figure out how I would be a working and breastfeeding mother. I knew I wanted to keep breastfeeding beyond my 12 week leave. Since I would be away from my baby for the entire workday, I would have to use a breast pump. I started asking some of the new mothers at my office if they had ever used a pump. I only found one co-worker who tried to breastfeed for more than a few weeks and she stopped breastfeeding before returning to work. Many of my co-workers seemed uncomfortable with the idea of breastfeeding, let alone working and pumping.

To me, breastfeeding always seemed like a wonderfully feminine super power.

I would be breaking new ground at my office, but I was determined to make it work. If I was going to be the first woman at my office to work and pump, I was going to do it right and set a good example for others to follow. I decided that I would be open and confident about my plan to work and pump. I would try to make everyone around me comfortable with my decision to continue breastfeeding after returning to work. The support of my co-workers would be critical to my success so I would make them part of my breastfeeding team and encourage them to share in my success.

Nearing my third trimester, I started looking for a space to pump. I had access to a computer equipment storage closet. My co-worker and I cleared out space near an outlet and set up a small desk for me to use as my pumping station. I talked to my boss, several co-workers, and my office manager about my plan to take two to three short breaks each day to express milk and I followed up our discussions with emails. Although this was a new experience for everyone, they did their best to support my decision.

A few weeks before my due date, my co-workers threw me a baby shower. I was truly touched by their show of support and excitement. I knew that they would do all they could to help me succeed as a working mother.

I gave birth to Clay a week before my due date. I was now a mother to a beautiful and healthy baby boy. I had finally given birth, but the journey had just begun. Clay and I battled through some of the common nursing difficulties such as painful latch-on and sore nipples. We persevered to become a great nursing team. Ron was constantly there, encouraging us and giving us confidence when we felt hopeless.

Nearing the end of my 12-week leave from work, I was feeling confident about breastfeeding, but anxious about my return to work. I looked at my breast pump with nervousness and disdain. I had used the pump several times, often yielding less than one ounce between feedings. I had tediously stashed away a precious 20 ounces of my milk. Would my husband have enough milk to feed Clay while I was at work? Would I be able to pump enough milk? Had I taken on too much? Would I be able to leave my baby? Would I really be able to make this work?

So much was at stake. Ron had already left his job. My baby was accustomed to and thriving on my milk. My co-workers were anxiously awaiting my return. So many people were depending on me to make this work. I had to set my fears aside and at least give it a try.

Recently, another woman I work with had a baby and to my delight, she decided to breastfeed.

I discussed my fears with Ron. He offered to bring Clay to my office for a nursing visit each day for as long as necessary to help ease my transition. Knowing I had this option made it all seem more manageable.

On the morning of my first day back at work, I felt as though I was starting a new job. I didn't know what to expect. I wondered if I would be rusty from my absence. I wondered if my co-workers would be discouraged by my pumping breaks. I wondered if I would be able to pump enough milk to replace the milk Clay would take that day. I wondered if I would be able to focus on my work and be productive.

My husband prepared my breakfast while I dressed for work and nursed Clay. We made plans to meet for a nursing visit over my lunch break. I kissed my family goodbye and joined the legions of working mothers.

I was received at work with hugs of encouragement and requests for baby pictures. My teammate instructed me to check out my pumping area. I was astonished to find that he had transformed the stark area into a mini-pumping oasis, complete with a tiny refrigerator to store my milk. At that moment, I realized that I had all the support I needed.

I believe that my decision to be open and honest about pumping at work enabled my co-workers to be supportive. While I never flaunted my pumping, I never tried to hide it either. On one occasion, I was pumping while on a conference call. One of the other callers noticed the sound of the pump and asked what it was. I responded that it was me, that I was using a pump to express milk for my baby. On other occasions, people would ask why I was away from my desk. I would just politely tell them. It's nothing to hide, just one more thing that I do each day.

Recently, another woman I work with had a baby and to my delight, she decided to breastfeed. I now take turns sharing my pumping oasis with another mother. I like to think that I have helped to make my office more breastfeeding-friendly for future working mothers and their babies.

As of now I've been working and pumping for five months. I breastfeed Clay right before I leave for work in the morning and as soon as I come home at night. Occasionally, Clay and Ron will stop by the office for a nursing lunch, but not as often as before.

I started by taking three breaks, but now I'm down to two 20-minute pumping breaks a day. Each day, I take home enough milk for Clay, plus a little extra to add to my frozen stash. My frozen milk stash has grown to well over 100 ounces. I recently contacted the Mothers' Milk Bank at Christiana Hospital and am undergoing the screening process to become a donor. Not too long ago, I was worried about having enough milk for Clay. As it turns out, I have enough milk to share.

I kissed my family goodbye and joined the legions of working mothers.

My breastfeeding success belongs to so many people, not the least of whom are my co-workers. The best advice I can give to other working and pumping moms is to build a support network of trusted co-workers. Be confident, straightforward, and honest about your plan to pump at work. Let your co-workers know that your decision to breastfeed is important to you and that it is also important that you do it in a way that won't be a burden to them or hinder your own productivity. As you become a working and pumping success, be sure to thank the people at work who support you every day.

UNITED STATES

Research Associate

Redefining Success

Ruth Tincoff, Massachusetts

I work to generate income to help meet the needs of my family. I am fortunate that my work offers personal fulfillment, intellectual stimulation, social interaction, and opportunities for solitary reflection and study. Breastfeeding my daughter also helps to meet the needs of my family. I am fortunate that mothering my daughter through breastfeeding offers personal fulfillment, intellectual stimulation, social interaction, and since she is now almost three years old, a few precious opportunities for solitary reflection! This situation would seem to be an opportunity for successfully blending two important aspects of my life. However, in my daughter's first year, despair and doubt surged in as my physical and mental energy were divided again and again by these two pieces of my life for which I felt incredible passion. As I near the end of my third year as a working breastfeeding woman, I have renewed clarity on what works well, what can go wrong, and how "success" is defined for a working breastfeeding woman. All women should have the opportunity to choose when and how to build their families, with breastfeeding providing important health and emotional benefits. All women should also have the opportunity to ensure economic security for themselves and their family. Why should we have to choose?

My Situation

The work that I do, academic research and teaching with a focus on developmental psychology, probably strikes many people as highly compatible with raising a family. Academics are privileged to have flexible hours and a high degree of independence. A PhD in cognitive developmental psychology prepared me for the scientific questions I wanted to ask and satisfied my curiosity about infants, their needs, and their development. Through my studies I first encountered reports of the benefits of breastfeeding and the prevalence of extended breastfeeding across cultures. I looked forward to being a mother. My husband and I got married shortly after I finished my undergraduate degree and we grew as a couple as we weathered the stresses of my graduate program. I believed that I had settled on a career that would allow me to achieve the work and family goals I envisioned. I completed my degree and began a three-year postdoctoral research fellowship. In the back of my mind were the questions, "When should we begin a family?" and "How would this work if I had a child?"

All women should also have the opportunity to ensure economic security for themselves and their family.

Gwen arrived at the end of the first year of my fellowship. The pregnancy was somewhat unexpected, but my husband and I were joyous about starting our family. At the time, my fellowship allowed for a 45-day paid maternity leave and then a choice between returning to a full-time commitment or an unpaid leave. Financial fallout from graduate school coupled with the high cost of housing in the Boston, Massachusetts, area made losing my salary an impossible option. I made the decision to return to a full-time commitment. I briefly surveyed child care and decided against it, partly due to the exorbitant cost of it (over $1,000 a month for an infant in full-time care) and largely because I felt a strong need to care for Gwen myself. We decided Gwen would come with me to work. I was fortunate to have a cooperative research sponsor, supportive colleagues, and a private office (though quite small and windowless!). Gwen spent the day with me at work, or I worked at home when possible. Daddy shifted his start time to the wee hours of the morning and picked her up in the afternoon, giving me some hours of uninterrupted work into the evening. For the first six months this was a manageable situation. At work we were a team, supervising undergraduate students who were conducting experiments, researching and writing experimental reports and literature reviews, and interacting with my colleagues. Gwen was an easy baby. She rode in to work with me on the bus, snug and tight in a baby carrier or sling. She slept in my lap, the sling, or a baby seat. She nursed on demand while we were together and easily took a bottle or two from Daddy when we were apart. My colleagues stopped to say hello, delighted in her progress, and did not complain about her as a disturbance. Her first summer we attended two scientific conferences at which I gave presentations; we attended one as a family and the other just Gwen and I attended along with two other academic moms. At night she slept with us and nursed on demand so that we all could get as much sleep as possible. During those early months I felt I was progressing on the traditionally defined academic tenure track while also meeting the needs of my breastfed baby.

She nursed on demand while we were together and easily took a bottle or two from Daddy when we were apart.

When Things Got Tough

When Gwen was around eight months old, the energy that sustained me during those early months began to wane and exhaustion and doubt started sliding in. I found myself constantly thinking, "Oh, it'll get easier when she starts eating some solid food…drops some nursings…starts sleeping through the night…we find child care…she can talk more." I could always find another milestone that seemed to offer some hope of change. Accomplishing work became more difficult as she became more active and socially engaged. We decided to have her spend several hours one day a week with a fun and loving neighbor family to give me some more focused time during the day. She enjoyed her new playmates but our separations were often tearful and difficult. Thankfully, our reunions were eased by immediate breastfeeding as soon as she saw me. Despite this help, I became frustrated with work and my increasingly slow progress. I began to believe that I was failing in the career for which I had trained so hard and enjoyed so much. I read that within five years after their PhD, women were less likely than men to be in the coveted tenure-track positions. In the back of my mind was the knowledge that women with more education are also more likely to breastfeed. I surveyed job ads knowing that I couldn't manage to be separated from my baby for the full day, often two day, interviews they entailed. I saw my belief in a family-friendly academic career slowly shattered during those months. My daughter needed me and I needed to be with her! My research projects needed me and I needed those projects to succeed. I realized I could not meet all those needs. I began searching for a new definition of success that might work.

Redefining Success

Now I am grateful for those months of turmoil. Hitting that wall helped me reach where I am today. I read a lot about academic career options and work/family issues. I sought out other breastfeeding mothers through La Leche League meetings and got involved with my local LLL group. I also consulted with a career coach who specializes in professional women with young children. They all combined to give me the nudge to embrace my intuition—step back, stay active in part-time positions, give myself time to embrace the intense relationship with my daughter, and most importantly, care for myself. I understand that success is what I define it to be. I embrace the La Leche League statement, "Happy mothers, breastfed babies." I am off the tenure track, I teach one or two courses a semester, I maintain contact with some of my research colleagues, and I am rebuilding my motivation to conduct and publish research. Certainly dropping to part-time adds financial constraints that can be especially poignant given the high cost of living in this area; the information on frugal living available through La Leche League helped us meet our new definition of success. Gwen is almost three years old and still loves nursing, which she calls "sides." She is joyous, independent, and socially outgoing. She enjoys her family daycare days and rarely do we ever have a separation protest. Nursing is still an important part of our relationship and we check in several times a day when we are together and still usually once at night. Nursing provides welcome shelter during some intense tantrums, and in her case, also seems to satisfy a persistent nutritional need. I am grateful that I realized when things weren't working well and found the strength to redefine success. I know our needs will change again in the future and that I have control over what we define as "success."

I am grateful that I realized when things weren't working well and found the strength to redefine success.

UNITED STATES

Scientist

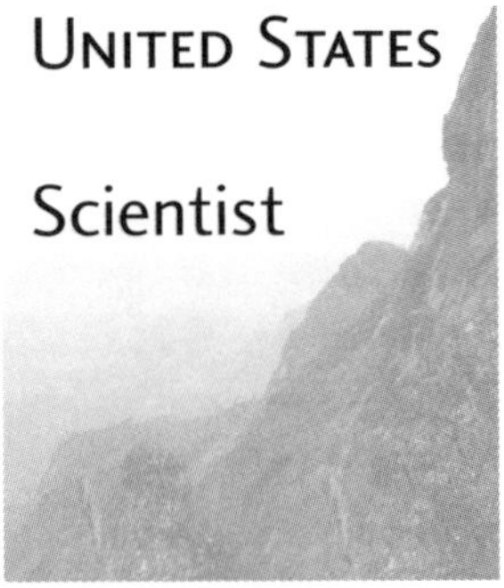

Moving Across the Atlantic

Nicola Evans, Illinois

I am both a quaternary scientist* specializing in palynology and the mother of nine-month-old Kellan. When Kellan was born, I decided that not only would I take a six-month break from working, but also that it was time to relocate. I wanted to find a job and a work environment that suited my new life as a breastfeeding mother. My husband and I were living in Britain and we had agreed that he would be staying at home with Kellan once I returned to work. At the same time, I was alerted to a palynology opening at the Illinois State Museum in Springfield, Illinois. After some negotiation about my start date, I accepted the job. We packed up and moved across the Atlantic, and I started work the week that Kellan turned six months old.

I have been working and breastfeeding for nearly four months now. I plan to continue until Kellan is at least two years old. Working at the

As a quaternary scientist, I specialize in the reconstruction of past environments through pollen and sediment analysis. This consists of looking at slides through a microscope and lots of work with the accumulated data on my computer. I construct age models, perform statistical analyses, make graphs, and write papers among other things.

Illinois State Museum (ISM) has allowed me complete freedom to breastfeed. Kellan is able to join me at work anytime at all. Many hours have been spent working at my computer while Kellan was latched onto my breast in total concentration. My co-workers especially enjoy the satisfied little sigh that he makes after each gulp of milk. I have my own room and a comfortable bean bag chair, used by past ISM nursing mothers, for expressing milk during the day. My work hours are completely flexible. I take a long lunch on Wednesdays so that Kellan and I can attend the local lactation support group where we spend two hours nursing, chatting with other mothers (another of whom also works at the ISM), and playing with other babies. Springfield is a small town. There is no traffic and my commute is less than ten minutes each way, allowing for maximum time to nurse at the beginning and end of my workday.

This is vastly different than my past job in Britain, where there was little to no flexibility. In Britain I worked as part of a "team" and our working hours were very structured. The work day was 9:00 AM to 5:30 PM, no exceptions (other than overtime). Lunch was from 12:00 to 1:00 PM or 1:00 to 2:00 PM, and each person's break had to fit in with those of the team as a whole. Holidays also had to be scheduled around those of the team. Overtime was expected. The environment was highly regulated; electronic passes and photo identification were required for entry to the building and again to the various floors. Kellan would never have been permitted to join me in the office, and certainly not to nurse while I worked. I would not have been able to take long lunches for lactation group meetings, to come in when he'd finished nursing in the morning (rather than at a certain time), or to leave early on a nice afternoon so that we could have some time at the park. Kellan would not have seen me often, I would have been exhausted, and breastfeeding would have been a scheduled, rather than natural and relaxed, activity.

I did speak to my previous employer in Britain before making the decision to leave, and they were entirely unwilling to alter the rules to accommodate me as a new breastfeeding mother. I resigned.

Before accepting a position in the US, I researched Springfield and found that it was billed as a "child-friendly" town. This was a good start. My work was going to be entirely independent, rather than team-oriented, and my employer had stressed the flexibility of the position. He had also informed me that I was expected to work 37 hours per week, and not a minute over. I could work these hours when and how it suited me. Because I work for the state, there are numerous holidays

ILLINOIS

Employers must provide a reasonable amount of break time for an employee who wishes to express human milk. If possible, the break time should run concurrent with existing break time. Any additional break time taken will be unpaid by the employer. An employer is not required to provide break time if to do so would unduly disrupt the employer's operations.

Employers must make reasonable efforts to provide a place nearby the work area that is not a toilet stall to express milk in private.

They were entirely unwilling to alter the rules to accommodate me as a new breastfeeding mother. I resigned.

and on top of that, the job started with four-and-one-half weeks paid vacation and 12 sick days. I also discussed breastfeeding with my employer who was immediately enthusiastic, talking about his wife who had breastfed their daughter and offering me a choice of three different private office locations in which to express each day, even alerting me to the existence of the bean bag chair. I knew that I had support even before I began the job.

So, we left all of our family and friends and moved to Springfield. We miss them dearly, but our quality of life here is much higher than it would have been had we stayed in England. We spend so much time together as a family and Kellan is thriving. With the support of my husband, my employer, and my co-workers, I have been able to combine breastfeeding and working without a single difficulty. My son is in the 97th percentile for height and weight, happy, healthy, and breastfed to his heart's content. I am happy in both my career and my family. I am relaxed, I am satisfied with my life; I am contented. I have always wanted to breastfeed my child for at least two years—that was my goal—and I wondered if I could make it work while at the same time having the career that I love as a palynologist. At the Illinois State Museum I can, I have, and I will continue to do so.

UNITED STATES

Dispatcher

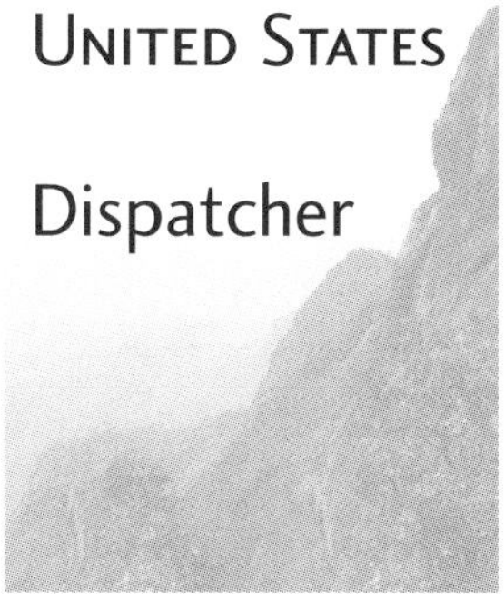

No Need to Worry After All

Thia Tomasich, Missouri

"Department of public safety, how can I help you?" "Yes, I was just.... Oh, I'm sorry I didn't realize what you were doing." "That's okay. He's not embarrassed. I admit I am, a little. He's becoming quite a messy eater. Now what can I do for you?"

I smile and silently thank God for my job, my understanding boss, and my 11-week-old son. I am a 24-year-old single mom. Working is not an option for me; it is a necessity. I am a dispatcher at a university in my hometown. I work in a small room filled with monitors, computers, alarm systems, and a small window. I chose this job originally, not for the mediocre pay, but for the great insurance and free tuition.

After working here only five months I found out I was pregnant. Immediately, I started to worry. I didn't have some of the usual worries. I knew I would be a great mother; I had been privately employed as a nanny for four years. I had no doubts my body was equipped; I come from a long line of women with "child-bearing hips." I knew at once that

I wanted to breastfeed. It might be the only time in my child's life that I could give him the absolute best without worrying about being able to afford it. My worries were about daycare. Nine months was not nearly enough time for me to find a breastfeeding-friendly infant care facility. It was not enough time to interview and observe caregivers. Not to mention, I knew I probably wouldn't be able to afford the caregiver I would ultimately choose. Three weeks was not enough time to establish breastfeeding before going back to work, yet it was all I could afford to take off.

It might be the only time in my child's life that I could give him the absolute best without worrying about being able to afford it.

I would just have to quit my job. I would have to give up the insurance and free education and find something that would pay even less, but that I could do from home. I went to my boss and voiced my concerns. He said, "Well why don't you just bring your baby to work with you—then you can feed him in my office."

After what seemed like an eternity of stunned silence on my part, he continued. "I used to be a Fire Chief in Nebraska. After our dispatcher gave birth, she brought the baby to work with her and kicked me out of my office every two hours to breastfeed. She was happy, the baby was happy. She never missed work due to a sick child or a sick babysitter. That made me happy. When the baby started crawling around and pulling stuff off shelves, she had to find child care. Until then, it worked out great."

So, three weeks after Ethan was born I went back to work and took him with me. Now I answer phones, monitor alarm systems, and watch security cameras while holding, feeding, and enjoying my son. I know that my situation is an exceptional one. I think that it is a great example of what some employers will do to support breastfeeding when they are fully aware of the benefits.

UNITED STATES

Professor

New Ways of Seeing the World

Laura Barbas-Rhoden, North Carolina

My work is a joy. Through my professional life, I have a chance to do what many of us hope to do as parents: to give, to communicate, to shape lives, to build community. I am a college professor, and my subject area is Spanish and Latin American studies. I am also a breastfeeding mother. Just as I cannot imagine not teaching my own child to see the world with eyes of understanding, so I cannot imagine giving up the opportunity to teach grown children to see and understand the cultures and peoples around them. That is why I am a nursing, working, income-earning mother.

Because I am a professor at a small liberal arts college, I have luxuries that many others do not. My college offers a very good family leave policy that allowed me to teach part-time for a semester while my son was between three and six months old (fortunately for me, he was born in the summer while I was off). My department chair is a former breastfeeding mother who helped me plan a schedule most conducive to raising a child and being a good teacher and faculty member. My departmental colleagues, most of whom are women, have been very supportive, and we joke that my little boy has a whole group of "tías locas" [crazy aunts] to greet him when he comes to campus. And maybe most importantly, I have the privacy of my own office for pumping at work—and for entertaining my son when he accompanies me during office hours!

During my first semester back at work, I thought long and hard about positive strategies for balancing all the new parent tasks. My husband was incredible, and a marvelous child care arrangement presented itself. A colleague on leave was writing a book and caring for his two-year-old granddaughter, and he offered to take my son, too, for three mornings a week while I taught my first semester back. Perfect, I thought, our son will hear German, too! Then, knowing the curiosity and persistence of students, I thought about how to let others know that I needed privacy when my door was closed for pumping sessions. I decided to approach the task with a sense of humor. I took a photo of a brown cow and attached it to a poster with a rhyming Spanish text that said: "No tocar ni entrar, cuando la vaca en la puerta está." (Don't knock or enter when the cow is on the door.) No one knocked when the door was closed.

I have the privacy of my own office for pumping at work—and for entertaining my son when he accompanies me during office hours.

I had other strategies and surprises. I hired a student to take my son for a walk in the stroller for Friday afternoon office hours, and when she was unavailable, he stayed with me and played on the office floor or my lap. He usually got "kidnapped" by one of my baby-loving colleagues and he would eventually make it back to me for a nursing session before we left campus. As my first semester ended, another child care solution presented itself as the first one drew to a close. My husband and I really wanted to find a Spanish-speaking nanny. I remembered a Honduran couple I'd previously helped with some document translations, and I contacted them, thinking they might know someone. It turned out that their little boy was now in school, and that the woman was willing to keep my son in our home while I went back for a full-time semester. We were delighted, and so far the arrangement has been fantastic. I'm even learning more baby words in Spanish.

My son enjoyed a water birth at home, nursed exclusively for more than six months, and has heard at least three languages from caregivers in his early months. None of these is the norm in our culture in the US, but I think they are all healthy, wholesome choices, and I'm not shy about sharing the experiences and decisions we've made as a household. In that way, I hope I've stayed true to my profession: to educate and to teach others new ways of seeing the world!

Averting Disaster

Cynthia Spidell, Florida

I have always been a successful career person. I never gave working and breastfeeding much thought before I had a child simply because I knew that I wanted desperately to do both, though I was not sure how. When I was pregnant and gave birth to Harrison, my colleagues were very supportive. They showered me with gifts and support and encouraged me to breastfeed during my maternity leave. Prior to returning to work, I met with my boss, the Human Resources (HR) Director, and another colleague for lunch and explained my plan to pump at work. I planned to pump twice at work and I would visit the daycare center during my lunch break to breastfeed in person. I specifically chose a daycare center within minutes of my work. My original plan was to do this for six months, though I ended up continuing for one year. My plan was welcomed and nobody said anything to the contrary. However, the difficulties started about two months after my return to work. I started feeling as though something was bothering my colleagues and I had the feeling they were talking about me at the daily lunches that I was no longer able to attend. Suddenly they all started acting differently toward me.

Then it happened. The HR Director came to my office, closed the door, and told me that she had to talk to me about something. She explained to me that someone had complained about me because I had mentioned the fact that I breastfeed my son during a meeting with an outside vendor. She said that he complained of feeling unappreciated because I had stated that I needed to reschedule a meeting until after 2:00 PM, because I spend my lunch breaks with my son to breastfeed him. He had complained to a colleague, who complained to the HR Director. By the time the story reached the HR Director, the story was that "all I talk about is breastfeeding and that is all I am interested in." She told me that some people might find breastfeeding "offensive" and that I should be more discreet and careful about how I discuss it and with whom. My first reaction was, "Oh dear! I am so sorry! I would never want to make any one feel uncomfortable! I had no idea that breastfeeding was so offensive!" I went home devastated and sick to my stomach. Tears come to my eyes even just writing about it now.

The next day one of my friends, another lactating mother, just happened to come to my house. I was upset and relayed the story. She was flabbergasted. At her urging, I visited the La Leche League Web site, specifically for information pertaining to Florida. I read that Florida was the pioneer state for breastfeeding legislation and that the word "breastfeeding" was exempted from the statutes and could neither be interpreted as offensive language or an offensive act. I also read that Florida is one of the first states to make the encouragement and promotion of breastfeeding a state policy.

Relief began to set in. I printed out a copy of the legislation and brought it to work. I tried to politely explain to my HR Director that if someone finds my attempts to balance breastfeeding and work offensive, then they are the ones that need to be sensitized, not me. She took the criticism but she sent it right on to my boss stating that I might file a complaint against the company. This caused the entire situation to explode. I had a meeting with my boss, the CEO. She in turn nailed me against the wall. She said that I misunderstood the message from the HR Director and that breastfeeding was not the issue, but that I was being offensive to people in general. She dug up things on me that I had said and done over a year prior to this incident. (Please bear in mind that I had been with the company for almost three years already and had received nothing but stellar reviews.) When I asked

Florida

Florida led the nation by enacting the first comprehensive breastfeeding legislation. The legislation not only exempted breastfeeding from criminal statutes, but created a new law that stated this important and basic act of nurture must be encouraged in the interests of maternal and child health.

There is no breastfeeding legislation in this state specific to workforce protection.

why these incidents were not brought up during prior reviews, she said that she just tried to blow them off not wanting to give it much thought. I then asked for examples of how I was offensive so that I could avoid being so in the future. My boss did not feel giving concrete examples would be productive.

Then it hit me. They had made a mistake and did not want to admit to it, for fear of litigation. In hindsight, I think that all I really wanted was an apology. "We are sorry—and thank you for bringing this to our attention so that we do not make the same mistake with other breastfeeding mothers." However, this is corporate America and corporate America never admits to making a mistake. I suddenly felt isolated and wondered, "Who are these people? Are they the same ones who showered me with gifts and support during my maternity leave?" Additionally I could not help but wonder, underneath that business front, do they all feel a bit guilty that they stopped breastfeeding to come to work...and perhaps they expect me to do the same?

She told me that some people might find breastfeeding "offensive" and that I should be more discreet and careful about how I discuss it and with whom.

This meeting was followed by a written email from my boss stating that I need to develop an action plan for either going part-time or taking a leave of absence. She also put in writing that I was taking too many paid breaks (this was the reference to my pumping sessions). I went home even more devastated. I called upon my support group, my husband, and a La Leche League Leader. Her kind words were wonderful and supportive. She encouraged me to come to an LLL Group meeting, which I did. My husband was also a great supporter. He picked me up out of the doldrums and said that now that I know what is bothering my boss, we can fix things. He helped me put together an action plan to appease my boss. I was not about to let the turkeys get me down!

My action plan was as follows:

I reduced my hours to 35 hours a week, seven hours a day. This extra hour per day really took a lot of pressure off of me.

I explained to my boss that she was misinformed. I was not taking two 30-minute breaks to pump. Rather, my pumping sessions were about ten to 15 minutes long, during which time I was also working. Having my own office allowed me to catch up on a lot of the reading and analytical work that my job required. I had learned to type, answer emails, and answer the phone while I pumped. In fact, I found the uninterrupted time in my office with the door closed to be quite productive.

In all fairness to my boss, I think that she was misinformed about my pumping and work attitude. I requested that we have a brief weekly meeting to discuss any issues that may be bothering her about my job performance.

I was so worried about how my boss would respond to this, but was pleasantly surprised when I received her response in an email. Suddenly her tone changed to one that was positive and supportive, specifically with respect to my decision to breastfeed and work. After a few weeks of hard work and dedication, tensions started to ease and things returned to normal. I continued to pump at work until Harrison's first birthday.

How do I feel now that I do not pump at work any more? It was a bit odd at first. I had become so used to my routine. However, I am still breastfeeding Harrison in the mornings and in the evenings and it is working out just fine. I can even rejoin the lunch crowd again for daily lunches and I have been having fun doing so.

Would I do it all over again? Of course. I would not change anything. We working mothers can feel guilty enough as it is by making the decision to leave our children with a caregiver and return to work. However, through my commitment to breastfeeding I feel as though I have made the most out of our first year. The following sums it up:

Through my commitment to breastfeeding I feel as though I have made the most out of our first year.

- By continuing to breastfeed after returning to work, I feel as though my work has not interfered with our relationship.
- By visiting him during my lunch breaks, I felt as though I was always a part of my son's day—no matter what.
- I have less time off due to a sick baby than the other working mothers. My baby is hardly ever sick. He has been exposed to everything at daycare, yet never brings anything home.
- Harrison has never needed an antibiotic. I always hear other mothers comparing stories about ear infections and antibiotics. This is one conversation that I am proud not to know anything about.

Without a doubt, the first year was challenging, but the ultimate reward is my happy and healthy baby. He is so healthy that people actually ask me what I am doing differently! I have returned to my usual highly productive state at work and have achieved every productivity bonus since "the incident." More significantly, I really feel confident that I have done everything in my power to have started my son's and my long-term relationship off on the right foot.

United States

Child Care Provider

Bartering Allows Me to Be at Home

Terry Magalhães, Iowa

I grew up with three younger brothers and learned from a young age how to be a wife and mother and run a household. No one ever discouraged me from pursuing a career. I hold a college degree and am quite confident I could make my way successfully through a career. However, I never had the drive to do that. I just wanted to be a stay-at-home mother. Fortunately, my husband, Eduardo's, career choice gives him a salary that makes that possible for me and he is in complete agreement with that desire of mine. While it is possible for me to stay home, it is true that we are a one-income family, not at an executive level, so it does take financial diligence, creativity, and fortitude to keep me at home. We were fortunate to stumble upon an especially inventive solution that would allow me to earn an income while staying home to care for my growing family.

We had three children and were moving to a new house when my youngest brother and his family moved to our town. We had purchased a manufactured home that was within our budget, but we wanted to add a garage, a front porch, and a screened-in back porch. In addition, two-thirds of the basement was left unfinished and we wanted to use that area as additional living space. My brother's first baby was eight weeks old and his wife had only four weeks left of her maternity leave. My brother works in home construction. It didn't take any of us long to connect the dots. They needed a daycare provider. We needed a carpenter. Neither of us had room in our budgets to pay for the services we needed. My brother told us what his wage would be, I told him what I would expect to be paid, we figured out an exchange rate and the deal was struck. I take care of my nephew about 50 hours a week, and we now have a garage, a finished basement, and a front porch.

Our barter system is pretty straightforward. My brother, Kyle, told us his expected wage, which is an average wage for a carpenter in this area. We decided to go with a ratio of seven of my hours for one of Kyle's hours, which brings my payment a little below other daycare options available in the area. I know, I know. The value of child care is never reflected in the actual wages! We are all aware of the fact that it is not really possible to pay me what the job is worth. We also had to take into consideration the fact that my nephew, Deikan, is here nearly 50 hours a week, so putting the ratio higher would create a debt Kyle would be unable to pay.

Our accounting system is very basic. Eduardo, always helpful, records the hours Deikan is here each day on a monthly calendar we use to track the family's schedules. When he pulls the old month off, he adds up my hours and converts it to Kyle's hours and writes that total on a dry-erase board we use for the never-ending grocery and errand lists. When Kyle works, Eduardo subtracts those hours from his total.

Besides the benefit of having work done on our house, my family has gotten to truly know my nephew. Deikan Ross is a blond, blue-eyed child, and my children are all brown-eyed and brown-haired, so it is a new experience every time I look down into his blue eyes. When I take them all to town, people often comment, "That one must not be yours. You must do daycare." I respond, "He is mine, just not in the same way as the others. He's my nephew." I don't want him to ever feel that he has less standing here than his cousins. I include him in conversations with my children about sharing and being kind and such by saying that Deikan is a part of this family, too.

The three littlest ones are stair steps in age. My two youngest sons

There is breastfeeding legislation in this state, but none specific to workforce protection.

are a year older and a year younger than Deikan. I doubt the older one, Elliot, remembers a time when Deikan wasn't here five days a week. Elliot and Deikan are particularly close and they often hug each other joyously on Monday mornings or when they see each other on the weekend. They hug tenderly before Deikan leaves for the day with his father. On those days when he would usually be here, but for some reason isn't, I repeatedly have to answer, "Where's Deikan, when is he coming, will he be here tomorrow?"

This routine is normal now for all of us, and I suspect that when Deikan reaches school age and is not here so much, the children will grieve the change. There are plenty of projects that need to be done here, so the house being finished is far enough into the future we haven't had a conversation about whether to terminate our "arrangement." Kyle is taller and considerably stronger than either of the adults here, so there is a healthy dose of plain old manual labor done here by Kyle and we count that as work we pay for. I anticipate that this arrangement will continue if Kyle and his wife decide to have another child. We will have to have a conversation about the time ratio at that time. One could argue that my rate should go up. One could argue that Deikan will be less work, and so my rate should remain the same. I keep my eyes on helping my family and the benefits this provides me and then I don't worry so much about it all coming out even. How can one truly calculate that?

I take care of my nephew about 50 hours a week, and we now have a garage, a finished basement, and a front porch.

Pointers to Others

I would recommend to anyone else adopting this system that you think it all through carefully and talk it over in clear, concise terms. The requirements for each party should be spelled out very clearly. I don't think lawyers need to be involved, but writing it all out so that everyone can see it is a very good idea. Misunderstandings about the expectations could lead to a family feud that would be a terrible outcome for the little ones involved! We put no claims on a certain number of hours being worked off in a certain amount of time and it probably would have been a good idea to do that.

Also, in the age of the new patient privacy laws, I would recommend at least a note in the child's medical file that indicates the caregiver can seek and authorize health care. We had an incident where Deikan fell off the couch and I thought he might need medical attention. I called but couldn't reach my brother or sister-in-law, so I called the doctor's office to ask the nurse. Her first comment to me was, "We need permission for you to receive information about him." I was so relieved to be able to say, "There is a note in his file for just that purpose."

As I consider the economics of the eight (and counting) years of nursing I have done, the impact is huge. Just the cost of formula and bottles would have been significant. (From the beginning Eduardo has helped to ensure a great breastfeeding relationship for our children, so he deserves credit, too. After the birth of our first child, Eduardo pumped my breasts while I lay in the hospital awaiting an emergency surgery.) If I had decided to have a career instead of being at home, and we add in the cost of a professional wardrobe and daycare and all of the other expenses that come with having an outside career, the money not spent becomes a staggering amount. Without all of that money saved, we would not have been able to afford this house and its larger mortgage payment. Without the arrangement with my brother, we would not have been able to make needed improvements. More profound than that, though, is the human impact. If I had not nursed our first three babies, we simply would not have been able to afford our fourth baby. In a very real sense, I earned having him with all of the hours I spent nursing his sister and brothers. It is the best return I can imagine for such an investment.

UNITED STATES

Business Director

Breastfeeding Road Warrior

Diane Cloutier, Florida

I am a self-proclaimed breastfeeding road warrior. When I became pregnant with my daughter, Valerie, I knew that I wanted to breastfeed because I felt it would be one of the best gifts that I could give her. I had read extensively about the boost it would provide to her immune system and her IQ, and how it would help us to form a stronger bond. In my career as a business professional, I travel extensively, so I wasn't sure how I was going to manage these two conflicting aspects of my life. But after making it through those blurry first few weeks of motherhood, I was hooked. I knew I had to find a way to make travel and breastfeeding work. I must confess that as exhausting as being a new mother can be, I actually looked forward to hearing my baby's whimpers in the night so that I could take her in my arms and put her to my breast. The closeness I felt to her as she nuzzled her warm little body into mine was, and still is, the most wonderful feeling in the world. I didn't want to lose that because of a business trip.

But as the end of my maternity leave was approaching, I knew that I would once again have to get on a plane, so the time came to devise a plan. I knew that if I could build up a "stash" of milk at home, and if I could find a way to refrigerate my milk on the road, I could bring home enough of a supply at the end of one trip to feed my daughter during my next trip.

What to Buy

My first investment was in a really good electric breast pump. I'm talking about a top of the line breast pump. Although the $300 price tag seemed high, it turned out to be the best investment I have ever made (and cheap compared to formula if you work it out over time). Next, we bought a freezer for the garage, which I proceeded to begin filling with little white bags of milk, all dated and inventoried with the oldest stock at the front for easy access by my husband or our nanny. Now the dilemma, how on earth was I going to travel with my computer, a suitcase, my breast pump (which is pretty much the size of a computer case and discreetly disguised to look like one), and some sort of cooler to store my milk, and still manage the logistics of only two pieces of carry-on luggage when I did not want to risk checking my computer, my pump, or my milk as luggage?

After quite a bit of creative shopping and several trial runs I am proud to say that I can now manage a business trip with only my two pieces of carry-on luggage! How? Well taking my daughter's stacking cups as an inspiration, I bought a soft-sided cooler that fits inside my wheeled bag and takes up about half the space. Into the other half I roll my clothes and tuck my small cosmetics bag. Granted I have become an expert in combining a few pieces of clothing into several outfits, which is an art in itself—but it can be done. I also purchased a large computer bag that I can actually squeeze my pump into, slipping my computer into the back pocket. When I pack for a trip I toss a bunch of large zippered freezer bags into my suitcase. Then while I'm on the road I proceed to fill each bag with a one-day supply of little white milk bags, and pop them into the mini-bar fridge. On the day of my departure, I fill another bag with ice, slip it into the little cooler with my milk bags, and off I go. When I arrive home, each of the one-day supply bags goes into the freezer and I'm ready for another trip.

Getting Creative

Now as you might imagine, there have been the occasional hiccups in my travels plans that have caused me to adjust my system. For instance, what to do when the hotel has no mini-bar or ice machine? One major hotel chain is actually incredibly accommodating and always rolls a little refrigerator into the room for me. (Trust me, it never hurts to ask.) And worst case scenario, I have gone down to the restaurant with my empty zippered freezer bag and asked for ice, which I then replenish daily to keep my little cooler cold enough to ensure my pumped milk remains fresh.

Dealing with Colleagues

Traveling with business colleagues always sparks interesting comments such as, "Did you pack your own lunch?" (This was before I began hiding my little cooler in my bag.) My favorite is, "Why do women always pack so much stuff?" (This they ask as they look at my bulging suitcase.) If they only knew that if I took out all of my breastfeeding paraphernalia, you could actually fit the rest of my things into a small briefcase!

But after making it through those blurry first few weeks of motherhood, I was hooked. I knew I had to find a way to make travel and breastfeeding work.

Airport Security

Some of my most amusing and stressful experiences have been at airport security checkpoints. It is always interesting to see the befuddled look on the face of the agent viewing the x-ray machine when I pass my pump through, as he tries to figure out what the heck he is looking at. Sometimes, as I lean over and whisper, "It's a breast pump," they just smile knowingly and let it pass. But often they insist upon doing a manual check to be sure I'm not bringing some dangerous device onto the plane. I have had wonderfully nice agents who in response to my request that they keep my pump as sanitary as possible, have changed their gloves, or even let me take my pump apart to show them, without touching it themselves. Unfortunately not everyone has been so sensitive. My most humiliating experience was with one particular agent who insisted upon taking everything apart and putting it on the table in front of all of the other passengers, coldly telling me that if I needed to keep this device sanitary I should seal all of the parts into bags. (I now do.) I remember crying as I ran into the airport bathroom and had to sanitize everything with anti-bacterial wipes so that all of the precious time I had planned to use for pumping was spent cleaning the parts.

No Regrets

But in spite of the lost lunchtimes, icky airport bathrooms, and the challenge of scheduling pumping time into my flight schedule, would I do it again? You bet. At the end of each trip as I arrive home and replenish our freezer, I feel proud that even though I might not have been able to spend the past few days with Valerie, I am bringing her the best gift I possibly can.

Travel Tips

So to any other mothers out there who want to keep breastfeeding even though they must travel, I offer the following tips:

- Find a travel system that works for you. I highly recommend the cooler, bag-in-bag approach and lots of zippered freezer bags.
- Sanitize your pump and assemble it ready to go after every use. That way if you are rushing for a plane and only have a few minutes, you won't waste precious time putting everything together. Every ounce counts when you need to arrive home with as much milk as your baby drank while you were away.
- Before going through airport security, zip everything you wouldn't want security guards to touch (remember their hands have just frisked another passenger) into freezer bags.
- Always keep a supply of antibacterial wipes in your pump bag. You can purchase them especially made for breast pumps to ensure you won't be leaving behind chemicals to mix with your baby's milk.
- If being away from your baby impacts your milk supply, try to pump twice as frequently as you normally would (even if each session produces less than a full feeding), keep pumping even after your milk has stopped flowing; it makes your breasts think your baby needs more food and they will start to respond. I have had good experience drinking herb tea like Mother's Milk Tea, and taking fenugreek herbal supplements. They really work! When you get home, breastfeed your baby as much as possible to restore your supply.
- Be sure to include time for however long it takes you to pump a full feeding into your travel plans. Ensure that you are scheduling sufficient time to pump as much as your baby drinks in a day.
- An airline club membership is a great way to spend some of your frequent flyer miles, and having a clean and comfortable bathroom to pump in is worth it.

Finally, no matter how awkward or inconvenient being a breastfeeding road warrior can be, remember the reward of giving your baby the most precious gift you have to offer. In a way, it is as if a part of you is always with her even when you are gone. And when you do get home, your extra effort on the road will allow you to continue breastfeeding for as long as you like.

In a way, it is as if a part of you is always with her even when you are gone.

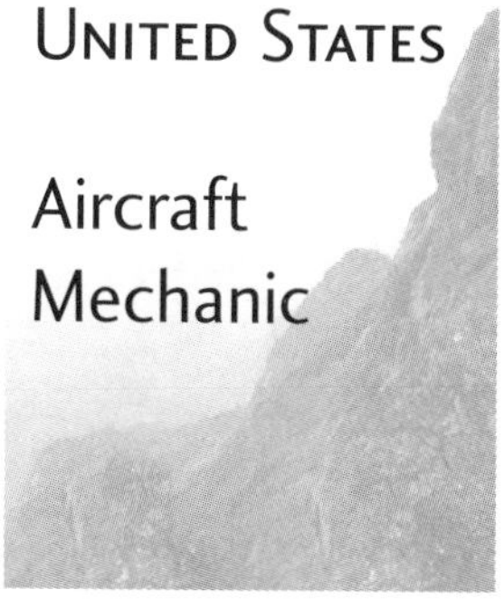

Breastfeeding on Active Duty

Robyn Roche Paull, California

I became pregnant with my son, Morgan, while on active duty in the US Navy. I had no idea how much life would change for me. I believed, naïvely, that nothing would be different after his birth. I really assumed I would continue on with my career and this baby would just fit in with my schedule. Little did I know!

Maternity leave in the military is six weeks, so just as I had finally resolved our nursing difficulties and began finally enjoying breastfeeding, it was time to return to work. I found I had a whole new set of problems to contend with! My LLL Leader helped me so much. She gave me a wealth of information on pumping and returning to work, a list of breastfeeding-friendly child-care providers that I could contact, and most importantly, the support to make this transition. I knew that I was doing what was best for my baby and me.

I returned to work full of mothering hormones and breastfeeding zeal. Unfortunately my co-workers and supervisors did not share my enthusiasm. I was an aircraft mechanic, working on jet aircraft. My job entailed dirty, greasy work in a male-dominated workplace, with long hours that coincided with the flight schedules. As the only female in my work area I found no support for my need to pump and was often the brunt of jokes about expressed milk in the refrigerator. While my co-workers took ten-minute smoke breaks every hour, I had to fight to take two 15-minute breaks twice a day for pumping. Oftentimes my break was not granted and I would become engorged and leak milk all over my uniform. I persevered though. Breastfeeding was too important to me and my baby to allow the juvenile attitudes of my co-workers or a lack of compassion by my supervisor stop me. I faced many time constraints, such as long hours (18-hour days), and fluctuating flight schedules. Worse than that were my watch-standing duties where I was required to stand watch immediately following a full shift of regular work. I also struggled with practical issues such as leaking milk on my uniform and having no place to pump.

The military did not and still does not have a policy on breastfeeding.

For lack of a better option, I found a corner in the locker room with an outlet where I could pump. Some days I could only pump once or twice for five to ten minutes, other days I could manage three or four pumping sessions for 15 to 20 minutes. It all depended on my workload and my supervisor. Fortunately, Morgan nursed a lot when I was home and at night, and my milk let down easily and quickly with the pump. I kept a picture of him in my locker and massaged my breasts while pumping to stimulate my let-down. I continued to breastfeed exclusively until Morgan turned nine months old, when he started solids. I pumped my milk for another three months until my Honorable Discharge from the US Navy.

I made breastfeeding work by finding a wonderful daycare provider close to my home who had breastfed all of her children. She knew how to hold my baby when feeding him, and she knew that he would get hungry quicker than his formula-fed counterparts. She knew the ins and outs of preparing human milk and she knew not to feed him right before I was coming to pick him up. My husband was my biggest support in combining breastfeeding and work. Since he was also on active duty in the Navy, he understood the difficulties I faced and cheered me on when I had a rough day.

I cherished every drop of my milk that Morgan received; he never had an ounce of formula during my time in the military. I especially enjoyed coming home to him after work. Oftentimes my milk would start letting down as I drove to the babysitter's. My son's face would light up when I arrived after a long day of work and he would reach for my shirt, in a hurry to nurse. In this way he thanked me, which made it all worthwhile.

I feel that I did the best I could under the circumstances. The military did not and still does not have a policy on breastfeeding.* Whether to grant time to pump and a place to pump was and is up to the Commanding Officer and more commonly, the direct supervisor. I would like to see the US Department of Defense write a military-wide policy on breastfeeding that covers all the ramifications of combining military service and breastfeeding. Maternity leave, uniform issues, pumping issues, eligibility for being deployed, and health issues all need to be addressed clearly and consistently across all of the services. With policies in place, maybe more mothers in the military would give their babies the mother's milk they need and deserve!

* The US Department of Defense has a policy that allows women to defer deployment until a newborn baby is four months old. It has declined to form a breastfeeding policy at this time. Currently, each branch of the military is responsible for its own breastfeeding policy.

Marine Corps

The US Marine Corps is the most progressive in support of breastfeeding and grants breastfeeding women a one-year deferment for deployment.

Marine Corps policy addresses training, support, and physical requirements for breastfeeding women in which breastfeeding officers must receive a secluded space, running water, and flexibility in work schedules to accommodate pumping. However, no extra time may be taken outside of normal breaks.

Navy

The US Navy makes it a requirement that women receive training about breastfeeding in some form.

Women are granted a secluded space, running water, and flexibility in work schedules to accommodate pumping. However, no extra time may be taken outside of normal breaks.

Women can defer their deployment period for four months.

Air Force

The US Air Force is in the process of implementing a breastfeeding policy but they do not currently have one in place.

Women can defer their deployment period for four months.

Army

The US Army has no breastfeeding policy at this time.

Women can defer their deployment period for four months.

More women are enlisted in the Army than any of the other military branches, with 169,900 women in the Army's active forces, Reserve, and National Guard combined.

UNITED STATES

Peace Corp Recruiter

An African Lesson in Motherhood

Mona Nyandoro, California

Before my child was born, I lived for two years on the island nation of Sao Tome and Principe in Africa as a Peace Corps Volunteer. Though technically I was there to help establish a national park, much of my job as a volunteer was focused on integrating into my local community. This meant learning such things as how to wash my clothes by hand, how to cook over an open fire, and how to sweep my home with a broom made from long grass. Like most volunteers, I found myself reaching out to community members to help me learn how to complete these everyday tasks. During the many hours that I spent in the village with the women, I managed to pick up some other unexpected skills. In the US, I had never witnessed basic functions of motherhood. In Africa, I learned how to diaper, bathe, feed, and take care of young children. It was only several years later, when I became pregnant with my own child, that I realized how valuable this experience had been to me—and to my new baby.

Once I became pregnant, I made the conscious decision to follow the African tradition of breastfeeding. I remembered vivid images of village women sitting together in the courtyard, avocado trees overhead, breastfeeding and talking. It was not rare to see a woman just plop her breast out from under her shirt and offer it to a wailing infant or an irritable toddler. Sometimes the child may not even have been hers! Additionally, everything that I read in preparation for motherhood indicated that it was in the best interest of the mother and child to establish a breastfeeding relationship. Why not make life easier on myself and give my baby the best food available?

I managed to take a total of three months off for maternity leave by combining sick leave, annual leave, and leave without pay. I believe this time with my child allowed us to create a successful breastfeeding relationship that was well established by the time I returned to full-time work. On my first day back at work, I was fully armed with a milk-pumping machine that I would switch on for about 15 minutes, three to four times per day. Boy, this was certainly different than anything I had seen in Africa! I wondered what those African ladies would think if they saw me doing this! Luckily, I had a private office and my boss and colleagues never interfered with my need to pump my baby's milk. On occasion, I would need to make a subtle exit from an office meeting, but no questions were ever asked. I never made any excuses or apologies for having to take time out of my day to collect milk for my baby. The way I thought about it was that I was doing them a favor by continuing to work full-time, while also managing the challenge of new motherhood. Besides, I could successfully type emails and answer phones without distraction. Only once did someone on the other end of the line ask me what that "noise" was. I simply responded that it was the "copy machine."

I never made any excuses or apologies for having to take time out of my day to collect milk for my baby.

Clearly one of the most beneficial things that resulted from my commitment to breastfeeding is that my child is amazingly healthy. Our pediatrician comments every time I take her in for a routine checkup that he "never" sees her. My favorite perk is the uniquely close relationship that I have established with my child. Though I am not able to spend the bulk of my days with her because of my work, I can be sure that when I finally make it through that front door my two-year-old will jump into mama's lap wanting to be cuddled and to drink "sum milk." At times, when I am sitting with my child at my breast, I think of those inspirational women back in Sao Tome. I really think that they would feel happy to know they were able to impart to me such a worthy skill. They taught me to choose breast over bottle and to feel no shame about breastfeeding in public.

Finding Value in Mothering

Kymberlie Stefanski, Illinois

Although I thought I was prepared to be pregnant, have a baby, and give up my career to be a stay-at-home mother, it wasn't until I actually became a mother and was home that I realized what my life was going to be like. My husband and I had always talked about how our lives would change when we had a baby. But we had no idea, really. With my first daughter, Moriah, I took the full leave of absence that my employer offered—a generous six months. A few weeks of it was paid but the rest was unpaid. We had built up our savings account in preparation for the unpaid time. During the time I was home, I felt so incredibly lonely. I went from "climbing the corporate ladder," working in technology for a growing telecommunications company, to holding a baby during every waking hour and many non-waking hours. I felt totally unfulfilled, yet I knew the time I was spending with my baby was valuable and would impact her for life. I was nursing on cue. She took her naps on my lap since she cried if I put her down. I called my husband daily, crying and saying that I wasn't doing anything with my life. He was so reassuring, telling me that I was doing something—I was mothering our daughter, which was more important than anything else.

Month after month, I hung in there, nurturing, holding, caressing, and playing with my tiny daughter. I paid the bills at the beginning of each month, first paying what I could from my husband's paychecks. For the bills that were left unpaid, I tapped into that savings account we had been building up. I learned how to skimp and cut corners and make lots of different stews from leftovers. Cooking became very creative. My father was paying for a diaper service. I knew that eventually our savings account was going to be down to nothing and there were no other corners to cut. Yet, we knew I should be at home with our daughter. Still, part of me wanted to go back to work for the sense of value that I was missing. When my leave of absence was coming to an end, I prepared my resignation. It wasn't an easy decision to make, especially considering the financial need we had. Having a very strong faith in God, we prayed for guidance.

I casually mentioned that I would be willing to be flexible on pay in return for being able to bring my daughter to work.

One evening we were watching the news and heard a blown-out-of-proportion story about breastfeeding and decided to look online to see if La Leche League had a position on the situation. My husband went to the La Leche League Web site and right there, on the home page, was a link for a position in the technology department. With nothing to lose, I submitted my resumé, prayed, and made a few phone calls to get some more information. I figured that if anyone would be flexible with children, it would be La Leche League. During the time that my resumé was being reviewed, I was offered a couple of part-time positions at other companies, but nothing was flexible enough to keep my daughter by my side. During my interview with La Leche League, I casually mentioned that I would be willing to be flexible on pay in return for being able to bring my daughter to work. I hadn't really thought about how to do that, but thought we could find a way to work it out as long as I was able to nurse her as she needed it.

We discussed scheduling and determined that it would be feasible to bring Moriah with me as well as work from home on occasion. She was seven months old when I started working two days each week. With a 30-minute commute, I was able to nurse her before we left the house, frequently throughout the day, and before we left in the evening. Many of her naps were on my lap or in her car seat. She learned to crawl and walk in my office where she had a set of special toys that were just for the office so she wouldn't get bored with them. She even spent a lot of time just sitting on my lap. Our arrangements made it easy for me to stick to my initial desire not to give her bottles, pacifiers, or anything other than my milk directly from me until Moriah was ready for healthy food. I also had an office full of very supportive co-workers who truly understood the needs of growing children!

Moriah became known as "the office toddler," and we continued this arrangement for two years, through my second pregnancy. She knew people by name and enjoyed sharing lunches with co-workers, as if I hadn't fed her just 15 minutes earlier. She attended meetings with me—sometimes nursing, sometimes coloring, and sometimes talking. I'm sure there were times when she distracted people and times when she provided a little "child relief" from the day-to-day office routines. The baby gate in the doorway of my office helped keep either of those times to a minimum.

Pregnant with my second child, I knew that it was becoming more difficult to keep my toddler occupied in the office. Moriah was a very normal, curious, and social child. She would still nurse on and off throughout the day and take her naps on my lap. She was also becoming very good at expressing her opinions and her growing independence. What was I going to do when the baby joined us? I couldn't even imagine working with two children by my side. I certainly couldn't imagine bringing two children into the office for two full days every week. What was I going to do?

When the time came to return to work with our new schedule, I had no idea what to expect.

I prayed. I prayed a lot. After some planning and discussions with my supervisor, we decided that in the last two months of my pregnancy I would work one day from home and one day in the office. This would allow me to demonstrate my ability to be productive from home while giving my co-workers time to adjust to my physical absence. After baby number two was born, we agreed that I would take a three-month leave of absence and then return to work on a work-from-home schedule. Working three hours each day from home equaled the same number of hours I worked when I was in the office two days per week. I would also go into the office as needed for meetings or certain projects. During those times, I would bring my children. I would work consistent hours unless there was a child-interruption, in which case I would just work later. It sounded like a good plan.

For two months, I worked one day a week in the office and one day a week from home. The week I went into labor, I worked in the office on Tuesday, and worked from home on Friday. In the wee hours of Sunday morning, my second daughter, Eliyah, was born. We took three months off of work to establish good bonding, grow as a family, and enjoy each other. When the time came to return to work with our new schedule, I had no idea what to expect. Moriah has always been a good napper. Eliyah cat napped, taking several ten or fifteen minute naps each day. I thought maybe I could encourage them to take naps together while I worked. No, that didn't work. Fortunately, Moriah had begun taking only one long nap a day, and the best time for that was in the afternoon. That would be the time I worked. Many days, I would spend the entire three hours nursing Eliyah and working at the computer.

As Eliyah grew, I realized how different she was from Moriah. Moriah is calm, focused, quiet, yet well-spoken. She nursed for comfort, whether a bump or a new tooth. Eliyah was trying to climb at five months. She is very physical and has a strong need to release energy that I never knew a baby could have. I truly cannot imagine having to work full-days or take her into the office on a regular basis. The plan we had arranged at work was exactly what I needed in order to continue doing the work I do. My children could nurse as they needed or wanted. I could tend to their every need. They could have my attention when they felt they needed it. Usually, Moriah would nap for most of the time I would be working from home. Sometimes Eliyah would. Other times she would watch an educational television program, or swing from the exercise bar in the doorway. Especially nice were the times she would stand behind me on my work chair with her arms wrapped around my neck, saying the occasional, "I love you, mom." Working still gives me a sense of value, but now I do it for both the money and to better the organization for which I work. I now have a sense of value from mothering.

The plan we had arranged at work was exactly what I needed in order to continue doing the work I do.

Eliyah is two and Moriah is four-and-a-half. To them, I have always worked and they have always been with me. When I am needed in the office, they go with me and we take along activities to keep them occupied. There are always people who enjoy playing with them if my undivided attention is needed. The arrangement that I have would not work without the support and encouragement of my dear husband and compassionate, understanding co-workers and supervisors. It also helps to have the surprise of a society that doesn't understand. Yes, that encourages me. I love the surprise when people find out I work with my children by my side. I don't need to supplement with formula or use a pacifier to calm my children. They nurse. They get all they need from me. They are learning they can count on me to meet those needs. I am spreading the word to society that mothers and babies do not need to be separated for women to contribute financially, for mothers to have a sense of self, or for babies to learn to be independent. They will learn that eventually. Until then, they need their mom right next to them.

United States

Pharmacist

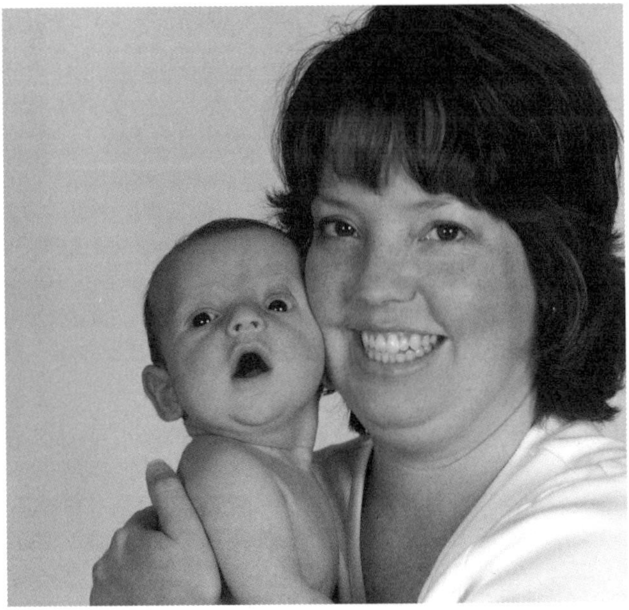

Working the Nightshift, Nursing the Dayshift

Melissa Hulse, Kansas

My breastfeeding experience began at the strong urging of my co-worker. I had actually planned on nursing my baby, but it was more of a passive decision than an active one. I figured that if it worked out then I would continue, and if my baby didn't take to it, then I would formula-feed. My knowledge of breastfeeding was limited as I had never been closely associated with a nursing mother. In addition, my husband and I were both bottle-fed babies in the 1970s, so our mothers weren't able to assist us with firsthand experience. My co-worker had successfully nursed her two children past the age of one and insisted that I give it an honest try. I'm forever grateful to her for the gentle nudging. When postpartum depression took over our lives, holding my little bundle in my arms while he nursed was one of the few bright spots in those early days. Then my doctor and extended family suggested that perhaps we would all benefit from my husband feeding the baby "a bottle or two of formula" so I could rest. It was my son's pediatrician who urged me to continue nursing and suggested that I contact a La Leche League Leader for support.

Before the birth of our son, who is now seven months old, my husband and I both worked full-time. We have always felt strongly that children should be raised with a stay-at-home parent. So, when I was five months pregnant, we decided that for financial stability, he should stay at home while I continued my career as a pharmacist. To minimize my time away from home, we decided that I would take the night position in our hospital pharmacy department. I returned to work after nine weeks off, where I now work 11-hour shifts for seven days in a row and then have seven days off. I am the only pharmacist on duty during the night, so when I leave for the pump room I carry a cell phone. At my urging, the pharmacy director installed an answering system on our department's phones, so that callers with non-urgent items could leave messages for me, and emergency callers could reach me immediately via the cell phone. The nursing staff has adapted well to this change.

I'm grateful for the support of my workplace, which enabled my son to receive only my milk for his first six months of life.

As a pharmacist, I have a variety of work environments from which to choose. I have found hospital pharmacy to be where I feel most at home. I am very fortunate to work for a hospital that provides its employees with a hospital grade pump to use free of charge and a quiet room dedicated just for pumping mothers. To my delight, I have found that I particularly enjoy the camaraderie of the night staff within our facility. I'm grateful for the support of my workplace, which enabled my son to receive only my milk for his first six months of life and will allow us to continue our nursing relationship for as long as we desire.

I believe that my night position has been a wonderful arrangement for breastfeeding. My husband bottle-feeds our son through the night with my expressed milk and then brings him to me while I sleep during the day for feedings and naps. Once we mastered the art of nursing while lying down, the whole process got even easier! The absolute best part of my particular schedule is that I get to spend seven whole days every other week with my family without pumps, bottles, or time clocks.

UNITED STATES

Family Lumber Business

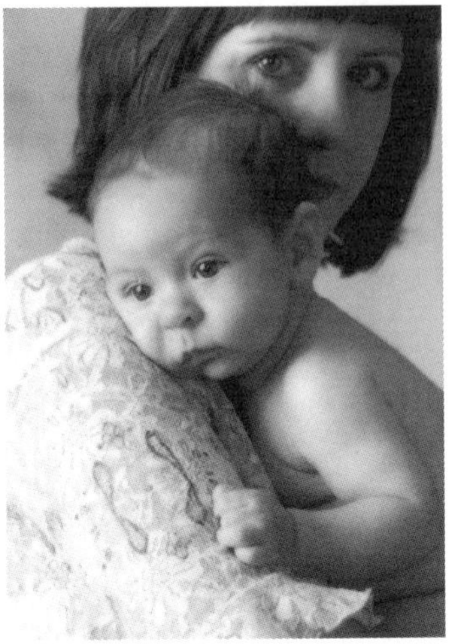

Working Mother, Disabled Father, Breastfed Children

Mary Joan Jordan Vacarella, Georgia

I grew up in a traditional family with a stay-at-home mom, working dad, and older brother and sister. My mother adhered to the medical practices of the day, being sedated during childbirth and feeding us formula and early solids. Still, she was an independent-minded sort, and I like to think she passed some of that on to me. My parents were unique in that they had both lost their mothers as children.

My father, who had his own lumber business, offered me a job. I accepted, married my husband, and bought a small house in Hickory, Georgia. That was 12 years ago and I am still working at my father's business, even though he has since passed away. My brother runs the place now, so I work for him. Don't assume that I work for a family-friendly business just because I work for a family business, however. My brother works long hours and has a wife at home to take care of his children and personal needs. I do not have this luxury. We seem to have reached a certain level of understanding though, that I am the primary caregiver for two young children, and that their needs take precedence. Still, one of their needs is financial support, so working at my job is also working for them.

My hours are from 8:00 AM until 5:30 PM with an hour for lunch, which I use to visit daycare. Other than our annual physical inventory, I rarely work outside of these hours. All of our office staff, including me, is salaried, and we are allowed to take time off as needed for doctor appointments or other needs, within reason. While I would rather be with my children, I have found that with reliable daycare, my hours are not overly burdensome and my work is sufficiently flexible. I have been able to pump my milk at work, take my children to the doctor, stay home with them when they are sick, and attend important functions for them. I know there are other women with more demanding hours, who must travel or work late night shifts, or who work on a strict schedule that allows little time to pump or to schedule personal appointments. These are all challenges that require negotiation, evaluation, creativity, and family support.

I am not only the sole wage earner for my family, but I also have primary responsibility for my children and my home. My husband's health began deteriorating soon after we married, and he was diagnosed with a degenerative brain disorder. For most of our marriage, I have been the primary wage earner. This was not an issue when we first got married, because I was sure I did not want to have children. My husband had considerable experience in fine dining as a server and cook, and he continued to work in this field at first, though his disability made this more and more difficult. At some point though, my mothering hormones kicked in. However, since I had to work and we were concerned about my husband's health, we put off having children. After about six years of seeing different specialists, I decided I did not want to not have children and I was tired of waiting. We had had no luck getting to the bottom of Frank's health problems, but we decided to try for a child.

Within a few months, I was pregnant, and we had our first child in 2000, a girl we named Sarah Frances. She is a high-need, outgoing, spirited, loving child. She challenges and rewards me. Knowing what I know today, I would still have decided to have a child, even though my husband's health began to deteriorate even more rapidly after Sarah's birth. I love my child so much; I knew in my heart I wanted more, but I also knew in my mind that it did not make sense to have another child.

Employers must provide a reasonable amount of break time for an employee who wishes to express human milk. If possible, the break time should run concurrent with existing break time. Any additional break time taken will be unpaid by the employer. An employer is not required to provide break time if to do so would unduly disrupt the employer's operations.

Employers must make reasonable efforts to provide a place nearby the work area that is not a toilet stall to express milk in private.

My second pregnancy was unplanned, and even though I was apprehensive about having a second child, our baby boy born in 2003, named Joseph William, has been an absolute joy. He is an easy, loving, happy baby.

For both my children, I followed a similar schedule. I did not take any time off other than necessary for medical appointments prior to giving birth. I negotiated an extended maternity leave of 12 weeks versus the standard six weeks my company provided. This leave was paid, but in order to extend it, I agreed to work part-time at home after two weeks. My company bought me a home computer and gave me a used fax machine. I did things like review paperwork, compile sales statistics, and call in the payroll. Once a week, I went into the office and signed checks. This schedule worked out okay with my first child and gave my husband a chance for one-on-one time with our daughter while I worked. With the second child, this schedule was more daunting, as my husband could no longer watch after the baby while I worked. I took my older child out of daycare during this time, so she needed attention, too. To make matters worse, I spent much of my two weeks of "free time" going back and forth to the hospital after my son tested positive for a newborn metabolic disorder. Repeat testing came back negative, but not without several stress-filled postpartum days. If I ever have a third child, I will try to take an extended leave, but I would choose to take it at half-pay rather than overload myself with commitments.

I am not only the sole wage earner for my family, but I also have primary responsibility for my children and my home.

When it came time to return to work, I eased back into it by scheduling an early return midweek, and then taking a day off midweek the following week. Both of my children took to their bottles of expressed milk just fine. Both had limited experience with bottles before going to daycare. I settled into a schedule of pumping mid-morning and mid-afternoon, and breastfeeding my babies during my lunch hour. Quite by accident, probably because they were cheaper, I used the type of bottles and nipples which are recommended for breastfed babies who must take bottles. I tried another feeding system that used bags for storage, but the bags were hard to fill with fresh milk without spilling and had to be thawed and put in a bottle before I could take them to daycare. My second child refused the nipple on this feeding system, so I just bought more standard plastic bottles and nipples, and stored all of the milk in bottles, frozen and fresh. My daughter had no problems switching from the bottle to the breast, and was obviously very attached to breastfeeding, as she is still nursing before going to sleep now at the age of four.

My son experienced some problems waiting for my let down, I

believe due to the instant gratification of bottle-feeding. Most of this occurred around month five, but after several frustrating feeding experiences, I read an article about communicating with your young baby, and I successfully talked my son into waiting patiently by speaking in a soothing voice, telling him what a good job he was doing, and patting and stroking him gently. I also experienced problems with let-down while trying to pump for my second child after the age of six months. After trying massage and relaxation, I tried a fenugreek supplement, and that seemed to get me over the hump.

Pumping and Daycare

My pumping situation at work was less than desirable. For my first child I used an empty office. For my second child, there was no office available, but a rough break room had been set up in the basement. I had to lock the door to the break room, which caused some inconvenience for my co-workers. I briefly tried pumping during my lunch instead of going to daycare, but this proved too inconvenient for the others at work. I found that total pumping time including setup and cleanup took about 25 minutes. Since I could not really make this time up, I made a concerted effort to look busy the rest of the time. Still, I received some criticism from my co-workers and my boss for taking time to pump and breastfeed. I tried to take it in stride and keep up with my work. That is, I pretty much ignored it. I knew I was doing what was best for my baby, and that I wouldn't be stopped without a fight. At one point my boss even said "I know that you are into breastfeeding, but..." as if it was just a hobby. All I could ever say in response was that my children would be healthier as a result, and that pumping was only temporary.

It is my belief that many women avoid breastfeeding or end it prematurely because of the difficulty of integrating it with their work.

Even though my situation was less than ideal, I was still able to pump and feed my children my milk exclusively. We do not all work for Fortune 500 companies with on-site daycares and lactation programs. For many of us who are working and breastfeeding, we are our company's first experience with a breastfeeding mother. Workplace legislation in this regard is woefully inadequate in the United States. At a minimum, businesses should provide enough time and an appropriate place to pump. It is my belief that many women avoid breastfeeding or end it prematurely because of the difficulty of integrating it with their work.

It is not easy to pump. It feels and looks awkward. There are bottles to clean and prepare, just like bottle-feeding. Milk must be stored and transported. The baby still gets the nutritional benefits of human milk, but loses the intimacy. Good quality pumps are expensive and can be cost-prohibitive, especially for the first-time mother who is unsure of her ability to successfully breastfeed. Still, I encourage any mother to pump if she works and feed her child her milk exclusively, because the benefits of maintaining the breastfeeding relationship far outweigh the inconvenience.

Thankfully, at around nine months of age, babies generally start to take in enough solid food that the working mother may be able to eliminate one pumping session. By the age of one, my first child quit taking bottles at daycare and breastfed only. It took a bit of creative scheduling to get me there when she was hungry, but we were able to eliminate her bottles one by one until she was nursing in the morning before I went to work, nursing once midday around the daycare's lunch schedule, and nursing when I picked her up. With my second child, I was also able to eliminate a pumping session at around nine months, but I kept bringing expressed milk for as long as he would take it, until about 14 months, because his weight was low on the charts. Now at 18 months of age, I still feed him at drop-off, midday, and pickup, and he nurses as frequently as he wants when we are together. Now that I am no longer pumping, breastfeeding is a breeze, and I wouldn't give up our special time for anything.

Combining breastfeeding and working... offers the reward of an intimate relationship with your children that is more important than any job.

Breastfeeding a baby at a daycare should not be a problem, but I have even experienced problems with that. There is no private, comfortable place to nurse at the daycare I use, even though more and more mothers are breastfeeding these days. After the age of one, my children moved into a room that had no adult furniture, so there isn't even a rocking chair. I usually sit on the floor to feed, which is hard on the back and provides no arm support. Using a baby sling helps. My practice of extended breastfeeding has led to some complaints from other parents. Still, rather than give up, I approached the problem from several different directions. First I worked with the daycare director to find the most agreeable place for me to nurse. Second, I consulted with La Leche League International to clarify my rights. Third, I worked with my La Leche League Leader, who in turn worked with the Area Professional Liaison Leader to write up a one-page information sheet for businesses and mailed it to my daycare.

Working and mothering are hard no matter what. For that matter, mothering alone is a challenge. Combining breastfeeding and working can be difficult, but it offers the reward of an intimate relationship with your children that is more important than any job.

Breastfeeding My Special Needs Child

Felicia Fogal, Texas

I never planned to become an advocate for breastfeeding and working. When my oldest daughter was born, she came to my office with me for the first three months. After those three months, my mother kept her; I pumped at the office and ran home at lunch to feed her. My company was very flexible with my hours and quietly supported my desire to breastfeed. I say quietly because it was never discussed too much. (It is hard to get a group of middle-aged, engineer-types to talk too much about lactation issues.) But nevertheless, they were a quiet pillar of support.

When I became pregnant with my son, I had planned all along to breastfeed. I did so with my daughter and I would do so again with the new baby. During my pregnancy, we discovered that there was a small percentage chance that the baby would have Down syndrome. But as the percentage was so small, my husband and I put it out of our minds. There was too much to do—renovate our house, raise our other children, and decorate the nursery. Jackson came into our lives three weeks early, just as we were finishing our renovation (good timing, Jax). And the moment he came pouting into the world, I knew. I just took one look at his face—those wonderful blueberry eyes and his kissable cherry nose, and his floppy limbs, and I knew. I knew our lives as we had known them would change forever.

Those first few days and weeks are still a bit of a blur. Hospitals, genetics doctors, fears, lost dreams, new wonderful dreams, and so many questions my husband and I would need to answer over the next few months—and still, here was this baby who needed to be fed. I began to breastfeed immediately in the hospital, and what I did not know at the time is that one of the characteristics of Down syndrome is low-muscle tone, which made it very difficult for Jackson to suck and swallow. I met with the hospital's lactation consultant, but did not receive much useful information for nursing a child with special needs.

I never planned to become an advocate for breastfeeding and working—but I did!

What I did learn, in the weeks to follow, through LLLI, a private lactation consultant, and some wonderful mothers who had nursed their special needs children, was that there were various techniques to establish a good milk supply and nursing pattern for my "little man." Those first few weeks I pumped around the clock, feeding him my milk swallow by swallow from a bottle, and slowly he began to gain enough strength to nurse directly. Now we jokingly refer to Jackson as our "Buddha-belly" baby, as he is at the top of the Down syndrome growth chart.

When Jackson was six weeks old, I began to go into the office for a few hours a week. I held him close to me in a sling, and nursed him. I typed with one hand and nuzzled with the other. My bringing my child to work was never something that we addressed directly, we just showed up at work, and once again, through the generosity of my company, we were accepted and supported. And so it has continued this way for many months now. Jackson and I go into the office several days a week; he has his play area in my office and is loved and adored by all of the women (and many of the men) in my company. He is fed when he is hungry, he is hugged when he is sad, and kissed when he smiles up at me with his blueberry eyes and his cherry nose.

I know now that though it can be more difficult to nurse babies with Down syndrome, it is not only possible, but is so important for their health and for their development. Breastfeeding not only helps bolster the immune system (babies with Down syndrome are prone to upper respiratory illness in their first year) it also helps develop their jaw muscles for help with their oral-motor skills. Most importantly to me, breastfeeding is providing my son with the best nutrition he can have. I am committed to breastfeeding Jackson for at least a year.

I don't know how much longer I will be bringing Jackson to work with me. I suppose it will be less feasible when he becomes mobile. But who knows, maybe he can practice his crawling down the long office hallway and into the arms of many wonderful middle-aged engineers!

UNITED STATES

Registered Dietitian

Surrendering One Dream Job for Another

Lisa Kopecky, Nebraska

Growing up in the 1970s, I clearly remember spending many evenings in a home filled with new mothers seeking support from other breastfeeding mothers. Listening to my mother encourage and educate women about the benefits and enjoyment of breastfeeding was an educational experience like no other. I always knew I would breastfeed my babies someday; I just never knew I would have to put so much planning and thought into making this natural occurrence a reality.

At the age of 16, I found myself in an unplanned pregnancy. With much support and direction, I selected a beautiful couple to adopt my unborn baby. It was during my sixth month of pregnancy that I picked up a copy of THE WOMANLY ART OF BREASTFEEDING and read it from cover to cover. I remember having a discussion with the adoptive mother about whether or not I was going to breastfeed my baby while I cared for her in the hospital following the delivery. Knowing what kind of bonding would transpire through breastfeeding, I opted not to do so, fearing that it might change my decision regarding the adoption process. It was during this time in my life when, feeling helpless, I made up my mind to focus on a career and a future.

Over the coming years, I doggedly pursued a career. In the process, my formal and work-based learning reinforced my early inclination that breastfeeding would someday be a beautiful, life-giving gift—one I would definitely give to my children.

Following my eventual college graduation, my new husband and I underwent a series of moves and changes so I could continue my training in nutrition. One of the courses I took during this time of study really stood out. It was in the class, Maternal and Infant Nutrition, that I relearned not only the importance of breastfeeding and the physiological how to's, but discovered the importance of breastfeeding until at least one year of age.

There is breastfeeding legislation in this state, but none specific to workforce protection.

Still later, in graduate school, I was working for a hospital as a clinical dietitian when I realized that if I wanted to breastfeed my babies for a year, I had to find a job that could support that. I was sharing an office with five other women and hated my job. Furthermore, I certainly did not feel there would be opportunities to pump milk for my babies in this environment.

I was offered and accepted my dream job—Assistant Coordinator of Performance Nutrition at the University of Nebraska. My job would entail putting together nutritional programs for the female athletic population, making meal arrangements pre and post competition, body composition testing, and occasional travel during tournaments. Although this job would be demanding at various times during the year, it was also extremely flexible.

A mere six months into my dream job, another dream came true. This time it was a planned pregnancy. I was reluctant to share the news with my predominately male co-workers. How would they react, how could I ever breastfeed and expect them to understand? Much to my surprise, as soon as the news of my pregnancy got out, three of the men in my department immediately started offering me advice on what type of breast pumps their wives had used when their children were born. Never in a million years would I have guessed that these very strong, macho men had a soft spot in their hearts for breastfeeding!

Landon Daniel arrived three weeks late following a wonderful pregnancy and delivery. With the assistance of my doulas, Landon was nursing within minutes of birth and as one nurse stated, "He could suck the paint off the walls!"

Eight weeks later I returned to work on a part-time basis and then went full-time at ten weeks postpartum. By this time my husband had changed from a day shift to a second shift at work so that he could be home with Landon most of the day. It was important to me to find a child care provider who would not only love and care for my child but who would also understand and support my decision to breastfeed. During my last trimester of pregnancy I started attending different La Leche League Groups in my community. Thank goodness I did. It was here that I found a friend and a child care provider for my son who held the same beliefs I had about nursing, even though using her would mean a one-hour round trip commute for both my husband and me each day.

Just because I wanted to breastfeed didn't mean that it was going to be easy.

I hadn't realized prior to returning to work that just because I wanted to breastfeed didn't mean that it was going to be easy. My first obstacle was that I could never pump more milk than what my baby needed for the next day. I never felt as though I could get ahead, and worried about what would happen if he should need more. Thankfully, I could slip away from work for an hour to nurse him if needed. During the busy fall-camp season, my sisters and my mother would stay with me and often accompany me and Landon to work so that I could nurse as we both needed.

In addition to job flexibility was a very large, comfortable staff locker room equipped with a recliner, couch, TV, and bathroom. It was not completely private, but I was not shy at all in letting everyone know what I was doing and why. I will never forget a comment made by a young woman named Michele. She said that she had never thought about breastfeeding before, but now she knew she could and she would be successful at it. That was one of my proudest moments as a new mother. Breastfeeding is an experience that you cannot give someone else; they have to experience it for themselves, and I was proud that I may have helped to encourage someone else.

After Landon's birth, if I needed to travel, my teams were very respectful of my needs. I always had a king size bed, refrigerator, and lots of help from the teams. And as Landon got bigger and more active, they respected my desire to avoid travel. I am proud to say that I have nursed my baby in every Division I athletic arena.

Thankfully breastfeeding was easy for us. I wasn't prepared for Landon to refuse to take a bottle at four months of age following his first and only nursing strike. Likewise, I was not prepared for what would be one of seven bouts with mastitis that I developed during this time. Looking back it would have been very easy to stop nursing, switching instead to formula, but I truly loved breastfeeding. Landon came into my bed permanently at that point. We started co-sleeping out of necessity, as he would nurse all night and take only sips of milk from a sippy cup during the day while I was at work. I continued to pump two to three times a day until Landon was nine months old and the volume of milk he needed declined.

As Landon was approaching his first birthday many family members and friends started asking me when I would stop nursing. I had mistakenly told them from the start that I would nurse until Landon's first birthday. I wasn't ready to stop; I had made it this far and I was going to continue as long as we mutually agreed. Landon and I continued our nursing relationship until his second birthday. To this day if Landon sees a baby, he assumes he or she is breastfed. He knows he is smart and strong due to the milk he received from me when he was a baby.

As I look back I am most thankful for enormous support during my first breastfeeding journey. First of all, my husband, who had no prior experience with breastfeeding, has given ongoing support for my decision to give our child the best nutritionally and emotionally. My new friend Sara, an LLL Leader in my community, gave me support not only at monthly meetings, but during the night, on the weekends, and for years to come. I remember her clear, calm words: "Lisa, don't make any decisions because of one bad day." I carry that advice with me today. If it had not been for my co-worker, Courtney, the only other full-time female staff member, I may not have been able to continue working in my dream job for as long as I did. Part of my job requirements included attending as many female athletic events as possible. Because I was involved in 12 women's teams, that meant I was attending events often seven days a week. At times, Courtney would pick Landon up from the babysitter and meet me at events so I could nurse him right away. Of course, my loving mother's support and encouragement for breastfeeding began when I was a girl, and it has continued through my adulthood.

Looking back it would have been very easy to stop nursing, switching instead to formula, but I truly loved breastfeeding.

A Priority Shift

By late 2001, my husband, Lon, and I wanted to expand our family. I had just taken over as the Interim Coordinator of the Performance Nutrition Team and I wasn't sure I could successfully raise another child in this fast-paced environment. It was through much soul-searching that I realized that I had lived my first dream job. Now I wanted to focus more of my time on my other dream job, being a mother. This was and is the most important job I have ever attempted to be successful at.

A job change was inevitable, so I accepted a position as assistant food service director for a 200 bed long-term care facility. Five years prior, I would have bet money that I would not have worked in long-term care, but this job was different. Tabitha Nursing and Rehab Center had just opened an on site intergenerational center. Providing care to 35 elders and a developmental playschool for approximately 70 infants and children, Tabitha's Intergenerational Center was one of a kind in our community. What a luxury it would be to have my children on site with me while I worked. At the time I accepted, I really didn't know the extent that it would benefit my children and me.

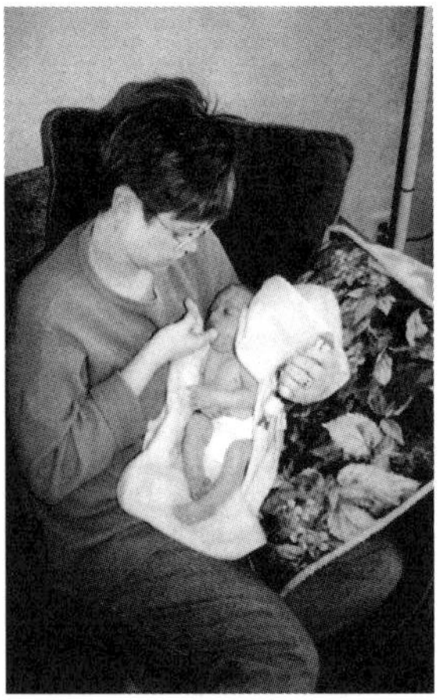

Soon after, I was pregnant again. Much to my surprise, I started having preterm labor at 28 weeks gestation. I took medication, worked half days, and even went on bed rest for a couple of weeks. It was my 36th week and I had been contraction-free for three days when I returned to work to finish training my replacement.

As my supervisor and I were heading to our offices on the first floor, I suggested we take the elevator instead of climbing the one flight of stairs. While in the elevator I felt a pop and announced "I think my water just broke." When we looked down we saw that it wasn't my water, but rather I was hemorrhaging. Shirley, my supervisor, immediately rushed me into her office which was right next to the elevator while she ran for her car.

My new baby, Lance, was born shortly after. It was a tumultuous time and he struggled in the NICU for a week. I fought hard to be able to feed him my colostrum and my milk, using a syringe at first, until he was eventually able to nurse from the breast. Once home, we continued to struggle when Lance's weight began dropping. I began finger-feeding him my expressed milk, until at last by day 12, he was nursing heartily and gaining weight.

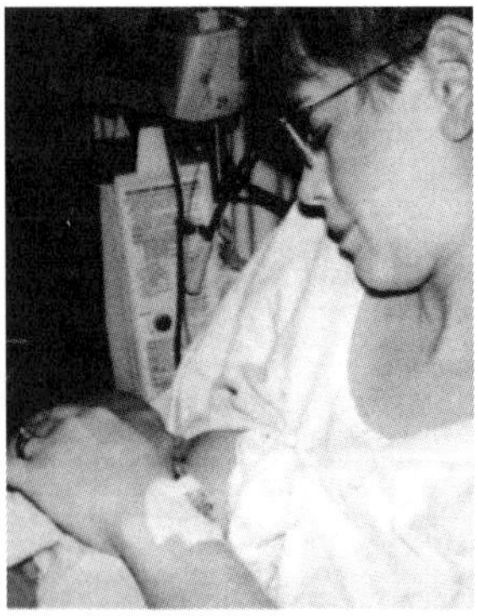

After 11 weeks of maternity leave, I needed to return to work. This time, though, my baby and preschooler would go with me! Although this was my second baby, I had to learn a new system. My plan wasn't to pump during the day; I was going to sneak across the street to nurse. Upon returning to work, my supervisor handed me a pager and announced, "Now I will be able to locate you." She knew and accepted that I would be spending a portion of my day across the street nursing Lance. I found it very interesting that within five minutes of my milk letting down at work, I would receive a page that Lance needed to nurse. Later I discovered that there was about a five-minute turnaround time on those pagers. To me that was mother's intuition.

To ease the stress of a hectic workday plus manage to nurse my baby four to five times, I extended my hours. I would go to work about an hour early each day so that I could sit and nurse while watching my older son play. I would often eat my lunch at my desk or on the way to a nursing session so that I could have that special time with Lance. In the evenings when I was the last mother to pick up my children, the director of the Intergenerational Center told me I could stay as long as I needed, if I would just lock up the center when I left. I brought dinner along for my older son to enjoy while I was nursing the baby.

Today, a happy, healthy two-year-old, Lance climbs up on my lap, grins at me with his big brown eyes, and asks, "I hold one nursie, mommy?" And I smile back and say "Yes, just one."

Because of my journey, I have had the opportunity to help other working mothers in ways I would have never imagined. Shortly after Lance's birth, I became heavily involved in city-wide efforts to help working mothers continue to breastfeed. In addition to my involvement within my city, I have made it my mission to support mothers at my worksite who plan to return to work and continue breastfeeding. As I write this story, I am proud to announce the opening of a Lactation Station for staff, families, and visitors located in our long-term care facility and a bill that is being introduced into our state's legislature later this month, which would guarantee a mother's right to breastfeed in public. I have enjoyed this adventure immensely, and I am eagerly awaiting the future to see where breastfeeding may lead me.

I am eagerly awaiting the future to see where breastfeeding may lead me.

Canada

Teacher

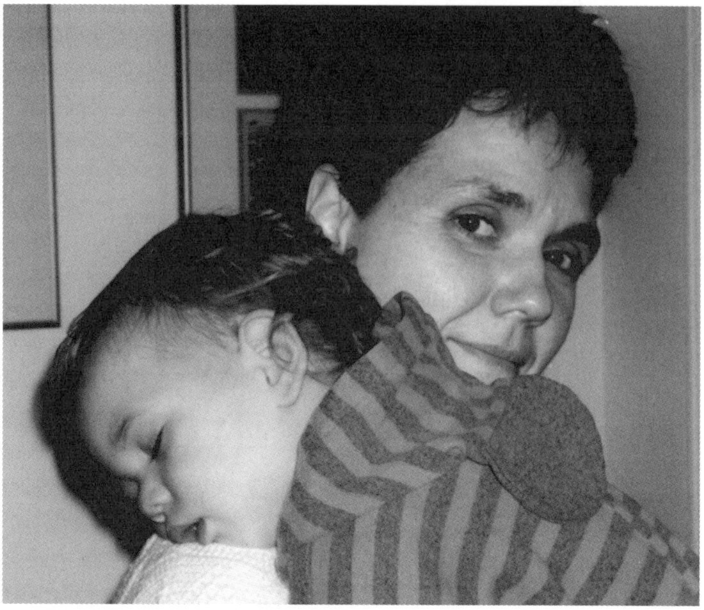

Sudden Illness

Roswita Dressler, British Columbia

In the summer of 1999, my life changed. My husband and I, along with our three children, moved into a new home. To help the movers remove the refrigerator, David took off the front door of our old home. Taking the door down the stairs, he slipped and landed on his back. Being a strong man, he got up and continued to work; however, we now believe that that fall was the pivotal event for the illness that was to come. This illness was the reason I returned to work.

Up until this time, I considered myself a “stay-at-home” mom. I had worked as a teacher, but we had moved a number of times and I had no permanent contract. I was a substitute teacher during my first pregnancy until approximately one month before the birth of our oldest son, Daniel. He nursed for almost four years, even through the pregnancy and birth of our daughter, Anja. In Canada, most women initiate breastfeeding, but fewer than ten percent are breastfeeding at one year, so our lifestyle of breastfeeding past toddlerhood was out of the norm. In fact, I hadn't thought I would breastfeed this long, but I started attending La Leche League meetings just before Daniel was born and soon had the knowledge and support to nurse past the original six months I had planned.

I was nursing Anja when we moved from our home in northern Manitoba to Vancouver Island in British Columbia. In our new town, I met a woman who was starting a tutoring agency. Since I was trained as a high school French teacher, she asked if I would be interested in working as a tutor. My first reaction was negative, knowing how often our ten-month-old still nursed. However, I decided to "float a trial balloon." I mentioned that I could work out of my home with a mother's helper (a teenager who looks after the children when the mother is home, but busy). I was clear that my daughter would need full access to me and my students and their parents would need to be aware that I would occasionally be breastfeeding while I taught. To my surprise, the woman responded that she had been a member of La Leche League and breastfed her children. She fully supported my working in this way. I worked for the tutoring agency for four years, seeing students in my home for two to three hours a week. I hired a reliable teenager who came after school a few days per week for three years. When Anja needed me for nursing or comfort, she jumped into my lap and we carried on as usual. When our second daughter, Kari, was born, I only had one student. I can't even remember when I started tutoring after I had the baby, because it went so smoothly.

In Canada, 57 percent of women are in the workforce; 17 weeks or more of maternity leave is paid by public funds; 245 days of parental leave is allowed; no breastfeeding breaks are allowed once a mother returns to work.

Working as a tutor had very little financial reward. Since my husband's income qualified, we received a monthly stipend from the government to augment our family income. When I declared my self-employment income on our taxes, our stipend was reduced. On top of that, I paid my babysitter. So taking all that into account, I figured out that I only took home $5 of the $18/hour that I earned. Still, it worked well for our family and I enjoyed the students and the opportunity to teach and make a difference.

When we decided to move outside of town, I knew it would be less convenient to tutor, but I was ready for the change. We were homeschooling and wanted to live where the children would have freedom to play outside and explore. We could finally afford a mortgage and we were thrilled to be homeowners. However, a day after the fall down the stairs, my husband, David, felt he was coming down with a cold. Within a few days, he was coughing constantly, experiencing arthritis pain, night sweats, and great fatigue. The doctor diagnosed bronchitis, but a month of antibiotics produced no relief. A second visit to the doctor resulted in an x-ray and a visit to an Internist. The resulting diagnosis was sarcoidosis. While acute sarcoidosis usually heals more rapidly that the chronic form, David was looking at two years of healing. While the cause is unknown, we hypothesize that the blow to David's spine might have caused the trauma that triggered the illness.

Although he coughed from May until October, David continued to work. With the permission of his employers, he cut back his hours. Even so, the work he did exhausted him completely. He spent his time at home napping. I became a single parent. If it weren't for the extended visits of my in-laws, I wouldn't have been able to manage.

The months of illness and working took their toll. Although he was physically healing, by December my husband was mentally worn out. We lamented our inability to qualify for the short-term disability insurance we took out with the mortgage. The fine print did not allow a claim for illness in the first six months of coverage.

When I chose to stay home with my children, I wasn't concerned about my career.

Hesitantly I suggested that I could go back to work. Our youngest was over two. Although I dreaded the thought of leaving "my baby," I knew she was easygoing and enjoyed the company of others. If I had been asked to leave our firstborn, I would have said "no way"; he was not comfortable outside of my presence until at least three years of age. Every child is so different!

Going back to teaching was the most practical idea. Substitute teaching provided the most return for the fewest hours and maximum flexibility. My skills as a French teacher were welcomed and for the next three months, I was able to work two to three days a week while David stayed home. One of the children went to kindergarten to ease the child care burden, but he had two others at home. Still he found himself recovering from the stress of the previous seven months.

The three months came to an end and David went back to work. We had borrowed from our retirement savings, so I continued to work one day a week on David's day off. The children once again became accustomed to an active father in their lives and enjoyed the spontaneous outdoor activities he came up with.

When I chose to stay home with my children, I wasn't concerned about my career. Unlike my sister who is a nurse, as a teacher, I was not required to maintain my professional status through a certain number of work hours in a given amount of time. Or so I thought. Upon reactivation of my certification, I discovered that since my training and work experience were from other provinces in Canada, they might not have been recognized if I had been out of the profession for more than ten years. I had been home for eight-and-a-half years. In addition, new regulations were no longer going to recognize my four-year degree. I qualified nine months before the change came into effect.

With this knowledge, I had to decide if I wanted to continue to work or return to staying home full-time. Since subbing was flexible and I could restrict my availability to my husband's days off, I continued to work two days a week during the next school year.

My husband and I were eager for another child. His illness had delayed our plans, but in the spring of 2001, I was excited to be pregnant with our fourth child. Both my mother and mother-in-law came for extended visits so I could work additional days, thus allowing me to qualify for our country's one-year maternity leave. With the baby due in October, it was easy to stretch my leave to sixteen months by including the summers on both ends.

Our fourth child, Matthias, was born at home in October 2001. He nursed exclusively for six months and enjoyed frequent nursing thereafter. When my maternity leave ended, I received a letter from my employer inquiring about my availability for work. No longer needing to work for financial reasons, I considered removing my name from the substitute teacher's list. However, in filling out the paperwork for my maternity leave, I had discovered that my interim teaching certificate would only become permanent if I taught 300 days in four years. If I allowed my certification to lapse, I would be required to return to the University if I ever chose to work as a teacher in the future. Deeply appreciating the ease with which I was able to go back to teaching, my husband and I decided that my working toward the goal of permanent certification would serve our family well.

My husband and I decided that my working toward the goal of permanent certification would serve our family well.

So, when Matthias was 12 months old, I went back to work. For the first few months, I limited my availability to half-days with advance notice only. Doing so meant that I could ask my mother-in-law, who had since moved to town, to watch the children at her house. Matthias loved spending time with Grandma, who is very loving and patient. He would nurse before I left and immediately upon my return. If I taught in the afternoon, he napped on her lap. What a fortunate boy! Grandma would set aside her other projects and sit in her armchair for one to two hours, just so that he wouldn't wake up. At home, he nursed to sleep, but with Grandma he cuddled to sleep. Having watched us with our other three children, Grandma was familiar with our extended nursing philosophy. Going to Grandma's is an extension of life at home. There are differences, but the children have developed a relationship with their grandparents that complements their relationship with us.

Gradually I returned to work full days, but limiting my availability to my husband's days off, and then only a maximum of two days a week.

More recently, I have given up substitute teaching for a quarter time teaching contract working twice a week for three hours. I also accepted an educational consulting contract that I fulfill from home. While less flexible, this work is more predictable and less stressful. Slowly I am working toward my 300 day goal. More importantly, I have found how paid employment can best fit into our family life. The consulting contract was appealing because of the flexible hours and potential for future growth. The school where I work has a small multi-level program. Often my children are welcome to accompany us on outings and if I have a meeting, Matthias plays happily with the kindergarten toys in the classroom.

Combining working and breastfeeding has worked well for me, primarily because breastfeeding and our parenting style were well-established before I began working. Challenges arise when this parenting style encounters resistance or a lack of understanding from others. When my consulting contract required a two-day meeting out of town (four hours away), I knew I couldn't leave my then almost two-year-old overnight. I also couldn't bring such an active toddler to all-day meetings in a conference room. The solution was to bring the whole family so that they could spend their day with Dad at the local Science Center and still have time with Mom in the evenings. For Matthias, it meant no interruption to those all-important night nursings. While my employer may have secretly questioned the arrangement, he didn't say anything to me. I paid for my family's share of the hotel room and was able to devote my attention to the subject of the meetings.

My personal challenge comes in remaining true to my convictions to be an active participant in my children's lives.

Still, there remains pressure to work more. So many people question that I can be content with such a small contract and wonder why I am not seeking full-time work. So few people nurse three-year-olds or acknowledge that children (from infancy upward) have a need to be with their mothers. I try to be an advocate in a strong, inoffensive manner, casually mentioning the needs of my family in a calm, unapologetic way as if it were the most normal thing in the world not to want to leave a nursing toddler overnight—because it is. In doing so, I find some people's attitudes becoming more understanding if not accepting.

My personal challenge comes in remaining true to my convictions to be an active participant in my children's lives. The lure of the money is great. Never before have I earned so much for so little time. I can imagine what luxuries earning more could bring and in some ways, this realization surprises me. When I was home full-time, I did not feel the need to make money, yet now that I do contribute to the family income, I have the urge to do more.

In addition, there are days when I receive more satisfaction from the work I do at school than at home. The interaction with adults and the chance to improve my personal skills is exciting. When these thoughts make me dissatisfied with my home life, I remind myself of the fond memories I have of my childhood with a stay-at-home mother. True, my children will always see me as a mother who combined working and being at home. But from my example, I hope they appreciate the importance of a mother's presence during that period of intense need that infants and children have. I hope they will understand all of that and appreciate that work can also be incorporated into a family's lifestyle.

United States

Assistant Food Service Manager

Nothing But Mother's Milk

Kim Johnson, Missouri

I always thought when I had children that I would be able to stay at home with them. Unfortunately, things have not turned out that way. Now I find myself a working, pumping mom—who is tandem nursing to boot!

My name is Kim, and I am a 24-year-old mother to nurslings Abby, age three, and Alaina, six months. I am currently working as an Assistant Manager at Baskin Robbins. Officially I work part-time, although with travel to and from work, I am away from my daughters at least six hours, sometimes seven or eight hours, a day. The first few weeks I worked shifts that were as short as possible, but gradually extended my hours to six- and eight-hour shifts. Even with my current schedule of six-hour shifts, both of my daughters were exclusively breastfed until the age of six months, and thereafter had only my milk and solids to complement their diet.

I had a very difficult time with the thought of returning to work after the birth of my first daughter, Abby. She was such an "easy" nurser, and a true delight; I just wanted to spend every hour of every day with her. Unfortunately her father was not very understanding of this desire, and insisted that I return to work when she was 12 weeks old, in spite of the fact she had balked at accepting a bottle since the age of four weeks.

With a heavy heart, I left her in the arms of my mother, and went off to work. I must have called to check on Abby at least four times an hour the first few days, and shed more than a few tears every day when I left her.

I made it a point to pump every two to three hours, rarely allowing more than three hours to pass between pumping sessions. I started out with a double electric pump, but because I am often the only person at the store, and have to stop pumping "on a dime," I found that using a good quality manual pump worked better for me. I've used the same pump faithfully (three times a day, five days a week) since my return to work in May 2002.

With a heavy heart, I left her in the arms of my mother, and went off to work.

Aside from a total lack of support from her father, there have been few obstacles that I have faced to overcome breastfeeding Abby while continuing with work. She flatly refused to accept a bottle. My mother, who is a breastfeeding educator and my biggest ally, took the bottle refusal in stride and fed Abby with a dropper. She offered the bottle every two hours, but didn't force the issue, just kept it gentle and non-invasive. Abby would decline, and mom would then just use the dropper. About eight weeks later, after this same routine every day, five days a week, Abby accepted the bottle. At that time she was almost six months old, and she only had the bottle when I was at work, never at any other time. At seven months, she learned to drink from a straw, and by one year, the bottles were put away. I continued to pump, however, until Abby was 20 months old and I was eight weeks into my pregnancy with Alaina.

I delivered my second daughter in June 2004 and continued to nurse Abby through the pregnancy, since she was not ready to wean.

Alaina has been quite a different nurser than Abby. We have had to overcome poor latch-on, oversupply, thrush, milk blebs, plugged ducts, and mastitis. Having Abby still nursing was a blessing when my breasts were so swollen that it was too difficult for Alaina to latch on.

I am lucky that my employers and co-workers are supportive of my need to pump while at work. Many of my co-workers are high-school or college students working part-time; working with a nursing, pumping mother has been quite enlightening for them. I calmly answer questions when asked, and I am discreet, so I have never had my employers or my co-workers faced with an awkward or embarrassing moment.

As I've mentioned, my mother has been my biggest support person. Without her encouragement, her knowledge, and her "hands on" help, I am sure I wouldn't have been able to continue to nurse as I have. My husband has never been supportive of nursing, in spite of my pleas for understanding and support. I have been lucky, however, in the last year to meet a few other nursing mothers with similar ideas, such as exclusive nursing to six months and continuing for the first year.

I have come to believe that, "where there is a will, there is a way." But, it sure helps to have at least one supportive, breastfeeding-savvy person in your corner. I would encourage mothers who must return to work to have a good support system in place, to have a good quality pump, to understand how milk production works, and to have a source available that can provide knowledgeable answers to questions or concerns that may arise. LLLI, a board certified lactation consultant, or a very knowledgeable health care provider can be worth her weight in gold.

I have been very fortunate to be able to provide each of my daughters with nothing but mother's milk for the first six months, though it hasn't been without a true commitment to do this. Through the difficult periods, the thrush, the plugs, and mastitis, it really took determination to continue. I decided long ago that nursing the girls is one of the most important things I can do for them. The help and support I have received from my mother, from my OB, and from my family doctor have made it much, much easier to stay true to my goal of child-led weaning.

UNITED STATES

Marketing Assistant

Driven from the Pump

Raquel Phillips, Washington, DC

When I returned to work at 12 weeks postpartum, I was a great breastfeeder. I'll admit it, though; I was a terrible pump user. I feared the pump. I did not start pumping and storing my milk until two weeks prior to returning to work.

Once back at work, I tried pumping for the first few weeks. I work out of my car most of the time, so I first tried to pump in a public bathroom. Other women came into the bathroom and were kept waiting. After a long while someone said, "What is that noise?" The next day, the battery went dead and I was unable to continue. The final straw was the day I had to pump driving down I-495 (a major interstate in the area). I had to find an alternative to pumping.

I knew I wanted my son to have only my milk for at least six months of his life, but taking the pump on the road was not going to work. I dug deep into my reserves of determination and discipline and worked out a plan that enabled me to continue breastfeeding. I began getting up at 5:30 AM every morning. I would pump either one or both breasts and save the milk for my son's second feeding of the day. My career requires me to move around to various locations in Maryland and Virginia. Because of that, I was able go home for lunch to feed my son, relax for an hour with him, and eat my lunch at the same time. I was able to supply a healthy meal for my son and I was eating healthier lunches, too. Of course, through all of this, I was very fortunate to have my mother as my live-in babysitter.

The evening feedings became very intense. I would feed my son when I first walked in the door and then he would take a nap. I would feed him several times later that evening. I did not feed my son solids until he turned six months old. He is currently nine months old and we are still breastfeeding. Most of our breastfeeding now happens in the mornings and evenings. It took some creativity once I decided to forgo pumping on the road, but I'm glad I found a way.

United States

Casino Dealer

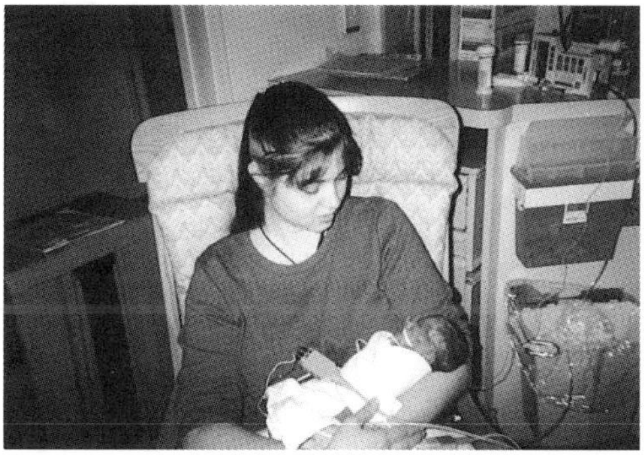

Fighting for My Son

Tammy Miner, Connecticut

I breastfeed because it is important for my son; I work because I need to. Breastfeeding is very cost effective and saves the time of washing and sterilizing bottles. It saves the time of having to get up in the middle of the night to warm a bottle and I never have to worry about not having enough bottles when going somewhere.

I pump while at work so my son can have my milk when I am away from him. When we are together, he breastfeeds, which is a great way to have time for just the two of us. I have worked hard to make this way of parenting fit my current job, having faced many obstacles from the time my son was born. Born prematurely at 27 weeks, I had to battle to keep my son on human milk while in the hospital. The hospital had my son on and off of formula without my husband's or my consent. I was furious and fought for two weeks to get him back on my milk. It took threatening to go to the chief of staff and remove my son from their care to get my expressed milk back into his feeding schedule.

New Obstacles

My struggles at work echoed those in the hospital. I work as a dual-rate floor person at a Tribal Casino. Whether I am working as a dealer or a floor supervisor determines what breaks I receive. For several months I was able to take two half-hour pumping breaks during my shift. When working as a dealer, the pit boss needs to get someone to cover my table for ten extra minutes until I come back from my extended nursing break. In theory, this should not be a hardship for my co-workers, my boss, or the work environment because it is a large company with thousands of employees.

However, a problem did occur. I was sent to relieve a co-worker who was leaving early, which meant that there would be no one to cover for my second nursing break. The shift manager was contacted, and then Human Resources. Rather than fixing the problem, they took away my second nursing break. I was handed a memo that stated I would be given only one half-hour break to express milk. If that was not enough, I would have to find my own solution, because their "policy" allows for only one nursing break per shift. So after nine months of expressing milk twice a day for my son, I was told I could only go once a day.

I wrote a three-page letter explaining difficulties I had as well as those that other mothers had, and I proposed solutions for every problem I presented.

There is one "Mother's Room" available for 10,000 to 13,000 employees and no written policy for breastfeeding whatsoever. I addressed my concerns with Human Resources and asked them why there was no written policy. I was instructed to write an incident report of any problems I was having. I wrote a three-page letter explaining difficulties I had as well as those that other mothers had, and I proposed solutions for every problem I presented. In addition I did the following:

- I contacted a local breastfeeding consultant who sent a letter supporting breastfeeding in the workplace, along with other useful information for my employer.
- I gathered supporting information from La Leche League and the American Academy of Pediatrics Web sites.
- I found legal cases concerning breastfeeding and the workplace and included those.
- I contacted many government officials including Congressman Rob Simmons, Governor John Rowland, Congresswoman Carolyn Maloney, but they were unable to offer any help.

I then scheduled a meeting with the director of Human Resources, provided all of the information I had found, and discussed what could be done to improve the current "breastfeeding program." I got nowhere. No changes were made.

Extremely frustrated, I turned to the CEO and the tribe for assistance. They turned the issue over to the assistant CEO. He spoke to the vice president of my department and it was decided that I could have a two-week extension to wean my body to once a day pumping. After one-and-a-half weeks of pumping in the bathroom for my second break, because they wouldn't allow me enough time to go to the Mother's Room, I said, "Enough." I wrote another incident report explaining that what they were doing was discriminating, a violation of my civil rights, and in violation of the Connecticut State Breastfeeding Law. I stated other times when workers are allowed to be away from their tables and consequently insisted that their concern of, "being fair to the other co-workers" was not a valid issue. I let them know that I would be contacting my lawyer to start a lawsuit if necessary.

I received a memo from upper management and it stated, "Please inform Tammy that a decision has been reached allowing mothers two (2) 30-minute breaks per day for breastfeeding purposes." This memo has never been posted or made public to my department so others only know about this "policy" by word of mouth. There is still no company-wide policy in writing, and to my knowledge no policy was ever made by the tribe.

My husband, my mother-in-law, and my best friend encouraged my assertiveness and ambition to fight for my right to breastfeed.

Team Effort

My husband, my mother-in-law, and my best friend encouraged my assertiveness and ambition to fight for my right to breastfeed. In addition, family members watch my son different days of the week so that my husband and I can both work. Because of the nature of the casino business my son was not allowed to be brought to me during the workday. My husband and I made sure to let caretakers know that we always breastfeed my son on demand and therefore he "makes" his own schedule. The family members who watch him go along with that.

I have been surprised how many mothers at work breastfeed. But I have also been surprised by how many will make sacrifices they really don't want to make just so they are not an inconvenience to their workplace. My advice to other women who want to breastfeed and work would be never lose sight of why you chose to breastfeed in the first place. If it's really important to you, don't let anyone discourage you. Federal laws are needed to allow mothers to breastfeed at work and fines need to follow if those laws are not honored.

I have persevered in the face of difficulties because breastfeeding is so important to me. I still breastfeed and work and will continue until my son self-weans because it is my son's and my choice to decide when to stop.

Canada

Traveling Performer

On Tour with My Son

Carrie Nimmo, British Columbia

I am a Canadian performer. I stilt-danced, sang, and acted on international tours while I was pregnant and I continued to perform while I was breastfeeding. I chose to continue to tour with my son in tow and as a result, Markus has had a rich and happy two-and-a-half years.

While I was pregnant I toured with Mortal Coil, a dance/theatre company, performing a show for young audiences called "Treemendous Journey." We toured the Eastern USA, including performing at the Kennedy Center in Washington, DC. I know that Markus enjoyed the movement and music from within because at six months pregnant I stopped performing and watched from the sidelines. Markus kicked during every scene where I used to dance—he wanted to move to the music!

Since his birth, Markus has traveled with me as I've toured to festivals across Canada. He even watched his momma perform in Croatia at the Modern Dance Festival in Zagreb. Airplane flights have been relatively easy due to breastfeeding. Markus latches on just after take-off and before landing, which seems to help him adjust to the changes in pressure. When on the road, we sing songs, create little puppet shows, and draw. I always have child care organized before arriving for performances because when I'm working I need to focus; it is exhausting work. Either my mother or my partner travel with us, or I have friends on the other end who can provide child care.

I do try to keep Markus on his routine while we are away. If he's awake he loves to watch performances. He runs a play by play for those sitting next to him, and always lets them know, "That's my momma in the dinosaur costume!" After the shows, he often tries on costume pieces or stilts. This exposure to live music, dance, and theatre is priceless.

What I have found challenging is when our schedule changes or days become long due to travel or technical problems. If I know a festival will be extremely challenging or travel will be too grueling, I choose not to go rather than have us all suffer. My colleagues are incredibly helpful while traveling and I often find it easier being on tour with the extra support than being at home alone. Overall, I love sharing this life with Markus. The arrangement is not as difficult as one might expect. Folk festivals are usually child friendly—providing changing stations, mother's rooms for nursing, and food. It's all I need. And of course, the social aspect of being around international performers is a definite bonus. Festival-goers and staff are educated, open minded, and supportive. In fact, I have never come across criticism at festivals for breastfeeding in public.

Festival-goers and staff are educated, open minded, and supportive.

That has not been the case at home, however. I have breastfed my son for two-and-a-half years despite ongoing criticism from my family. My son is one-quarter Vietnamese and his grandmother ("Ba Noi") was convinced that I was harming his health by breastfeeding. She is sure that I have "an abnormal relationship" with Markus because I have breastfed him past six months. I'm not sure if some of her reservations about breastfeeding are cultural, but I know that she did not breastfeed her children. She has not been open to hearing about the benefits of breastfeeding. She has boycotted visits, and she would tell my son, "Yuck! You're too old to breastfeed!"

I did not want my son to stop breastfeeding out of guilt. I decided to breastfeed in private when she was visiting and my husband asked her to speak to us about it, not our son. My sister-in-law also decided to join the anti-breastfeeding bandwagon and criticized us constantly. My son loves his Ba Noi and Aunty so I wanted to continue having contact with them; however, I was feeling drained. I developed positive imagery to counteract the criticism. As I traveled to see them I would imagine that I had a reserve of strong and supportive women surrounding me. I even named them: Muriel, Clara, Kirsten, Bonnie, Ann, Mimi, Denise, and Joy. Dealing with the criticism was a challenge, but now I bring in the reinforcements whenever I need some support.

I am no longer doing as much traveling, since I am now working more in the office as Artistic Managing Director of Mortal Coil in order to have a more stable income and routine. Since Markus is past two, his flights need to be paid for and my company does not cover any of his travel expenses. Our life may change as our needs do, but I have no regrets about breastfeeding and parenting my son on tour. On the contrary, I highly recommend it!

Part Two

Latin America

Dominican Republic

Veterinarian

Animal Care—a Family Affair

Ada Frias de Torres, Santiago

My husband and I are veterinarians. Since we were newly married, we have always worked together. We started out as employees together in an animal clinic. We worked long hours, from 8 AM to 8 PM daily. I enjoy my work very much.

When I became pregnant with our first daughter, Ana Maite, I continued working and I did fine until the third trimester of pregnancy when I began to feel fatigue from the long work hours. My husband and I decided that I should quit my job for a time.

The joy of the arrival of my daughter and the pleasure of nursing her completely were sufficient to make me forget my career for a time. I was attached soul and body to my baby, focusing only on mothering her.

While Ana was still an infant, my husband quit his job and launched out on his own. He began to provide veterinarian home visits and soon his clientele increased to the point that he began to need my help.

I began to work part time, taking my daughter with me in a front pack and sometimes setting up a portable crib in a client's home while we checked or treated a pet. Our clients seemed to enjoy our visits, often asking to hold the baby. Ana thrived. She was always with me, nursed when hungry, slept when tired, and was continuously stimulated by the changing environments. She has been healthy throughout her whole childhood despite many people warning us that being around animals would be dangerous to her health.

Our veterinary practice continued to grow as did our family. Our second child, Anabel, arrived a few years later. Our lives became a bit more complicated. We needed to make some adjustments in our practice so that our children would continue to have their full share of our time. We set up a small clinic in our home for sick animals, which enabled me to stay at home and care for our daughters as well as continue serving our clients. We hired a housekeeper to help with washing and cleaning so that I could be free to care for our daughters and the animals in our home. Now and then things get really crazy and work piles up or I have a very ill animal that needs my focused attention. My mother helps during those extra busy times and cares for the girls for a few hours.

My husband recognizes the many benefits that breastfeeding brings to our children. He has always supported and protected that aspect of our lives. I am still breastfeeding my two-and-a-half-year-old, Anabel. She does not seem the least bit interested in weaning as yet.

I encourage other working mothers to be creative in looking for solutions to working and breastfeeding. Though it is not always easy, I have found that it is very worthwhile. I think my daughters will someday recognize that I always tried to give them the best of myself, something money could never buy.

Dominican Republic

In the Dominican Republic, 31 percent of women are in the workforce; 12 weeks of maternity leave is paid by public funds and the employer; paid breastfeeding breaks are given once the mother returns to work.

GUATEMALA

Computer Specialist

United for a Better Life

Angela Bailon, La Esperanza

I am very thankful to La Leche League because I was able to breastfeed my third child even though I had to return to work very soon after delivery. My third child was born after I had been accredited as a peer counselor in Guatemala, helping other mothers learn to breastfeed. It was good timing, because I had the knowledge and understanding that breastfeeding is the best for any child, and I knew it was especially important for a child who was born with respiratory difficulties, as my son was. I know that it was my milk that helped him to survive and be healed.

Because of lack of opportunities, I wasn't able to finish my studies. I was able to learn how to use the computer, so I became the person in charge of inventory, quality control, and accounts in UPAVIM (Unidas Para Vivir Mejor or United for a Better Life). This is an organization where very low-income women gather to make crafts to sell and sustain other health and education activities for their community.

Twenty days after my third child was born, I had to return to work, but I was blessed to do it with my baby in my arms. I would lay him on top of my desk or improvise a crib with the materials we use for sewing. Every time he needed me, I was close by. I would just bring him to my breast and he was happy. Sometimes I would nurse and type at the computer at the same time. He was happy and I was happy, too, for I knew he was receiving the best food and attention. No other person, no other milk, could have substituted for what we had. I was able to exclusively breastfeed Daniel till he was in his sixth month.

Luckily by then, the nursery in UPAVIM was available for those of us working at the center. This made working and breastfeeding simple. The person in charge of the nursery would call me every time Daniel needed to breastfeed and we would share a break together. He also started on solids and that helped to space feedings a bit.

Guatemala

In Guatemala, 28 percent of women are in the workforce; 12 weeks of maternity leave is paid by public funds and employer; 2 days of paternity leave; paid breastfeeding breaks are given once the mother returns to work.

A few times I had to express my milk when I had to attend a conference or attend a sale outside. He took my milk from a cup, for we had learned that it was best to avoid bottles. When he was ten moths old, I was invited to attend a conference in the US and I was able to travel with him. His "chichita" was always ready to comfort and nourish him, in the plane or sitting at the conference, or even seated in his car seat. He was always well behaved and quiet because his needs were met by me and by breastfeeding.

It was breastfeeding that kept us close. He nursed for almost three years; it was the best.

Teaching Life Lessons

Viana Maza, Ciudad de Guatemala

Translated from Spanish by Natalia Smith Allen

I am a single mother. I have to work to make money for myself and my baby. Ever since the moment I knew I was having a baby, I worried a lot about my financial situation, because I knew it meant I would have two jobs—raising my baby and bringing in money. I was very frightened because my wish was to breastfeed her exclusively, but because I had to work, I thought this would not be possible.

During the pregnancy, I finished my university coursework so I did not have anything pending when my baby arrived. My mother was a constant support during this whole time. At last the moment I had always waited for arrived and my little baby was born. I named her Ariana. I continued to worry about finances, but when I was with her, she filled anything that was lacking in my life and she was the only thing I wished for during those moments. I was delighted that being with her allowed me to breastfeed her exclusively. (It was also nice not to spend money on formula.) She was a very healthy baby and there were no medical expenses. I was given baby clothes during my pregnancy, and all in all, I felt that no money could buy the happiness I felt by being with her.

When Ariana was two months old, a friend commented that she was giving classes at the University and that they were urgently looking for a professor. She told me to give her my resume and that they most probably would hire me. I wasn't too enthused about this because I could not imagine leaving my baby; my heart hurt just with the thought of it. But because I needed the money, I told her I would think about it and I would let her know. After consulting with my family, the conclusion was that I should go for it. Since the position only required me to work on Saturdays, my mother would be able take care of Ariana, as that was her day off. I expressed my milk and left it with my mother to give to Ariana in a finger feeding device.

I never had a problem teaching class with Ariana around—to the contrary, having her there calmed me and allowed me to do a good job.

My first day arrived and I was very nervous. The previous day and that morning I had expressed and managed to collect about five ounces of milk. I left Ariana asleep and as I gave her a kiss I could not help but cry. It was the first time we would be separated. I cried the whole way to my work and I wished to go back home as soon as possible. My breasts were engorged and I kept leaking. When I returned home, Ariana was crying and so was I. She began breastfeeding immediately, and we both felt relieved. My mother had no luck with the feeding device, as Ariana wanted only to nurse.

My mother and I realized that the separation had not worked well. Ariana did not want anything but my breast. We decided that the best option was for them both to come with me to work, which would allow me to continue with breastfeeding.

When Saturday arrived, we got ready as if we were going for a walk and the three of us left the house. I took the sling with me so as to leave my hands free while I taught my class. Ariana always remained calm. Her grandmother took her for long walks and during recess, I breastfed her. Again, we were happy. My students got used to seeing me with her in the sling and they watched her grow. They were amazed at how good she was. Since she was a baby with all her needs met, she was contented.

I never asked at work if I could do this. I simply did it and my supervisors soon realized that it brought good results. I never had a problem teaching class with Ariana around—to the contrary, having her there calmed me and allowed me to do a good job. Of course I never would have managed without the help of my mother. She played a very important role in helping me successfully breastfeed my baby and take her with me to work.

I am a clinical psychologist at a university in Guatemala. I give classes to fourth and fifth year psychology students. The majority of my students are female. They have learned a lot from my experience and they constantly ask me about breastfeeding. Currently there are two students who attend class with their babies, as they realized from watching me that it was possible.

My job is about one hour away from my house, which adds an additional two hours to my workday. The day I left Ariana at home, I suffered the whole trip and tried to drive much faster. In contrast, when the three of us are together, I drive with less of a rush because I have her right there beside me.

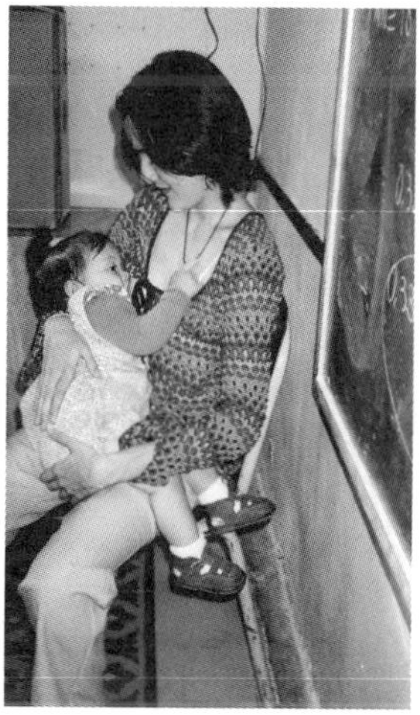

I am the daughter of a La Leche League Leader. I grew up surrounded by support groups and meetings of Leaders. I never questioned how I would nourish my children. For me it was always a given that I would breastfeed until I was faced with the difficulty of having to take care of my child and financially support my family. I thought it would be impossible for one person to do both these jobs. Thanks to my parents' support, especially my mother, I managed to work and breastfeed.

The advice I give to any mother who would like to work is to first consider whether there is truly a need. For me, spending time with our children is more important than any economic luxuries. What a newborn baby needs is to have her mother close by to provide love and nourishment. Many times, a mother has to pay a large part of her salary for someone else to take care of her children. If it is absolutely necessary, as I believe it was in my case, try to find alternatives to be able to take the baby to work. People are always surprised when they see breastfed children because they are happy babies and seldom cry.

Ariana and I were together during the first six months of exclusive breastfeeding and beyond. Eventually she became more interested in crawling around the floor than sitting in the sling. Little by little she made me realize that she was ready to stay at home on Saturdays while her Mummy worked. One day, she was crawling around my students' desks and began putting into her mouth anything she found on the floor. At that moment, I knew I could no longer manage to take care of her while teaching class. That is how my 12-month-old girl and my mother began staying at home. By then Ariana was eating enough solids to wait to breastfeed until I returned from work.

In her first year, many people interacted with Ariana, but I was there to satisfy her needs all the while.

Even today, my students ask about her and miss her. But now she is a little two-year-old rascal who would be impossible to handle in a classroom.

What surprised me the most in all of this was the relationship that was established between the two of us during the first few months that we were together. I was surprised at how difficult it was the day I had to leave her. It made me realize how strong our bond is. Breastfeeding allowed me to build this beautiful bond that will unite us for life.

The work I do makes me very happy, especially because I work with people who are in the process of learning, and I am the channel for such a process. In regard to psychology, I have taught them a variety of topics such as history, technical skills, and theory. But in regard to breastfeeding, I have left my footprint with a real example they experienced every Saturday. It fills me with joy to see my students continue studying after having a baby, especially with the knowledge that they do not have to leave their babies with someone else.

I suppose that for Ariana it was also a great experience. She was close to Mum, seeing new people and new places. She went out together with her grandmother while I taught my class; they also formed a close bond. Most special is the realization that in her first year, many people interacted with Ariana, but I was there to satisfy her needs all the while.

MEXICO

Quality Engineer

The Wisdom of Nature

Guadalupe Vega, Tijuana

I think the most important birthright that I can offer my baby is good health. Nature is so wise. If breastfeeding is not the ideal, why is a mother's body prepared to do it? Maybe it is simplistic logic, but my common sense told me that I should be feeding my baby with my milk for a year-and-a-half; no formula.

It is sometimes difficult for women to decide to breastfeed since it takes a lot of time, and the logistics may be complicated. I am the only working woman that I know who breastfed a baby for a long time. Other working mothers are combining human milk and formula during the working hours and then doing it for just for a few months. I was determined not to do this.

I work as a Quality Engineer for Cardinal Health. I'm the liaison between the production process at the company and many injection molder suppliers. About 25 percent of the time I travel either to Europe or within the USA. One co-worker was very supportive and insisted on handling all the European travel for me, which meant that I would only have to travel in the USA while I was breastfeeding.

Knowing how important "the details" would be, I began to investigate the technology, logistics, and resources available in order for me to pump at work. I read the Mexican laws regarding the rights of a breastfeeding, working mother, and I found that a mother is allowed to breastfeed the baby for two 30-minutes periods during the working day, but even this is not enough time if the baby is not close to you. When I asked for this benefit, it was denied to me until I revealed to the Human Resources Department that I knew about the law (with a copy of the Mexican law in my hand!). The benefits are hidden from mothers and there are no facilities available to express the milk.

My mother would be my baby's caretaker. It took a lot of time and patience to prepare her to handle and warm my frozen milk, but she was willing to learn it.

In Mexico, 31 percent of women are in the workforce; 12 weeks of maternity leave is paid by public funds and employer; paid breastfeeding breaks are given once a mother returns to work.

Prior to my maternity leave, I negotiated with my boss to decrease my usual ten-and-a- half-hour day by two-and-a-half hours for the first six months. He agreed, though all the hours I used would need to be my vacation hours. This extra time has helped me to understand the language of my body, the features of the pump, and the needs of my baby.

When Celine was born, I was already prepared with my fantastic acquisition: a Nurture III pump. It is an electric pump that allows me to pump both breasts at once. Around the second week I started to express my milk and freeze it. When Celine was six weeks old, I had in the freezer around 250 oz (7,400 ml) of mother's milk, conveniently stored in six-ounce plastics bags. I worked from 7:00 AM until 5:30 PM daily, except Saturdays and Sundays.

Since there was no place in the company set aside for mothers to express their milk, every day I had to find interesting places to pump: a conference room, a private office, and believe it or not, I once did it in an aisle! One male co-worker arrived when I was expressing my milk, and he seemed both surprised and embarrassed. He very quickly said hello to me and left. He never asked me what I was doing.

The most memorable situation that happened to me was during an all day Quality Meeting in a big casino in San Diego. Around 300 colleagues were attending the meeting, and the only place for expressing milk was the sound room, which was directly behind the main speaker. Every time I went there to express milk everyone watched me leave with the questioning expression on their faces, "What are you doing in there, and what is inside your black suitcase?"

During my frequent travels and visits, all of the suppliers were supportive. I interrupted more meetings than I can remember. At a certain point, I began to feel guilty. Still, I never regretted doing it. I found that in the USA, people are more knowledgeable about breastfeeding than in Mexico. Since most of my visits and travels were throughout the USA, most of my colleagues made me feel respected as a breastfeeding, working mother. It may have helped that I had a long working relationship with all of them.

Unfortunately, I did not receive much help from the company I work for. Though there were times I was angry with them, I never thought about quitting. In fact, I had a second baby and I am following the same logistics to combine breastfeeding with work. It is fantastic to see how beautiful and healthy my daughters are. My husband and mother were especially supportive in this adventure; without their help, it would not be possible. I enjoy experiencing motherhood through breastfeeding while developing my career. Breastfeeding, without a doubt, is the most wonderful experience in my life.

ARGENTINA

Physicist

A Bicycle Ride Away

Veronica Garea

I had breastfed my older daughter while I was in graduate school in the US. I managed to defend my dissertation with her waiting in the hallway, and I was able to delay work until she was eight months old. But when my husband and I decided to have a second child, we were back in Argentina. I was working and my family could not manage without the income from my job.

I have a PhD in Engineering Physics and at the time we made the decision to have a second baby in 1998, I was working for an engineering company. The company does not have on-site daycare and I could not come up with an arrangement that would satisfy my need to be near my baby. After discussing it with my husband, I decided to apply for a postdoctoral research position at a research center that has a daycare facility on campus. My husband worked in that same research center, and our daughter was currently attending the daycare center. They were breastfeeding-friendly and did not mind holding babies that needed to be held. We live far away from our extended family, so we did not have the chance to have one of the loving grandmothers taking care of our babies. Neither of us could take time off work to stay with the children at home and we felt that it would be very difficult finding a caregiver we would be satisfied with. We had a happy experience with our daughter at this daycare center and felt this was the best option for our family.

I was fortunate to obtain the postdoctoral fellowship and we were blessed with a pregnancy that very same year. Leonardo was born in April 1999. The fellowship did not include maternity benefits, but was flexible enough to allow me to negotiate a paid leave with my advisor. I took two full months off to dedicate myself completely to getting to know this new love of my life. And after two months, I started working part-time from home. We coslept, Leo was worn either by his father or by me during all his waking hours, and we breastfed happily.

When Leo was four months old, I went back to work. We took two weeks for him to get used to the daycare center. A teacher and two assistants staffed the babies' room, all of them loving, patient young women with experience caring for babies. I bought a bicycle and rode from the laboratory to the daycare center to see Leo and feed him. I had described his feeding cues to the staff and they picked them up immediately, so Leo was rarely crying by the time I made it to the daycare center. I brought Leo's sling so that the teachers could wear him and keep him happy on the days he needed a bit more contact. My lunch hour was spent walking around the campus with Leo and his older sister, Muriel, or watching Muriel in the playground with her friends. Argentina's law gives the mother one hour per day to breastfeed during the first year, but taking more than an hour when adding all the times I went to nurse Leo was not an issue. Since I was doing research, I imposed the pace of the work, and if I was running a bit slow I was able to catch up at home during the children's naptime on weekends.

I was not alone while breastfeeding Leo. The babies' room had no separate place for mothers to breastfeed, but had three comfortable chairs in the same room. And sometimes there were so many of us breastfeeding our babies that one of us had to sit on the floor or lie on a mat with the baby. The community in the research center is pro-breastfeeding and it is not uncommon to have a majority of the babies in the babies' room being breastfed. Nursing time was a wonderful time with the baby, but it was also a wonderful time to share with the other mothers.

Breastfeeding is more common in Argentina than in many other

ARGENTINA

In Argentina, 33 percent of women are in the workforce; 12 weeks of maternity leave and 2 days of paternity leave are paid by public funds; paid breastfeeding breaks are allowed once a mother returns to work countries, but unfortunately not all babies are breastfed. The law gives the mother 12 weeks of paid maternity leave and one hour to breastfeed per day during the first year. And all companies with more than 50 women on staff have to provide on-site daycare or have an agreement with a daycare center close to the place of work. Sadly, our country has this ability to have great laws that are not enforced, and sometimes employers do not comply with these requirements and the mothers do not know their rights.

I was able to breastfeed exclusively for six-and-a-half months, when Leo started eating solids. He continued to breastfeed on demand, and I kept going to feed him for as long as he wanted. He breastfed frequently until he was 13 months old, so I rode my bicycle to the daycare center several times every day. When he was 16 months old, I was offered a position at the company I was working for before he was born. It was an excellent opportunity for me and we decided that our family was ready for the change. We adjusted our working hours so that I would get to work early and my husband would take the children to the daycare center. Then I would be able to leave work early so I would pick them up and take them home. I nursed Leo before leaving home in the morning and still went to breastfeed him once during the day in addition to spending my lunchtime with him and Muriel. He nursed during the night and while we were together at home, and I sent my milk to the daycare center for him to drink from a cup at snack time. On weekends he nursed on demand. He came to me one day at 30 months and said, "I don't want 'teta' today." That was the beginning of the weaning process that took about a month.

I am convinced that being close to our babies is important to be successful in combining work and breastfeeding.

I have had two wonderful and happy experiences combining work and breastfeeding. I would not have been able to do it without the full and constant support of my husband. He shared my conviction that this was important for our family and he supported my decisions. I am thankful that my country has laws that support a woman's right to give her best to her baby and a baby's right to receive it. I am also thankful that I found a community of breastfeeding mothers in my workplace as well as experienced and breastfeeding-friendly staff in the daycare center. I am convinced that being close to our babies is important to be successful in combining work and breastfeeding. I would like to see the day when all working mothers have access to dependable daycare of top-notch quality close enough to their place of work that they can feed and hold their babies as many times a day as they both need it.

BOLIVIA

Agronomist

Mountain Mothering

Victoria Escobar, La Paz

My work specialty is Andean crops and I like working in rural areas much more than working in a city. My grandfather was a farmer, and we used to travel to his place during vacations. I am also a mother. Working in a job I love does not prevent me from being with my child.

I am an agricultural extensionist worker for Save the Children US/Bolivia. My position is called a "supervisor of income generation." My main work consists of meeting with the farmers in the rural communities. Mostly the men participate in these meetings, but some women do as well, especially those who are widows. During these meetings, I teach farmers about crops, specifically about how to prevent the worms that affect their main crop, potato. I also supervise when they work terraces or use irrigation systems. Currently, I work in the rural municipality of Patacamaya, and I am in charge of 11 communities with each community containing anywhere from 35 to 200 families.

When Yamiel was two months old, I had to go back to work. At first, I had a room in Patacamaya that was without running water. Since I have had a baby, I decided to rent a hotel room that has water and a shower. My baby loves showering with warm water, so I had to spend a bit more money to rent this room.

Because the rural families I visit are far apart, I travel a lot. I have to walk sometimes two or three hours to get to the communities. At first, it was hard because I couldn't find a caretaker who would come along to help me with my son. When I did finally find a girl, she did not like all of the walking, so she left. Then I had a girl who was separated from her husband, but after a couple of weeks, they reconciled and she also left me. Now I have one from Potosí, another region of Bolivia. When she is watching my son, I sneak in now and then to observe her. I look for someone who knows how to treat a child. Sometimes caretakers beat the children, which is frightening. I never want that. Neither do I want to see someone psychologically mistreat my boy. So, I stay close by, always.

In Bolivia, 40 percent of women are in the workforce; one to 12 weeks of maternity leave is paid for by public funds and employers; there are paid breastfeeding breaks once a mother returns to work.

I live 22 days during the month in Patacamaya, while I am working. The rest of the time, my free days, I spend in La Paz. The two towns are about two hours apart, by bus. So when I am not working, Yamiel and I travel home and we live with my mother in La Paz.

There have been times when it was difficult to keep up the exclusive breastfeeding. I did try to express milk. I left it in a cup, and the girl was to give it to my son with a spoon. But he didn't take it. So I began to take him with me to the communities on my back, in an aguayo (a typical Bolivian cloth used to carry children on the back). Sometimes, especially after four months of age, my son would get bored on my back in the aguayo. Or he wanted to get down and sleep somewhere. Then there are the rains—I had to buy him special clothes for the rainy season. (The climate on the Andean Altiplano is one of the harshest and coldest worldwide. At 12,000 feet altitude, it is very cold, very windy, with a burning sun most of the year and three months of continuous rainfall.)

More difficult than the physical obstacles was the time when my boss scolded me and said I shouldn't bring the baby during staff meetings. "You get distracted," he said. "Leave him at home!" Once I tried, but my breasts became hard and painful and my baby was screaming when I got home. I was very sad and began crying, wondering what I was going to do.

The director of our program saw me and asked what was happening. I told him. He said, "Bring your baby. Don't worry." He had always asked me how the baby was doing and supported me more than anyone else. "Go see your baby," he would say if we stayed long hours in the office. Working with Save the Children helped, because our advisor from the central office in La Paz also encouraged me. She often said, "Bring your baby along—that is fine."

Some of my co-workers surprised me. All of my agricultural extensionist colleagues are men. And some are really very "macho," or so I thought. Many, especially those who are fathers, became very supportive. They even got into a fight once among themselves. Some said, "Let her go early, she has a little son." Others objected.

It is worth any trouble to offer these gifts to my Yamiel. It is worth any trouble.

When I travel, the mothers in the communities also help me. When my boy gets tired or bored, they say, "Bring him here, I will let him sleep in my house." In addition, the health education nurse who works with me in Patacamaya for Save the Children uses me as an example to others. "Look at this woman; she is a professional, and she only breastfeeds!" She says this to the mothers, some of whom are bottle-feeding. This makes me feel proud. In the Bolivian Altiplano, breastfeeding is universal and exclusive breastfeeding is around 70 percent according to Save the Children surveys in the area.

I want my son to only breastfeed so that he will become superintelligent. I also want only natural things for him, no additives, no drugs, and no vitamins—just things from nature. I have heard that you should breastfeed up to two years, but the pediatrician and the dentist tell me to stop when he is one year old. My nephew breastfed until he was two years and seven months. He is incredibly intelligent—he learns everything, he knows the colors, he talks well, and he is happy. This is proof enough for me. It is worth any trouble to offer these gifts to my Yamiel. It is worth any trouble.

Mexico

Foreign Service Officer

Things I Never Thought I Would Do...

Elizabeth Power, Ciudad Juarez

I never thought I would be grateful that my baby woke four or five times a night to nurse. I never thought I would carry my pump into the Uruguayan Foreign Ministry and duck into a bathroom to use it between meetings. I never thought I would bare my breasts and hook up to my pump at a sink, while strangers came and went, chatting, washing their hands, checking their makeup. I never thought I would find myself leaning over a toilet with my dress unzipped, top around my waist, hand-expressing my aching breasts and cursing the fact that I had left my pump at home. Little did I know what wacky things I would do for the sake of my baby!

My working and pumping journey began almost four years ago, when my daughter, Maggie, was born. I pumped for her until she was 20 months old, and I'm now on maternity leave nursing my two-month-old son, Liam, and building up a freezer stash of milk for him. I am a Foreign Service Officer with the US Department of State. As a working, pumping diplomat, I have served in Montevideo, Uruguay, and am currently working in Ciudad Juarez, Mexico. My job requires me to change positions and locations at least every two to three years, and sometimes more frequently. I began pumping for my daughter while at a government training facility in Washington, DC, pumped throughout an entire year as a political officer in Montevideo, Uruguay, and then pumped there for several more months as a consular officer. Because of all these changes, I have dealt with pumping around a fixed training schedule that gave me no flexibility in setting my pumping sessions. I learned good office etiquette for pumping in a shared workspace, and I have had the luxury of having my own office and being able to set my own schedule. I have been so lucky in how this journey has worked out so far.

Breastfeeding was not really a conscious decision for me. My mother breastfed all five of her children and was a La Leche League Leader in the 1970s; having grown up around lots of nursing babies, I just assumed that since this was the best way to nourish my child's body and spirit, it was the only way for me. I am lucky to have had lots of support in my choice to breastfeed, both from my family and from friends I made in a natural childbirth class. I also had a working and pumping role model in my older sister, who had nursed both of her children for several years and pumped for each of them at least until their first birthday. Yet despite all of the support and information I had, combining working with breastfeeding became the first real challenge of my nursing relationship with my daughter.

I have been so lucky in how this journey has worked out so far.

Struggling with Milk Output

After my daughter's birth, I did not want to return to work, but for a variety of reasons, I had to continue. My negative attitude about having to leave my daughter every day fed into my natural procrastination and it wasn't until the week before my first day back on the job that I gave any serious thought to how I would handle the logistics of pumping. Formula-feeding wasn't an option for me, and I felt that if my sister had been able to pump, surely I would be able to, also. She sent me bottles and two battery-operated hand-held pumps, so I figured I was all set. Actually using those pumps was a different story! Before returning to work, I somehow managed to get 20 ounces of milk in the feezer for bottles while I would be away, but I struggled for every drop. I couldn't get my milk to let down, the pumps pulled my nipples too hard, and I couldn't regulate the suction or pumping cycles. I ended every pumping session with no more than two ounces, despite still having an oversupply of milk at this point. I leaked so much while nursing that I could soak an entire cloth diaper in two minutes, but my body simply did not respond well to the pump. My struggles proved that pumping output is not a reliable indicator of supply.

Once back on the job, things were even worse. I was still only getting about two ounces each time I pumped, and I had to do all my pumping standing at the sink in the crowded bathroom at a large training facility. My husband, who cares for our children at home, was quickly running through the small freezer stash I had managed to store while on maternity leave, and I was desperately trying to meet my daughter's ravenous appetite. Almost in tears, I called my sister for help, and what she said stuck with me and kept me going throughout the next year and a half. She reassured that I could do this, and reminded me that I only needed to stay one bottle ahead of Maggie. Having lots of ounces of milk in the freezer was a nice luxury, but as long as I could keep the next bottle coming, we would make it through. Viewing pumping as a step by step process was just what I needed to make it seem less of a problem and more of a workable challenge.

Viewing pumping as a step-by-step process was just what I needed to make it seem less of a problem and more of a workable challenge.

Around this same time, I also discovered a message board for pumping mothers on the Internet. It was here that I learned that my current pump had a reputation for poor quality and painful suction, and I decided to invest in a highly regarded double electric pump. Hearing about the accommodations other employers had made for other mothers to pump, I was encouraged to approach my own employer and ask for help in finding a place other than the training center's crowded bathroom to pump. One of my supervisors immediately offered his own office to pump in on my breaks from class, so that every day I would go to his office, find it empty, and quickly pump before rushing back to my training. And probably most important for my milk output, the message board reinforced the suggestion of breast massage that I had heard at a local La Leche League meeting. Within a few weeks, I was pumping with my new pump in a private office and getting an immediate let-down—it was no surprise that my output suddenly doubled from two ounces each pumping session to four ounces. Suddenly my nightmare of having to resort to supplementing with formula started to fade away.

I probably still could not have kept up with Maggie's demand for milk during the day, though, if she hadn't cooperated with me by reverse cycling.* After I had been at work for almost two months, she

**See a discussion about reverse cycling in Part Seven.*

all of a sudden slowed her bottle intake during the day and started nursing more often at night. Sometimes she would only take six ounces of expressed milk during the ten hours that I would be at work, and then she would make up for it by nursing for up to an hour after work and waking as many as five times in the night to eat. I was worried that this pattern would hurt her—who ever heard of a baby hardly eating during the day and thriving? But my friends at La Leche League and on the message board reassured me that this was normal. And as my daughter continued to grow and develop well, and my freezer stash slowly started to grow again, I settled into this new routine, happy that we had found a way to make it work and proud that Maggie was receiving all of her nourishment from my milk.

Once my milk output problems were solved, the only changes that occurred in my pumping life involved location. As I shuttled between classrooms, offices, and bathrooms looking for pumping sites at the training center, I found other pumping mothers, and we would frequently pump together in our borrowed spaces. We all agreed that there needed to be a permanent solution to this problem of space, so I talked to the center's management and requested that they convert an office, a closet, or some other place to a pumping room to accommodate all of the pumping mothers in training. The managers were sympathetic to the need for a dedicated site, and one of them was a former pumping mother herself, but they were unable to give us the permanent solution we wanted due to overcrowding at the facility. However, they agreed to incorporate such a room into the building plans for future buildings at that site, and as an interim solution, they added outlets and shelves in handicapped bathroom stalls for mothers to have some privacy while pumping.

I found other pumping mothers, and we would frequently pump together in our borrowed spaces.

Pumping at the US Embassy and Beyond

After four months of borrowing offices and pumping in the bathroom when necessary, we moved to Montevideo, Uruguay, where I was a political officer at the US Embassy. It was very easy to work pumping sessions into my flexible schedule of meetings and other tasks, and I quickly adapted to pumping at my desk in a shared office. My office mate was a man who had no children, and lucky for me he was both curious about pumping and breastfeeding and willing to work with me to give me privacy when I needed it. He readily left the office for 20 minutes at a time to let me "do my thing," and we came up with a code of sorts to let him know when it was safe to come back to his desk. If my special magnet was in the middle of the door, I was still pumping, but if the magnet was back in its place by the door handle, he could come in. After a year of this arrangement, I moved into the Embassy's consular section, where I had my own office, but had to work my pumping around work that involved set public hours for visa and passport applicants. By this time, Maggie was 18 months old and had really started enjoying eating solids, so I was only pumping once or twice a day, and it was easy to simply pump at my lunchtime or to work a quick pumping session into lulls in our applicant workload, if necessary. After two months of this, Maggie no longer took any expressed milk during the day, so I weaned myself off the pump. After 18 months of struggling to pump enough milk, worrying about where and when to pump, and sometimes resenting having to lug that big black bag with all the bottles and pump parts, my last day pumping was surprisingly bittersweet, as it meant the end of one part of my breastfeeding relationship with Maggie—she no longer needed me as much as she once had.

After 18 months of struggling to pump enough milk...my last day pumping was surprisingly bittersweet.

Throughout my pumping journey, my husband, Conor, has been my greatest champion and supporter. He stays home to care for our children while I'm working, which was reassuring when I was having trouble leaving Maggie to return to work. I was comforted knowing that she was being cared for by the only person in the world who loved her as much as I did. Conor learned about pumping along with me, especially how to store, warm, and feed expressed milk. He encouraged me when things were rough, and celebrated with me when I got my pumping output up, never doubting that I could make pumping work, and never once thinking that it might be easier or better to just use formula. On a day-to-day basis, he took charge of my pump after work hours. He would take the pump bag from me as I walked in the door, and while I sat down for a "welcome home" nursing with Maggie, he would store the milk I had expressed that day, clean the pump parts and bottles, and pack up the bag again for the next day of work. But the most important thing he did for me was bringing Maggie to my office for lunch a few times a week. Seeing her in the middle of the day was a great pick-me-up, especially on the days when I questioned my decision to return to work or when I had doubts about my ability to pump enough milk for her. Her chubby baby face always cheered me up, and nursing her during lunchtime was not only a great way to reconnect, but it also saved me from having to pump and try to fill another daytime bottle for her. Although I was the one expressing the milk, becoming a successful working and pumping mother was really a team effort.

Now we're starting all over again. I am currently tandem nursing my two children and I have two weeks left of maternity leave following Liam's birth two months ago. No procrastinating this time around! Conor introduced a bottle when Liam was six weeks old, and he's had one to two bottles a week since then. I am pumping just once a day while nursing so that I don't exacerbate my oversupply problem. Once I return to work, I will have a boss who supports my need to pump, my own office, and the ability to set my own pumping times. I have been through this before, and I know what to expect and where to find help if I need it. I am confident that I can and will make pumping work for my family again.

I am not excited about the physical aspect of pumping, especially since I still labor over every ounce of that liquid gold. But I am so grateful to the pump that has allowed me to maintain my breastfeeding relationship with my babies, and I am proud and pleased that as a working, pumping mama, I can still nourish my children, body and spirit, by breastfeeding. I could never have foreseen how blending my career and motherhood would turn out, but I am thrilled with the results.

Sharing Some Hard-Earned Wisdom

Here is what surprised me about working and pumping:

- I was surprised by how hard it was for me to pump and keep up with my daughter's demand. Before going back to work, my breastfeeding experience had been very easy: no latching-on issues, no supply issues, lots of support for my choice. Pumping became the first challenge for me, and I was not prepared for that. I expected that pumping would be easy, just as nursing was, and I had to adjust mentally and physically to being a low-volume pumper—figuring out that I needed a dual electric pump to maximize output, and learning relaxation and massage techniques to assist my let-down reflex to respond to the pump.
- Another, greater surprise was how much I came to treasure my pumping sessions at work. I started off my pumping career dreading pumping time, particularly since I agonized over every ounce I was able to produce. But once I increased my output and settled into a good routine at work, my pumping sessions became important breaks in my busy days, times when I could sit back from my work and concentrate on my beautiful daughter. I would look at her picture, read NEW BEGINNINGS or *Mothering* magazines, and feel confident and proud that I was able to give my daughter my milk even though I couldn't be with her. Once I finally stopped pumping, I found I actually missed those quiet 15 minute breaks in my day where I sat back and focused on Maggie.

I am proud and pleased that as a working, pumping mama, I can still nourish my children, body and spirit, by breastfeeding.

Here are some interesting places I have pumped:

- In the chilly, drafty bathroom of the restaurant at a Uruguayan highway rest stop, listening to the cheers and commentary of the rest of the diners, who were watching Uruguay and France play in the World Cup. Being a soccer fan myself, I lost track of my milk output trying to decipher the score from the crowd's reactions.

- In my own office, unaware that the mirrored, one-way security window I sat in front of was actually a two way window if my office light was on. I quickly learned to turn off my light before plugging in the pump!
- At the sink in public restrooms around the Washington, DC, area. I regularly got positive comments from other women, who stopped next to me at the sink to tell me about how much they had enjoyed breastfeeding their children.

Here are my tips for low volume pumpers:

- Invest in a good quality, dual electric pump. Your body might respond better to the increased suction and the adjustable cycling of a quality pump.
- Learn to nurse one breast while pumping the other. This will take advantage of your body's natural let-down, which may give you more milk than the let-down you get from simply pumping.
- Massage your breasts prior to pumping to encourage a quick let-down, and if the milk flow slows, you can massage again to bring on a second let-down. If your body doesn't respond immediately to the massage, try gently tweaking your nipples with damp fingers to mimic your baby's mouth.
- Sleep with your baby to encourage her to nurse more often when you're together and reduce her demand for bottles when you're apart. This is also a great way to maintain a bond while working.
- Visit your baby at lunchtime or have the care provider bring her to you, if possible. You both get the comfort of nursing and that will be one less bottle you have to worry about filling.
- Make sure you pump for a full 15 minutes each session.
- If you pump at home, do it in the morning when your milk supply is greatest.

GUATEMALA

Field Biologist

Jungle Love

Raquel Sigüenza de Micheo

Translated from Spanish by Nicole Austin Daleiseo

Before having children, I was a biologist in Guatemala who worked long hours, often traveling to remote areas to work in the field four or five days a week. When my husband and I decided to start our family, and I became pregnant with Diego, I knew my life would never be the same. I was faced with the dilemma of choosing between my job and a life at home with my baby. As a biologist, I knew that breastfeeding was clearly the best choice for my son, mainly for health reasons, but also because I felt that it would be most convenient. In Guatemala, the law gives women three months maternity leave, so most women give up breastfeeding when they return to work, which I wasn't willing to do. Also, my husband and I both strongly believed that we didn't want to have children just to have somebody else raise them. After Diego's premature birth by emergency cesarean, I chose to stay home with my son.

I had a very difficult start to breastfeeding. I had no knowledge of how to do it, nobody to help me, and few resources available to me. All I had was my family's support of my decision, and my "stubbornness." It wasn't until six months later did I learn about La Leche League. How many problems and tears I could have saved if I had only had their support at the right moment! Now, as a La Leche League Leader, this is my principle motivation to help other mothers.

After a year of staying home with Diego, I decided to accept a job offer as a university professor. For someone who was used to a professional life, I was in need of a break from my day-to-day routine at home. Although the job paid less than expected, at least I felt the hours and nearby location would make it possible to balance my responsibilities.

I still felt confined being in a classroom, and eventually I arranged to travel on the weekends for class field trips. Later, I took on other jobs that would allow me opportunities to work out in the field again, but this time with my husband and son accompanying me. Because of my husband's undying support, and because of my continued breastfeeding, travel was possible and easy when my milk was always available. Diego was getting older, but my being nearby was comforting to him in strange or uncomfortable situations. As part of my job, my family and I often traveled to remote areas, jungles, and other ecological reserves in Guatemala where most people would not consider bringing their child. I would like to relate several interesting adventures.

I advise mothers who work to evaluate all their options fully in order to achieve the maximum gain for their work and for their families.

One time I had to hike up a mountain with my group, while my son and husband waited at a small hotel down below. I had fed Diego before leaving, and planned on returning before lunch, but the distance was much farther than I had expected. I began to panic and found myself running down the mountain. Others around me were amazed at my ability to do that, but they did not realize why I was running and what a strong motivation a mother's love could be. When I returned, I found my son and husband doing just fine, and realized I could have saved myself many blisters if I had only known he was okay.

People often comment to me that my son is very well-behaved, even in situations where adults would run out of patience. I always like to follow that comment with a story about a time we were stuck waiting on a bus in Ecuador, and waited two hours more in the airport. My secret, which always did the trick to calm my son, was to nurse him.

As Diego grew, I began to work more and more. At one point, when Diego started to have some difficult times without me, and when I became pregnant with my daughter, Rebecca, I realized I had to re-prioritize my life again. I felt that family must always come before work. With two children now, I do consulting work from home. Eventually, when my children are older, I hope to be out working full-time in the field again. Until then, those plans are on hold. But I feel proud to be a mother and proud of the choices I have made in order to do what I feel is best for my family.

For my success in my motherhood and my career, I give credit to two "star actors," my loving husband who has always supported me, and breastfeeding, which has been one of the better-paying investments of my life. I advise mothers who work to evaluate all their options fully in order to achieve the maximum gain for their work and for their families.

MEXICO

Live-In Maid

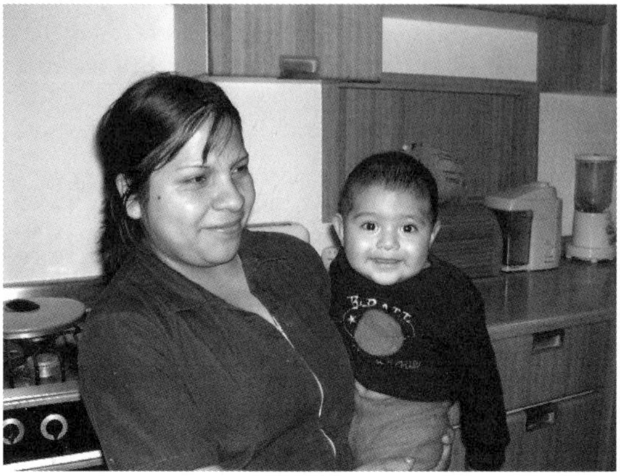

A Return to My Milk

Margarita Santiago Ramirez

Interviewed and translated from Spanish by Paulina Smith

I have worked as a live-in maid since I was 14 years old. I come from a small community in the State of Oaxaca. My parents work the crops and I am one of seven children. I am now 23 and have a little baby, Cristian. I was worried when I knew that I was pregnant. I worked at my job until I was finding it difficult to walk—a month before the baby was born. I then left my job because my boyfriend had said he was going to look after me and the baby, but he didn't. He was with us for a few weeks and then left. I knew he had done this to another woman but thought it would be different this time. My father made him promise he would send us money but he only did this for a few weeks. The lady I had worked for had given me lots of information on breastfeeding; I breastfed Cristian when he was born but then mostly stopped as I was not sure if I really wanted to. I went to visit the family to show them

Cristian and the lady was upset when she saw I was giving him a bottle. She talked to me strongly and said it would be best for Cristian if I gave him my milk. That same day I decided to stop giving him the bottle and breastfeed him only. Though he had been having a bottle much of the day, my milk was plentiful. Now he also eats other foods as he is seven months old.

A few days later I called the lady to see if I could go back to work for her as I saw at that visit that she had not hired another maid. She said yes! Working for the family and having my baby right here feels good. The baby does not cry anymore—he is happy and well. I am at peace and so is Cristian. I keep thinking of the difficult days I had while giving him the bottle. The milk had spilt, the milk had got too hot, and Cristian was sad all the time. My mother worried that I would not attend to the baby properly if I went back to work. But I like to work. When Cristian cries I stop what I'm doing and give him my milk. I like to see that he doesn't cry anymore and that he is contented.

Now I can care for my baby and do my work.

Brazil

Organizational Development Consultant

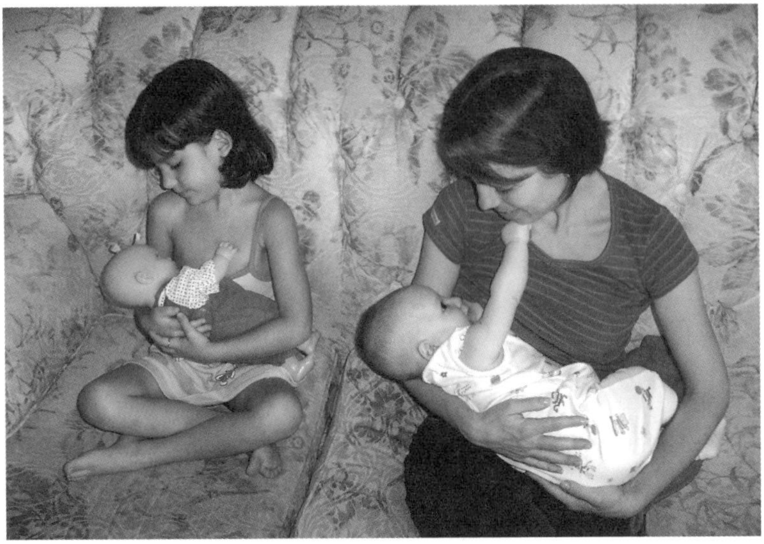

Grounded in More Ways Than One

Ana Raquel Bueno Moraes Ribeiro

Translated from Portuguese by Andréia Mortensen

It was Sunday, and my second son, Tomás, was just 24 hours old when two good friends of mine came to the hospital for a visit. We talked about the things we would usually talk about in this kind of situation—how the second birth had been much faster than the first, how wonderful the arrival of a new baby in the family is, and how well he was breastfeeding already.

It was a very special moment for all of us. After all, Marli and Glaucia, presidents of the consulting company where I work, had shared every emotion of my pregnancy as we worked together all over Brazil developing consulting work and doing training in the area of organizational development.

As my belly grew bigger, our routine began to change. Eventually, I could only board the plane with a physician's statement giving me permission to fly. Every month as my pregnancy progressed, Marli, who usually organizes the teams for work travel, would ask me in a very caring way if I could take one more trip. It continued like this until the ninth month, when ten days before Tomás was born, I took a break from travel.

But on that Sunday our conversation about nursing and diaper changing shifted when Marli asked, "When can we schedule your next trip?" Very calmly, I answered her, "In two years." She was obviously very surprised! Marli knew of my intention to breastfeed my son; she knew I thought breastfeeding was the best choice, both in terms of the nutritional and emotional health benefits to my baby. But she didn't imagine I intended to do that for so long; she was assuming that six months, or certainly one year, would be enough.

We continued our conversation and I made it clear that I wanted to breastfeed Tomás exclusively for six months and continue doing so for two years. It was the same thing I had done with Mariana, my first daughter. I also told her clearly that I did not want to quit my job. I just did not want to go on trips during this phase. All of the office work and other preparations I could easily handle at home, with no problems.

And, that is what happened.

Today my son is one year and nine months old and still breastfeeds. I have never given him a pacifier or a bottle, though I did end up traveling again when he was just under two years old. To my surprise, even though I was away for some days, my milk did not dry up. Tomás resumed nursing when I was back home, and my milk production returned to normal, as if I had never left.

I cannot say that everything was easy on this "breastfeeding project." I faced my share of (somewhat) traditional problems: sleepless nights, feverish episodes, and problems with excess milk.

In the end, for me, breastfeeding and working have not been incompatible. Both are fundamental aspects of my life. I cannot imagine myself away from my work; in the same way I would never think of motherhood without breastfeeding. I think it is in this confidence that I get the strength to face problems that can come my way. There were difficulties that challenged my conviction, but by looking at the healthy and happy eyes of Mariana and Tomás, and by feeling the affection of our skin touching, I feel sure that breastfeeding was our best choice.

I cannot imagine myself away from my work; in the same way I would never think of motherhood without breastfeeding.

Peru

Social Development Consultant

Making Space for My Baby

Silvia Valderrama Sanchez, Trujillo

Translated from Spanish by Nicole Austin Daleiseo

Nowadays I find that many women like me work in order to survive. I work because in the deepest part of my heart, I like it a lot. Really, I get paid to do what I like to do. I have been working for almost nine years in my field and will continue working. I will also continue breastfeeding—combining both is a challenge for me. In fact, it is the greatest challenge of my life.

I am currently mother to an eight-month-old daughter. I work and breastfeed because it strengthens the bonds of love I have for my baby. Just because I do it, does not mean it is easy. I work in Peru as a CARE consultant. I work in projects promoting social development, helping people to take care of their health and giving them innovative strategies to better develop health care skills. My job requires a lot of travel to different places. When I travel by bus, my baby spends the time attached to my breast. When I travel by plane from Cajamarca to Lima, my baby is always nursing. I take advantage of the traveling and breastfeed more.

To be able to bring my baby along on trips and into the office with me, some things had to change. I negotiated with the project coordinator that I needed to have an hour for breastfeeding, which is the law in my country. I also arrived early and stayed later than the normal hours. Besides this, I negotiated that my daughter would be by my side, along with a support person from time to time, to help care for her. I talked to the CARE director, who is a marvelous person, and said that I would produce the same or even better work than before. He understood me, and gave me the support. But always at work, there are people who just don't get it, and they make life difficult for women like me. We mothers should persist and eventually they will become accustomed to it. Then we will change their points of view.

There are few facilities to accommodate me and my breastfeeding baby. I asked to make a space for babies at work, and though it seemed like people accepted the idea well, there was no push to change things. However, for my baby, I will make space. My boss didn't like the idea much, but she didn't say anything because I work hard. Colleagues also gave me disapproving looks when I had to breastfeed my baby. But later they became familiar with the routine and it wasn't so difficult. I take the responsibility for doing my job and caring for my baby, so they did not say anything more to me. In fact, we stole all of their hearts. They now call my daughter and me "Super Powerful Girls."

In Peru, 56 percent of women are in the workforce; 13 weeks of maternity leave is paid by public funds; no breastfeeding breaks allowed.

Our Shared Adventures

While working with my daughter in tow, I have served as supervisor of a large project that was created in order to strengthen social networks for the Health Departments. In my role, I traveled to many different communities. I traveled with my baby, because she is my heart and my life. When on the road, she often needed to nurse. When that happened, I would pull the truck over a moment and enjoy it. She sleeps and wakes. Everyone tells me that I am lucky that my baby is so calm and that she doesn't cry and she likes to travel.

When we are not traveling, we often have meetings in the office where my baby looks for the breast in front of everyone. I am not ashamed, and I breastfeed her. My co-workers used to say, "Give her a bottle, and leave her with 'the girl' (nanny) at home." I told them that the most important thing for the life of a baby until six months of age is her mother's milk. We cannot take this away from her.

When giving a conference for the local government officials, the health department, or for the women of the communities, my baby and my mother also occupy a place in the auditorium. People see this and tell me, "I could not do what you do." I reply that in some ways it has been simple. I never have to schedule. She nurses when she asks, whatever the place: in my job, in the street, in the car.

Finding a good balance is not always easy. There are times when I've had to do things I really did not want to do. I remember clearly the time that I had to go to a community where there were people infected with Carrion's disease (a bacterial infection transmitted by sand flies), and I had to go by foot. The trip was long, but no matter what, I had to do it in order to ensure that the project went well. With pain in my heart, I left my baby. I took out all the milk I had in my breasts, kissed her, and I left. I recommended that she be spoon-fed my milk which I had left in a covered glass in a cold thermos in the health clinic. When I returned, I changed my clothes and reunited with my daughter who attached herself to my breast, nursed until she got tired, and fell asleep.

There are times when I've had to do things I really did not want to do.

A Family Effort

It would be much harder to persevere without my support system. My greatest support so far has been my husband, a marvelous person. Because it is a part of my job to travel from one place to another, together with my baby, my kind husband, who is very busy himself, would say over the telephone, "Take good care of yourself and the baby. If you get tired, quit your job, and what I earn will be sufficient. We will see what we can do here together." In addition my mother-in-law and my mother, two beautiful and good women, often accompany me on my routes. One of them stays at home cooking for my older daughter and husband and the other grandma accompanies me and my baby.

Besides caring for our physical needs, my mother is a great source of emotional and inspirational support. She affectionately reminds me to care for my baby and for myself. She once told me, "My little daughter you have to feed yourself and try to rest when the baby is sleeping in the day." Besides this, she has led through example, having breastfed six children and worked as a college professor. For me, she will always be the best example. She is a woman who always offers tenderness and much love to her children and grandchildren.

Here is my advice to other mothers on how to succeed at combining breastfeeding and work:

- Think always that it is a new challenge that you have to face for the benefit of your baby.
- Be creative. Each day look for new ways of satisfying your baby and organizing your work.
- Seek and have a balance between your life as a mother and as a worker.
- Make sure that the quality of your work is not sacrificed. On the contrary, try to be better at your job each day.
- Negotiate with your boss, stressing that providing facilities that enable you to bring your breastfeeding baby to work will affect your work in a positive way. (As opposed to leaving your baby, which can affect your work in a negative way.)
- Speak to other mothers who have had the experience of breastfeeding or who are pregnant and promise to be their allies.
- Make sure that your boss is contented with the work that you are doing once you have baby nearby.
- Be patient. Life is not always going to be rosy when you are breastfeeding your baby at work. There are people who don't understand and will try to bring you down with your efforts and your accomplishments and they tell you: "When I had my baby I gave him a bottle and he is alive and well just the same." But you must persevere. Do it for your baby, and one day she will appreciate you, just as I appreciate my mother for doing it for me.
- If you have to travel far for work, take advantage and take your baby along. She will have more time with you, and will enjoy the best food that a mother can give.
- Try to maintain contact with other mothers who have had the experience—they are motivating. Establish a network of support for mothers who breastfeed and work in order to facilitate this ambitious goal.

I have learned that really nothing is impossible for a mother when she knows what she has to do to give the best to her baby. However, more working mothers will be better able to breastfeed their children when we:

- Give mothers who breastfeed and work more time to breastfeed, and provide on-site facilities that allow for the support of child care.
- Improve the levels of communication through strategies of communication and empowerment.
- Break down "machismo."

- Focus on self-esteem and the value of the woman.
- Focus on literacy for women.
- Address extreme poverty that exists in certain areas.

I work now and I will continue working. When my daughter grows up, she will know a lot about how to help women and children and how to save lives because she has watched her mother do it every day. Because I made room for her, I like to think my baby has learned a great deal. I know that she will someday recognize that although I have had to work a lot, I have not denied her needs.

PART THREE

EUROPE

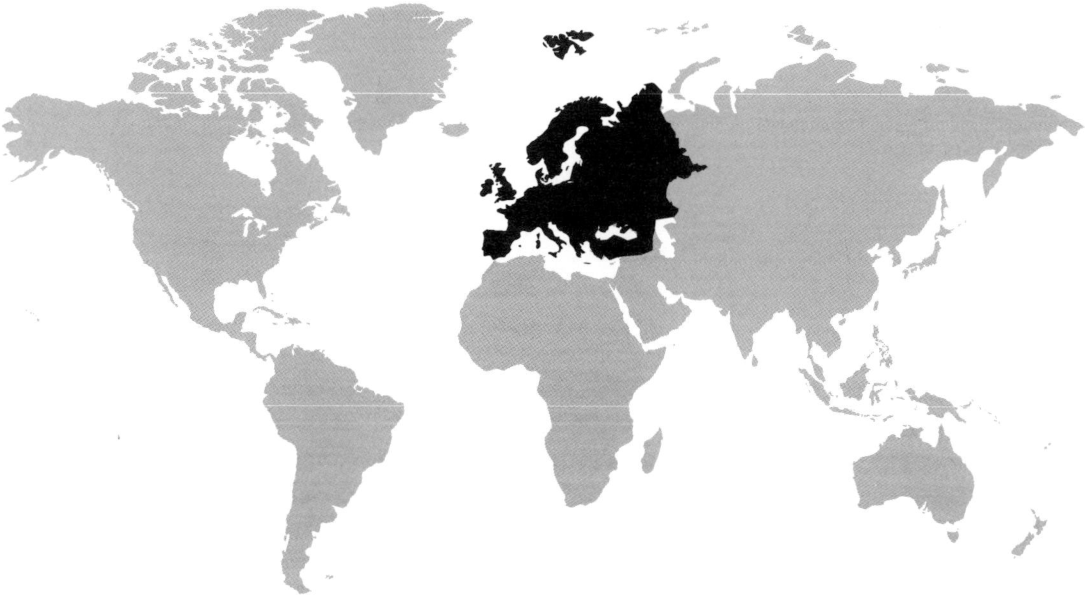

UNITED KINGDOM

Graphic Designer

The Best of Both Worlds

Sue Low, Hampshire

I am very lucky. I have a beautiful, healthy 13-month-old daughter and a loving husband who is a doting father. All three of us have shared a very special first year in my daughter's life. A combination of the maximum one-year maternity leave for me and part-time hours for my husband has created not only a strong bond between mother and daughter, but also between father and daughter.

I have been a graphic designer for over 15 years and love my job, but my aim all along was to return to work on part-time hours. Financially it would be a struggle. Emotionally there was no other choice. I was lucky—the UK recently passed legislation making it almost impossible for an employer to reject a claim for part-time hours from a previous full-time employee. My bosses and I quickly agreed on a three-day workweek. Daddy would take care of Mae on my three days at work and vice versa.

Everything seemed to be clicking into place, except my one biggest concern—her food! Since she waited until six months to start eating solids, Mae completely bypassed the stage of baby food and purées and went straight to finger food. However, at ten months she was still exclusively breastfed with the odd "meal" explored through play more than hunger. As my return to work loomed ever closer, I finally had to admit to myself—I was going to have to express milk for her. It had always been something I strenuously avoided, setting myself the goal of not introducing a bottle. But now I had to find answers: how would I do it, where would I do it, how often would I do it, and would Mae cope without breastfeeding? I scoured the Internet and asked around for advice but there didn't seem to be any firsthand experience of combining breastfeeding and working with an older, almost exclusively breastfed baby.

My husband and I decided to do some trial runs. We discovered very quickly that Mae was happy to be with daddy for a good six hours without me or my milk. During my absence she was content to drink water and "nibble" on food. I bought a breast pump and was immediately encouraged by the speed and ease of expressing when I was nice and full! The only drawback: every possible serving suggestion for feeding her mummy's milk was steadfastedly rejected!

My journey to work is about 30 minutes by car. I feed Mae before I leave. Sometimes she's asleep, but sometimes she's up and she happily waves me off as she snuggles with her daddy. I use the First Aid room at work to express my milk. It has a couch and a lock on the door. I need to express twice, once at midday and again at 3:00 PM. Each pumping takes about 15 to 20 minutes. I take the time out of my lunch and tea breaks, which has more to do with me learning to manage my work load than anyone clock watching. I store the milk in our department's refrigerator.

I have now been back at work for nearly two months and, "so far so good." I work in a large corporate office building but in a small department. My two bosses are both mothers and the company philosophy believes strongly in the importance of family. Even so, I think I am the only mother who is doing what I am doing in terms of feeding. My bosses are supportive but I don't think any of them can relate to it personally. Most people I know gave up breastfeeding way before their babies were a year, or the baby adored soilds and the milk consumption was dramatically reduced. I think the fact that I am different has actually made me more determined to continue for as long as need be. After two weeks back at work, Mae was doing poorly so Daddy drove her to my workplace where I could feed her in the car. This has now

United Kingdom

In the United Kingdom, 57 percent of women are in the workforce; 26 or more weeks of maternity leave is paid by public funds; 14 days of paternity leave is paid by public funds; an additional 26 weeks of unpaid maternity leave is available plus 91 days (x2) of unpaid parental leave; no breastfeeding breaks are allowed.

become a regular lunchtime event. A nearby park and cafe provide us with food, fresh air, and ducks to watch! Mae happily has her milk, feeds the ducks, and waves bye-bye—homeward bound, full, rosy-cheeked, and I think very secure in the knowledge that she really does have the best of both worlds at that moment.

As I said at the beginning, I am very lucky. I get to leave the house guilt-free and actually looking forward to work. Everyone benefits. A happy, healthy child means less stress all round, at work and at home.

France

Professor of History, Architecture, and Design

Museum-Bound Babies

Anne Betting

Translated from French by Jo-Anne Elder

After breastfeeding five children and working full-time, I have a few experiences I can share to prove that it is possible to bring babies everywhere you go. Breastfed babies cuddling with their mothers are extraordinarily easy to look after. They're quiet and calm, especially if their mothers are relaxed. It's the people that can be hard to handle sometimes! Often colleagues would ask me: "Why in the world did you bring your baby here?" I simply replied that the baby needed his mother, without mentioning that he needed to breastfeed which can lead to negative comments. I might add, "It's for health reasons." Usually, in that case, people didn't ask any more questions; they thought he was gravely ill and couldn't be left at home.

Before I share my stories, here are the pivotal things that have made this arrangement possible:

- I negotiated flexible schedules, without specifying that it was for breastfeeding, to reduce the time spent away from the baby (I am never away more than six hours at a time).
- I went home at noon if necessary; it is more tiring, but helped me avoid the need to pump, so the day seemed shorter.
- I shortened the time the baby was at the babysitter's by having a caregiver as close to home as possible, ten to 12 hours a week. I explained to the caregiver that the baby did not need anything to eat. The baby nursed right before I left, and food was an accessory. She played with the baby, took the baby out for walks, etc. The baby's father managed to convert his vacations and breaks into longer periods of time away from the office, which meant he could take half-days off.
- I took the baby everywhere with me, except into the classroom: conferences, exhibitions, even places where people didn't expect to find children, as long as there was no law against it.

So, here are some of my stories, some of which by now are very dear memories.

When Camille was eight days old, I took her to a special concert performed in an abbey; she was hidden in a big wool sweater. Later Camille, at eight months, came with me by bus to take some 50 students for an all-day trip to visit galleries and museums in Paris. The driver recommended that I keep the baby bottles in his portable fridge, and I thanked him politely, although of course I didn't have any bottles. One of my students called out: "You'd have to put the whole professor in the fridge!"

Ever the traveler, Camille, at 14 months, went on a five-day trip with me from Lille, France to Barcelona, Spain. I only let people know the night before that I would be taking the baby. By then, it was too late to cancel the trip! Everything worked out fine, and she ended up taking her first step in Spain. With the baby in a sling, traveling was so much easier: no folding bed, no stroller, no bottle-warmer, just a few disposable diapers (instead of the cloth diapers we used at home) and we were all set. I took her with me when I met with the people in the construction industry (men only, naturally!) and there was never any problem. I'm sure my students would never think that it was strange to see a baby nurse; I'd always had my baby around them. Camille weaned herself when she was three.

Amélie was born in 1997. She became my companion quite early. From the age of eight days through five months, Amélie came with me when I volunteered at her brothers' and sisters' school, giving work-

In France, 55 percent of women are in the workforce; 16 weeks of maternity leave is paid by public funds and 7 days of paternity leave is allowed; unpaid breastfeeding breaks of one hour per day are allowed until the baby is one year old.

shops on building and art. I only missed one session when I was in the hospital having my baby! I would prop Amélie up in a nest of pillows and look after two groups of eight children for an hour at a time, with a ten-minute nursing break in between.

Amélie also took part in a two-day conference on ecological architecture when she was three-and-a-half-months old. There were doorkeepers who seemed a bit worried at first, but I reassured them that a baby that age slept half the time and that I would leave the minute she disturbed anyone; but that never happened. She usually played with her toes or with quiet toys. I always made sure I didn't bring rattles or any other noisy toys. I keep my babies on my lap in these situations, and make sure they are only lightly dressed because it is often quite hot in the rooms they use for conferences. I think that babies who scream in department stores often do it because they are really hot. (Have you ever noticed the stores are stuffy and the crying babies are often wearing heavy coats?)

Thomas is the fifth of the family and the fifth of my children to accompany me everywhere, even to work.

Amélie was exclusively breastfed for seven months and then started table foods. She never had any strained or puréed baby foods. She didn't get sick until her fifth birthday. She had weaned at four years old, and she is our most independent child. At two years, she wouldn't let us help her get dressed: no way! She did everything on her own.

Thomas, born in January 2004, is the fifth of the family and the fifth of my children to accompany me everywhere, even to work. By his birth, I had a lot more experience. But every child is different. This week he'll be celebrating his first birthday and he still gets about 90 percent of his food from breastfeeding. He'll take tastes of all kinds of things but only a little bit at a time. He likes things that are in little pieces: omelettes, ham, clementines, and grapes.

At 15 days old, Thomas went to his first conference at the School of Architecture. At one month old, he went on the express train with Camille and Amélie for the first time to attend a day-long exhibition. The gallery staff members were a bit curious, and so were the visitors. Not very many women take such young babies. There was only one negative remark, by a 60-year-old visitor, who said I should be ashamed to expose an infant to so many germs. I used a pass to avoid the long line up. In France we receive these passes in the sixth month of pregnancy and can use them until our child is three years old. These make toting a baby much easier.

Thomas also went on an architects' tour with me to see wood building designs in Belgium. We travelled 1,000 km in two days, and the organizer was furious when we got on the bus because I hadn't let her know about the baby. I explained that the baby wouldn't disturb anyone. The bus was half-empty. The Belgian organizer was just as surprised: "It's as if a gentleman decided to bring his dog or a lady brought her pet canary! This is a business trip after all, and we're professionals!" I replied calmly that we would try not to bother anyone. Two hours later we were welcomed into an amazing house where his parents lived, and he told them, "I've never seen such a well-behaved baby!" At 10:30 the next night, an architect asked me if I had changed my baby—he couldn't believe that he didn't hear the baby crying, see a lot of paraphernalia, or smell anything!

The day I started back at work, I was called to a meeting 600 km away. I asked for two more days of maternity leave and my doctor gave me a slip that said, "The mother is not to be separated from the baby." A breastfeeding permission slip! It was useful, and I could have had another two weeks at home, but I wanted to see my students before they left for their work-term. I think that if you don't abuse your vacation days, the day you do need to stay home no one will get too upset. In fact, I've only taken one sick day for any of my children in the 12 years I've been teaching (and mothering) in this school, when one cut a finger and had to be hospitalized.

My husband and daughter tried to give Thomas my hand-expressed milk in a bottle and in a spoon but Thomas wanted nothing to do with that.

Recently, because of the many commitments I had approaching, my husband and daughter tried to give Thomas my hand-expressed milk in a bottle and in a spoon but Thomas wanted nothing to do with that. He still nurses every three hours; it's his own personal rhythm. He can skip a nursing and wait for me, but will never go more than six hours at a time. With important work around the corner, and important work at home, I did what I have always done—took the baby along.

I had to go to serve on an examining committee and took Thomas with me, letting my colleagues know that I would have him there during the exam. He spent six hours going from my lap to my breast to sleeping on a table. He's a very physical child who walked a week before he was eight months old so this day required some flexibility.

Eight days later, we went to sit on another jury, but this time I was a bit apprehensive, because it meant giving oral exams to ten candidates. I was expecting negative remarks and had prepared my answer: "If I didn't bring my baby with me, you would have had to find another examiner at the last minute to replace me." But I was met with: "Oh! And this year you're coming with this beautiful baby in tow!" I didn't have to apologize for anything. I gave oral exams for three hours without any break. I had worn a cardigan so that the baby wouldn't shock anyone while nursing, but in the exam room you could hear little "glug

glug glug" noises as it was 34° C and Thomas needed a lot of fluids. I've never counted how many times my children nurse in a day, and tell people, "If you have a drink of water, do you count that as a meal?"

Defending my choices has not always been easy. By preferring direct breastfeeding over pumping, I was often breastfeeding in an environment that wasn't always breastfeeding-friendly. My colleagues never breastfed more than a month or two. However, my partner was supportive, because it made life simpler for him.

By preferring direct breastfeeding over pumping, I was often breastfeeding in an environment that wasn't always breastfeeding-friendly.

Despite all of that, here is why I continually choose breastfeeding. It makes for easy living and easy travelling. It saves time and money, as I buy no formula and little medication. Of course, it is better for my children's health, but also for my health. (We often forget that.) Finally, the closeness of the mother and child is hard to beat. Breastfed children are more secure and mothers know their children well.

In the end, I have enjoyed taking the babies everywhere I go and I think they've enjoyed it, too. Check around you; you'll see it is never specifically prohibited to take a child into a place. So enjoy it! Introduce the baby to daily life. The more babies are taken on trains, into galleries, and among the world, the less surprising it will be. I fondly remember the time we toured a textile mill. The baby was in a sling and was nursing very peacefully at the time. A lady who was 75 or 80 years old looked at me with a big smile and said, "It's so nice to see that, and it's so rare these days."

My New Swiss "Entitlement"

Linda Hooper

I consider myself to be a very lucky mother. I am "entitled" to nurse my baby for up to two hours each day until her first birthday. I can leave my place of employment and take the bus to my daughter at her day-care and spend, on average, 25 minutes with her, twice a day. That does not even include my lunch hour, which I also spend with her. This special policy through my employer, the United Nations, has enabled me to strive to do my best, both as a mother and an employee

Although I pursued academic studies and went to work after graduate school, I always thought I would be a stay-at-home mom when I had children. Most of the jobs I had were not fulfilling enough for me to imagine working while I had children. Of course, there was always the "dream career" of working at the United Nations. But, dreams often do not come true and I did not think this dream would ever be a reality. Nevertheless, before I was pregnant, I was accepted to the United Nations' examination process.

During my pregnancy with our daughter, Hadley Sophia, I was offered a position to work in Geneva, Switzerland at the United Nations. My husband and I decided that I would accept the position. I was supposed to start when the baby was four months old.

When the baby was born, I was in for a surprise. I quickly realized that it was impossible to sell the house, move from Virginia to Geneva, get ready for a new job, and learn to be a mother in the short four months we had allotted! Luckily, I was able to have the start date pushed back, so that I could take care of all the things I had to get done in the USA while getting to know my baby. I started my position at the United Nations in Geneva when Hadley Sophia was almost six months old.

As a new mother starting a new job, I asked where I could express milk for the baby. I was amazed at the answer I received. As a nursing mother within the UN system, I was "entitled" to two hours a day to go to my baby and nurse her! If I chose to pump my milk, I was "entitled" one hour to do so. Whenever someone asked me about what I was going to do with the baby while I was working, I told them she would be in daycare, but I would still get to nurse her for the first year of her life. They were usually amazed. No one had ever heard of such a policy, not even members of the LLLI Group I attended.

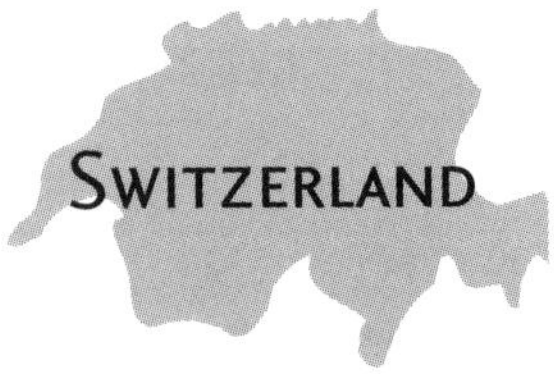

In Switzerland, 52 percent of women are in the workforce; 14 weeks of maternity leave is paid by public funds; no breastfeeding breaks are allowed.

One critical thing that really makes this possible for me, besides our awesome daughter and some great pro-breastfeeding policies at work, is my husband. He has supported my decisions about childbirth, co-sleeping, nursing, taking this job, and moving to Switzerland. In many ways, it is he who makes it possible for me to work and breastfeed our daughter. To minimize the time she spends at the daycare, he is the one that drops her at 9:00 AM before he goes to work. He also leaves work early to pick her up at 3:30 PM.

In the mornings, I get myself ready for work and then dress and nurse Hadley. During the day, I leave work around 10:30 AM, 1:00 PM, and 4:00 PM to nurse her in person. If I cannot make it to the daycare or back to the apartment for the afternoon nursing, my husband will often bring the baby to me, so that we can nurse at work. This was especially true during the first month or two, when we were just getting used to working and nursing. More recently, if I cannot get to her, I will express milk. Luckily, I seldom have to do this. In these cases, I leave the caretaker my milk to feed to Hadley in a cup. Hadley has never taken a bottle. She never liked the bottle, and because I went to her in person, she never needed to like it.

Hadley's daycare center is a private crèche (French for daycare) located very close to our apartment and a five-minute bus ride from work. The care providers speak to the babies in French—they also speak to the parents in French, which is one of the difficulties for me. My husband speaks French, which helps. The general attitude in the crèche toward breastfeeding is positive. Most mothers in Switzerland nurse their babies for some time during the first six months. At the crèche, there are some other mothers who come to nurse their babies during the course of the day. One mother who works with older children at the crèche would nurse her daughter three times a day in the baby room, but now that her daughter is over six months old she no longer nurses her as often. I find it sad that she was told that she does not make enough milk for her daughter and is stopping their nursing relationship. I am the only mother who physically nurses her baby to provide the primary means of milk.

When I get home from work, we nurse for as long as she wants and as often as she wants. When I am not at work and on weekends, Hadley nurses on demand. We also cosleep, which allows Hadley to nurse when she needs to at night. Cosleeping really helps strengthen our bond. I think it also helps lessen the pain of missing my daughter all day, since she is next to me all night. Of course, I miss her anyway.

I am still aware of and grateful for the extremely close bond I have with our daughter, developed I think, from our nursing relationship.

I don't want to make it seem like everything has gone off without a hitch. There have been some difficult times for us. In the beginning, during the slow adaptation process to the crèche, it was painful for me to leave Hadley. I was sure that they would not know what to do with her. I was worried that she would not adapt to being away from me. Of course, she did. There are days it is still hard to leave after I have nursed her. She clearly wants mommy. On these days, I try to stay a little longer and make sure that I hand her over to one of the care providers, who usually can distract her from my leaving.

Like everyone, we cope with ongoing difficulties. We struggle with having a very limited support network here in Geneva, which makes it harder for me to combine working and nursing. I really miss my LLL Group from the USA. When my daughter was born, my younger sister, an LLL Leader, was one of the most helpful people in establishing my nursing relationship with Hadley. Margaret was always there to answer any question I had about nursing—she still is. It is also hard that we do not have grandmothers and aunts or cousins who can help out.

However, I am still aware of and grateful for the extremely close bond I have with our daughter, developed I think, from our nursing relationship. I am also thrilled about the relationship my husband has developed with our daughter. Had we stayed in Virginia, they would never have spent so much time together, because I would not have been working.

There are times when I feel as though I have too much work to do to leave the office for a couple of hours. On these days I remind myself that Hadley will only be a baby for a short time. Once she is a year old, I can no longer leave work in the morning and afternoon to nurse her. If we continue nursing as I plan to, we will still be able to nurse at lunch time during the day. These precious times are very important to me, perhaps even more so because I work.

NETHERLANDS

Social worker

Working a 24-Hour Shift

Titia Vanderwerf

I don't see breastfeeding as a choice, but rather something dictated by nature. Of course I would give my son my own milk. I never gave it a thought when I was pregnant with Jillis.

Like breastfeeding, working for me is also not a choice, but rather something dictated by financial necessity. We need the money and cannot live off of the income of my husband alone. I was not excited to work again, not because I don't like my job, but because I found it hard to be away from Jillis. In the end, I needn't have worried, because it all worked out.

I am a social worker, employed as group leader with mentally disabled children ranging in age from 11 to 16 years. These children have behavioral problems in addition to their mental disabilities. They live in a group together and have been taken away from their homes for reasons such as child abuse and neglect. In my group, there are 11 children. So, while I would prefer to be home with my son, I do find my work gratifying and important.

In addition to much needed emotional readiness, I prepared to return to work by renting a Medela pump that allows me to efficiently empty both breasts at the same time. I went back to work with "the blue box" as my colleagues call it, and a cooler-bag. I was worried about expressing milk at work, because we don't have breaks. When I take a break, I leave my colleague alone with 11 behaviorally challenged children! As far as I know, I am the first one to ever come to work with a "blue box." Colleagues and children are most curious, but I never hear negative comments. Some of them might find it just a bit strange and make stupid jokes about it. But I don't care; I joke along with them. To be honest, it did seem like a strange thing to do in the beginning. I felt like a cow! After months of doing it, everyone sees it just as one more thing I have to do a few times a day.

Workplace acceptance is helpful, but it can't solve all challenges. I must work night shifts and 24-hour-shifts, which are very tough. The first time I had to work a night shift, I found it agonizing to be away from my son for such a long time. And I worried. What if he wakes up at night and there is no breast available? I trust his father and have no problem leaving my son with him. He is a really concerned daddy—but he has no breast! My colleagues try to give me as few night shifts as possible. When I am forced to work one, I make do. Luckily, I have my own bedroom with a locking door. The children go to bed at about 10:00 PM, and then I go to bed at 11:00 PM. I express my milk and leave it in my cooler-bag. The alarm goes off again at 6:00 AM and I have to express milk again quickly, before waking "my" 11 children. When I finally go home, I am absolutely exhausted. I always enjoy an afternoon nap with Jillis drinking and sleeping at my breast. It is such a nice reunion for the two of us.

Unfortunately, people around me are now starting to say that it is time to stop breastfeeding, especially as Jillis is getting a bit of banana and carrots. Six months is plenty, they think. My son is eight months old and we both still feel happy with breastfeeding; it is the best part of our daily routine. When he wakes up at six in the morning, I take him out of his bed to nurse, and we happily return to sleep until eight or nine in the morning. Fortunately, I never work early in the morning. We get to take it easy and enjoy quality time together.

Netherlands

In Netherlands, 55 percent of women are in the workforce; 16 weeks of maternity leave is paid by public funds; 65 days of parental leave; 2 days of paternity leave; paid breastfeeding breaks are given.

SLOVENIA

Technical Engineer

The Politics of Life

Karmen Mlinar, Kamnik

Most Slovenian mothers work. The first reason for this is economical; the second is cultural. We are a little country in Europe with only two million inhabitants. Out of those inhabitants, only 17,000 children are born each year, with the average family having only one to two children. Our nation's birthrate is extremely low.

Slovenian women are granted one year of fully paid maternity leave! Officially it is called "maternity leave" for the first three months and "parent's leave" for next nine months. These nine months can be equally used between a mother and a father.

Due to our nation's low birth rate and to encourage breastfeeding, the Slovenian government grants legal acts to help families. The acts entitle:

- One year (12 months) of fully paid maternity leave to either parent.

- Parents of three children, who are younger than eight years old, receive 13 months of maternity leave.
- All mothers receive a "gift" for birth worth approximately 300 dollars in cash or baby equipment.
- Parents of three or more children receive a yearly stipend of about 400 dollars.
- If a baby is ill or has development problems, maternity leave can be prolonged to 18 fully paid months.
- One parent has the option to work part-time until the baby is three years old. Because this lowers the family income, the government covers the difference by contributing the full payment of social, health, and retirement contributions and taxes.
- Kindergartens (daycare centers) are very well organized. There are enough of them and babies can be enrolled before they are one year old.
- Parents can get a sickness leave when the baby is ill that pays 80 percent of the regular salary.
- A breastfeeding mother has a legal right to use one hour per day for feeding a baby or expressing her milk.
- A breastfeeding mother has a legal right not to work at nights and in certain work environments (e.g., with chemicals or radiation).
- A breastfeeding mother legally cannot be fired from her job!

Great isn't it? But still, most Slovenian mothers have to work because most Slovenian families cannot survive on only one income. And despite the good family policies, an average Slovenian family has few children.

As an LLL Leader, I receive specific questions about working and breastfeeding. Some mothers call and ask how to wean a baby around one year because they think they must do it before returning to work. After I talk with them about their options, most mothers decide to continue breastfeeding. Some mothers need to pump their milk at work, but most mothers don't even need to.

Now, I'd like to tell you more about my personal experiences with my three babies and my plans for the future.

I'm an electro-technical engineer. Before children, I worked as a computer systems engineer. In the afternoon, I worked my second job teaching computer basics and programs at the Medical University in Ljubljana. I had very good job conditions and my payment was a little bit more than the average Slovenian wage. My husband and I lived well. We rebuilt his parents' house, so we could live together in one house

In Slovenia, 67 percent of women are in the workforce; 365 days of paid parental leave is allowed for either parent; a breastfeeding mother has a legal right to use one hour per day for feeding a baby or expressing her milk.

but each have separate flats, we traveled a lot, and we had many hobbies. Then, we decided it was time to have children—we wanted at least three.

I went back to work with an extremely heavy heart when my first son, Luka, was one-year-old and still breastfeeding. We are lucky that our in-laws live in the same house. My husband and I decided we would like my retired mother-in-law to take care of our baby and she was very happy to do that. It was great, because Luka could sleep longer and did not need to wake up early to go to kindergarten (daycare). We have a big garden around the house so they spent most of their days outside. My mother-in-law loves her grandson, and they have a great relationship.

I started to prepare my baby for my absence a few weeks before I went back to work. I went to the bank or post or shopping and left him with his grandmother. We had no problems at all. I gradually prolonged the absence and one week before I went back to work he slept his lunchtime nap for the first time in his grandmother's bed. She read him stories and he easily fell asleep without his mommy for the first time. When I came back I gave him extra attention and everything was okay.

Most Slovenian mothers have to work because most Slovenian families cannot survive on only one income.

At work I had to pump milk just to release the pressure. I was lucky to have my own office. I simply locked the door and expressed some milk every three to four hours. I asked my boss if I could come to work earlier so I could leave earlier to have more time with Luka. He was very supportive. Our usual working day was from 8:00 AM to 4:00 PM, but I worked from 6:00 AM to 2:00 PM. Luka ate lunch at his grandmother's and when I came home shortly after, we had afternoons and evenings to ourselves for playing, walks, baking cookies, etc.

Luka was very happy with his grandmother as his babysitter. When I came home, he usually wanted to breastfeed immediately. But after one month he completely weaned himself. I was the one who was not prepared for that!

It was hard for me to go back to work at that time. But I was a graduate and my job meant a lot to me. In the computer business, one year of absence is a lot, and I had some problems getting right back into the business. Of course, my child was also very important to me, so I felt such pressure. I was pretty relieved after nine months of working to discover that I was pregnant with baby number two. During that pregnancy, I had many problems, so I stayed home almost all nine months on sickness leave until the birth of our daughter, Naja. I remember these nine months as a most beautiful time, spending it with my growing toddler son. We really had a nice time together despite my pregnancy problems.

After Naja was born, I was at home with her and Luka for 17months. Luka had recently started kindergarten (preschool), and attended four hours a day, until lunch. He loved the activities but had some minor problems with socialization with the other children in the beginning. At that time he was sick a lot and we were also having very severe problems with Naja's health. Naja is highly allergic and, consequently, we spent many days in hospitals. (A breastfeeding mother can be with her baby all the time in Slovenia. She is allowed to sleep and eat in the hospital for free.) Because of Naja's severe allergies, my maternity leave was prolonged.

After maternity leave was over, Naja was in good care with my mother-in-law and Luka was in kindergarten at that time.

I struggled hard to find other ways to stay home with my children. Unfortunately that was impossible. I earned twice as much money as my husband did and we were deep in debt. I was extremely unhappy with the situation as Naja was sick a lot and I was often home on sick-leave.

I struggled hard to find other ways to stay home with my children.

Because of her allergies, Naja was fully breastfed for 13 months and started solids very slowly after that. That is why I was still expressing milk for my 17-month-old daughter. I put milk in storage bags in the freezer and carried milk back home to use for cooking for Naja. She weaned herself at 26 months with a little help from me. I was pregnant at that time with baby number three and extremely sick. I couldn't handle it all—two little ones, a full-time job, no sleeping at night. The weaning was very kind and slow. We kept our morning breastfeeding for several months.

And then Jaka was born. At that time, both of the older children went to kindergarten (preschool) for four hours a day. I had a really nice time to spend with my new baby before picking up the older ones. In the afternoon, we would have time for all of us to be together. In the beginning of this maternity leave I started to search for other options. I knew that I could not go back to work full-time. I started to write articles for two Slovenian parenting magazines and parents loved them. My husband changed his job and started his own business, together with his brother. The first years were really hard—there was little money in addition to my husband's increased absence. He worked from morning to late night. During this maternity leave, we decided that I would only return to work part-time, for four hours a day.

When my maternity leave was over, I started to work part-time. Jaka was in good care with my mother-in-law, Luka had just started school, and Naja was in kindergarten. In the morning I drove the older two to school and kindergarten and came home just after lunch. We had more time in the afternoons for us to be together.

After that maternity leave I lost some privileges at work. I no longer have my own office anymore. I no longer have a parking place, and I have little chance for promotion. But I don't mind. Working part-time is important to me. While I do keep up with my profession, I have no time to socialize with my co-workers. But I don't mind—spending time with my children is much more important. We do live now on quite a lower income, and I have to think twice about every bit I spend. But I'm also much happier. I have more time for my children, I am more relaxed, and we don't live at such a fast tempo anymore.

In June 2005 I'm going on my fourth maternity leave. I'm seriously thinking about quitting my job for good this time. With the freelance work I've done, I have learned many new things: Web design, writing articles, editing and publishing books, etc. I would like to become a freelance writer and Web designer, working from home. Though we know it will be financially difficult, my husband is very supportive of the idea. We have made the right decisions for our family in the past, and trust ourselves to do so again.

We have made the right decisions for our family in the past, and trust ourselves to do so again.

SPAIN

Music Teacher

A Father's Foresight

Marta Marina González Pérez, Méntrida

Translated from Spanish by Natalia Smith Allen

Since I was a little girl I was certain I wanted to be a mother. I felt joy observing the sweetness, honesty, and spontaneity of children. Furthermore, my mother made me the happiest child in this world, which gave me the dream of trying to repeat this story with my own child.

Finally my most awaited day arrived in January of 2004. I was able to meet my new baby, Pablo. I had read and been told that health centers have the obligation to promote breastfeeding, and because of this I was eager for them to place my child close to me to breastfeed him—but this did not happen. They took him away to clean him and to make sure he was in good health. I was not able to see him for more than half an hour. After that they did not allow us to take him out of the crib for two more hours. Between one thing and another, I was not able to breastfeed Pablo until four hours after birth. I have to admit that those were among the worst hours of my life. My child was hungry and he didn't quickly learn how to latch on. During the next two days everything continued the same. Pablo cried and cried, and the only solution others offered was to give him formula. I cried together with him and asked that they dry up my milk, but my husband remained calm and asked me for one last opportunity before giving up. He said he was certain that we would be successful in the end, and reminded me that my milk was the best thing for Pablo. I became extremely upset with him and told him he was selfish. Today Pablo and I have a lot to thank him for because he was right—we succeeded!

Unfortunately this is not the happy ending of the story. During the following months Pablo suffered from colic and associated his discomfort with me. As a result, he wanted to be with anyone except me. He would cry every time he was in my arms. I felt I was a bad mother, and that my child did not love me. But my instinct kept on telling me not to give up, that I had to continue. That is what I did. After three-and-a-half months I was expected to go back to work, which created an even more difficult situation. I wasn't feeling well, and to wean Pablo would have made everything worse. Because of this, the doctor decided I should have an extended leave of absence. At seven-and-a-half months I returned to work; I could not sleep. What was going to happen now? My child was finally happily breastfeeding! As soon as I arrived at work I went to talk to my Director and I gained permission to leave during recess to breastfeed Pablo. I think it made a difference that she saw Pablo and was amazed at his physical and intellectual development, not to mention his sociability. It was as if he knew he had to smile!

In Spain, 43 percent of women are in the workforce; 16 weeks of maternity leave is paid by public funds; 2 days paternity leave; paid breastfeeding breaks are given when a mother returns to work.

His daycare is only two minutes from where I work, so I was able to meet him everyday. There was no assigned place for breastfeeding, since the convention in Spain is for children to breastfeed only for three or four months. Weaning usually occurs when a mother goes back to work. Still, I am very grateful to the daycare for accommodating me. I can tell you it is a wonderful feeling to see my child's face full of happiness when I arrive at his school to breastfeed him.

The reason I continue with working and breastfeeding is because combining both is incredibly fulfilling. I work as a music teacher, which is my choice: I love music and I love to teach. And of course, I love my son and the closeness breastfeeding gives us. The distance from my work to my house makes this feat very doable.

Even though I am happy with my decision, working and breastfeeding is not without difficulties. Among my colleagues, the fact that

A million times over I know my husband's help and understanding have allowed me to continue to work and breastfeed.

I breastfeed is a source of conflict. Every day someone asks me when I will stop nursing my son. My response is: "When he wants to." They continually tell me again and again what bad experiences they had when they breastfed their babies.

It would be very hard to face these disparaging attitudes without my husband, Jose. A million times over I know his help and understanding have allowed me to continue to work and breastfeed. I cannot thank him enough.

Unfortunately, success at breastfeeding and work is not that common because society demands a woman's presence at work, while being insensitive to nature's reality—the need of children to breastfeed. In Spain, the government is questioning the need for a maternity leave of a mere 16 weeks. It is so unfair, that this has been my main reason for submitting this story.

By speaking out, I hope to inspire all mothers around the world to overcome every single difficulty they encounter to enable them to breastfeed their child. One has to have patience, perseverance, and a little bit of imagination, just like other challenges in life. Why not attempt to combine breastfeeding with work? I can assure you that the reward is enormous; a baby's laughter has no price!

In the end, I cannot take full credit for all of the love and fondness that has grown out of mine and Pablo's breastfeeding relationship. Pablo and I both know that we owe much of it to a father who is so sensitive and special that he has made this story possible.

ENGLAND

Mental Health Nurse

Thriving on Mummy's Milk

Lisa Marrett

I am 39 years old and I have two gorgeous girls, Saskia, four years, and Mischa, 19 months. I am now employed by the National Health Service of Great Britain as a Training and Staff Development Facilitator; I work four days per week.

I am breastfeeding and working because when it was time for me to return to work, I did not feel that either Mischa or I was ready for weaning. Mischa was almost 12 months old at that time but she had been in child care for three days per week since she was seven months old for unusual and traumatic reasons. Mischa is an identical twin and her twin sister, Esther, was admitted to a hospital when the twins were six months old. Esther had an undiagnosed congenital condition that affected her muscle function and breathing, but not her intellect, and she died in Intensive Care in the hospital on the sixth of February in 2004. In order to devote myself more to Esther during her last precious few months, I chose to have Mischa cared for in nursery (daycare) three days per week, the same hours as Saskia was attending. I was on compassionate leave and therefore full pay at the time and decided that Esther was worth the expenditure in the absence of family having the time and capacity to look after Saskia and Mischa.

So Mischa was introduced to nursery at a very young age and when I finally returned to work three months after Esther's death, she and I were very used to her being there. That did make returning to work easier.

I did not make a conscious choice to parent in this way. I had to resume work for financial reasons. I had received far more than the usual fully paid time off for maternity leave because of the situation with Esther, and if I had quit my job, I would have had to repay most of that leave salary, which I did not have the means to do. I also thought it might be good therapy to return to my career since spending a lot of time at home seemed to be contributing to my low mood and grief; having some intellectually stimulating daytime occupation could offer me some relief. So I actually went back to work gladly, nervously, and excitedly!

The staff at the nursery is incredibly supportive, they have all learned about the merits of breastfeeding in their training.

The job I was returning to was a new one. I had had an interview before Esther became very ill while I was on normal maternity leave, and I had been offered a new post. My previous post had been shift work, front line mental health nursing in the inner city. Even in that post I had managed to breastfeed Saskia for a few months. My new post is on a 9:00 AM to 5:00 PM shift and it has moved me away from seeing patients. Now my responsibility is to train staff to be better able to function in their jobs. I really enjoy the job that I have now. My colleagues are great to be with, my intellect is truly stretched. My responsibilities vary from developing training programs to writing training strategy reports. I also commission training from external independent trainers, which is a big financial responsibility. But my managers entrust me with this and are very happy with my work.

On workdays, I breastfeed Mischa two or three times a day, always first thing in the morning and at bedtime, and sometimes immediately after we get home from work/nursery. On the three non-work days, I feed her at least five times a day, basically whenever she asks for it. (Our code word is "MM" which stands for Mummy's milk, so that we can be discreet if required to be.)

Sometimes I attend meetings near the nursery and do take the opportunity, unofficially, to pop in and enjoy a quick feed. The staff at the nursery is incredibly supportive, they have all learned about the merits of breastfeeding in their training, and while they have no official policy, they do everything they can to help. Expressed milk can be stored and given to children at the nursery, and mothers can come in and breastfeed whenever they want to—there is a proper breastfeeding rocking chair for the purpose. Even though feeding a 19-month-old is quite unusual in our society, I have never felt embarrassed or judged in any way by the nursery staff (or indeed by the children there). Most women who chose to breastfeed at all in this country have stopped by the time their babies are 12 months old, and it is a rare sight to see an older child being fed by his or her mother in public.

A Supportive Network

I see very little of my parents as they live almost four hours away by car, but I see my in-laws most weekends. Both Nana and Papa are very supportive of my breastfeeding and think it's marvelous when we use it to cope with very demanding situations. (An example of this was the time we were together on a plane for two hours with a very tired, crying Mischa, who was able to have a lovely sleep in the sling on the way to Spain thanks to "MM.") Saskia helpfully suggests "MM" if Mischa is spoiling her puzzles or artwork, so she very clearly appreciates the benefits of breastfeeding in her life.

My husband, Steve, is definitely the most supportive person in all of this. He is an amazing man. He initiated reducing his hours at work to spend more time with the girls. I have fully supported him with this and he now has a Daddy Day on Monday. In fact, Steve said the loveliest thing just the other morning. He commented that he had observed Mischa breastfeeding a lot more often in the daytime recently, and he thought in some ways it was more important to her now than it has ever been, and that it is a very significant time in our breastfeeding relationship. That was such a wonderful supportive observation and I agreed, commenting that she is probably becoming more aware of herself as a separate person from me and is anxiously forming her own identity. In the end, she knows that all is right with her world when she is able to have her "MM."

I have persevered with breastfeeding because I love it, because at the end of the day work is only work, and because I know I am not going to have any more children and this is my last chance ever to do it. I am someone who enjoys rising to a challenge. (And my job certainly has made it challenging!)

Where More Support Would Help

There is no corporate policy on breastfeeding and work in my particular job. If any breastfeeding or expressing goes on during paid work time, it is done unofficially and at the individual manager's discretion. The National Health Service (NHS) is the largest employer of women in Great Britain, so I believe that this really needs to change with some urgency. I think I should be allowed paid time off to go to the nursery and breastfeed during the working day. I do not think there should be an upper limit on the child's age to be allowed this time off, because when an age limit is specified, it encourages the wider societal view that breastfeeding should stop, and that it is unacceptable beyond a certain number of months. And certainly, I think that a huge organization like the NHS should have on-site subsidized nurseries to encourage women who are going back to work to continue breastfeeding.

Many of my friends have said that they are stopping breastfeeding because they are going back to work. I persevered longer than most with breastfeeding Saskia while working nursing shifts but ultimately gave "going back to work" as the excuse for stopping. Because of my very different experience with breastfeeding Mischa, the most heartfelt advice I would give to anyone in this situation is to get in touch with those feelings. If you want to stop breastfeeding, do not use work to justify your decision. Work does not automatically mean the end of breastfeeding. If you want to stop, that is absolutely fine and it is then the right thing for you and your child, but you should not use work as an excuse for doing this. This advice is crucial if you want to avoid regret over stopping feeding in future months or years.

She wants the closeness, the intimacy, and the sucking satisfaction more than the milk.

People ask me how it is possible to combine breastfeeding with a four-day-a-week job, and I say it just works out somehow. I don't think Mischa cares that much anymore about the quantity of her Mummy's Milk. She wants the closeness, the intimacy, and the sucking satisfaction more than the milk. Her nutritional needs can be met fully when we are not together. She is happy drinking organic milk from a cup at nursery or on Daddy Day. I have persevered because it is so useful in emergency situations to calm a fretful child or to soothe a sick or teething child. Ultimately, I like breastfeeding because it gives me a greater repertoire of comforts.

I think if Mischa could write this story she would say that she loves being with the other children at nursery but the highlight is seeing Mummy sometimes appear at funny times of the day to provide some "MM."

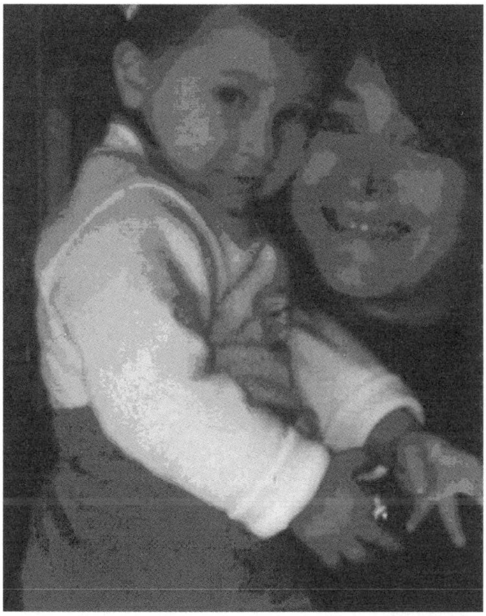

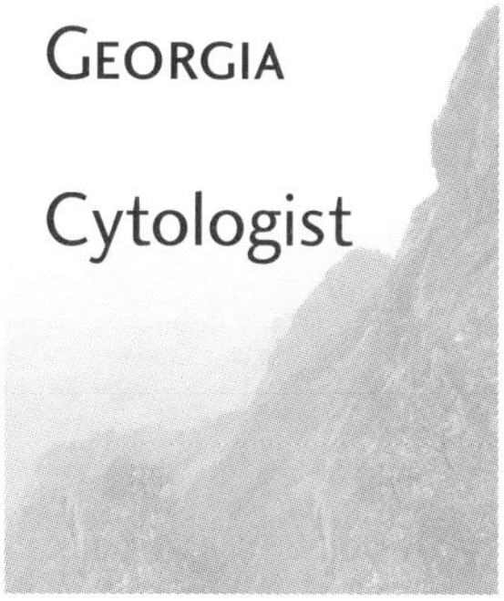

GEORGIA

Cytologist

A Month-Long Absence Quickly Erased

Tamar Kaloiani

Interviewed, Narrated, and Translated by Maya Sartania

Before one can understand the story of a Georgian woman, one must appreciate the society in which she lives. The former Soviet Union country of Georgia was once famous for tourism and hospitality. Thousands of tourists visited and were enchanted by the country.

Now, the situation is quite different. Political unrest, civil war, and other events have brought Georgia severe economic distress and crisis. Unemployment is rampant, as are refugees for whom the state can do nothing. Pensioners have not enough money to purchase bread. Seventy percent of the population lives in poverty. Many people have left Georgia seeking a better life in other countries.

In 2004, as you may know, Georgia gained a new government. We are hopeful that the new authorities will improve our life…someday. They have accomplished several reforms. Among them is a reduction of employees coupled with an increase in salaries. Due to these reforms, however, the unemployment rate has risen dramatically.

Of course there are some people who do still hold jobs, and among them are some breastfeeding mothers. I want to tell you a story of one such working mother, Tamar Kaloiani.

I asked Tamar's permission to tell her story and she kindly agreed saying, "If my story will help another mother to breastfeed, I will be most pleased and happy."

Tamar's Tale

I work as a cytologist, a leading professional for the Georgian National Oncology Center. My job consists of studying the structure and function of cells. For 40 days I was able to leave my job to stay home with my new baby girl, Nana. I hired a babysitter for my return to work, as I am not married and did not have a spouse to share child care in my absence. I breastfed Nana at night, in the morning, and like many others, I left pumped milk for the babysitter. I worked 10:00 AM to 3:00 PM, and spent the rest of my time with Nana.

Notwithstanding my attempts to introduce Nana to additional food at six months, she was exclusively breastfed for 11 months. When Nana was one year and ten months old and still breastfeeding, I received an offer to go to qualification courses abroad. It was very important for my career and I could not reject such a proposal. The certification is required for my career and without it, I would have no job. So, sadly, I had to leave Nana with my babysitter for a month.

I called twice a day every day and the babysitter assured me that Nana was having no problems. During the first week, I pumped my engorged breasts but I had no additional problems outside of missing my baby like one would miss an arm or a leg, suddenly and abruptly removed.

In a month, I was able to return from my courses. There are no words to describe how happy I felt coming home. It was nighttime when I arrived. Nana had a high temperature and was deeply asleep and motionless. I took her into bed with me. She leaned her head against my breast. Then, she put her hand on it. I did not think that she would breastfeed after a month had passed since her last feeding but she started to suckle. I did not know if I had milk either and thought she was just playing. Soon, she became more alert, as if she just realized what was going on, and she started sucking more enthu-

In Georgia, 71 percent of women are in the workforce; 17 or more weeks of maternity leave is paid by public funds; 540 days of parental leave is paid by public funds, or up to 3 years unpaid leave; paid breastfeeding breaks are given.

siastically. I had a feeling that Nana instantly erased the month that she had spent without my breast. In an hour or so, I took her temperature and found that it had decreased though I had not given her any medication. The following morning she was fine—alert and lively—and extremely happy that I was at home with her.

Since then, we have carried on breastfeeding as we used to. Nana is three years old now and my milk is as dear and nice for her as it was when she was very small.

Germany

Financial Officer

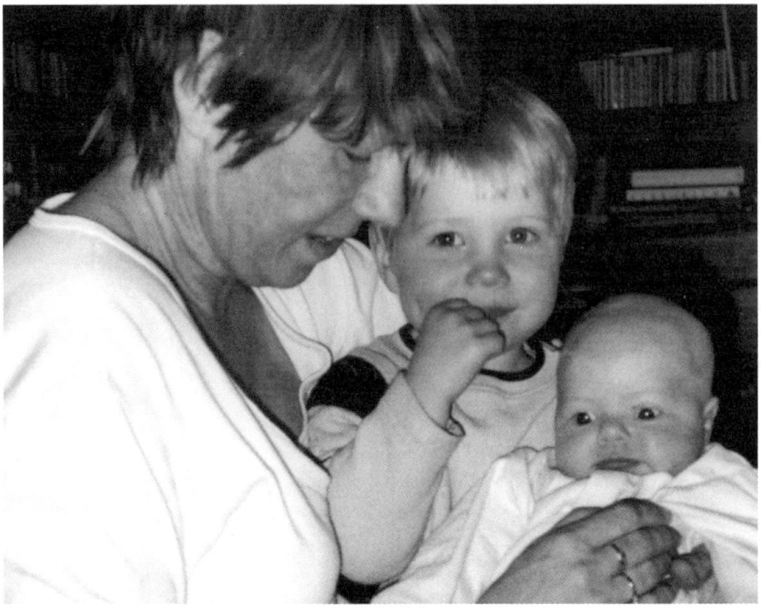

A Home Office Helps

Julia Zantke, Wedel

Having grown up with a mother who did not work, it was very important to me that one parent stay home with our children at least for the early years. However, it was clear to me that if we chose to have children, my husband would be the one staying at home; I would be the one going to work. As head of finance for a subsidiary of a bank, I earn almost twice as much as my husband, an editor of a local newspaper. In addition, I had trouble seeing myself as a stay-at-home mom.

Three years after our wedding, we were expecting our first child. In Germany, mothers are not allowed to work for eight weeks after giving birth. I planned to extend this period by taking four weeks of paid vacation. (A total of six weeks annual paid vacation is typical in Germany.) At this point my husband was going to stay home with our child for at least two years. It was always clear to me that I would breastfeed, and that I would be pumping once I went back to work.

During my pregnancy my mother warned me that postpartum hormones might make me change my mind and suggested that I leave some options open. On the surface I did so, but I am pretty stubborn and very focused, so straying from my plans would have meant losing face to myself in a big way. Down deep inside, there was no other option.

Breastfeeding went well right from the start, especially once I ignored the advice of my midwife, who told me to wait at least two hours between feedings. When Otto was seven weeks old I expressed some milk with a hand pump and left him alone with Daddy. Otto drank the expressed milk out of the bottle with no problems. By the time I went back to work we had found a breastfeeding schedule that worked well for us. We had started out breastfeeding on demand, then I began keeping track of the times he was "demanding" milk, and managed to find a good pattern.

When arranging the three-month leave with my boss, I asked if I could spend some of my time working from home. I knew of others who had the ability to go online from home. Some of the work I do involves just me and the computer or telephone, so it seemed feasible that I could do it, too. It worked out so well that I continued to put in some hours at home even after I officially returned to work.

I bought a good electric pump that would allow me to express from both sides simultaneously, then headed back to work. Since I have my own office I put a "do not disturb" sign on the door and pumped once a day around 11:00 AM. Some days I would be too stressed and tense and would need to wait an hour before trying again. I left work around 3:00 PM. Half an hour later I would nurse Otto. By 4:00 PM, I was back "at work," this time from home. Since my phone calls were routed home, many colleagues didn't even notice that I wasn't at the office. I remember getting a call at 6:45 PM one Friday evening and hearing, "Thank goodness you're still there. I can't reach anyone else at headquarters." Little did they know!

While working from home it was really important that I had a separate room and that I was very strict about the hours. Not once did I not work in the afternoon, though several times friends or relatives who were visiting would suggest it. "You can make it up on the weekend," or "If the phone rings you can still answer it." Working from home is all about trust, and I never wanted the slightest doubt to surface as to whether I was really putting in my time. In fact, I still tended to put in more than the required hours.

After seven months of exclusive breastfeeding we began trying out "real food." Otto loved bananas and so I was pumping less and less.

In Germany, 56 percent of women are in the workforce; 14 weeks of maternity leave is paid by public funds and the employer; 730 days of parental leave is paid by public funds; up to 3 years of unpaid parental leave is allowed; 2 days of paternity leave; paid breastfeeding breaks are given once the mother returns to work.

During this transition I sometimes had difficulty pumping enough at work. I think it had to do with let-down as I usually had more than enough milk when I got home. Thus, I would occasionally hand-express milk from one side while Otto drank from the other in the afternoon.

Soon I stopped coming home from work earlier, and by the time Otto was one year old, we cut down nursing to twice a day. Now Otto is almost three and tandem nursing with his eight-month-old sister, Marta.

Two Is More Than One Plus One

Although Marta, like Otto, is a very happy baby, things have been much harder this time around. First of all, two is more than one plus one. Since my husband's paternity leave was up right around the time Marta was due, he went back to work and left a very pregnant mother with only weekend parenting experience to take care of a lively two-year-old. It didn't get any easier after Marta arrived. I was exhausted. My mom blamed it on tandem nursing, but there was no way I was going to give that up, since it allowed me to have some peaceful time with both my children.

I keep reminding myself that the day will come when I will look back fondly on these times.

Three months after Marta's birth, my husband started his next paternity leave, and I went back to work. We kept the same pattern as with Otto, only Marta was still waking up to nurse two to three times a night. All I did was work, eat, sleep, and nurse. I had hoped things would get better once I was in my familiar environment. It is still hard at times. Sometimes I yell at Otto for no reason because I am just at the end of my wits. Sometimes Marta wakes up for the third nighttime nursing session and I hope that Dad can appease her with cuddling. After half an hour of getting Marta back to sleep, then having her wake again five to ten minutes later, I finally give in and nurse her. Some days I can go with the flow and accept everyone's needs—then it is easier. I keep reminding myself that the day will come when I will look back fondly on these times.

And it sure is nice to come home to Otto meeting me at the door and telling me "Otto and Marta want to have nummies on the couch!" As soon as Marta hears me, she crawls over at lightning speed. Sometimes when they are nursing together they suddenly both start laughing. Then I have to laugh, too, and it makes it all worthwhile. Even though I am working, I feel extremely close to my children, and for me that has a lot to do with breastfeeding.

Spain

Lawyer/
Publisher

Nature's Law

Monica Tornadijo Sabate, Barcelona

Translated from Spanish by Natalia Smith Allen

Breastfeeding a child is one of the most enriching experiences that a mother can have. Everyone agrees on its innumerable advantages. It contains all that is necessary for a baby's development: it is cheap and easily accessible, and it is always at the right temperature. Why then do only 23 percent of all mothers in Spain breastfeed their children until six months of age? Why do 90 percent of those who are breastfeeding stop during the fourth month? The reason is clear; problems arise when a woman has to return to work.

The half-hour break that all women in Spain are entitled to use to breastfeed does not actually make things any easier. What are the solutions? For starters: maternity leave should be extended until the introduction of complementary foods—nine months minimum. Mothers also need reduced workdays and lactation rooms. All of these are very difficult to put into practice in today's world. And some people will say, "What about a breast pump?" The Spanish workday is from 9:00 AM to 2:00 PM and then 4:00 PM to 8:00 PM—few employers will allow a mother to pump milk every three hours.

I consider myself privileged. I have been able to combine working and breastfeeding for my baby girl, allowing her to be fed my milk exclusively for the first six months. I am a lawyer and the director of a publishing firm. Combining this career with breastfeeding my little girl has not been easy, and of course I would not have been able to manage if not for unconditional help from my mother and sister. My parents' house, where I leave my child every morning, is not too far from my office, which easily allows me to come and go without having to use a breast pump.

For the first four months, I worked from home on maternity leave while my baby continued to grow strong and healthy on my milk. Not surprisingly, things became more difficult during the fifth month when I had no option but to return to full-time work. I did not want to give up breastfeeding, but at my work nobody was aware that my little one had to eat every three hours and was waking up various times during the night, and that this, without a doubt, was affecting my productivity.

Things were not going well at work. I had been reprimanded various times by the board of directors for not making magazine deadlines. The magazines were late getting to the stores—much later than usual—and they insisted that my performance was affecting the interests of the company's shareholders. I resolved that I would try to accomplish everything as before, but that I was not going to work any afternoons; the afternoons were to enjoy my baby!

Now I have acclimated some to being away from my daughter. I continue to breastfeed my baby girl in addition to offering the usual foods. Work is now going well, but the best moment of my day is when I arrive in the afternoon and see my little girl smile as I walk through the door. If the laws of nature grant my daughter any right, it is to be loved and well fed, which she is. I make this happen despite obstacles, because through the struggles, I see the days go by quickly. I can't help but see that my girl is growing strong, healthy—not one single cold or colic—and above all, she is happy.

BULGARIA

Operations Manager

Bulgarian Baby Boy

Silviya Zaharieva Andreeva, Sofia

When we decided to have a baby I knew it wouldn't be easy. My partner was unemployed and I earned the money in the family. However, nearing our 30s, we were sure that a baby would add joy to our lives, which is the whole point of living, after all! After three short months, I was pregnant. We were so happy. My mate even found a new job. Everything was wonderful and I was sure that I would stay at home and take care of my baby for at least the first eight months. My husband's salary was much less than mine, but we decided that we would manage somehow for at least eight months. It was clear that after that period, I would have to go back to work.

Some background on my country's laws will be helpful here. In Bulgaria the Labor Code permits mothers nearly four months paid maternity leave. The days are broken down like this: 135 days are permitted, 45 of which are before the baby is born, 45 after the baby is born, and 45 days for maternity leave. After these 135 days expire, the mother can go back to work or stay at home for unpaid leave until the baby is two years old. In both cases, the government pays the mother a monthly financial aid or maternity benefit. The financial aid during unpaid leave equals around 60 Euro per month. When a mother goes back to work, she is entitled to half of this sum or around 30 Euro. For this sum in Bulgaria you can buy a couple of jumbo packs of diapers.

Unfortunately, dreams do not always come true! Just before our baby was born my partner lost his job and we were back where we started. Despite all this, we were so happy to have our baby boy born in April 2004.

It is a pity, but in Bulgarian hospitals, no one tells you what to do to successfully breastfeed your baby. They do not give the baby to the mother to breastfeed right after birth. I saw my new baby, Georgi, long enough to kiss him, and the next time I saw him was the following day at noon. It was then that he was breastfed for the first time. In Bulgarian hospitals, babies are automatically fed with formula from the first day. I was seeing my boy every three hours (he was in a separate room) and the midwife was giving me a bottle with formula to feed him after he was breastfed. Fortunately, Georgi refused the bottle and started to nurse very easily and quickly without any problems.

In Bulgaria, 70 percent of women are in the workforce; 17 weeks or more of maternity leave is paid by public funds and 1,095 days of parental leave is allowed; there are paid breastfeeding breaks when a mother returns to work.

I was sure that I wanted to breastfeed my baby. This helped me a lot after a tough start in the hospital, and it is helping me now that I am back at work. I had several problem periods with the baby; during these times his physician recommended formula as a "top-up," but I never gave him anything other than my milk. I also had a difficult time standing up against the pediatrician's recommendations to introduce solids in the third month. Like most Bulgarian doctors who follow the old Russian protocol, she told me to give him water from birth and juice in the second month! Thanks to the Internet (http://forum.bg-mamma.com) and a new pediatrician who was aware of all the newest research and WHO recommendations, I was able to exclusively breastfeed my baby for the first six months. To overcome all the confusion and hesitation of the early months, the support I received from my husband and my mother, who was and still is here to help me with the baby, was crucial.

Georgi was 18 weeks old when I had to go back to work. I was so afraid of this moment! I was concerned that going back to work would cause me to stop breastfeeding. First, I wasn't able to express more that 100 ml from one breast. Second, at work I shared a room with two male colleagues. Our office was small and we didn't have a room that I could use to express milk. Unfortunately we don't have a refrigerator at the office, but I bought a thermos box to store my milk. (I read that human milk can be kept at room temperature for four to five hours.) Of course, I'm lucky to work at about 5 km distance from home and I have a car, so I can go back home for 20 minutes in an emergency.

Practicing the Return to Work

Despite these problems, I continued to breastfeed. In my country, under the Labor Law a breastfeeding mother is permitted to take two hours each day of paid leave to breastfeed until the baby is eight months old. The mother is then granted one hour until the baby's first year. Even though this is the law, most employers do not follow it. In fact, I didn't even know that I had this right. It was while searching for other information that I accidentally found this information.

After my discovery, I spoke to my boss and he agreed that I could take these two hours leave every day. This allowed me to start my workday at 11:00 AM instead of 9:00 AM. That was perfect because it allowed me to breastfeed Georgi all morning everyday, reducing the number of times I would have to pump each day. Until then I was breastfeeding my baby on demand. Returning to work made it necessary to create some kind of a schedule, so I started to put him on the breast during the specific times that would be my normal "work hours." Our activities soon started to follow a particular order and became routine.

I practiced returning to work while I was still at home. I expressed each afternoon and my husband or my mother gave my milk to Georgi.

I practiced returning to work while I was still at home. I expressed each afternoon and my husband or my mother gave my milk to Georgi. I was afraid that he would not take the bottle or he would wean from the breast if he felt the bottle was easier. Lucky for us, we have the best baby in the world! He had no problem with the bottle and was able to feed from that or the breast with no problem. This practice week helped me feel comfortable about Georgi's limits and it also allowed me to get comfortable with the breast pump. After a few more practice days, I began to express around 200 ml from both breasts—plenty for Georgi's feeding at lunch time. I also had about five liters of my milk stored from late night pumping sessions.

When I went back to my small firm to work, I met with all ten of my colleagues. I told them that I wished to continue exclusively breastfeeding, which meant I would need to express every day at lunch time. I wanted them to be aware of what I was doing and to know that I was doing it because it was the best thing for my baby. All of them were very supportive.

Practice Makes (almost) Perfect

So, every day around two o'clock I went to my female colleagues' office to express. They locked the door for me and arranged their meetings so that I did not worry about someone interrupting me. It was a good experience for them, too, because they asked a lot of questions about breastfeeding and I was able to explain the benefits. It's funny because if a colleague calls the intercom to ask for something, they answer, "Silvia is nursing now—so we'll do it later!"

My work requires that I sit in front of the computer about 80 percent of the workday. I also hold staff meetings to coordinate our activities. The entire schedule is coordinated with my "nursing" time. My colleagues make it very easy for me. Of course, all this is possible because my boss is a very decent person, and is so supportive. Our small office is like a second family and this made it much easier to arrange things this way.

One of the prerequisites to accepting their offer was that they support breastfeeding and make it possible for me to express at work.

While my return went smoothly, nothing is ever perfect. I had one devastating, depressing accident two months after I went back to work. One morning I went to the freezer to take the daily portion of expressed milk for Georgi and I saw that the door had been left open. Everything inside was defrosted, including every drop of my milk. It was awful! I sadly threw away around 7 liters of expressed milk. My heart hurt! I sat down and cried like a little baby. Then I found the solution. I called a friend of mine whose baby girl was born on the same day as Georgi. I was very grateful to Sunny, because when she heard the story she suggested that I take some of her expressed milk. I know her well, and trust her, so of course I agreed.* She gave me enough frozen milk to feed Georgi once a day for a week. I doubled my pumping from one to two times a day and eventually built up a new supply. This was the worst experience that I had with breastfeeding and working.

Adapting to Another Change

Now I am in the process of changing jobs. I'm going to work for a big telecom here and one of the prerequisites to accepting their offer was that they support breastfeeding and make it possible for me to express at work. The company has waited three months for me to start to work until Georgi is old enough for me to come in at 9:00 AM every day. I was firm that I must continue to stay at home in the mornings for the next three months because my baby still needs me, and they have complied.

**Editor's Note: LLLI recommends that women use only human milk screened and distributed by a milk bank. If that is not possible, LLLI suggests having the prospective milk donor screened by a physician.*

The only thing that I can say to mothers who plan to work and breastfeed is: It will not be easy, but it is worth it. Don't give up. Your child will return the favor with less illness and more smiles!

I have changed a lot over the past few months. I learned that being a mother is a hard job, and being a working mother can make it even harder. But even the struggle of combining breastfeeding and work is worth it for the first smile that you receive when you return from work and your baby sees you at the door. I have never been as happy as I am now while holding my baby in my arms and nursing him after a long day at work. It is the best anti-stress medicine ever.

ENGLAND

Business Owner

Breastfeeding Is Not a Barrier to My Business

Lucy Cokes, Cornwall

I own my own business, so quitting work was not an option when I had Roxy. My partner and I set up a search engine marketing agency five years ago, and we now employ nine full-time staff members. We promote clients' Web sites on search engines so they can generate business and sales via their Web sites. I look after the company accounts, manage the staff, and generally ensure the clients are happy and the work is done on time. Most of my time is spent at my computer, either on the phone or on the Internet, chairing staff meetings, and holding interviews and reviews for staff. I have had the luxury of being able to tailor my hours at work to fit into the way I want to parent.

Mum's "Nursery"

When Roxy was just two weeks old, I was able to work from home.

It was easy then; she slept so much that I could easily use my laptop as she slept next to me in her Moses basket, or nursed in my arms. Until she started rolling and sitting up, I would take her with me into the office on one day a week. I breastfed her sitting at my desk, and then would have her play on the floor next to me. Eventually, a friend began looking after her three mornings a week, three hours at a time, as I needed to devote more time to work and it was no longer practical to bring Roxy to the office with me. I would feed her, drive to work, and get back just after noon, ready for the next feed. After she started solids, this became easier and I would leave her for four hours, three days a week.

I have been in some funny situations at work when Roxy was little, as she came with me everywhere. She would sit on my knee at the head of the table during our weekly staff meeting. She came along with me to meetings with important clients and was even present when I was interviewing for new staff. On two occasions, she was actually breastfeeding during the interview! I never really thought to ask if they were comfortable with me doing this; I am sure it may have raised a few eyebrows.

I would have personally found it impossible to have gone back into full-time work and breastfeed Roxy when she was three months old as some mother do, because I have never mastered the art of expressing milk and I would not have been comfortable leaving her for that length of time at such a tender age. For me, breastfeeding also means quality time with my daughter and there is a need to separate breastfeeding (where you need to be there) and feeding your child mother's milk (when you could be miles away). Ideally, mothers would be able to begin going back to work gradually, or work from home as much as possible in the early days.

Ideally, mothers would be able to begin going back to work gradually, or work from home as much as possible in the early days.

Day Nursery

Starting at nine months, I left Roxy at a local day nursery from 9:00 AM until 1:00 PM five mornings a week. This allowed me to be in the office to manage staff and respond to important issues, but allowed for quality time with Roxy. At two years old, she still has a feed in the morning and a feed as soon as I pick her up from nursery. This is our nice "Welcome back to Mummy time!"

Luckily my workplace is only a ten-minute drive from home. I drive 15 minutes to her day nursery, then five minutes to work. It is far easier to continue breastfeeding if your child care, home, and work are in close proximity to each other. I don't like my daughter spending too much time in the car each day, for me the half hour a day spent going to and from her nursery is enough.

Making It Work

My main inspiration has been my own mother who breastfed my younger brother until he was four (and I witnessed this as he is five years younger than me). I myself was breastfed until I was two. My partner is also my business partner, so it has been completely necessary that he supports my belief that Roxy should be breastfed for as long as possible. My partner was breastfed until he was two years old.

Ideally, breastfeeding for an extended period should be the norm. This will not be possible until half-days are an option for all mothers for the first year back at work. The government should also contemplate supplementing the income for breastfeeding mothers who choose this option, as it would save them loads of money in long and short term health care costs.

Because of my flexibility, combining breastfeeding with work has been manageable.

My partner and I are the only members of our staff who currently have any children. When other members of our staff start a family, we intend to assist them in as many ways possible to ensure they can breastfeed for as long as they want.

To be honest, because of my flexibility, combining breastfeeding with work has been manageable. The main issue for me has been working with a young child. In many ways, I think breastfeeding has made it all easier—from looking after her while traveling, to bonding with her and having a good night's sleep by sleeping with and feeding her while lying down. The real challenge has been juggling the needs of my little one and running a business. A supportive partner along with friends and family living close by have all helped with those emergency situations that crop up from time to time.

NETHERLANDS

Physician

Nam-Nam in the Netherlands

Tanja Schulin

When I get home from work, the first thing my son and I share is a "nam-nam" session (his word for breastfeeding). We settle down and get connected again after our separation. This is a very special, very dear, and very easy way to get together again. I am a medical doctor and work in a university hospital laboratory in the Netherlands. In this country, mothers have to return to work three months after birth. Most children are taken care of in daycare centers, but we were in the very lucky situation to have found a wonderful daycare mother (who is also his godmother), who is very much in agreement with us regarding childrearing and breastfeeding.

So, after three months I started working four mornings per week. After another six months, I began to work 80 percent, which meant my child was at his daycare mother's house four days a week for eight hours each day, and one day until noon. Two days a week, my husband picked him up early. I was finally reunited with him each day after about nine hours. Because I commute 45 minutes, bringing my son to work for breastfeeding was not a practical option. I decided to pump at least once every four hours. We had to adjust our day planning, which meant getting up at least 45 minutes earlier than usual to be able to have a relaxed breastfeeding session in the morning. My son never hesitated to take the bottle with my milk, which we introduced a few weeks before my return to work; it was given only by his other care providers. After the schedule changes, the nights were more difficult than usual. He sucked the whole night, needing to get back the security and closeness that he had missed from me during the day. We cosleep anyway, so that was not much of a problem.

Breastfeeding and pumping milk are quite common in the Netherlands, though usually mothers stop within six months.

In the beginning, I got terribly stressed out pumping in the little bathroom at work. It didn't help that my pumping skills were poor. With time, I learned some tricks (stimulation of the other nipple while pumping, etc.), and I pumped until my son was 19 months old. Culturally, I faced little resistance. Breastfeeding and pumping milk are quite common in the Netherlands, though usually mothers stop within six months. My son was exclusively breastfed until he was about eight months, and after that, he remained very skeptical about solid food until around 17 months old.

As a medical specialist I often attend professional meetings, and my son and my husband frequently accompany me. This way, we travel a lot together, all over Europe, and always manage to fit in plenty of "nam-nam" on the trains. In addition, my husband comes to the meetings during the breaks so I can breastfeed my son, which is really important for me in times of stress, too.

I was and will remain very proud that I could give my child my milk despite working. I still remain so very close to him. My son is almost three years old and continues to nurse; I am expecting my second child in a few days. This time, I made arrangements to continue working again only after the sixth month. It still feels very early to me, but because of the great experience my son and I have shared, I am optimistically looking to the future.

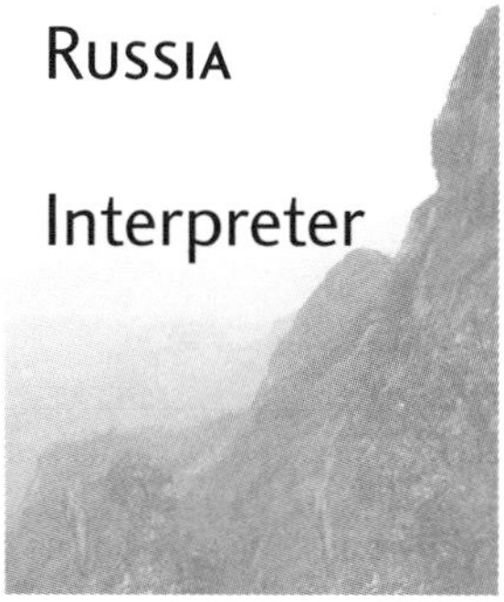

RUSSIA

Interpreter

Perfect Nutrition in Any Language

Tatyana Zorina, Murmansk City

When I was pregnant with my third child, I knew that I would breastfeed her. I am an interpreter and have been working in an international company. Because of work-related constraints, I had to return to work when my baby was only three weeks old. My dear friend is a neonatologist and specializes in treating premature babies. She gave me much information on exclusive breastfeeding. I owe my friend my deep gratitude, as she helped me understand that it was possible to combine exclusive breastfeeding with work, and she told me how. What a gift she gave to my baby and me. I have learned there is no real substitute for human milk for a human baby!

When I work, my mother-in-law cares for my baby. I have an eight-hour workday and am able to go home to breastfeed during lunchtime. Otherwise, I breastfeed my baby at home—morning, evening, and night! After a month, my baby adapted to this regimen and slept in the afternoon when I was at work. Believe me, it gets easier with time and will definitely be worth it for both of you, especially if you breastfeed for an extended period of time. Newborn babies do not have a fully developed immune system. One of the best benefits of breastfeeding, I've learned, is the presence of antibodies in the mother's milk that help to boost the baby's immune system.

Some women are lucky and have babies who are complete naturals at breastfeeding, even when combined with work. This has been the case with my daughter. Of course, I have still faced some obstacles. For reasons I cannot understand, my mother, stepmother, mother-in-law, and stepmother-in-law are still firmly entrenched in the idea that formula is better, easier, and the only way to go. Worse was the surprise I faced when I took my daughter to the clinic. When I told the doctor about our exclusive breastfeeding combined with work, she criticized me. Then she tried to find my baby's "developmental lags." Of course, over time, she has learned that is a futile pursuit!

In Russia, 75 percent of women are in the workforce; 17 or more weeks of maternity leave is paid by public funds; 365 days of parental leave is allowed; no information available about breastfeeding breaks.

I have learned to warmly embrace the people who support my goals and dismiss those who do not. If it were not for the support of my husband, children, friends, and colleagues I could never have breastfed exclusively, despite my strong motivation. My husband brings me to work every day, and my colleagues at work encourage me. When I have to be on two-day business trips, I travel together with my husband and baby in order to breastfeed at will. In addition, my husband also handles all the housekeeping.

While it is true that breastfeeding gives a mother and baby a close bond, a working mother especially values the important health benefits a baby receives from a mother's milk. My children have hardly ever been sick. My daughter is now ten months old (still breastfeeding) and has only had her first cold at the age of nine months.

I would like to advise other women who want to make breastfeeding and working a reality to do it, regardless of anything. Of course, this is more feasible if our medical providers, family, and society start to support exclusive breastfeeding and truly understand its value.

The benefits for mother and baby are a treasure, one too valuable to surrender because of work. Because of the nature of breastfeeding, a mother needs to spend a lot of time with her baby. This makes natural sense; when a baby is young, the most important person in that child's life is his mother. Besides, anyone who has seen a baby breastfeeding or has seen that child fall asleep at the breast has seen the closest thing to heaven on this earth.

Northern Ireland

Wildlife Site Manager

Easing the Transition

Judith Montgomery-Watson

Few women breastfeed in Northern Ireland. When I had my son, only one other person on the ward chose to breastfeed. Among those women who do breastfeed, most only do so for the first six weeks and very few do so past six months.

Before I had my son I planned to breastfeed, but had thought this was something I would do for about six months, until returning to work. Of course, I also thought the baby would sleep in a cot in the next room!

Adam never slept in his cot or in the other room. He only slept when he was right on top of me! He also had terrible reflux and I spent a lot of time feeding him in the first four to six months. I had planned to return to work after six months, but due to ill health, I did not return until Adam was eight months old. As my breastfeeding relationship with Adam developed and I shared information from other LLL mothers, I decided to follow my own heart and give Adam what he was telling me he wanted. I would continue to feed Adam despite returning to work.

When preparing to return to work, I tried to get Adam to take expressed milk, but he flatly refused. I tried to get him to drink water, which he also rejected. His interest in solids was very poor, too. Nonetheless, I had a chest freezer bursting with expressed milk and I found a child minder who was prepared to feed it to him. She had two other children, but had not breastfed because, "fair skinned people cannot breastfeed." (This must not be true as you can't get much fairer skinned than me!)

My employer allowed me to return to work on a phased return, over a 15 week period, working one day the first week, and building up to five days. After the phased return, I reduced my hours to 8:00 AM to 4:00 PM, which still meant leaving Adam for longer than I would have liked.

Despite all my fears and worries, Adam really loved the company at the child minders. He never would use any of the expressed milk, but drank water for her and ate solids. Since he slept with me he was able to feed through the night, and he always had a big feed when I came home. For the first month I expressed at work, but as Adam was not using the milk, I stopped without much discomfort.

Having a transitional period of phased return to work, and not returning to work until Adam was eight months old, made it much easier to continue to breastfeed. It also helped that he slept with us. I continued to feed Adam at night throughout my second pregnancy with Esther Rose.

In Northern Ireland, 35 percent of women are in the workforce; 17 or more weeks of maternity leave is paid by public funds with an additional 8 weeks of unpaid maternity leave allowed; 98 (x2) days of parental leave; paid breastfeeding breaks are given.

Lessons Learned

Esther Rose has benefited greatly from my experiences with Adam, though she is a different feeder. She feeds a lot less, never vomits, and is a very good eater of solids. This time I didn't return to work until Esther Rose was ten months old. I have also changed to a child minder who comes to our home. She has a daughter the same age as Esther Rose and also still breastfeeds. She could not find a job where people were happy for her to breastfeed in front of their children. My children do not mind at all, and neither do I.

As with Adam, I went back to work on a phased return and I expressed milk for Esther. Once again, she wasn't interested so I stopped expressing. As with Adam, Esther has showed no distress at me going to work.

The reasons I still breastfeed are:

- My children still want to be fed.
- I believe it gives my children comfort and confidence to know their mum loves them and will meet their needs, despite going to work.
- It reaffirms our bond when I return from work.
- The health benefits to my children are immense.

The reasons we have succeeded at combining breastfeeding and work:

- My children were over six months old when I returned to work.
- They both were happy with the child minders and enjoyed the company of other children.
- I had a phased return to work.
- I sleep with my children, so they can feed on demand at night.
- I only ever work two days in a row.

FRANCE

Senior Technical Officer

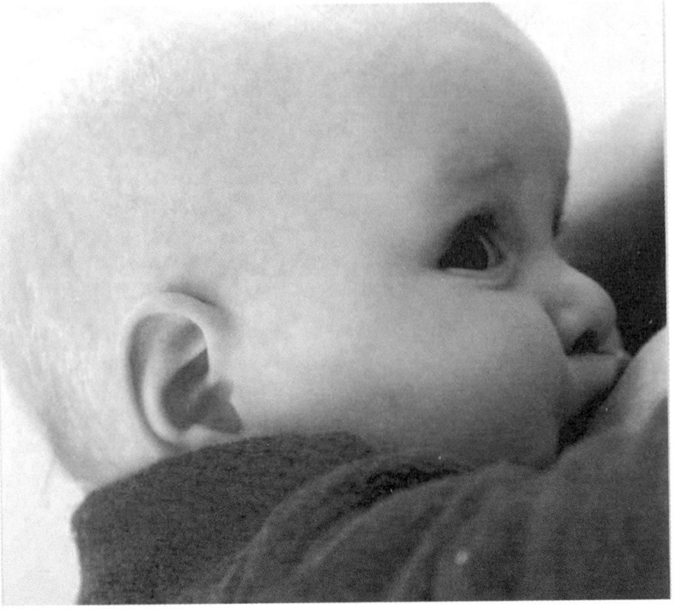

Open Arms, Uncompromising Ideals

Catherine Mulholland

My educational background is in the area of political science, development studies, and public health. I am currently working on strategic planning, policy change, and effective action strategies to protect children from environmental risks to their health. I am also the mother of three children, all of whom have been breastfed over the course of my career.

Combining breastfeeding and work takes a lot of inventiveness, negotiation, and organization. This must also be joined with courage and personal conviction. But it can be done. I hope this book helps spread the information to help other women do the same. Their lives will be changed forever.

I made a conscious decision to breastfeed and to work. I know that many women have no choice. When I had to return to work after my four-month maternity leave, I set myself the challenge of continuing to exclusively breastfeed my first child for as long as I could. Having done it once, there was no question that I would do it again for my other children. As it turns out, each and every time I combined breastfeeding and work was different.

My First Child

When I returned to work after the birth of my first child, I was working 40 hours a week in addition to two hours of commuting time each day. I was separated from my baby for at least ten hours a day. For the first few months, my son was in a "crèche" (municipal day-care), which I quickly decided to take him out of. It was difficult to get the crèche to understand and accept the different handling of a breastfed child. About 95 percent of the children in daycare in France are bottle-fed and there is very poor understanding and acceptance of breastfeeding. This is changing a bit, but very slowly. I would get telephone calls at work to tell me that my son had diarrhea only to rush back to find a diaper with evidence of the perfectly normal bowel movement of a breastfed child. I was also told that the crèche was going to put my son on a "substitute" for my milk to deal with the diarrhea. Of course, he was also more frequently ill in the crèche environment.

Christopher categorically refused to take my milk from a bottle, sipper cup, or spoon.

So, from the age of nine months, my son was taken care of by a "nounou" (day nanny) in my home. I would take an electric breast pump to work and pump several times a day in my office, which I was lucky enough to have to myself. As there were no refrigerators available, I stored the pumped milk in a cooler bag with ice blocks around it. I did this until Michael was over a year old, at which time I stopped pumping but continued to breastfeed when I was with him. He was on solid foods during the day and I no longer had to supply my milk when I was absent.

My Second Child

After the birth of my second child, I managed to negotiate working only three days a week. However, the child care situation was more complicated. My son, Christopher, categorically refused to take my milk from a bottle, sipper cup, or spoon. I ended up bringing him to work with me for the first two months in order to continue to exclusively breastfeed until he was ready for solids at around seven months old.

My Third Child

Working and breastfeeding was different again for my third child, as I was self-employed and working mostly out of my home. I gave myself an unpaid six-month maternity leave in order to manage the organizational aspects of three children. However, part of my time was taken up with the final coursework for a graduate certificate in public health. Though it was distance-based learning, my plate was still rather full even though I was not engaged in paid work. I began to accept some contracts when my daughter was five months old, which allowed me to work when she slept and the others were at school. (And I worked into the night, of course!) I increased my workload gradually, taking on as much as I could handle. Working from home, I no longer had to pump. Caroline probably had two to three bottles of expressed milk in her entire existence. I went back to a three-day-a-week arrangement with World Health Organization, when Caroline was two years old.

In the case of all my children, I had to travel while they were still breastfeeding. I did not travel for the first year after the birth unless they traveled with me. For all the other travel times, they were taking solid foods and I simply took a manual breast pump with me to keep up my milk supply while I was gone. All of the children resumed breastfeeding quite happily when I returned from my travels.

All of the children resumed breastfeeding quite happily when I returned from my travels.

Working for WHO

I have always tried to ensure that my colleagues are not unduly or unfairly affected by my desire to breastfeed and "materner" (mother) my children. But it is a difficult balance and I am sure that there are times when it has been difficult for them. I try to be open about my priorities, my desire to always contribute to the maximum of my ability, and to have open and frank dialogue to ensure that different perceptions do not become problems between colleagues.

One would think that combining breastfeeding and work would be the easiest thing at a place like WHO. However, it is a difficult balance—no matter what organization a woman works for. We do have a breastfeeding room at WHO which is equipped with armchairs, refrigerator, freezer, sink, change table, etc. In an ideal world, we would also have an on-site crèche or other facility, which would allow babies to be close to their working mothers.

As is likely the case with most mothers, the largest and most difficult obstacles I can remember included things like major breakdowns in child care arrangements coupled with Christopher not taking my milk from a bottle, thus necessitating bringing him to work. I got through this obstacle by simply doing what I had to do and struggling to make it as easy as possible for both the baby and my co-workers.

Without a doubt, it is difficult to combine the demands of work and the demands of a breastfeeding body. I still remember the pain of my overfull breasts as I rushed out of an all-day meeting at coffee breaks or lunchtime feeling incredibly stressed, knowing that I had only 30 minutes to relieve those breasts and get something to eat and drink to keep my body and brain going!

Embracing a Support System

The obstacles, while unavoidable, become manageable with help. A pediatrician who was an uncompromising advocate of breastfeeding helped tremendously with the breastfeeding. As he also advocates that mothers stay home with their children rather than work outside the home, I had to listen to him on that score and then just do what felt right for me.

Without a doubt, it is difficult to combine the demands of work and the demands of a breastfeeding body.

My immediate supervisor was an extraordinary woman. She valued my work and would therefore do almost anything to make sure that I could continue to work. Not many people would have accepted having a baby in the office for two months. She even made a play space in her office for my son and would have meetings with very senior staff while bouncing my son on her knees!

My husband was probably the single most important person who quietly but solidly supported me in my decisions regarding breastfeeding and the way I wanted to "mother" my children. He just naturally seemed to find the most warm and loving ways of being a special part of the breastfeeding experience and of being close to his children without ever giving them a bottle. His unstinting support definitely made it easier.

My third child is now four years old. She breastfed until she was three-and-a-half, at which time she solemnly announced that she no longer nursed. I was able to combine work and breastfeeding in different ways for all of my children and for as long as both of us wanted and needed. I practiced baby-led weaning for all of my children.

Cultural Context and Constraints

France, where I live, has one of the lowest rates of breastfeeding in Europe. Very few women breastfeed beyond three months. Even fewer attempt to combine breastfeeding and work. As the legal maternity leave consists of six weeks prior to the baby's birth and ten weeks after the baby is born, most French women are already thinking about weaning by six weeks if they plan to go back to work.

Almost a whole generation has been lost to the bottle in France. There is very little support (in many cases quite the opposite!) among the grandmothers, grandfathers, aunts, other female family members, and even fathers of babies being born at the same time as my children. Children brought up in the 1950s, 1960s, and 1970s were almost exclusively bottle-fed. Breastfeeding nowadays seems to be seen as something fashionable that one does with newborns, but shouldn't really continue beyond the first few months of life. Breastfeeding in public and breastfeeding of children one year or older are often looked upon as an aberration.

Encouragement for Other Women

Know that for every problem and every obstacle encountered, there is always a solution.

From my experience, the best advice is to give very little of it. It is best just to encourage other women to be strong, and to do what feels right for them (it will always be the right thing for the baby), regardless of what everyone else is saying. Know that for every problem and every obstacle encountered, there is always a solution.

Persevere. Being convinced that this is the best thing for me and for my baby has helped me get through everything. I just never gave up and tried always to surround myself as best I could with people who felt the same way I did about breastfeeding and mothering. I created my own personal support group.

What has most surprised me about work and breastfeeding is how surprisingly easy it really is. Just fit it in as you do any other thing as you organize your day. Work out the big and little hiccups as they present themselves, and never compromise the baseline, which is, "I will do this!"

Both attitudes and practices must change. Which is easier and should come first is not an easy thing to resolve. We can certainly change the logistics of combining work and breastfeeding into something easier for women through on-site child care and breastfeeding-friendly facilities. Let's make it logistically easy for women—their lives are complicated enough as it is. When it is logistically a little easier, perhaps more women will be encouraged to do it. More women combining working and breastfeeding will create the critical mass that will certainly change attitudes. Then all the barriers will begin tumbling down.

In the end, none of us can know what our children would say or think of their upbringing. Maybe what they say is less important than who and what they are. I can only hope that somewhere deep down inside each of them they have a strong and indelible image of a mother whose arms were always open, where the warmth, nutrition, and comfort of a marvelous breastfeeding relationship helped them grow into the wonderful people they are today.

Part Four

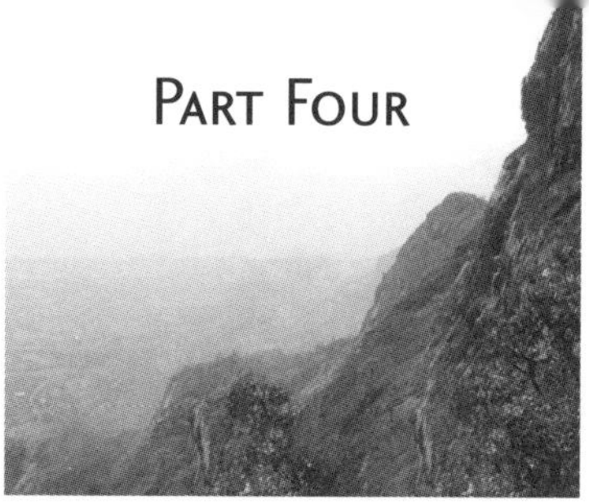

Africa
Middle East

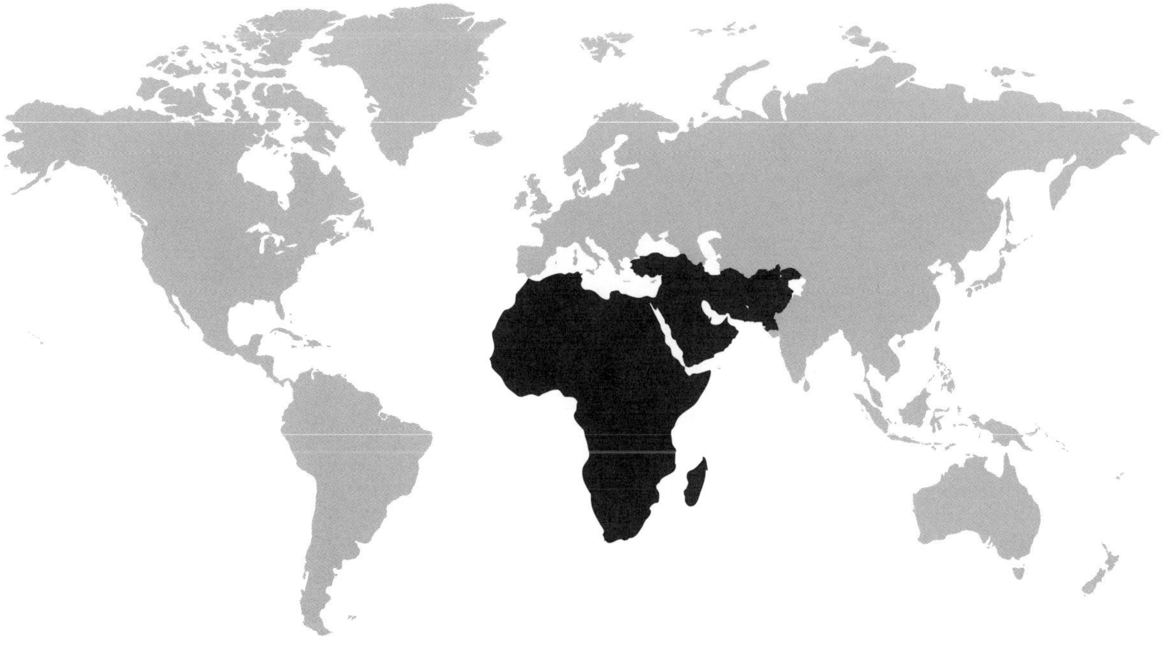

PAKISTAN

International Development Relief Worker

Supporting My Extended Family

Anita Cole, Islamabad

The international development field is loaded with single men and women working flat out for a cause. I was one of those women until my son, Rehmat, came along. Prior to his birth, my Pakistani husband was often working or sorting out his extended family responsibilities and I frequently worked late into the night without upsetting anyone. I was blissfully unaware of the demands that a family makes on your time.

While I can no longer continue the long hours, the insight I have gained through having and raising my child makes my contributions to program development much more informed. A native Australian, I myself have now given birth in a less developed country, have had my son admitted to the public hospital with neonatal sepsis, have suffered through non-supportive unsolicited breastfeeding advice, and now breastfeed my son while working to earn an income that supports my husband's extended family, in addition to my husband and son. I earn quite a lot in comparison to my husband's seasonal income and

In Pakistan, 28 percent of women are in the workforce; 12 weeks of maternity leave is paid by the employer; no breastfeeding breaks are allowed.

between the two of us we support his four brothers, three sisters, mum and dad, and many others among his poorer relations. Since I began work and helped my husband to support his family, I have seen their standard of living rise dramatically. They once resided in a single room mud house with no bathroom, and now live in a well constructed home with three bedrooms and three bathrooms. If I chose to stop working, the drain of meeting a huge family's basic shelter, clothing, food, and medical needs would mean that we would eventually all return to living a hand-to-mouth existence. The opportunities that have opened up with regard to education, investment, and sustainable livelihoods for many other family members would dwindle. Despite all of that, I like working and I believe that my contribution makes a small but significant difference.

I am convinced by science that breastfeeding is the best option for babies; however, I do still need money. If it came to having to choose between breastfeeding or working, I would have to consider giving up breastfeeding. Luckily for me I don't need to make that choice. My employer, Save the Children, not only promotes exclusive breastfeeding in Pakistan, it enables breastfeeding for me and three other colleagues.

My role at Save the Children is really nice. I support program staff to document and plan their work. It is very flexible and I have had no trouble fitting in breastfeeding. In addition to the fact that my son stays on-site during the workday, the atmosphere is one that fully understands and encourages me to breastfeed Rehmat. During a regular workday, I simply go to the children's room at work to nurse him. If there are more restrictive meetings that demand my time, I try and feed him prior to the meeting. When Rehmat was younger, I asked for a break during any meeting that was longer than two hours. In fact, I have had whole meetings and interview panels take 20 minute breaks so I could breastfeed. I have always been made to feel that the timing was convenient and that everybody could use the break. At most meetings, there is a special room for breastfeeding, and among women-only groups, it is not unusual or uncomfortable. At outside functions, the Chador (large shawl) enables modest breastfeeding, though often a room is made available. The culture of Pakistan usually allows for private places for women wherever you go, anyway.

The emotional support at work is crucial, but the practical, logistical space is equally important. Save the Children provides us with a furnished room to meet the needs of our families and our work. We working mums have a cozy room with a chair, change table with drawers, a cot, and a bed. We often end up in the baby room at the same time and dream up ways to make the baby-friendly space better for our growing children, now aged eight months and ten months. This is important to us since we want to continue breastfeeding for up to two years. My co-worker, Shagufa, and I often discuss how lucky we are to have been able to return to work so easily and to have a safe place nearby for our contented breastfed babies. We bring our own sitters to watch after them, however, so it can be quite crowded.

My babysitter is also my brother-in-law—a unique situation. My 17-year-old brother-in-law helps me and I help him. He has missed out on school but has learned English since living with me. He looks after Rehmat during the day and then goes to a language center at night. He has been with Rehmat since the day I returned to work, when Rehmat was two months old, and he actually hates holidays because he can't be with Rehmat! The two of them have a lot of fun together.

It is not just the mothers and the sitters who enjoy having babies at work. Other, non-mums take time out for babies, too. In fact, I have been surprised by how many of my male colleagues visit the babies for mini-work breaks. So in addition to being able to breastfeed comfortably, our babies are socially adjusted. As a result, the office is a really nice place to be for mums, babies, and colleagues.

While working with Rehmat on-site is as ideal a situation as possible, Save the Children also allows me flexibility to work from home. Family Leave for all staff is a standard part of our entitlements, so no one even questions our need to stay home when a child is sick. I can access my email online from home, and I have been considering a high speed Internet connection to make it easier for me to do networking from home.

As nice as my office is, it is still work; and it is not easy being a working mother. In my case, all the pressure to be the perfect mother and super employee comes from my own internal standards. Save the Children has made allowances for my new mother status and I must accept that being a working mother means that sometimes I take time out for my baby. I am never made to feel unprofessional.

My biggest challenge is to reduce the feelings of guilt I have when I ask for something that will help me to continue to breastfeed and work. Now that my son is older the baby room is no longer suitable for his developmental stage. I have asked for an indoor play area for the three to four babies, soon to be toddlers, who routinely come to the office. I also want to support the emergency response in Indonesia, but have asked that my husband accompany me as babysitter, which will add extra expense to either myself or the project. I have offered solu-

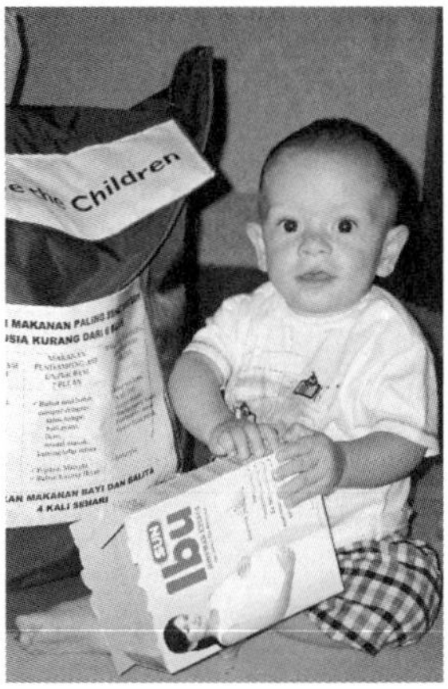

The bag in the photo was used for emergency distribution of food for babies from six to 18 months of age after the Tsunami. The message at the top says that exclusive breastfeeding is best for babies up to six months of age. It then gives a list of locally available foods that are appropriate for different aged babies. It contains some manufactured powdered baby foods as the local food supplies were all disrupted by the Tsunami.

tions that involve innovative ideas and cost sharing. I know my workplace will be responsive, but I still hesitate to mention my extra needs. This is my own internal struggle even though the office has never treated my requests as being unreasonable or unwelcome. It is simply one of the dilemmas that professional mothers face when trying to do two jobs well.

My personal culture is somewhat confused; I have my modern Australian ways, I live in a modern Islamic city, and I have family from a rural Pakistani village. In the village where my husband is from, women do breastfeed. I remember a gathering of about 50 women who all started screaming at me to feed the baby when he started to cry. My son was only tired and fell asleep after two minutes of crying but the women were incredulous that I didn't immediately start breastfeeding him. At the office we promote breastfeeding, so I think if I had chosen not to breastfeed, that could have been a problem. Indeed, our office is proud to have three breastfeeding, working mums.

Of all the people who benefit from my workplace's generosity and flexibility, Rehmat is near the top. He loves the piles of used paper I have behind my desk. He enjoys going to work, seeing different people, and visiting his mum. I think he also feels that solid food is okay, but breast is best!

Editor's Note: We received a follow-up message from Anita after she was sent to Indonesia to help with relief efforts for the 2004 Tsunami. Here is what she told us about working as a relief worker in a disaster area:

I am now in Indonesia with Rehmat for the emergency response. Save the Children worked out a way to utilize part of my vacation pay so my husband could come and look after the baby. The Indonesian office is as helpful as the Pakistani field office. With two more babies soon to arrive with their mothers, the Indonesian office is planning to incorporate breastfeeding and play space into their existing space, even as it works to meet the needs of the huge emergency efforts. In the meantime, my baby stays with another staff member's nanny and I can be taken to him for feeding anytime. The office will also pay for a hotel babysitter after hours if I have to work late in my room. I feel great about being able to continue to contribute in a crisis response.

Third Son's a Charm

Ghada Sayed

I am Ghada Sayed, an Egyptian pediatrician. In 2003 I was preparing for the Egyptian Board of Pediatrics when I first learned about the International Board of Lactation Consultant's Exam (IBLCE) and joined the local courses to prepare to take the exam and become certified as an International Board Certified Lactation Consultant (IBCLC). I was amazed with everything I learned and so sorry about how I had managed breastfeeding with my eldest two sons, now 15 and 13 years old. It was at that time that I got pregnant!

By the end of the course I was very determined to exclusively breastfeed my coming baby. I had a baby boy, Ahmed, who was born in September 2003. When he was one month old I was bringing him with me to the courses and he was training with me. After three months I had to go back to work. It then became really challenging for me to continue because I live 15km from work, so it takes over 45 minutes to commute every day. I took Ahmed with me and left him with a lady who was caring for the doctor's dormitory. I was so happy that my baby was a few meters away from me and that I could go and breastfeed him at anytime. By the time he was six months old, his growth chart was over the 95th percentile and he never fell sick.

By the end of the year I managed to enter the Egyptian Board exam and the IBLCE exam and passed both very successfully. I am convinced that breastfeeding and having my baby with me at all times probably gave me the strength to accomplish challenges in my life that I may never have been able to achieve if I hadn't exclusively breastfed my baby. I am sure that any woman determined to exclusively breastfeed her baby for six months, even if she is working or studying, will do so. If she has a strong will combined with faith, then she can do it!

In Egypt, 29 percent of women are in the workforce; 12 weeks of maternity leave is paid by public funds and the employer; 219 days of unpaid maternity leave is allowed; paid breastfeeding breaks are given once the mother returns to work.

Israel

Attorney

Hand-Expression Works

Tsviya Shir

I tried at least five different types of pumps: manual, electric, even a double pump. Nothing. I could not find a pump that worked for me. Output was nil, and even worse was the severe pain. It was so extreme that after a few minutes of pumping, the pain would continue the entire day and even interfered with nursing. Pumping was something I would not be able to do. However, I would be returning to work when my daughter, Yuvaly, was 18 weeks old. She had been fully breastfed and I did not intend for that to change.

Thankfully, my wonderful breastfeeding forum entered the picture, specifically Esther Grunis, the IBCLC who serves as the moderator. She helped me understand that hand expression of my milk is a natural function that could provide enough of a supply, if I was able to master the technique. And so I did. I enjoyed it and succeeded almost from the beginning.

So I had milk, my problems were over, right? Wrong! A few days before I returned to work, I tried giving Yuvaly a bottle of my hand-expressed milk. I tried all the tips from the forum on bottle refusal—every one! Nothing helped. Fortunately, Yuvaly's babysitter, who had known us for ten years, was quite relaxed. It was the first time she had ever needed to feed a baby expressed milk, and one reluctant to take a bottle to boot. Still, she got to work and read all the material I had found on the Internet until she became an expert on handling expressed milk. (There were a few mishaps, but that's for another story!)

Before retuning to work, I left Yuvaly with the babysitter for three hours. She didn't eat and didn't cry. The babysitter wasn't concerned and I came home dripping, to a satisfying and relaxing nursing session for both of us.

The second time I left her, I was gone for the whole morning. I promised not to call and went to look for clothes for work. The time passed slowly and I missed Yuvaly terribly. When I returned, the surprised babysitter reported that Yuvaly hadn't wanted any milk, hadn't cried, and waited patiently. Again, Yuvaly eagerly saved me from my overfull breasts and immediately fell asleep.

In Israel, 42 percent of women are in the workforce; 12 weeks of maternity leave is paid by public funds; 365 days of parental leave; paid breastfeeding breaks are given once mother returns to work.

Then the weekend came, which passed with trepidation about what would happen on my first day back at work. I had asked to begin working short days, where I would leave home at 7:30 AM and return at 1:30 PM. For five days, Yuvaly refused to drink from a bottle. Each day passed like sand in an hourglass while I sat practically bursting in my office. Everyday I came home expectantly, only to hear that the baby didn't eat. She would hold the bottle in her mouth and not suck. The babysitter began to take it personally, and to worry. On Thursday I got a joyous phone call at work: "She ate, she ate!!" All at once the matter was solved. When I came home the babysitter explained how she had used an ancient Polish trick—she told Yuvaly that if she wouldn't eat, she wouldn't come tomorrow. And apparently it worked.

We continued this way for three months. Yuvaly drank expressed milk from a bottle. I alternated between fresh and frozen milk.

I continued hand-expressing and no longer tried to use a pump. Still, I never expressed more than 150 ml in one session. It was very important to me that Yuvaly never get formula, and I struggled to make this happen. I connected my previous pumping problems and pain to an inner feeling I couldn't suppress, that my body had somehow reacted to the pain by producing less milk. I still don't know if that was true, but that was the feeling that haunted me then.

When Yuvaly was six months old we tried solid foods. It was a failure. Solids continue to be problematic, but we are working on this issue and hope things will improve in the near future.

When Yuvaly was seven months old, I got very tired of expressing. Things at work picked up and I was asked to return full-time, even though I had an agreement for a shorter workday in exchange for giving up my lunch break. This enabled me to finish work at 3:00 PM and be home by 3:30. The milk I prepared was already not enough. Even worse, Yuvaly didn't want bottles anymore and the babysitter would leave unfinished bottles of milk on the kitchen table. The combination of not being able to supply enough and the reduction in the amount of milk Yuvaly ate was very hard on me, and I cried to the forum constantly. My stock began to go down and I didn't know what I would do when it was finished.

Even with an occasional tough day, the time has certainly passed quickly!

Then a miracle happened—Yuvaly agreed to eat a jar of baby food. She was seven-and-a-half months when she began to eat solids and quickly stopped drinking from a bottle. Until this day, at 14 months old, she eats only solids with the babysitter.

Today we number about four or five nursing sessions a day and a few more at night. I still haven't allowed Yuvaly to have formula, and don't intend to. Through the many challenges, I find myself surprised to look up and see we have already made it to Yuvaly's fourteenth month! Even with an occasional tough day, the time has certainly passed quickly!

Israel

Computer Programmer

Going to "All That Trouble" for My Son

Avital Mulay

Translated from Hebrew by Hannah Katsman

I was an experienced breastfeeding mother of three, but a beginning pumper. A friend helped out by giving me a Medela pump as a gift. I was not aware that there were differences between pumps. When my baby, Amir, was three months old, I began to stock up on bags of frozen milk. My output was not impressive—70 to 80 cc at each pumping.

Formula was not an option for me, so I hoped my stock would last until I added solids to my son's menu.

Before returning to work, I informed my wonderful babysitter that Amir would only be drinking expressed milk and told her how to warm it. Despite the fact that she hadn't nursed her own children, she responded with cooperation and admiration.

I didn't acclimate Amir to the bottle because it was hard for me to forgo a breastfeeding session when I was with him, and I also didn't want to waste any of my precious stockpile. The babysitter accepted this. My return to work was very traumatic for me, but Amir surprised us and took the expressed milk with no problem.

Less than Perfect Privacy

I dragged a big bag to work each day fully stocked. It contained my pump, milk bags, ties, a newspaper (to read during the pumping), and a cooler with ice, a bottle, and a large "room occupied" sign. Each time I pumped I had to find a different room, usually an unlockable meeting room on my floor. I was surprised a few times despite the big sign I hung on the door when co-workers would barge in. Pumping in the office of my managers proved equally unhelpful, as even they would occasionally come to the door and "remind" me that they were waiting. Regardless of the room, I was always uncomfortable imagining that everyone could hear the noisy pump.

The few supportive reactions I received came, surprisingly, from men.

After pumping I washed the parts in water and rinsed them in boiling water. My husband sterilized them at home in the evening and prepared the cooler for me each day.

At work I received many different reactions. The few supportive reactions I received came, surprisingly, from men. Most of my co-workers were shocked, appalled, or disgusted by the act of pumping and no one could comprehend why I would "go to all that trouble."

At about six months, Amir began to eat solid food with pleasure. At seven months I decided, after consulting with the babysitter and Dr. Mira Leibovich, MD, IBCLC, that the amount and variety he received during the day was adequate, and thus I stopped pumping. Since then, and currently at 20 months, he nurses frequently when I am home.

I think having more support at work would have made continued pumping easier, although I don't think Amir suffered. The babysitter reported that he often didn't finish the bottle and she had to throw out the remainder. Still, I am glad that I chose to "go to all that trouble" for my son. I would do it again.

WEST BANK

Documentation Manager

The Other Side of the Wall

Jennifer Moorehead, East Jerusalem

I work in an area of Jerusalem through which a Separation Wall is being constructed. My office is on one side of the Wall, and my babysitter is on the other side of the Wall. The Wall is not yet completed, so there is currently an opening through which I can drive to drop off and pick up my baby. Lately, I have been reluctant to leave Leila in Bethlehem, where I live, since there are three checkpoints between my office and home. At any moment the checkpoints could be closed and I would be trapped outside. There is no way I want to be trapped away from my baby so I bring her with me, and am living with this terrible uncertainty about what to do when they close the Wall.

My job is fairly demanding, and since my husband is unemployed (given the catastrophic economic situation here), I really do need to keep working. Though my commute into Jerusalem with checkpoints and occasional clashes is intensely difficult, I do feel good about my babysitter, her understanding of my baby's nutritional and emotional needs, and my ability to provide milk for my child even after returning to work. I am also fortunate to have a great employer.

Save the Children in Jerusalem hired me while I was seven months pregnant, so that definitely gave me an indication that this office was baby-friendly! I returned to work when my eldest child, Leena, was only two months old. She stayed with me at work until she was five months old, was exclusively breastfed, and attended every management meeting with me. I even facilitated meetings while breastfeeding! When necessary, I pumped my milk at the office, using an old-fashioned hand pump, until she was a year old.

In March of 2004, I gave birth to Leila Julia Issa, and decided that I wanted to take a longer maternity leave. I took all of my vacation plus a full maternity leave and came back to work when Leila was five months old. I also changed my pump. I bought a Whisper Wear hands-free pump to replace my hand pump for use at work. Now, I work and pump at the same time. I don't even have a door to my office, but other than exceptionally large looking cleavage and a funny pumping noise, it's tough to tell that I'm doing anything at all! I do put up a Japanese screen so my male colleagues can avoid seeing me pump if they prefer. My female colleagues, on the other hand, enjoy visiting so they can see how it works. The Whisper Wear pump has changed the way I work, since it is 100 percent more efficient than my old pump.

I have to say that I never really considered it difficult to continue breastfeeding and pumping while working. What I really find difficult is to keep working. I so much would prefer to be at home with my children! Since economically that is not an option, I try to do the next best thing.

There is no way I want to be trapped away from my baby so I bring her with me.

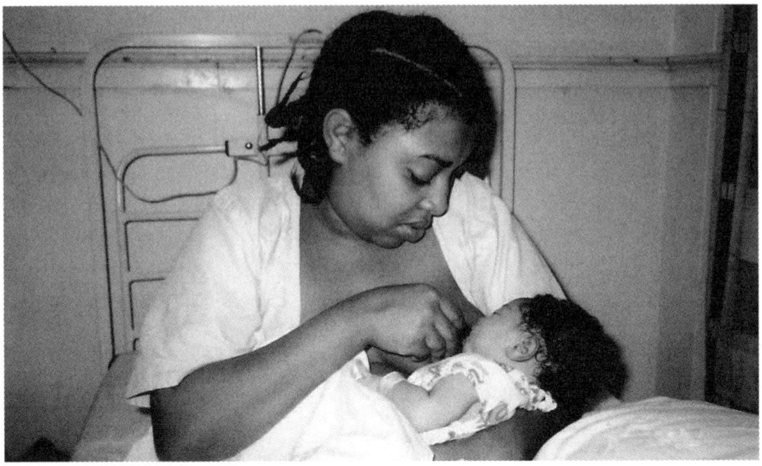

Silencing the Cacophony of Advice

Victoria Kisanga, Dar es Salaam

Combining breastfeeding and work requires listening to your own voice and following your own path. As it was with my daughter Nicole's birth, so will it remain that the rest of the world has opinions on the best way to rear your children, especially where nutrition is concerned. Despite having told the nurses that I planned to breastfeed my daughter, she was taken to a private room immediately after birth. I asked for her repeatedly and was told that I needed my rest and the baby needed to be fed immediately. I insisted on receiving her, and luckily, they brought her to me hungry. She had refused the bottle, which they desperately wanted to give her to prevent "yellowing."

In the first few weeks, all sorts of people continued to give advice to me, because I was a new mother. Some would tell me to give warm water; others said to give gripe water. Some even suggested giving other food because mother's milk alone was not enough. Others said I would gain too much weight or get too thin. But, because I had the support of my husband, plus a nutritionist and family friend, and because I had read quite a lot about exclusive breastfeeding, I simply listened to the cacophony of advice, and followed what my trusted sources and my instincts said.

In the end, despite all of the "noise" from others, I was able to breastfeed exclusively up to the end of the seventh month. It worked for me because I was home most of the time and I took my baby with me when I went out. After seven months, I began to work from home in several capacities, and by using creativity and flexibility, have been able to provide my milk as Nicole's main source of nutrition. Primarily, I work as a home caterer. I do catering for small functions, not more than 100 people, as most cooking is done in my small house kitchen. Most of the events that I cater are home functions such as engagement or birthday parties, or larger family get-togethers. For many of the events, clients prefer traditional African foods, but I will occasionally follow a client's more time-consuming request for a special menu.

In Tanzania, 86 percent of women are in the workforce, from 1 to 11 weeks of maternity leave is paid by the employer; paid breastfeeding breaks are given.

I cater about three times per week. I start preparing things well in advance, usually while Nicole is sleeping. If she happens to wake up while I am in the midst of things, I will breastfeed her and then let her play in the corridor where I can monitor her. Most events happen in the evening and my husband either remains at home with Nicole, or escorts me and helps deliver dishes to the function. Then he remains in the car with Nicole. In total, I am only physically away from home for about three hours per event.

In addition to this business, I look after our few cars that are used as taxi cabs here in the city. I have also been paid from time to time to design gardens for others. All of these undertakings afford me income with the flexibility to adjust to my family's needs.

In the last year, a few lessons I have learned are:

- My baby will have enough milk, even up to seven months, if I breastfeed as often as the baby wants it.
- Having the support of someone who knows about breastfeeding was critical to me, as it is to every new mother. If not for this, I would have made many mistakes or followed some of the poor advice I had been given early on.
- Manual expression is possible but time-consuming; a breast pump is sometimes helpful.
- Having a flexible working schedule is very important. This was

doable because I was working for myself.

- Influences from outside are many, and often misleading. I have seen my two neighbors fail with exclusive breastfeeding because of well-intended but bad advice from friends. I was able to help one of them relactate, but the other one was not successful.
- Family support is very important. My husband and nanny were instrumental in seeing that I had time to feed myself, the baby, and get more rest than normal.
- I carry my baby along wherever I go! I could afford this because I have a car and do not have a fixed time to work.

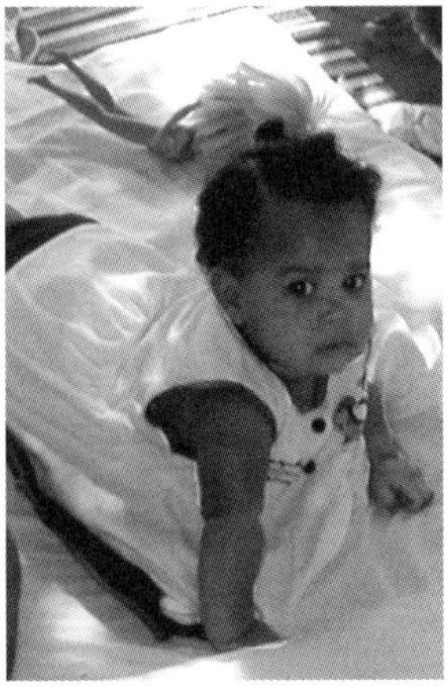

My Nicole is now one-and-a-half years old, eating well, and taking my milk and other milk in a cup when I am working. Following my own path and not doing full-time work has been a big advantage for me in maintaining my close breastfeeding relationship with Nicole. I do not know if I would have succeeded with exclusive breastfeeding if I had gone back to full-time work after having my daughter. I think women need a lot of help and support to breastfeed successfully. When I was young, I never knew the extent of breastfeeding's benefits. Now I know. My child has never suffered from diarrhea or other diseases that I know little children suffer from. She is vibrant and precocious, walking and talking like a bright little light.

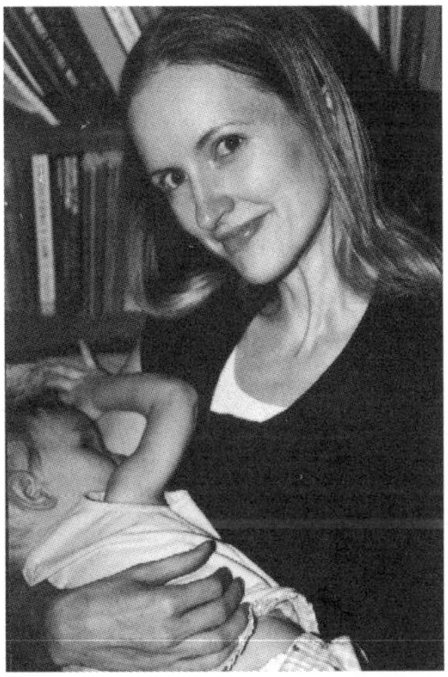

The Nanny from Heaven

Ena du Plessis, Johannesburg

It was my initial decision that my baby would have to be weaned around the age of three months, prior to my returning to work. I had heard of the option of expressing and thereby continuing breastfeeding, but it sounded like a terrible hassle. All the working mothers I knew had simply put their babies onto formula and it seemed to have worked fine for them. To breastfeed while working seemed to be reserved for extremists with lots of time.

Then, when I started reading about the countless benefits of breastfeeding, this "extremist option" started to make sense. I became determined to make it work. At the breastfeeding workshop I attended as part of my antenatal classes, the lactation consultant explained in detail how to express and store milk. I was relieved that it did not sound nearly as complicated as I had feared.

Because of early latching-on difficulties when Colleen was born, I developed an enormous fear of nipple confusion. Though I knew that

Colleen would eventually have to be partly bottle-fed, I was extremely cautious not to introduce a bottle too soon. The lactation consultant had recommended that we wait at least six weeks, and that was exactly what we did. During those six weeks Colleen became so proficient at latching on that before I knew it we were managing to breastfeed lying down. That was heaven!

Even so, the mere thought of "The Day of Introduction to the Bottle" created a knot in my stomach. What if that would mean the end of my breastfeeding days? An ideal opportunity for this introduction happened to arise on the very day that Colleen turned six weeks. A friend invited us to her birthday party at a restaurant. My mother was more than willing to babysit, and so we dropped Colleen off with a bottle of expressed milk. I felt a slight heaviness in my heart as we left. What if Colleen instantly develops into a bottle-lover and refuses me when I return?

My fears turned out to be totally unfounded. We had barely finished our meal when my dad phoned to summon us back. On arrival at my parents' house, we found my mother and Colleen both in tears. Colleen was obviously hungry, but bluntly refused to take the bottle. My mom had managed to feed her a few drops with a spoon, but this method soon upset her even more. I reclined onto a sofa with my baby and felt her relief as her jaws sunk into the familiar. I myself was relieved at not being refused, but, at the same time, I felt a tinge of worry—was Colleen ever going to accept a bottle?

That tinge of worry grew into a major concern over the next couple of weeks. On a few occasions I left Colleen with my mother or my husband for short periods, and without fail our efforts resulted in a hysterical baby and a very upset granny or dad. Both my mom and my husband time and again found themselves rocking Colleen to sleep without her having had a single drop of milk. As my husband put it, "If you want to see her really angry, you must bring that bottle near her."

During all this time, I never thought of trying to leave Colleen with the nanny who was going to look after her once I returned to work. Barbara is a lovely, grandmotherly African lady with an exceptionally calm manner. Besides having raised her own four children into adulthood, she had worked as a nanny for three families before becoming employed by us. We had started off the arrangement by her helping out with the domestic work once a week during my maternity leave. Although on such days she would play with Colleen in between, I never left Colleen alone with Barbara for long periods. I thought that either my mom or my husband would first have to convince Colleen to take a

In South Africa, 47 percent of women are in the workforce; 16 weeks of maternity leave is paid by public funds and employer; 3 days of parental leave; no breastfeeding breaks are allowed.

bottle. The problem was that neither of them was having any success, and the expiration of my maternity leave was drawing closer at a frightening speed.

One particular day, about two weeks before I was due to return to work, out of sheer despair I started telling Barbara about our battle. As I was expecting little more than a sympathetic ear, my surprise was great when she simply said, "Leave it to me; we will manage." She proceeded to tell me about the little boy that she looked after previously. She had taught that boy to drink from a bottle. She felt sure that no baby could be a bigger challenge than he had been. Barbara said I should stop worrying; she and Colleen would be fine.

So I stopped putting my mother, my husband, Colleen, and myself through the agony of trying the bottle. I forgot about the issue and simply carried on breastfeeding until two days before I was supposed to return to work. On that day I took a deep breath, prayed that everything would be all right, and left Colleen and a bottle of expressed milk with Barbara. I visited my mother at the office in an attempt to kill the five hours I had resolved to devote to the exercise. No amount of chatting to her or her colleagues could distract me. I spent those five hours praying, panicking, and watching my cell phone. Barbara did not phone once.

I found Colleen playing happily and Barbara reporting that she had finished 100 ml of milk from the bottle!

The five hours had barely elapsed when I pulled my car into the carport in front of our flat. I half-expected to hear Colleen screaming as I opened the door, but no, everything was quiet. I could hardly believe it when, on stepping into the living room, I found Colleen playing happily and Barbara reporting that she had finished 100 ml of milk from the bottle! She had had so much milk, that she did not even want to breastfeed immediately. I was so relieved, so grateful. My baby was going to be fine.

My return to work went smoothly. Even though my boss's first question upon seeing me after the birth was, "You're not breastfeeding, are you?" he has been very supportive. Before returning to work, I asked him whether he would mind my taking a few short breaks every day to express my milk. His reaction was, "So this child is going to be drinking mother's milk for a heck of a long time!" He has had absolutely no problem with the arrangement, although he makes a point of regularly teasing me about my breastfeeding!

I express in the ladies' room, as I find it convenient to wash the equipment in the basin directly afterwards. I then sterilize everything with boiling water in the kitchen. My bottles of expressed milk go straight into my cool bag, between two ice packs designed for cold

drink cans.

Initially I had to express three times a day at work, as well as once in the morning before work and once in the afternoon on returning from work. When Colleen was about six months old and started having solids, I was able to eliminate the before and after-work expressing sessions. Another two months later I was able to produce enough milk by only expressing twice at work. This arrangement still stands.

Colleen is now nearly 11months old. We returned a couple of days ago from a two-week Christmas holiday at the seaside. It was pure bliss to have been able to leave the pump and bottles at home and simply breastfeed wherever, whenever. We are now back at home and Colleen is once again happily combining breast and bottle. She clearly enjoys being with Barbara while I am at work. I am truly blessed to be able to continue nourishing my child emotionally and physically at the breast and through my milk.

Part Five

Asia, Australia, New Zealand

INDIA

Actress

Jungle Expression

Utkarsh Naik

Being an actress, I could not be replaced from a television serial. I was shooting up until the delivery and I had to go back to work when my baby girl, Gahna, was not even a month old. Unfortunately, I have long working hours—from 9:00 AM to 9:00 PM, sometimes beyond. I was very keen on breastfeeding my baby. However, there were many problems to work through. How would I be able to do it? My family was predominantly dependent on my income for our livelihood, and there was a lot of pressure at work.

Initially, I carried Gahna to work and took my mother with me to care for her. This could not work in the long-term because of the small make-up rooms and poor hygienic conditions at the studios. I needed a better solution. Fortunately, I met good doctors throughout this process who encouraged me to find a way. Dr. Oak motivated me with his enthusiastic support of breastfeeding.

I tried a breast pump, but to no avail as it was hurting and hardly

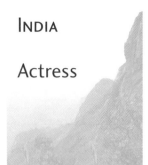

In India, 48 percent of women are in the workforce; 17 weeks or more of maternity leave is paid by public funds and the employer; 15 days of paternity leave; paid breastfeeding breaks are given once a mother returns to work.

helped. (The breast pumps that are available in India are not of good quality.) The next pediatrician I met was Dr. Vaidya. He guided me well, and told me to try hand-expression, which I found worked.

The first six months were very tricky as Gahna was breastfed exclusively. My working hours were erratic and shooting locations would sometimes be far away. I hired a maid who played an important role in caring for Gahna the way I wanted. I would express milk after Gahna finished having her share and her stomach was full. I also expressed whenever my breasts were full; whether I was at a shooting in a studio or in the middle of the jungle. Yes! Once I was shooting for a mythological serial in the jungle setting of film city. I told my hairdresser that I needed to pump my milk and we went behind some bushes. She helped me remove the costume and all of the heavy jewelry. She was very cooperative when she understood my motherly instincts.

I used to keep the expressed milk in small steel containers in a cooler box, and put it in the freezer when I came home. Sometimes if the location was near the house, I would send the cooler box home with my driver. Then, because I had a heavy milk flow, I would express practically every night so Gahna would have extra milk the next day. My maid would warm the steel container in water and feed Gahna.

But problems did arise. Once I was shooting at Madh Island and had arranged for the milk stock to last till midnight. But at 10:00 PM my husband called to say that the stock was depleted. I had finished shooting, but would need a little more time to pack up and get home. Gahna was howling with hunger. I recalled my doctor telling me that it's criminal to keep a baby hungry. I became frantic to rush back, and the situation turned into a great drama. Only it was a real drama.

Since we were on an island, I had not brought my car, but had traveled by ferry. But to reach the ferry landing, I needed a vehicle. The office vehicle was out. I ran to the road only to realize that even a rickshaw was not available. The only option was to request a lift from a stranger. Imagine me standing alone on a dimly lighted road at 11 o'clock at night. Obviously nobody would stop for a mysterious lady asking for a lift on a lonely island. Finally, I stood in the middle of the road and succeeded in stopping a car. I screamed through the window and told the man inside about the situation. Fortunately the man could understand my plight, probably because he was a doctor. He took me to the ferry.

My husband was standing with the baby on the other shore with only a small creek separating me from my baby. The distance by water to the other shore was hardly five minutes, yet I was suddenly faced with another problem. While I was waiting anxiously for the ferry to start, it was determined that the ferry would not be able to leave for another half-hour due to a high tide. It is hard to imagine how I spent that frustrating half-hour, and in what state of mind I crossed the creek. When I finally reached the other side in the middle of the night, I found Gahna fast asleep in her father's lap. It was agonizing for me to learn that she had cried and cried and had fallen asleep out of sheer exhaustion. I can never forget the moment when I snatched her from my husband and woke her up for the feed.

Things became much easier after six months when she started on complementary food. I went on to feed Ghana till she was four-and-a-half years old. During that period, I often had to go for out-station shooting. I thought that milk flow would stop during these breaks, but it never did. For those four-and-a-half years, milk kept on flowing to fill Gahna's needs. I could succeed in feeding Gahna because of my maid, Basanti, who played an important role by following my instructions rigidly. My husband's help was also crucial. In the end, the milk flow ceased only after I made a conscious decision to stop breastfeeding Gahna in her fifth year. Such is the power of mother's love.

Cambodia

Housekeeper

Exclusive Breastfeeding, a Family Effort

Chim Sophorn, Chhlong District, Kratie Province

Interview by Mr Ya Saroeun, PFD Community Officer
Translated from Khmer by Kim Chadwick

I work full time as the housekeeper of a non-governmental organization, Partners for Development (PFD), in Chhlong, Cambodia. During the first three months after delivery of my first son, Chandee, a family member had to perform my housekeeping duties at PFD, to ensure that I would keep my job.

Now Chandee stays with his father at our home, which is a five-minute walk away from the office. My husband is called Deuk Seang; he works as a rice farmer. During the year there are two main seasons for rice so the workload is varied throughout the year. Most of the time he is able to take care of Chandee himself with some help from my mother, who also lives with me and my family.

I work five days a week, starting work at 7:00 AM and ending at 5:00 PM, with a lunch break from 12:00 to 2:00. But if Chandee needs my milk during my work hours, Deuk Seang or my sisters will brings Chandee to the office, or I will go back to the house. It is sometimes difficult because I want to exclusively breastfeed and so occasionally, I must leave work for short times, but I know that mother's milk is very good for my boy's health. Now I am beginning to give him complementary foods such as special rice with egg yolk, green leafy vegetables, oil, and meat or fish.

I am happy to give good care to my child, and I also like to use my time to tell other mothers who live nearby about the benefits of exclusive breastfeeding and how it has protected Chandee against illness and made him grow to be healthy.

In Cambodia, 85 percent of women are in the workforce; 13 weeks of maternity leave is paid by the employer; there are paid breastfeeding breaks once a mother returns to work.

PHILIPPINES

Professor

College, Career, and Chemotherapy

Melissa Reyes

I am a 39-year-old Filipina, a wife, and mother of Agnes, Marcus, Frances, and Nicholas. Between my four children, I have logged seven years and four months of breastfeeding. To date, I still would not know how to prepare formula, how much it costs, or how much of it would satisfy a baby's hunger for food and love.

I am also a full-time faculty member in a leading private university in Manila, Philippines. Prior to that, my home was Iowa, USA, where I worked for my PhD, taught courses, and assumed a part-time post-doctoral research position. Academia is the only workplace I have known and the only workplace to which I wish to belong.

Four Different Breastfeeding Experiences

With four children, I have had more than enough opportunities to improve my craft of breastfeeding. When we had only Agnes I had fewer professional involvements, my schedule was simpler, and so were the logistics of breastfeeding. Yet, as my family and career grew, so did the challenges and complexities of breastfeeding. Because I am committed to breastfeeding for the long haul, I persevere through new problems, often by drawing on prior experiences.

When I gave birth to Agnes, I had already finished all the degree requirements except my dissertation. I wanted to stay home to exclusively breastfeed Agnes. I could write the dissertation at home, but my teaching assistantship would have to stop. It was hard to break the teaching habit and I needed the money. Hence, when the offer for a one-hour-a-day summer teaching position came, I grabbed it, still clueless about the logistics of leaving a nursing baby at home. Three weeks after a cesarean birth, I was back at the university.

Agnes and I managed. Our student apartment was just a pleasant ten-minute walk away from the university and the hours that I would be gone from home were few and far between. Thus, I was not overly worried that there would not be plenty of my milk in stock or that Agnes would never learn to feed from a bottle. She took my milk from a dropper or from a teaspoon or sometimes she simply waited for me. At other times she became stubborn and she cried inconsolably. Knowing that she might do so when I was gone made it hard for me to concentrate in the classroom or during meetings. I tried to nurse her long and well before leaving for work although there were times when I was in a rush and failed to do so. Once she was taking solids at six months, she adapted to having them when I wasn't home and to feasting on milk when I was. As she grew, she got used to playing during the times when I would be gone. I learned to enjoy, even savor, the times I had for myself at the university.

Once she was taking solids at six months, she adapted to having them when I wasn't home and to feasting on milk when I was.

New Baby, New Country

Marcus was born four months before we resettled in the Philippines. My husband, Tristan, and I had to attend to the myriad details that went with leaving a place that already felt like home, only to begin anew in Manila, where economic realities and typical living arrangements dictated that we both work full-time in the city and live in the suburbs.

Tristan and I accepted full-time teaching positions at the same university in the Philippines. We were excited, but I was anxious about leaving Marcus for the whole working day. I knew I would be nostalgic for those hours of intimate times with my children. I anticipated that adjustments to the Filipino way of living would take time, and I was doubtful that Marcus could subsist wholly on expressed milk while I worked, especially given the crazy traffic situation that Manila is notorious for. For these reasons, I asked to postpone my start date, giving me time until Marcus was seven months old.

The most-prized possession I took home from the US was a Medela Pump In Style, an electric double breast pump. I stored expressed milk like ants hoard food in anticipation of rainy days. I slowly became better at following the do's and avoiding the don'ts. My breast pump continues to be a constant and reliable servant, faithful and uncomplaining, asking only that a few parts be replaced through the years.

Frances, Baby Number Three

Breastfeeding and working with my third child, Frances, was similar to working with Marcus. This time, however, I was already in a full-time position and I could not bargain for more than the standard two-month maternity leave. The timing of Frances' birth worked in her favor, however. When I came back to work there were only two weeks remaining of classes before the summer vacation. Except for some hectic working days, vacation was happily spent nursing Frances and saving up my milk for another stretch of rainy days.

Struggling after Chemotherapy

Nicholas was conceived two months after my last chemotherapy session. With a breast on my right side but only a heart on my left, I still wanted to nurse Nicholas and hoped to do so exclusively. Long before his birth, I consulted my obstetrician-gynecologist and my pediatrician about this concern. They said that although exclusive breastfeeding was not out of the question, I might have to supplement. But then I thought of mothers who have nursed twins exclusively, of wet nurses that I had read about who had kept their babies and those of others peaceful and contented, and of women who, despite an earlier breast reduction surgery, breastfed their babies on their own terms. Through the La Leche League Web site, I sought counsel from a lactation adviser. Across the Atlantic, Kathie wrote to tell me that I should be able to nurse exclusively as I had done in the past; she did not mention formula supplementation. I clung to her words and believed in them with all my heart.

But Nicolas and I did not have a good start. Although I nursed around the clock, my milk was not coming in. I continued to nurse because Nicholas continued to suck. When the milk finally came in, my

PHILIPPINES

In the Philippines, 46 percent of women are in the workforce; from 1 to 11 weeks of maternity leave is paid by public funds and 7 days of paternity leave; no breastfeeding breaks are allowed.

breast was sore and heavy, and I was tired.

This time my cup did not run over. There was no surplus milk as there had been in the earlier days. There was no extra milk soaking my nightgown or seeping through my nursing pad or frustrating my child with its strong flow. I now saved much more feverishly for the rainy days.

Working again after two months, I pumped more often and saved every drop. When milk was no longer coming, I would stop and massage my breast, hand-express to yield about ten drops, and then resume pumping with the machine. Sometimes, I just relaxed and let the machine run; never mind there was no milk coming. It was during one of these times that I discovered that second let-down—milk coming in long plentiful streams. I watched in awe this soothing blessing from nature that now I am almost sure my babies had long known, experienced, and taken for granted. Through the months, there were many other second let-downs. My cup never ran over, but it was never empty either. Just when it seemed half-filled, it would fill itself just a little below the brim, giving my child what he needed.

It was during one of these times that I discovered that second let-down—milk coming in long plentiful streams.

My husband gave up his own room in a computer laboratory at work so that I would not have to express in my appointed small cubicle during my frequent pumping sessions. I expressed milk in between classes and meetings and before going home. I tried expressing milk immediately upon arriving at work and was pleased to discover that I actually could express a lot at this time, and it was the heavier, thicker kind (hindmilk that is rich in fat). These pumping sessions helped increase Nicholas' milk store. I continued to express milk until each of my babies was about one-and-a-half, then nursing continued only when I was at home.

My Priorities

My teaching and research work at the university is challenging and demanding. Although my university work eats up a big chunk of my time, it affords me flexibility in work arrangements and schedules. I choose my class schedules, I arrange my own appointments, and I can spend 15 of the 40 hours worked in a week outside of the university. While I am responsible for and feel committed to the work assigned to me, when I am outside the classroom or not called for meetings, really, my time is mine and I can go home to nurse or retreat in my pumping room. Work commitments will just have to wait until I am finished nursing or pumping. Moreover, there are several breaks—a short mid-term break, a summer break, and a Christmas break. I also have a four-day teaching week so that on Thursdays, I pretend to be a full-time stay-at-home mom.

For flexibility in scheduling and for the satisfaction and fulfillment I derive from my work, I owe the teaching profession and my university employer. I try to work with order and focus and I'd like to think that my colleagues and students respect me for the work that I do. Still, the demands of my profession and my family are more than what can fit in 24 hours a day, seven days a week. I know this, I accept this. I cannot be married to my career as others are. I cannot let it run my life and I cannot turn it into my life's dominant passion. I do not excel in it as much as I want to, as much as I think I could, or as much as many colleagues do.

Breastfeeding and mothering slow me down professionally. Sometimes I count the months of my married life when I was not pregnant or not nursing (or both) and all I come up with are the first two months of marriage and my seven-month bout with a mastectomy and chemotherapy. Then, I count how many more years of childbearing I have, and how many more years before the youngest turns ten. I figure children grow up fast and that pregnancy, breastfeeding, and mothering are not forever. I can live with this.

I figure children grow up fast and that pregnancy, breastfeeding, and mothering are not forever. I can live with this.

The Nursing Mother's Reward

How precious are the moments I have spent nursing my babies. I hold in a special corner of my memory the moments I spent nursing my children during their first minute, hour, or day of life. I held my bloody and crying newborn babies, put them to my breast, and sang to them. They held on to me quietly as though they were back in the comfort of my womb. When they were better at focusing their eyes, they looked at me with an adoring look reserved for me alone.

Filipinos are master-singers. We sing when we are happy, we sing when we are sad, we sing when we are in love. In various Philippine dialects are written many lullabies handed down from mother to mother through many generations.

Occasionally, a song comes along that speaks of the composer's love for his or her mother. "Sa Ugoy ng Duyan," a well-loved Filipino song with lyrics written by Levi Celerio and music composed by Lucio San Pedro, is one such song. It has a lullaby-like melody so even though it is meant to be sung by an adult son to his mother, I imagine that mothers sing it to their babies. Its melody, is as hauntingly beautiful as its lyrics, perfectly conveying the lyrics' message and sentiment. If you listen to it even without knowing a word of Filipino, you would still understand every nuance of meaning.

It sings of the sweet gentle swaying of the cradle, of the longing for those days when as a baby, I was in the presence of "Nanay." " I wish to hear again that song of love sung by Nanay while the stars watch over me, by the sweet gentle swaying of the cradle."

I wonder what memories my babies hold of the cradle I have carved out for them and whether, someday, they'll create memories from the love they feel for me.

JAPAN

IT Engineer

The Sound of Mother's Milk

Yuriko Inukai

I never considered powdered milk an option, mostly because my milk always worked well for my children. My way of working and feeding mother's milk, however, has not always been the most inconspicuous.

I expressed my milk with my first baby before going to work. In addition, during the day, at lunchtime, I would go to the bathroom in the office and hand-express more milk. I put this milk into a freezer bag and kept it in a portable freezer, which I had provided because my office had no such equipment. I expressed completely by hand until Erika's first birthday because I did not like to hassle with sterilizing pump parts and such and it seemed the simplest, most natural method. I would take my milk home at day's end then provide it to the caregiver who was looking after the baby the next day.

As the seasons changed and the temperature rose, my portable freezer needed to work quite hard to keep cool. Unfortunately, the freezer made a ghastly noise in summer, increasingly so as the heat increased. Daily, that freezer cranked noisily away, a constant groan in the background of the office environment. Though my colleagues teased me, they were altogether kind about it. They called my freezer "the office beast." The noisy groan was an audible reminder to all that I alone provided my child her nourishment.

Toward the seventh month, the caretaker asked for 400 cc of milk, which she felt the baby needed, but I could manage pumping only 360 cc a day at best. I had her give the baby other fluids such as Japanese tea and water, which the baby seemed happy with. She seemed to make up for any lack by nursing frequently when she was with me.

Despite my freezer sounding like "the office beast," and in spite of time-consuming milk expression, I continued with breastfeeding because I never considered powdered milk an option. Why would it be? I had no problem feeding with my own milk!

In Japan, 44 percent of women are in the workforce; 14 weeks of maternity leave is paid by public funds and employer; 365 days of parental leave; 8 weeks of paternity leave; paid and unpaid breastfeeding breaks are allowed, up to one hour per day until the baby is one year old.

MALAYSIA

Environmental Control Officer

Support from Around the World

Azleena bt Wan Mohamad, Ehsan

My daughter, Aisha, is eight months old at the time of writing this. We live in Malaysia where I work with the Malaysian Department of Environment.

From my informal observations, both breastfeeding and formula-feeding are common in Malaysia. Generally, stay-at-home mothers breastfeed while working mothers formula-feed. However, with the importation of good-quality pumps, there is an increased awareness of the possibility of providing mother's milk for babies, even when the mother is working.

Awareness of the importance of breastfeeding is also increasing in Malaysia, with support from the government and some local breastfeeding support groups. Most hospitals finally have lactation consultants and breastfeeding policies, and almost all major department stores have nursing rooms. Companies are encouraged to set up crèches, but this is not much practiced yet.

The main thing that has made breastfeeding, working, and pumping so successful for me is the wealth of information and support from the Internet. Thanks to Web sites like LLLI, askdrsears.com, kellymom.com, and the iVillage breastfeeding and working message boards, I have been able to start breastfeeding easily, conquer any breastfeeding problems that have come up, select a good pump, and schedule pumping times appropriately. Most significantly, just knowing that so many other mothers around the world are able to work and exclusively provide their babies with human milk is reassuring and inspiring. I have also been able to pass on information, tips, and advice to several friends who are breastfeeding and working. Of course, support from my husband and mother has been invaluable.

Before Aisha was born, I made a decision to breastfeed her, for economic and convenience reasons. I did not want the cost of buying formula or the hassle of carrying insulated bottles when we would go out. But since then, we have discovered what a wonderful feeling and close bond breastfeeding has brought us, making me all the more determined to continue nursing for as long as possible. Furthermore, she is the healthiest baby I have ever seen and I have not needed to take any time off work due to illness. This is why I have chosen and will continue to pump at work—in order to provide her with my milk while ensuring my supply is maintained for nursing her when I am not at work.

In Malaysia, it is quite common for working families to employ an Indonesian maid to look after the baby and the house, and this is what my husband and I have done. We live with my in-laws, so they are able to supervise. Thus, Aisha stays at home while I am at work, and drinks my expressed milk. After she was six months old, she started solids. She now gets most of her solids while I am at work, so when I am home, we mostly nurse.

My work as an environmental control officer is mostly managerial, with several weekly meetings, occasional site visits, and courses that often last several days. I am fortunate that my position allows me my own office room, although I have heard of other staff having to use the small prayer room to pump. I installed my own window blinds, and with the permission of my bosses, I take some time off during the workday to pump. I arrive early to work and get my first pumping done, so I am free from pumping during the busiest part of the day. My staff is aware of this, and takes messages for me while I am pumping. Sometimes I have to juggle pumping times around meetings. Occasionally when I go for courses held in training facilities, I've had to rush to pump during

Malaysia

In Malaysia, 43 percent of women are in the workforce; from 1 to 11 weeks of maternity leave is paid by the employer; no breastfeeding breaks are allowed.

tea and lunch breaks, sometimes in my car or in toilets, though occasionally organizers are able to find a room for me. I store and transport the expressed milk in a small cooler box with freezable ice-packs.

I have learned that what made working and pumping easier was to be willing to talk about options and ask questions.

I have learned that what made working and pumping easier was to be willing to talk about options and ask questions. Too often there is the unfounded embarrassment of talking about breastfeeding and expressing milk, when it is the most natural thing in the world. In a working environment, most men are already fathers, and will understand that you want to give your child the best. Although you may feel embarrassed to ask for certain accommodations, if you don't ask, you won't get anything.

Ideally, all workplaces would have a crèche or in-house child care center, so that mothers could breastfeed their children during breaks in the workday. Practically, a small but comfortable room with electrical outlets and a small refrigerator with guaranteed privacy should be allocated for the convenience of mothers, and would serve as a statement of the company's commitment to helping working mothers maintain their nursing relationship.

Choosing to combine breastfeeding with work is a decision I do not regret. Admittedly, it is troublesome to carry a cooler box to and from work every day, and pumping regularly is a challenge, especially when I have to attend courses away from my office. But to come home and have my daughter reach out for me and demand to nurse immediately, to see her eyes close in nursing ecstasy, and then to see her milky smile of satisfaction—that is priceless.

MONGOLIA

Accountant

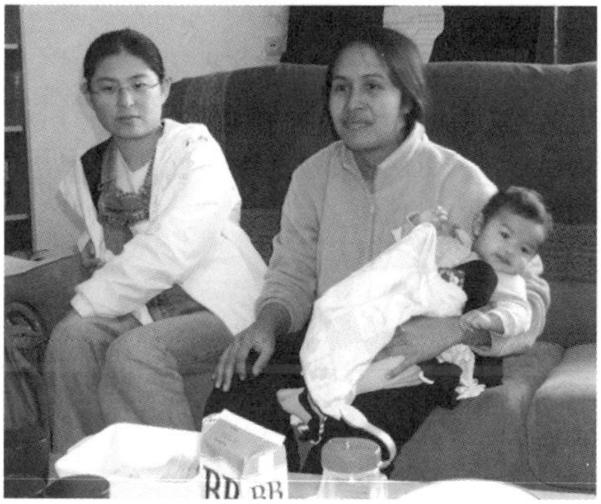

My Greatest Accomplishment

Eunie 'Lou

Interviewed by Melanie Wilson

I considered myself a workaholic and an efficient accountant for the Seventh-Day Adventist Christian Mission in Cambodia when I became pregnant with my son, Bradley. My husband and I had just gotten married, and before I could even get my hands on some preventive pills, I was already pregnant.

I was a new wife and soon-to-be new mother—an overwhelming feeling! My first thoughts were of guilt. I felt guilty to be pregnant so soon after working for less than a year in that mission. I felt guilty to have contributed only several months' work before the organization would have to bear maternity costs. From that point on, I was determined that I would maintain the same efficiency level in my accounting work, even after having my baby. It became my ultimate goal to prove that it is possible to be a great worker while also being the best mother to my baby.

The other women missionaries were so supportive that slowly my guilt decreased to a point that I was beginning to finally enjoy being pregnant. My co-accountant, who had a baby the year before, loaned me a book entitled, The Womanly Art of Breastfeeding. The timing was perfect. I had an answer before I could even ask myself whether I should breastfeed my baby or not.

I went home to the Philippines during the seventh month of pregnancy since that was the latest time in pregnancy that the airlines would allow me to fly. After a week in the Philippines, my baby was born quite premature. I am a disciple to any well-written book (!) and so, The Womanly Art of Breastfeeding became my Bible. My son had to stay in the nursery for only one week. I was always there to breastfeed him, with the mind-set that my milk was the only perfect medicine for him to reach the health level of being a normal "term" baby. I believe God sustained my baby through the natural gift of human milk, so that after a month, when we flew back to Cambodia, he was normal and very healthy.

In Mongolia, 76 percent of women are in the workforce; 17 or more weeks of maternity leave is paid by public funds; 730 days of unpaid parental leave is allowed; paid breastfeeding breaks are given.

I had only one month of maternity leave. The bulk of it was all spent flying, walking, having premature labor, breastfeeding at the nursery, passport processing, and quickly visiting family and relatives on different islands in the Philippines by boat, by bus, or by plane. Boy was my body tired!

It is hard to understand how my son could change in one month's time from a sleepyhead to a colicky two-month-old. My plan was to bring him to my office, breastfeed him, lay him down on the crib near my table, and let the sounds of the printer, the typing, and the air conditioner lull him into a deep slumber. Reality hit me hard. He would not let go of my breast, much less lay in the stroller or sleep. When his mouth was not busy sucking, it was busy wailing! The fulfillment of my goal—to maintain the same work efficiency level, being the best possible worker while at the same time being the best mother to my son—seemed impossible.

It would have been worse had the people around me been unsupportive. The president told me as long as I met my deadlines and my 40-hour work requirement there was no problem. (Their policy allowed for two hours daily to nurse the baby.)

My routine in the daytime consisted of walking and climbing, walking and climbing. I was constantly getting exercise by running from our small apartment on the third floor of the mission building, down to the basement office when the baby was asleep. I would go up again when the babysitter rang for feeding time, which was about every 30 minutes! His wailing schedule was from 6:00 to 8:00 PM, so I let my husband get his after-office-work relaxation and "bonding time" while I returned to the office for work. There were days when I would even go down to work at midnight or 2:00 AM when my baby was (finally!) in a deep sleep. When did I sleep or rest? Easy. When my baby was sucking, I was also napping! Sunday was a work and family day, too. We would all relax together in my office. While I worked, my husband played with the baby on the floor or watched a cartoon musical on the other computer.

To be a full-time working mother and at the same time a full-time breastfeeding mother for one straight year was the most challenging task of my life. It is also the greatest accomplishment I could ever claim. And it was only possible because of the understanding and supportive people that surrounded me in that mission compound.

To be a full-time working mother and at the same time a full-time breastfeeding mother for one straight year was the most challenging task of my life.

In 2002, my family decided to transfer missions from Cambodia to Mongolia. Before we accepted the work, we told the president of the Mongolia Mission that I was pregnant with my second child. They were very positive about it. I later learned that my being a mother was even one of the reasons why they hired me. They assumed that if I managed to be a full-time accountant with a baby, and still have good recommendations, then I was qualified for the job. It was a good move made even better when I learned that the LLL Groups I had read so much about in THE WOMANLY ART OF BREASTFEEDING, actually held meetings in Mongolia!

My baby girl was born in Mongolia on July 2, 2002. I would bring her to the office, feed her, and she'd be asleep in the stroller until my lunch break. She would then eat again and sleep until time to go home. She was a much better "working baby." When she became more mobile, I would leave her at our director's apartment, which was in the same building as our office. His wife and their teen age daughters enjoyed watching her. They brought her to me during feeding time and I would simply close my office and feed her—people were very respectful about it.

In Mongolia, breastfeeding in the open is quite normal, sometimes so normal that even when you cover yourself, people will peep inside! I would have loved to breastfeed my baby girl in person for a whole year, if only the Mongolian climate was cooperative. December through February is an extremely cold season in Mongolia and we had to walk from our apartment to the taxi station. I thought if I was cold, then my baby was probably cold, too. I decided it was time for my baby girl to stop working.

I've never liked using the freezer. Even now I have a lot of irrational thoughts about it and cannot be reconciled with giving frozen milk to my baby. So, I pumped milk during the early morning feedings to leave for my baby that day instructing the babysitter to only give my expressed milk and plain water until I returned in the early afternoons. I never became an expert on milk expression by hand or by any pumping gadget.

Success as a working breastfeeding mother depends largely on the kind of people one works with. Our children and families are the most important part of our lives. If companies cannot value this universal truth then we must choose family loyalty over company loyalty—no matter what.

Taiwan

Preschool Director

Changing Society's Collective Consciousness

Crystal Hui Man Lai

The first time I saw a woman breastfeed her baby in public was in the Montessori Infant-Toddler Assistant Training, in Chicago USA, in 1990. I was very impressed by the phenomenon of a highly educated woman breastfeeding her son in public while giving a lecture to a full room of students. It was so amazing to me. I never saw a woman in Taiwan breastfeed a baby in public. This is when I realized that a woman can work and breastfeed her child at the same time. I could hear a voice come up from my heart, "I want to be like her, to work and breastfeed my child at the same time."

My first son was born in the United States, where I happily breastfed him for three years. I felt free to breastfeed him in public and was surrounded by a group of breastfeeding mothers with whom I shared all kinds of family activities. It felt great to be supported by other

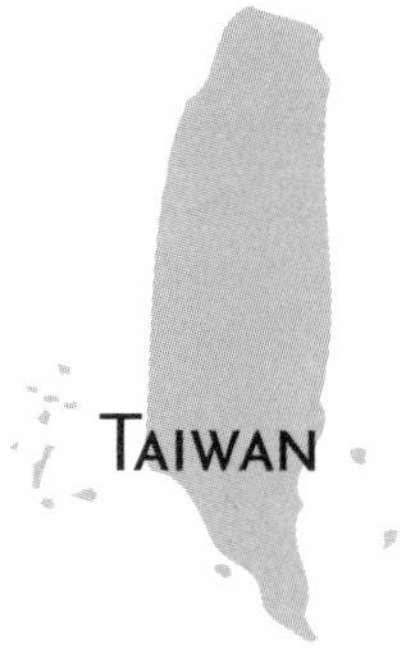

In Taiwan, from 1 to 11 weeks of maternity leave, 730 days of parental leave, and 2 days of paternity leave are offered; paid breastfeeding breaks are given.

breastfeeding families.

Yet, everything changed when we returned to my homeland. I could no longer breastfeed my son in public and would be ashamed if people knew my three-year-old boy still breastfed! Fortunately, my son was almost weaned. He only needed to be breastfed before going to sleep at night. At about four-and-a-half years, my son completely weaned himself. During the day, he was in kindergarten while I worked as an instructor at a university.

It was not until my second pregnancy that I truly realized what a dire lack of support I had with respect to parenting choices, especially those viewed by my society as "alternative." The norms in Taiwan, I was quickly learning, are: "Husbands must be segregated when a woman is delivering the baby," and "The newborn cannot be breastfed right after birth." In the first five months of my pregnancy, I visited almost every obstetrician in my town—not one of them agreed that my husband could be present at my child's birth. Breastfeeding right after birth was an impossible issue to discuss with the doctors, too. The doctors were clearly annoyed and irritated with my questions and concerns. Eventually, we decided to find a midwife and have the baby at home.

These difficulties foreshadowed what I would experience when returning to work as a preschool director. We had a beautiful home birth and a great time together during my two-month maternity leave. Then I had to return to work. I had arranged to leave my baby with a nanny right next to the preschool. I thought I had planned everything well. My baby was adjusting nicely, and I had a wonderful, experienced nanny taking care of her.

Despite that, there were problems. My colleagues complained to my boss that it was "not professional" to leave the school at naptime to breastfeed at a nanny's house. It was also decided that I was abusing "my position as a director" by leaving for a 20-minute lunch break (during which time I also breastfed). Then, one day, a colleague confronted me with great jealousy saying that I spoiled my baby and would someday regret letting my daughter take charge of my whole life.

I could not understand why the situation was so out of control! I decided to pump my milk and let the nanny bottle-feed it to my daughter. In the beginning, my daughter accepted this arrangement. Yet, one week later she started to refuse the bottle. Crying and crying, she kept expecting me to come during my lunch break. One day, my nanny showed up at the front door of the preschool with her. I heard my baby crying, and sadly handed my nanny a bottle of expressed milk. I asked her to feed my daughter with a spoon. Life continued like this, and it was a terrible struggle for a couple of months until my daughter finally adjusted to my milk from a bottle. How could she possibly understand that her mother was expected to be the "perfect model" of a professional director in the eyes of her colleagues? Still, every night, I went home with her crying and the next day I went back to work again. I hoped as time passed that things would improve. I prayed to God that I wanted to have my job and breastfeed my baby at the same time, and I wanted to do well at both.

Yet, I think God had his own plan, which was different from mine. My daughter had an accident when she was around six months old. We went to a traditional Chinese food store to have breakfast. The food store offered hot soybean milk and dumplings. With all the work-related stress, I was feeling sick and dizzy. When the hot soybean milk was served, my daughter reached out and spilled it on herself before I could push it away. She started to scream and cry. I ran to the restroom for cold water for her wound, while my husband called the ambulance. We sent her to the hospital emergency room. That 20-minute car trip was the longest one in my life. I can still feel the burning pain on her skin and hear her heartbreaking cry.

I wanted to have my job and breastfeed my baby at the same time, and I wanted to do well at both.

I took ten days sick leave to be home with my daughter. I felt happy being home with her and began to think about quitting my job. When I went back to work again, one of my colleagues teased me saying, "You took a long vacation and must feel refreshed!" She also raised a question. "According to the guidelines, when a family member dies, one can take seven days leave. Why did your daughter need you so many days?" I did not say a word, but just looked at her. I decided to quit my job starting at the end of the semester. I would find a way to work part-time, so I could stay at home and take care of my baby.

For the first month after quitting my job, I cried a lot. I did not understand why I had faced so many obstacles in my work. Then, as more and more young mothers came to me needing breastfeeding support, I began to realize that my society's collective consciousness needed to be reformed! I decided to write articles for newspapers and parents' magazines promoting breastfeeding as a mother's and baby's right.

When my second child went to kindergarten, I led a breastfeeding support group with the Public Health Department in my town. I joined the first government-based pilot research analyzing breastfeeding rates in relation to community support for new mothers.

I don't know how much difference I can make in Taiwan. I do know as long as I can fuel and protect my own fire, I can and will share it with others. More and more women breastfeed successfully on this tiny island. More and more doctors have changed their attitudes toward women who breastfeed their babies. More and more hospitals are becoming baby-friendly hospitals, encouraging young mothers to breastfeed. The government is about to make an official Health Policy related to women, infants, and children. I hope that 20 years from now, the majority of Taiwanese babies are breastfed. This is my dream now and I pray for it every day!

Finding the Right Child Care Center

Midori Fujita, Matsuyama, Ehime Prefecture

Translated from Japanese by Toshi Jolliffe

I was happy that I could stay home with my daughter for a full year after she was born. When I was supposed to go back to work as a district health nurse, my main concern was finding a quality caretaker. I checked through the Internet to find a place where I could leave my baby, Yukika, and selected a few possible care centers. I took Yukika to visit one of them, which was a private center without certification, and I talked at length with the senior caretaker.

This center, unlike many in Japan, welcomes breastfeeding mothers as if it were their second home. I was lucky to be able to leave Yukika at this place.

When I mentioned that she had never been separated from me,

and that while she was away from me I wanted Yukika to receive only my expressed milk, they agreed with me straight away. This was such a relief! It is interesting to note that there are very few child care centers in Japan that will accept expressed human milk for a baby. Most insist on formula use.

Now when I am at work, I look forward to the end of the workday. As soon as I come to pick her up, it is such a special "reunion."

I call to her "Yuki," and she answers "Mama!" Often other children rush to see Yukika and me breastfeeding, and they say "Yukika is having paipai!" Some little girls sit beside us and nurse their little baby dolls.

Shortly after Yukika had turned two years old, the director of this center said to me, "Yukika is such a contented and lively girl because she has you as a safe base." I felt so honoured with this comment.

I feel lucky to have found a care center that entirely supports breastfeeding. My hope is that there will be more breastfeeding-friendly centers available in the future.

India

Newspaper Editor

Searching for Balance

Shubhada Chaukar, Mumbai

I started working when Mallika was five-and-a-half months old. I worked part-time for two weeks, thus I could feed Mallika exclusively for six months. Subsequently, work pressures compelled me to be away from her for almost eight to nine hours at a stretch. At this juncture, I started giving her rice, pulses, fruits, and vegetable juices along with mother's milk. Whenever I was around, my milk was her only food. Other eatables were served during my working hours. I used to send Mallika to the mavshi (babysitter), with a bag full of clothes, a bed, a blanket, and four to five containers of her special food cooked by me.

To continue breastfeeding after returning to work was a challenging task. I had no support at my workplace. I work for *Loksatta*, a leading Marathi daily of Indian Express Group. Print media is still a man's domain where the proportion of men to women journalists is ten to one. There were only four other lady colleagues and only two of us were married. Hence my office was not at all aware of the importance of breastfeeding. Our office was not mother-friendly. There was no crèche, no room to relax and express milk, and no storage facility for expressed milk. Milk had to be expressed and stored in a basin, which was just in front of a toilet. I continued to express milk for about two weeks in these unhygienic conditions but could do it no further. My breasts acclimatized to function without emptying during the daytime. Before coming to the office, I would express sufficiently for one feeding and hand it in an airtight container to the mavshi. Initially, her reaction was odd. She had never heard of such a thing and was hesitant. But I successfully convinced her to feed my expressed milk and fortunately she followed my instructions. She also agreed to feed it by wait-spoon (teaspoon) and assured me that she would not use the bottle.

The suburban area where I work gets flooded very easily and that's what happened that day. I got stranded in my office.

In October, when Mallika was just seven months old, it suddenly rained heavily in Mumbai. The suburban area where I work gets flooded very easily and that's what happened that day. I got stranded in my office. Earlier, in such times, I used to spend the night in the office or at a friend's place. But now, I was a mother. I had to get home to feed Mallika. She wouldn't have slept without me. A newspaper delivery van dropped me halfway to my house, and I traveled the remaining ten km by rickshaw. My colleagues were discouraging me to do so. It was not so safe to travel in a rickshaw after 10:00 PM, but I was not ready to listen to anybody. I had to reach home to feed Mallika. I managed to be at home by 11:40 PM. My beloved baby was waiting for me eagerly. My husband had arrived earlier and he was trying to put Mallika to sleep, but she was refusing to be pacified by him. I fed her at midnight and all my fatigue withered away. Even Mallika slept comfortably after breastfeeding.

When she was almost a year old, I had two good opportunities, which would have enhanced my career. One was to participate in a three-day convention in Delhi. I flatly refused. Mallika's breastfeeding might have been hampered. Opportunities will come in the future, but my child's needs were my top priority in those days.

Soon after, there was a chance to cover the Malaysian tourism festival, which was of eight to ten days duration. I refused that, also. Some of my colleagues made fun of me for not accepting such an opportunity. But I was committed to my child, so Malaysia did not attract me. Here I should compliment my boss and management because they never pressured me to go outstation in that specific period. They finally became sensitive to my efforts to care for my child.

When Mallika was two-and-a-half years old, again there was an out-of-town opportunity. This time it was a chance to cover the

International Film Awards Ceremony in Genting, Malaysia. That was a four-day tour. I accepted the offer. I talked about it to Mallika and asked her if she could mange without breastfeeding for four nights. She reluctantly agreed. For the first night, she was restless without me. Back in Genting, even I yearned to breastfeed her, missed her dearly, and slept with tears rolling down my cheeks. I could imagine her eager and helpless face and that made me even more restless. Somehow Mallika managed without milk and without me for those four days. She came to the airport to receive me. She hugged me and immediately asked, "Aai, (mom), will you feed me more tonight? I am missing you," as if she wanted to make up for the lost time. The first thing I did after reaching home was to feed her. I had brought many gifts for her, but that night she did not give the gift packet even a glance.

I do not have fixed working hours. I often reach home late at night, sometimes as late as 11:00 PM. My husband picks Mallika up from the babysitter in the evening. She would comfortably play and dine with her father, but always waited for me and never slept without breastfeeding. However tired I would be, I always looked forward to this opportunity to get close to my dear child. For Mallika, mother's milk was always the first choice of food.

When she was three months past three years, we had been to our hometown for a week. Plenty of relatives had gathered in the house. By that time she had started feeling awkward to ask to breastfeed in front of others. So lack of privacy and tiredness compelled her to sleep without feeding. I was not well after returning home, and was unable to breastfeed. The long gap finally terminated breastfeeding for us.

It was a bit difficult for me to adjust to that stage of hers. I felt as if my child was no longer a baby; she had grown up. Her babyhood was over and her childhood had started.

My profession as a journalist is time-demanding and I love it. I can't think of leaving it. Somehow, I am trying to balance my profession with my family life. I try my best to offer Mallika "quality time" when I am at home. Breastfeeding has helped with that, and has proved a great boon for my family in many ways. Mallika has been quite healthy throughout. The three of us—Mallika, my husband, and I—are very close. Mallika is not yet five, still I do talk to her about almost everything and anything. She is very sensitive and shares her feelings. Amazingly, she also understands my feelings very well. She is a happy child. She is intelligent. She is confident. Perhaps most importantly, she trusts me a lot and loves me a lot. I could not ask for more.

AUSTRALIA

Management Accountant

The Value of a Happy Employee

Carolyn Rushworth, Lindisfarne

It was very much my choice to return to work; it was a family decision as to how to implement that choice. My husband, Matt, was supportive and we both wanted to provide the majority of early care for our new baby. So, the first big change of 2004, having Nick, led to the second big change: Matt negotiated part-time work for the next five to seven years, and I made plans to return to work in a new position.

I did not want returning to work to be detrimental to Nick's and my relationship—it is hard enough leaving him for the day. I proposed an arrangement that would allow my family the time to adjust to our new roles and it was very fortunate that my employer agreed.

Matt and I both work for the same corporation, Hydro Tasmania. This is Australia's leading renewable energy business and supplies hydropower to the Tasmanian market. I work within the Energy Business, and provide financial management reporting to management and project managers. Matt is a Senior Technical Officer in our

Telecommunications Group, which provides the telecommunications infrastructure for the corporation. Though our ideal situation would be for both of us to maintain our career paths and skills while enjoying weekday parenting of Nick, my position is not part-time. I was deeply concerned with how our breastfeeding relationship would fare with me working. I was also conscious of needing additional time at work to express my milk and I did not want to leave Nick for whole days. We agonized over the mechanics, but in the end, all you can do in these situations is make a decision, try it out, and see how it goes. I was able to negotiate a gradual return to work, including some hours from home where possible, allowing the adjustment for all of us to be as smooth as possible.

Here is what we worked out:

- Nick at five months:
  I returned to work initially one day per week in mid-July, which was enough time to be back in the swing of things, but not enough time to be given too many tasks.
- Nick at seven months:
  In September, I increased to working two days a week.
- Nick at nine months:
  By November, I was working three days a week.
- Nick at 11 months:
  As of January, I worked four days a week, a few of which were worked from home.

In Australia, 52 percent of women are in the workforce; 26 weeks or more of unpaid maternity leave is allowed; 365 days of unpaid parental leave is allowed; no breast-feeding breaks are given once a mother returns to work.

Currently, I have Wednesday at home, while Matt has Monday and Tuesday at home. We travel together to work on Thursday and Friday while Matt's mum looks after Nick at our house. There have been quite a few occasions where Matt has brought Nick in to work for one of the two daytime feeds. (One was when I forgot the all-important valve for the pump and wasn't yet hand-expressing.) I have also ducked home to feed him on occasion, again when I forgot my "gear."

Expressing at Work

Expressing at work was (and still is) interesting. I work in a field office, which doesn't even have a first aid room, so on my first day back, I arranged to pump in an old tea room. It was more than big enough, had an outlet, and most importantly a lockable door. Add one chair from our facilities people, and I was set. At first the pumping was okay—much better than I expected. I was expressing at the times I would normally feed Nick and getting "enough" milk to give him for the next time I was at work. The hardest part initially was judging how much milk I should be leaving.

Surprisingly, as the months pass, I find that expressing has become more difficult. I am not as easily able to get a let-down and so find that Nick drinks more of my milk than I can express in a workday. I have made up for the shortfall by expressing a little after each feed when I am at home. Obviously as Nick is getting older the milk feeds are lessening. (His first birthday is next month!) In the end, I have given up on the electric pump and just use hand-expressing—it seems more effective and quicker.

Leaving expressed milk with Matt is no problem. He knows more about it than me, really, as I never have to use it! I was a bit more nervous (okay, paranoid) about leaving my expressed milk for other people. Matt's and my mum have done well, and tolerated explicit instructions being left by me! As Nick gets older I am trying to be less panicky, which is easier to do now that water and solid food amuse and distract him.

In the end, I have given up on the electric pump and just use hand-expressing—it seems more effective and quicker.

The Corporate Culture

I have very supportive co-workers and have had no problems dashing off to express my milk, usually by warning, "I'm just going downstairs!" We have a "family officer" in our Human Resources team, and other mothers have also returned to work while breastfeeding. The corporation has a generous 12-week paid maternity or paternity leave, and my manager has been extremely flexible in allowing me to suggest my staged return to work and allowing work from home. My manager is supportive of me and others in our team and conscious of the impact our home life has on our work. In fact, we currently are working with Nick to try and establish better sleeping patterns and my manager has allowed me to take a week of unpaid leave on short notice. In addition, my work makes arrangements for child care and reserves places, allowing me to skip huge waiting lists.

I take Nick to work on occasion, too. When we were forming the larger team I am part of, we had a two-day session to discuss our group, our values, and our behaviors. Nick came with me and he was extremely well-behaved and accepted. The session was held at a venue within driving distance for me, instead of the more normal "get away" location that is usually used. Working in a team like this is great.

My Suggestions to Others

If possible, find out how your employer can help you before going on maternity leave. Talk about the need for appropriate space, privacy, power, a sink, and the need to take breaks at appropriate times. (Suggestions might include splitting your lunch break, taking additional time in a day, or working a longer day to accommodate pumping breaks.)

To make life easier for those to come, employers will do well to realize the make-up of a happy staff: employees who are relaxed about returning to work, able to express or feed their babies at work, and can take necessary time off. Employers will do well to remember that a happy staff is more productive. This benefits everyone. I don't think all employers really think through the value in retaining staff. The costs for a company are enormous, not just in finding a replacement, but in possible relocation, training, and a possible need to temporarily staff a role. The benefits of retaining skilled staff and making the workplace an environment people want to return to are not to be calculated purely in dollar terms.

Employers will do well to remember that a happy staff is more productive.

New Zealand

Early Childhood Development Specialist

Early Childhood Policies

Sarah E. Farquhar, Wellington

The good thing about being a woman today is that there are fewer obstacles to participation in the world of work. New Zealand was the first country in the world to give women the right to vote. Today all the top government positions in the country are held by women, including a female prime minister. It is not such a good thing for young children, however, because this usually means reduced opportunity to be breastfed and cuddled by their mothers, especially since there is not widespread support for breastfeeding in New Zealand child care services.

One would think that people with knowledge of child development, working in a profession that exists to support families with child care and early education, would be strong advocates of breastfeeding for young children. One would think people in this field would actively support mothers in developing this nurturing bond with their children. Unfortunately that is not the case. I have seen the barriers firsthand while trying to breastfeed my own children and working in the field of childhood development. Of particular surprise were the negative reactions I received to having my baby with me at an early childhood research conference. I was horrified when I read these comments on feedback forms:

- I would have appreciated it if you could have organized support/child care so that the baby wasn't at centre-stage.
- Found having a baby on stage distracting. Apart from that, great.
- Crèche? (daycare). Difficult to focus when baby is in front of audience.
- I would prefer not have babies, very distracting—also seems unhelpful for the presenter.

I quickly put the comments into perspective with the following thinking:

If it wasn't for me, the conference would never have happened as no one else was willing to put the work in.

My baby had sat on my hip and been delightful in the two or so hours prior to the opening of the conference when I was running around and organizing. At the end of the day as I put her in her car seat, she gave me a great smile and I knew she had enjoyed it. I felt great about having had her with me.

Because my baby was used to being breastfed on demand, when she wanted to nurse, I fed her. She preferred to fall asleep at the breast. I would not have considered introducing her to artificial formula and feeding from a bottle, not to mention learning to sleep on her own, just so she would be out-of-sight at a conference.

I think some were likely disturbed because I was publicly breastfeeding while simultaneously opening the conference and introducing the speaker. Out of an audience of 180, only a small number stated that they had a problem with my baby's presence.

I also gain perspective by remembering how my feelings about breastfeeding have evolved over time. When I reflect on the 23 years I have been working with young children, teaching the teachers, and researching early childhood education, I feel ashamed of my own lack of recognition of breastfeeding support as a fundamental issue for young children. It was not until after carrying out a small research study for Dr. Judith Galtry, who was researching breastfeeding and employer support, that I even realized breastfeeding support was an issue in the quality of child care services. Further, I assumed that the

New Zealand

In New Zealand, 57 percent of women are in the workforce; 14 or more weeks of maternity leave is paid by public funds; 91 days of parental leave is paid by public funds or up to one year unpaid leave; 14 days of paternity leave; no breastfeeding breaks are allowed.

lack of recognition for breastfeeding support in early childhood education policy was an unintentional oversight. However, I've come to realize that the issue of breastfeeding support is being intentionally ignored by the early childhood education community.

Breastfeeding is a major health concern and is a legitimate reason for families to have a genuine choice as to where and by whom their child will be cared for.

You see, the history of the growth of the child care movement in New Zealand mirrors the growth of the women's movement. Any official promotion that required early childhood services to implement supportive breastfeeding policies could be interpreted as a negative blow to the feminist, political, and economic interest in women's labor market participation. In other words, if the Ministry of Education or Government came out and said to all early childhood services that they should put in place policies to support mothers' breastfeeding—or if anyone suggests the possibility that perhaps there should be caution in the recommendation to place young infants in child care because of issues such as breastfeeding support—it would likely come under heavy criticism from trade unions, including the teachers' union, and liberal feminists. It would be perceived as reinforcing traditional social ideology that women's role is in the home with baby, and infringing on her right to participate in the labor market. But I hate to see women giving up breastfeeding because they are returning to work, they do not have support from their child care service to continue breastfeeding, and they do not know that they could be demanding that the child care service be breastfeeding-friendly.

And many are not breastfeeding-friendly. Because of the prevailing cultural beliefs in New Zealand, encouraging exclusive breastfeeding could be interpreted as a challenge to the political mantra that says good-quality child care provided by trained professionals can only be helpful and beneficial to children. However, we are not recognizing or acknowledging that a more cautious approach to promoting child care participation is needed, especially for infants. We know it is best for infant development and learning to receive one-to-one care, close parental contact, and to be breastfed. Breastfeeding is a major health concern and is a legitimate reason for families to have a genuine choice as to where and by whom their child will be cared for.

Going forward, I would like to see frank and honest discussion of biases surrounding breastfeeding. As I have become personally aware of them, I realize they had always surrounded me. About 12 years ago, before having my four children, I worked in a position as an early childhood lecturer at a teachers' college. A female student asked the college director to be allowed to continue her studies and bring her baby to class when it was born. There was a staff meeting to discuss this. The student was considered to be unreasonable in making this request because babies did not belong in class and it was assumed that it would be a disadvantage to other students whose learning would be distracted by the baby's presence. I sat in silence listening to the discussion and thinking that I needed to find a job somewhere else if I wanted to start a family. I wish I had spoken up.

I continue to notice at early childhood conferences and other meetings that I go to that it is rare for a young child to be present, and if there is a child it's usually mine. I still hear people saying things like, "It's too distracting and not fair on others who attend and want to be able to listen." But when I went to a La Leche League Conference last year, I was delighted to see so many babies and noted that indeed participants can still have serious discussions and be learning at the same time that they are breastfeeding and caring for their children. One mother was breastfeeding twins—one on each breast—and she was asking very thoughtful intelligent questions of the presenter. So to my early childhood colleagues, to education officials, and to the world, I say, "Please recognize that we can and must support breastfeeding for working women."

So to my early childhood colleagues, to education officials, and to the world, I say, "Please recognize that we can and must support breastfeeding for working women."

Part Six

Breastfeeding Friendly Employers

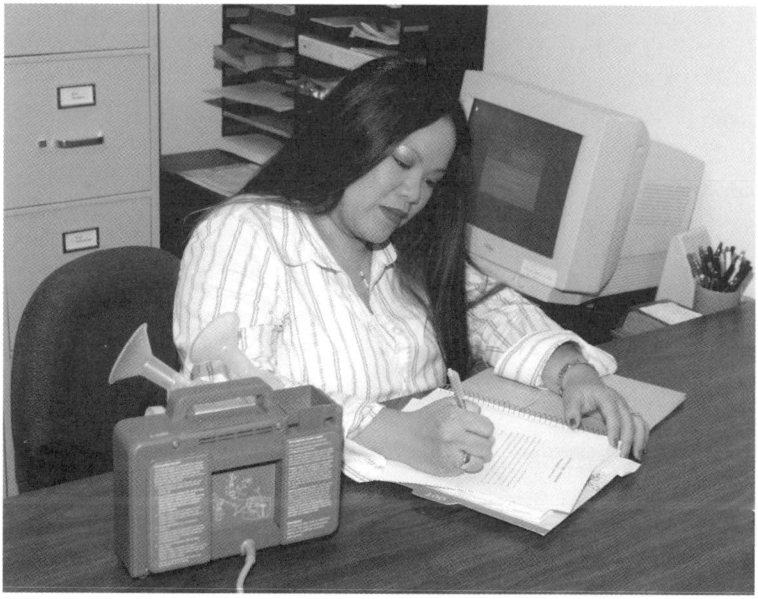

Pioneering a Better Workplace

The Los Angeles Department of Power and Water is a well-known employer in the world of corporate lactation, with good reason. They implemented a lactation program in the late 1980s and found surprising results. The department gained a three to one return on their investment due to savings from less parental absenteeism. More surprisingly, LADPW saw a 35 percent reduction in health care claims. Simply put, more breastfeeding mothers meant fewer sick babies. When illnesses did occur, only 25 percent of the absences were among mothers of breastfed babies—the other 75 percent were among women whose children were formula-fed.

Though these and similar results from other companies are impressive, many employers still are not rallying behind their breastfeeding employees. Decision-makers are not clued-in to the few simple changes it would take to reap significant financial benefits while helping nursing mothers and babies in the process. Many working, breastfeeding women instead lack a place to pump, work long hours away from their children, and often are misunderstood or discriminated against in the workplace.

Not all businesses are so uninformed. There are admirable employers worldwide that do support their breastfeeding employees. Altruism and core philosophy play some part in their motives, as a handful recognize the value in sustaining family-friendly policies. Some, like LADPW, see the benefits extend well beyond a clear conscience. In addition to reduced sick leave, implementing pro-breastfeeding policies also bolsters morale, increases retention rates, and in the end, saves piles of cash.

Enacting policies is important to success, but the policies must be backed by a company culture that deliberately encourages breastfeeding. Chris Mulford, Co-Coordinator of Women and Work Task Force in the World Alliance for Breastfeeding Action (WABA), emphasizes that it is also helpful for employers to keep these short-term needs in perspective. "Breastfeeding is not something to make a fuss about. It's something to help the employee with. After all, it's only a short period of time out of the time the company is going to be employing her."

In addition to reduced sick leave, implementing pro-breastfeeding policies also bolsters morale, increases retention rates, and in the end, saves piles of cash.

This section offers a glimpse at workplaces that are truly breastfeeding-friendly. Their efforts to accommodate nursing mothers are praiseworthy in the context of countries, companies, and laws that are often inexcusably ignorant of the benefits of breastfeeding to mothers, children, and workplaces.

We have highlighted a few of the ways that these companies support their employees in combining breastfeeding with work. Many of these efforts would be reasonably easy for others to consider.

Maternity leave. Providing paid maternity leave or offering additional leave to supplement the nationally mandated leave makes establishing the breastfeeding relationship much easier in the crucial early months.

Allow children at work. Permitting mothers to bring their children to work enables nursing on cue, and though complicated at times, can simplify life by alleviating the need for bottles, pumps, and scheduling. Most importantly, perhaps, it eliminates the concern and stress of being separated from a breastfeeding baby. Chris Mulford notes that the greatest difficulty a working, nursing mother has is worrying about whether or not her baby is being well cared for. Bringing the baby along is the surest way to eliminate that concern, which not only benefits breastfeeding, but can improve workplace performance.

On-site daycare. On-site daycares can provide women with ready access to their breastfeeding babies. With flexibility and encouragement, employees can breastfeed their babies on cue, decreasing or eliminating the need to pump. In addition, intermittent visits for mothers and babies can relieve some of the stress of separation.

Telecommuting and flex-time. Both working from home and/or having a fluid schedule allows mothers more flexibility and proximity to their children while lightening the stress of a rigid workday in which scheduled pumping is necessary.

Lactation facilities. Constant or intermittent proximity to the baby is not always possible. To maintain the breastfeeding relationship without frequent proximity, a woman must be dedicated to pumping. (At least in the early months.) Providing clean, private rooms for pumping is incredibly helpful to breastfeeding employees. By offering easily accessible lactation facilities and a culture supportive of using them, employers make breastfeeding success much more likely for their employees. A study by the *American Journal of Health Promotion* found that providing lactation programs for working women can increase their breastfeeding rates to the same level as non-working, breastfeeding women.

Lactation equipment. Some employers also provide complimentary breast pumps or other supplies. This supports the employee financially, but also sends a positive message about an employer's support for the breastfeeding relationship.

Mother-to-mother support. Employers can facilitate mother-to-mother support in several ways. Some employers allow lactation group meetings in which employees are permitted to meet during work or lunch hours.

Employers may also offer Intranet database systems that allow breastfeeding employees to communicate on issues as general as milk supply, or as specific to their workplace as corporate maternity leave policies.

Professional support. Some employers hire professional lactation consultants for breastfeeding employees to seek advice from. This is a helpful back-up for mothers, especially new ones, who may have questions or concerns.

References

Chen, R., Mrtek, M.B., and Mrtek, R.G. Comparison of maternal absenteeism an infant illness rates among breastfeeding and formula-feeding women in two corporations, *American Journal of Health Promotion*, Nov/Dec 1995,

Cohen, R. and Mrtek, M.B. Impact of two corporate lactation programs on the incidence and duration of breastfeeding by employed mothers, *American Journal of Health Promotion*, July/August 1994.

Washington, F. Los Angeles Department of Water and Power: Men have babies too. *Innovative Practices*. 13-14.

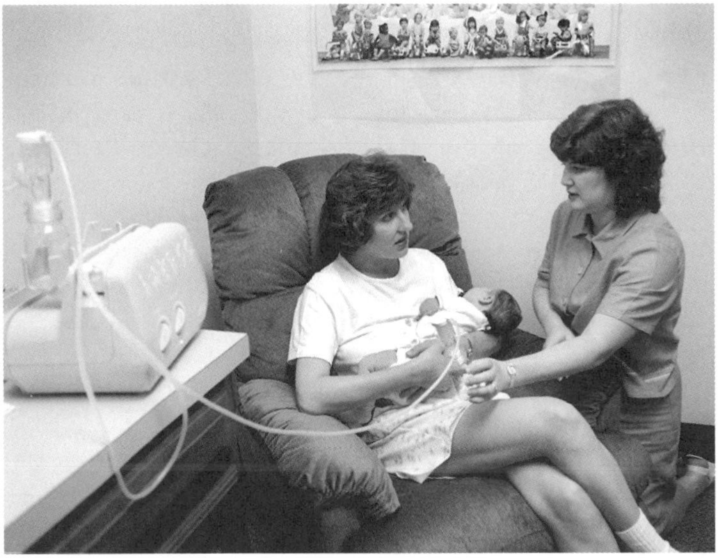

Award-Winning Workplace, Home to Healthy Families

Working mothers, you may want to sit down before reading this. There is an international software company based in North Carolina that is going to make you feel a little (okay, a lot) envious. SAS is a privately owned corporation that believes that a work/life balance makes for vibrant and productive employees. Get this. SAS employees enjoy a 35 hour workweek, receive free on-site health care, have a break room fully stocked with free snacks, plus an on-site gym and aquatic center. The list of benefits starts to look incredulous somewhere between an on-site farmers' market and the spa where employees can get lunch-hour facials, massages, and leg-waxing. That's just the beginning. SAS is unabashedly, shout-out-loud supportive of breastfeeding. The company culture does not whisper, "If you breastfeed, we will support you." It screams, "We want you to consider breastfeeding and we'll help you do it!"

And they do. SAS has a health care model that Corporate Health Services Manager, Gale Adcock, likens to a BMW. Some of the breastfeeding program options include: on-site Montessori daycare, five lactation experts, private offices, a lactation room equipped with a full-size electric pump, childbirth and breastfeeding classes, an active listserv for nursing employees, Nursing Buddies (a SAS network akin to a breastfeeding support system), breast pumps offered at cost, and company-wide recognition of World Breastfeeding Week. Really, the only difficult thing about the nursing program is finding someone to agree on which piece is most helpful.

At the top of everyone's list is the daycare. Breastfeeding employees at SAS are able to visit their children on-site in what all agree is a spectacular child care center. Not only do employees rave about the quality of care, they get a bargain. Comparable daycare in the area costs around $1,000 per month, per child. SAS parents pay $300.

Mothers are issued pagers and can be contacted when their baby shows signs of hunger.

Mothers are issued pagers and can be contacted when their baby shows signs of hunger. Women are then able to nurse in the breastfeeding lounge any time of day. (Non-breastfeeding mothers are free to come in to feed a bottle as well.) The nursing room, an ad-hoc support group at times, is equipped with seating for approximately eight mothers and has comfortable chairs, foot stools, and toys for older siblings who might also leave daycare to be with their mothers during the nursing breaks.

Sabrina Poteat, a project manager at SAS, has two daughters in SAS daycare and has breastfed them both without needing any bottles. Though not the case for all women, Sabrina's job makes it reasonably easy for her to zip over when her pager sounds. Daycare employees have accommodated her desire to breastfeed both girls. "They are very supportive of the fact that I want to nurse my child. They're very happy, too, because that is one less bottle for them to fix," she says.

With a higher than average ratio of 2.5 teachers for every six infants, plus the Montessori philosophy that every child has an individual set of needs, a child's unique needs are detected pretty quickly. Daycare Manager, Mary Brown, says that contrary to what one might believe, allowing for different feeding, sleeping, and playing schedules actually makes teachers' jobs easier. Unlike some daycares, SAS teachers do not mind having mothers pop in and out at different times of the day. In fact, the Montessori-certified teachers would not want it any other way. The teachers, many of whom have been at SAS for over 20 years, enjoy the varied pace of the day and find that children are happier all around. "I would never say that it is any hardship on us to page the mom. It is just not an issue," says Mary. In fact, Sabrina was once paged by a teacher with a friendly message: "You have got to come and see your child, she is playing in a mud puddle."

Of course, there are also the sick-kid phone calls that every working parent gets from time to time. When SAS employees have a sick child, they take a short walk to the free on-site health care center where their child is seen by one of four physicians or one of ten family nurse practitioners. Those same health practitioners may have seen their baby from birth and may have helped them to establish breastfeeding in the early days. Nancy Register, Family Nurse Practitioner, breastfeeding guru, and the woman credited with fueling SAS breastfeeding programs, feels this model of health care is ideal. "Because we are nurse practitioners, we can treat the mom and baby at the same time, on-site. If mom and baby have thrush, we can treat them both."

And both mother and baby will benefit from unlimited lactation consults whether they are on-site or regional. In fact, Sabrina Poteat credits Nancy Register with her early breastfeeding success. "I wasn't sure if my milk had come in. When my first child was one or two days old, I came in and Nancy weighed her for me. She made sure Alyssa was latching on right. She made sure my milk was coming in. And she called me afterwards to see how everything was going."

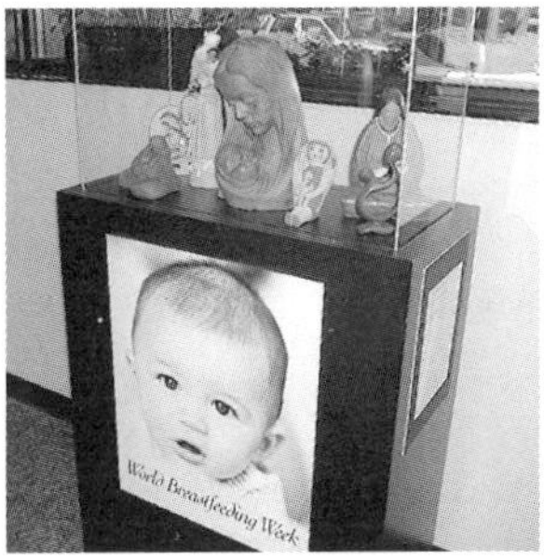

The health care team doesn't just make lactation consults, however. They honor World Breastfeeding Week once a year, often through displays of mother/child artwork and other activities that change annually. In addition, Nancy and others regularly teach the "Hey Baby Series," a succession of classes on birth and breastfeeding. The sixth and final class is for men only and helps husbands learn how to support their breastfeeding wives. The class is enormously popular, and according to Gale Adcock, has SAS veteran fathers waiting in line to be on the panel. "They all want to talk about breastfeeding success because, of course, they're so proud," she says. (At most recent count, 25 SAS babies are soon to be born.)

It's not just fathers helping fathers at SAS. Two simple but effective programs are in place that offer mother-to-mother support, without costing a dime. Nursing Buddies was created, and is largely run by, SAS employees. This program pairs new breastfeeding employees with experienced partners who can answer breastfeeding-related questions or offer moral support. Nancy Register coordinates the buddy selection process and makes deliberate pairings based on each woman's situation. A mother of twins, for instance, is often placed with another mother of twins. Or like Manya Mayes, women with similar concerns may be linked. "I had a cesarean birth and got hooked up with a Nursing Buddy who had also had a cesarean. She was able to offer me advice on positions that were good for avoiding the cesarean incision and those sorts of things. You've got that one-on-one with somebody that you can just call on and chat. It's a good line of support."

And if a Nursing Buddy can't answer a question at SAS, undoubtedly someone on the breastfeeding listserv can. This electronic bulletin board allows women to send queries out to the entire SAS breastfeeding population via computer. Sabrina Poteat laughs when she recalls the help she has sought over the years. "The listserv is just tremendous. I had an issue with my first child where she had gone nine days without having a bowel movement. I sent out a notice that said, 'Help my baby poop!' and I got 25 to 30 responses."

In addition to facilitating peer support, SAS offers employees a host of pump supplies, all at a discount. Women can buy breast pumps at cost and have them deducted through payroll. They can also purchase nursing bras, pump supplies, books, and other materials at a discount. For employees who pump, SAS will gladly put a lock on their office door before they return from maternity leave. (Yes, SAS culture dictates that almost all employees have their own private office.)

Not surprisingly, the SAS emphasis on work/life balance fares well with employees. "The whole philosophy of the company is that you have to keep the employees happy. And everyone here is happy. I've worked at IBM, AST Computers; I've worked at companies that were going under, companies that were starting out, and this is the only company that cares about its people. If you spend that amount of time and money training people, you want to keep them," says Sabrina Poteat. And keep them SAS does. Where normal turnover rates in the software industry range between 18 to 20 percent, SAS has turnover rates of three to five percent.

Not surprisingly, the SAS emphasis on work/life balance fares well with employees.

Employees know they have a good thing. If they should forget, a quick venture outside the SAS campus reminds them. "I don't tell people I work here anymore. They always say, 'Get me a job, man!' I used to dread going to parties, going out to picnics with my neighbors. You could just see the glint in their eye. They were hunting me down from across the room. Oh, and when I forget and wear a SAS t-shirt—you might as well put a bull's-eye on me," jokes Poteat.

Clearly no small secret on the East Coast, SAS has also been featured on "Oprah," "60 Minutes," and continually receives awards such as *Fortune* magazine's "100 Best Companies to Work for in America." It has been repeatedly listed by *Working Mother* as one of the 100 best companies for employed mothers. But SAS programs are not as out of reach as one might think. Gale Adcock often speaks to corporations about the SAS model. She reminds others that though it resembles a BMW now, it looked more like a Hyundai when it began 20 years ago.

"There are so many things that companies can do that add to the bottom line in terms of health care costs and in terms of productivity and loyalty that are so inexpensive. Breastfeeding is the one example that I always use. It is a very inexpensive program. A full-size electric pump and a private place to express milk—those are inexpensive things to do. But the goodwill that they engender is priceless. You just can't put a price tag on that," says Gale.

In fact, Nancy Register estimates that after the one time cost of a thousand dollars to set up their lactation room, expenditures to support the breastfeeding program are less than several hundred dollars per year. "Finances should not come into play as far as a company's support for breastfeeding. And some of the best features are free: the Nursing Buddies, the listserv. I think the least concern is financial." Her approach to breastfeeding support is pragmatic. "You see a need and you brainstorm, 'How can we fix this?' Then you figure out a way and you make it happen."

"Finances should not come into play as far as a company's support for breastfeeding."

Like Nancy and Gale, Sabrina Poteat thinks more employers should create family-friendly workplaces. "I hope companies actually see that people want more than just a high-paying job. Family life is important to a lot of people. There is no point in earning all of that money if you can't spend it. Or you wake up one morning and your kid is a stranger. SAS gives me the best of both worlds. I'm able to fulfill my career and I'm able to fulfill my family life, which to me, is more important than a career."

In fact, Sabrina says a company would have to triple her salary to entice her to leave SAS. Manya Mayes is an even tougher recruit. "To be honest, the likelihood of my leaving SAS...is zero. I'd have to win the lottery."

Winning the lottery? Many working mothers would say that she's already hit the jackpot.

MINNESOTA

Mayo Clinic

A Prescription for Happier, Healthier Working Mothers

"Breastfeeding and working at the Mayo Clinic have been going on for a very long time," says Tripp Welch, Mayo Clinic human resources section head. "Some of our lactation rooms date back to the early 1970s, and some of our buildings were clearly built with those rooms in mind."

Today, this world-class health care center features 26 lactation rooms purposefully placed throughout the Rochester campus. In 2003, the rooms were standardized, so breastfeeding employees can count on the same amenities in every room. That includes a lock on the door, at least one full-size Medela Classic pump, a recliner, sink, paper towels, sanitizer, soap, telephone, wall clock, consistent interior and exterior signage, and counter space for organizing pump parts and pieces. Women only need to bring the universal pumping system and their personal tubing or attachments. And they can purchase these things at two on-site Mayo Clinic stores.

"The goal was that no room would be greater than a five-minute distance from any work location," says Mayo Clinic lactation consultant Elizabeth LaFleur. "We want this to be something women can easily accomplish during a break."

Jenika Johnson, a nurse working 12-hour shifts in the neuroscience intensive care unit, appreciates this strategic planning. She credits the convenience of the rooms for the fact that she is still nursing her 19-month-old son, Cade. After all, it would have been impossible for Jenika to express milk three to four times during every busy nursing shift without plenty of pumps in proximity.

And Jenika isn't the only happy new mother at Mayo. By all accounts, the lactation rooms are busy. Very busy. In fact, in some work areas, women have started posting sign-up sheets on the doors of "their" rooms, so everyone in the area can schedule pumping time in advance.

Lactation support doesn't end here, though. The Mayo Clinic stores rent Medela Lactina electric dual pumps for a month at a time, so women can pick one up before a business trip or vacation. Breastfeeding women also benefit from Mayo-approved educational materials on pumping, storing, handling, and transporting milk, as well as prenatal and postpartum breastfeeding classes and two full-time, on-site lactation consultants. These registered nurses help with all sorts of pumping predicaments—such as when to start pumping before returning to work, how to configure baby's feeding schedule, and what to do about changing milk supply.

"We haven't spent time tracking data on our lactation rooms, because our board of physician-scientists has never questioned their value."

New mothers at Mayo have other benefits, too. They're offered six weeks paid or partially paid maternity leave, plus a child care referral program, backup child care, a sick-child child care center staffed by registered nurses, and a 24-hour nurse phone line for those middle-of-the-night maternal worries.

"When you're a mother, it's already a tough decision to come back to work, and if a mother is forced to choose between a child and work, we know which one will win," Tripp Welch says.

Are these programs good for business, too? Tripp believes the answer is yes, but he has no numbers to prove it. "We haven't spent time tracking data on our lactation rooms, because our board of physician-scientists has never questioned their value," Tripp says. "They've been a no-brainer from the beginning. And these policies aren't a public relations thing. We didn't implement them with too much hoopla, and we don't expect a lot of acknowledgement for them. If you're not a breastfeeding mother or her spouse, you probably haven't even noticed our lactation rooms. We intentionally put them in discreet locations and discreetly identified them. We do it because it's the right thing to do. We're a health care institution. We understand why it's important to support a mother in her decision to breastfeed."

That view is part of the value system that exists throughout Mayo Clinic. And employees like Lacey Hart, a planning and process analyst in the human resources department, say that kind of support and open acceptance is even more important than the well-stocked lactation rooms.

"I read about women who were afraid to go back to work, because they weren't sure how to approach their managers about breastfeeding, but that's not something I had to think about at all," Lacey says, in front of her male manager. "I knew I wanted to breastfeed, and I started talking about it before I went on maternity leave."

"Since this is a medical institution, people are much more aware of the benefits of breastfeeding—but also the detriments of not breastfeeding."

In fact, when Lacey had a problem with excess lipase in her milk at eight months, she found a solution by asking around the office. Now, she's still nursing 13-month-old daughter, Clara. "When I discovered the problem, I started asking questions at work, and I immediately had physicians, lactation consultants, and co-workers helping me," Lacey says. "Since this is a medical institution, people are much more aware of the benefits of breastfeeding—but also the detriments of not breastfeeding. And that openness and encouragement make me more committed to being here. It allowed me to come back to work full-time. It also means that I have less guilt being at work, because I'm able to work and breastfeed my child."

Jenika Johnson understands this sentiment well. She spent much of her maternity leave feeling guilty and nervous about returning to work, because she wasn't sure she could successfully juggle breastfeeding and working. Luckily, she didn't have any reason to be concerned. "When I think about all of the time I have put in pumping milk, keeping track of milk, cleaning my supplies, and everything else, I can't believe how many hours it must be," Jenika says. "But all of that work makes me feel good because I'm doing it all for my son. It would be easy to give up and just buy a can of formula, but there is something special about the fact that while I'm away, my child is getting bigger and fatter, and I know he's not eating anything but what I'm giving him. And I feel Mayo is making a huge effort to help me to do this."

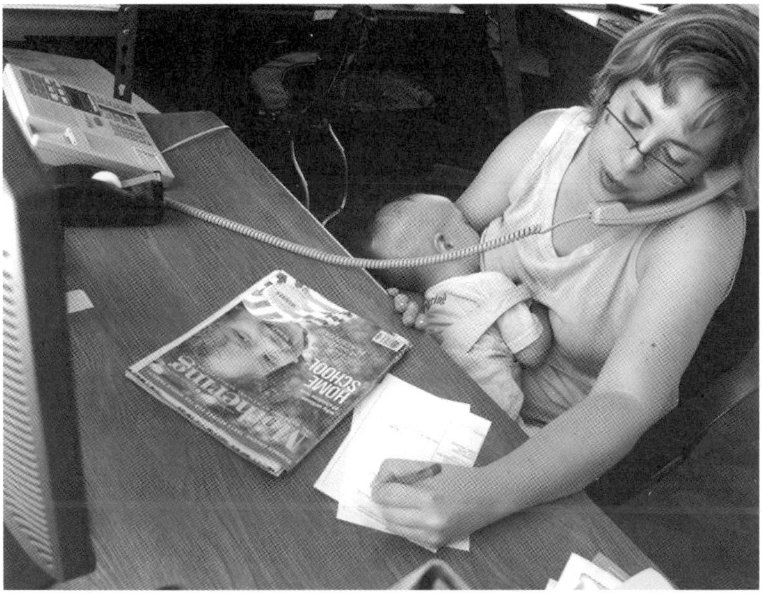

Mothering Mamas Enjoy a Progressive, Productive Workplace

This is not your ordinary workplace. Yes, there are computers and desks and filing cabinets, but there is something else, too. There is a basket of toys, a pile of children's books, and laughter. Most strikingly, there are babies and children milling about who play with those toys and read those books.

A Natural Family Living magazine with a readership of 250,000, the *Mothering* magazine office is a warm, familiar place to its employees' children. And why wouldn't it be? Parents bring their children with them to work as often as they like. In the most progressive and mind-bending policy imaginable, Peggy O'Mara, Editor and Publisher of *Mothering* magazine, tailors each employee's guidelines to his or her individual needs. That need, especially for a breastfeeding woman, is often to be with her child. A job at *Mothering* makes that possible. While some employers accommodate breastfeeding employees to help with recruitment or to reduce parental absence, Peggy does it because she feels, quite simply, that it is the way the world should work.

As a result, a job at *Mothering* magazine is a highly coveted prize, and a tough one to surrender. *Mothering* is a great employer for a breastfeeding mother, who can be with her baby all day, and can kiss that pump goodbye. Perhaps most ideal, it allows Peggy to advance her deeply held notion that mothers, with their children beside them, can be part of a productive workforce.

It allows Peggy to advance her deeply held notion that mothers, with their children beside them, can be part of a productive workforce.

"Bringing children to work is definitely something we encourage. I've never been able to put a policy in writing because it is something I have to work out with each mom," says Peggy.

One policy that is official is maternity leave. *Mothering* employees are granted eight weeks of paid leave, an almost unprecedented gift for a US mother. (And Peggy is considering increasing it to 12 weeks.) Once maternity leave is over, employees enjoy varied work schedules. Some work from home, some work at *Mothering* headquarters during the hours their children are in school. Other employees, especially those with young children, tote the little ones along every day.

"When I first bought the magazine we met once a week, brought our kids, and then went home and did our work. I've kind of always had that model and that's the way I ran the business and why I wanted to have a business. I just wanted to be with my kids. I want to give others that opportunity, too," says Peggy.

Candace Walsh, who works at *Mothering* as the product fulfillment manager, is seizing that chance. A former freelance writer, she says she would not have considered a job that required her to be separated from 11-month-old Nathaniel and so far, she has been pleased at how well it has worked to bring him along. "It's pretty simple. Right now Nathaniel is sitting on the floor playing with a toy, having a cracker. He's coming over to me and is probably going to want to nurse. And I'm still getting my work done," she says.

To many employers, the idea of having a baby crawling around the workplace, or nursing in the break room seems radical. Peggy insists that it is the severance of mother and child that is a new and odd phenomenon, not mothers working with their children.

"The modern workplace segments those two parts of our lives. It's not about work, it's about being separated. Women have always worked—in the fields, as hunter gatherers, but they have had their babies strapped to them. They were never separated. We have always worked—when we were making food, cleaning things around the house. Having our kids with us is what I believe in really strongly and how I want to lead my life."

As a result, *Mothering* magazine headquarters is buzzing with little feet, tiny voices, and breastfeeding mothers. Though idyllic sounding, the arrangement requires honest communication and constant evaluation to succeed.

"I think it would be hard for people who weren't comfortable having real conversations with their employees. The manager and the moms have to be able to talk quite honestly, I think. They must be willing to cooperate and work problems out, which I find most people are."

That kind of honesty goes a long way in working through a range of issues from a wandering toddler to a constantly crying baby. Though there is no realm in which children are off-limits, Peggy does not hesitate to ask someone to leave if the kids are being disruptive. Mindful of everyone's rights, the children are not allowed to rule the workplace.

Peggy finds, like La Leche League meetings or life in general, some women and children fare better in a group than others. Among managers and employees, between colleagues, and especially from parent to child, candor and negotiation are paramount. The flexibility works well when boundaries are known, set, and constantly evaluated. Despite occasional problems or mismatches, Peggy is committed to fostering a workplace that does not insist on separating mothers from their children.

Candace Walsh, who is also mother to three-year-old Honorée, brings both children to work when her daughter is not in preschool. Things can get, "a little more hectic," with two children. Because she is a new employee, Candace and her daughter are still settling in. And Honorée, like most children, is exploring her boundaries. When necessary, Candace explains plainly to her daughter, "If you act like this, Mommy won't want to bring you here next time. You love it here, so how can you act so that mommy wants to bring you again?"

Fortunately, Honorée is so pleased to be playing with her friends, Candace says she does not often interfere with her work. "[The children] really just have their own little community. As long as she's got buddies to play with, forget it—she's gone!" Clearly a benefit for the children, the socialization many learn in daycare is available here, with the added perk of having mother within arm's reach.

Ana June, publications editor for *Mothering* and mother of four, enjoys being close to her kids during the day, but acknowledges that organization and foresight are needed to bring children to work. In fact, she feels most of the problems she encounters can be avoided by planning ahead.

"My bad days are usually my own fault because I am not prepared or I have not taken care of myself.... Having a routine helps. If I really prepare ahead of time for a day with kids in the office, it makes things go more smoothly," says Ana. There have been days when Ana has been so busy getting her four children out the door that she has forgotten to feed herself. By packing school bags for the older children and gathering office toys for the youngest each night, the whole family has a better start to the day.

As summer approaches, Ana's older three children will be out of school. Rather than having all four kids in the office, Ana will spend the summer months working from home. She admits that having the flexibility to manipulate her schedule around her children's lives is a privilege. And it is one that she does not take for granted. "I do appreciate my job, very much," she says.

Ana is not the only grateful one. *Mothering* magazine's breastfeeding employees are able to nurse on cue. Neither the mothers nor their babies suffer from worries about separation. The magazine, as one might expect, has no problem retaining qualified employees. In fact, Peggy jokes, "I can't get rid of people!"

The magazine, as one might expect, has no problem retaining qualified employees.

Colleagues develop bonds deeper than ordinary co-worker relationships. A large "family," they routinely keep an eye on each other's children when one of them has to run to the printer or the bathroom. Even those who do not have children enjoy holding and playing with the kids, and many report that stress-levels plummet at the sight or sound of a giggling baby.

The magazine editor who began a business 29 years ago on her living room couch has stayed true to her founding ideals. "I don't want the parents to dominate, but then I don't want these precious children running around to think the world revolves around them, either. I just want to bring them into life, and then they learn to be part of life," says Peggy.

What she has always felt and doggedly models is, "Look, we can still be with our kids and get a lot done. Isn't that great? "

Yes, it is. It is indeed.

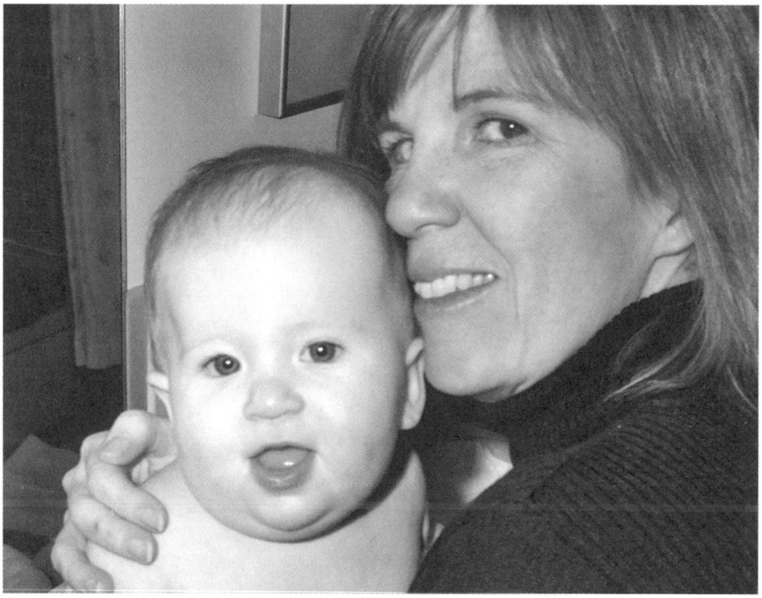

Cost Savings Promote Health

CIGNA Corporation is saving tens of thousands of dollars every year. Their money-saving secret? A corporate lactation program that is backed by a positive corporate culture. If it sounds simple, that's because it is. Like any good insurance provider, this one knows about cost-savings gained through health promotion.

"We're a health care company, and it's pretty obvious that breastfeeding is a health-promotion effort," says Catherine L. Hawkes, CIGNA's benefits strategy director. "I think it's pretty easy for us to get behind it."

CIGNA's lactation program, which was established in the early 1990s at the request of female employees, is designed to support women even before they give birth. "That's an important feature of our program compared to some of the others I've seen," says Catherine. "It's really important that people get accurate information about breastfeeding early on in the process."

The lactation program is well-advertised within the company, and a one-year study conducted by the UCLA Center for Healthier Children, Families and Communities in the late 1990s found that women enrolled in the program ranked it second behind their spouses as an influence on their decision to initiate breastfeeding.

"The other thing that our study showed is that breastfeeding has historically been limited to college-educated, middle-income, and upper-income women, and that by offering a program such as the one we have, we actually eliminated the cultural disparity," says Catherine Hawkes. "We see that we have breastfeeding occurring in all of our different salary levels."

Women who choose to enroll in the lactation program do so during their second or third trimesters and are given educational materials and immediate access to a lactation consultant. This ensures that women who experience problems in the early days of breastfeeding have the support they need.

Women enrolled in the program ranked it second behind their spouses as an influence on their decision to initiate breastfeeding.

Jacqueline Hennessy, a product manager and the mother of an 11-month-old daughter, benefited from that early support. She was unable to nurse for a couple of days because of post-delivery problems, and her daughter was fed from a bottle in the hospital. "In the beginning for me it was pretty difficult and scary," she says. "I was afraid she would never nurse, and I was very weak, and it was helpful to have an advocate."

Her daughter did learn to nurse, and when Jacqueline returned to work, she was given access to a lactation room and a full-size breast pump, all the supplies needed to use the pump, a carrying case, and access to a refrigerator for storing her milk. She also found that her co-workers viewed pumping as no big deal. "They really set it up that in our culture here at work that is accepted and normal," she says. "You see a lot of women running around in our building with a purple bag. You know where they're going."

The women are free to manage the lactation rooms however they see fit. When the rooms are in high demand, women set up a schedule and start reserving times. There is no formal peer mentoring program at CIGNA, but women form those relationships on their own, according to Rebecca McClain, a financial analysis senior specialist who is the mother of a two-year-old with another child on the way. "You get to talking and hit the room at the same time every day and really build some friendships that way," she says.

All of these things combined—the educational materials, the availability of a lactation consultant, the lactation rooms and equipment, the company culture that views breastfeeding as natural—result in six- and 12-month breastfeeding statistics that are much higher than the national average. The UCLA study found that breastfeeding duration for women enrolled in CIGNA's lactation program was 72.5 percent at six months compared to that year's national average of 21.1 percent of employed new mothers. At 12 months, 36 percent were still breastfeeding, compared to the 10.1 percent national average of employed new mothers.

Rebecca McClain credits the convenience offered by the on-site breast pumps with helping her breastfeed longer. "I had originally set a goal that I would breastfeed my daughter for 12 months, and that after that we would see how it goes," she says. "And I not only continued to breastfeed her past 12 months, I continued to pump and use the lactation room until she was about 17 months, and then I weaned her at about 21 months."

That figures out to be a lot of pumping sessions. According to Catherine Hawkes, there is the occasional question from a new employee about all the pumping going on in the lactation rooms. "We'll walk through the program and talk about the fact that this is something we're committed to as a corporation and that I have seen no mother take advantage of the time," she says. "I think that women are very grateful to have the opportunity to do it, and once I explain how efficient it is, and how the work gets done, I don't hear anything else," she says.

"My message to people is that these programs are not difficult to administer, and they're not expensive."

The mothers are, in fact, very grateful and very determined not to take advantage. "I think it was always in the back of my head that I felt like I was getting special treatment, and I tried to make sure that other people didn't feel that way," says Rebecca McClain. "I just rearranged my schedule to make it so that I was still putting in the hours that I needed to, and I would work from home if I had something big going on."

Jacqueline Hennessy is also careful to get in all her hours, even going so far as to print out emails to read while she pumps, but she feels that employees are not the only ones to benefit from the program. "Now it's 11 months after my daughter was born and seven months since I've been back to work, and I'm a functioning, contributing, productive member of this team. To replace me would have been costly for them," she says. "I think it really benefited CIGNA as well. I think they would say so. Obviously, they say so by continuing the program."

Catherine Hawkes agrees. "My message to people is that these programs are not difficult to administer, and they're not expensive," she says. "If you want to have a program that builds employee loyalty and gets people who are productive at work, this should be one of the programs that you consider."

Companies may stand to gain more than employee loyalty and productivity. According to the UCLA study, CIGNA realized an annual savings of $240,000 in health care expenses for breastfeeding mothers and their children and $60,000 through reduced absenteeism among breastfeeding mothers. The study also found that pharmacy costs for breastfed children were lower because they required 62 percent fewer prescriptions.

"Breastfeeding is a natural part of the cycle of life."

However you measure it, one thing is obvious, as stated so eloquently by Rebecca McClain: "Breastfeeding is a natural part of the cycle of life, and if companies embrace it instead of sticking [employees] in some dark corner and ignoring them, it's to everyone's benefit."

Guatemala

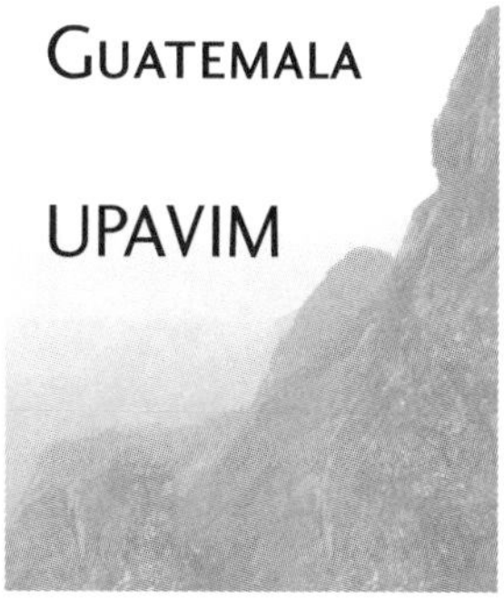

UPAVIM

Employing Women, Improving Lives

Picture a household where the one thing stopping a mother from having running water for her children is the amount of money needed to buy a shovel and a pipe. Next, add a shortage of jobs, lack of reliable child care, and a baby who needs to nurse. Suddenly a simple solution seems out of reach. Many such dilemmas exist in the small community of La Esperanza, outside Guatemala City, but that is changing. And it is changing, thanks to UPAVIM.

This nonprofit group, which stands for Unidas Para Vivir Mejor, or United for a Better Life, was founded by ten women in 1990, with an ambitious goal: to empower area women and improve their quality of life. It's working. Women of La Esperanza are gaining control of their lives, even in the face of rampant unemployment, lack of affordable health care, and malnutrition. How is this small nonprofit turning the community around? By allowing women to work—with their children at their sides.

And in La Esperanza, being able to bring a baby to work is more than a nice perk. Most women are not able to work outside the home for lack of affordable child care. In addition, there are few jobs available; those that do exist require a long, costly commute by bus. Many of the community's unemployed men struggle with alcoholism, and as a result, add to the already heavy family burdens.

For these reasons, UPAVIM never debated whether to "permit" women to bring their babies and children to work. It is understood that without that privilege, the women simply would not be there. Mimi de Maza, Training Coordinator of La Leche League International Child Survival Project in Guatemala (1988-1992) states it clearly, "Mothers have no other option. If they want to work outside their homes, they have to take their children."

UPAVIM employees, with their children beside them, perform a variety of jobs. Some make crafts such as baskets, jewelry, and dolls; some sell the crafts. Others run the nonprofit administratively. Regardless of their position, all of these women bring their children along. And they do so gladly.

UPAVIM never debated whether to "permit" women to bring their babies and children to work. It is understood that without that privilege, the women simply would not be there.

"We are happy and we work well because we know our babies are safe," says Angela Bailon, a bookkeeper at UPAVIM. Until they crawl, babies are always with their mothers, often sleeping atop a desk in a handmade basket or playing with one of the nearby handmade toys. When babies are hungry or tired, mothers simply stop their work and nurse. Naturally, there are times when having an infant nearby is challenging. Angela notes that it is not always simple. "Sometimes my baby cries for other reasons besides hunger and I have to stop and rock him. Or, sometimes I am on the phone when he wakes up and I can't go to him immediately." Despite the difficulty, Angela says she feels very fortunate to always know her baby is safe and well-nourished. And, being well-fed is not something that can be taken for granted in this community. Maryanne Stone-Jimenez, Director of La Leche League International Child Survival Project in Guatemala (1988-1992), says many homes in La Esperanza do not have running water. Under these circumstances infant formula is not a safe option. In addition, because formula is so expensive, the powder is sometimes diluted to make it last longer. This dangerous, potentially life-threatening practice makes UPAVIM's support for breastfeeding a truly lifesaving gift.

The organization is supportive of older babies and children, as well. Once little ones are crawling, they are moved to UPAVIM's on-site daycare for safety reasons. The daycare, which currently cares for 65 children, is an inviting room staffed with one caretaker for every five babies. It is a short walk from the work area. Employees are encouraged to breastfeed their babies as often as needed, with no limits on their daily breastfeeding breaks. In fact, daycare providers gladly call mothers to nurse when a child shows signs of hunger. Always mindful of breastfeeding's health benefits, administrators encourage it as much and as long as possible. "If a mother is hired, she automatically can use the day nursery. We know breastfeeding is best and therefore we support it," says Mimi de Maza.

UPAVIM is structured to sustain a healthy community. Children are cared for and educated from the proceeds of this nonprofit, a direct result of the employees' efforts. Older children benefit from a Montessori preschool free of charge. The cost of running and maintaining the preschool is paid for entirely out of UPAVIM profits, which makes the employees' work all the more meaningful.

Once their children have reached school age, they can attend UPAVIM's Alternative Learning Center. According to Mimi de Maza, The Alternative Learning Center was created by UPAVIM "to offer children from La Esperanza and neighboring communities a school that aims to inspire in children a desire for learning so that they will keep studying their entire life." It also aims to teach them "to resolve interpersonal conflicts, to respect their peers without discriminating according to race or gender, and to create within them a commitment to their community and their country."

Always mindful of breastfeeding's health benefits, administrators encourage it as much and as long as possible.

UPAVIM employees can send their child to Alternative Learning Center for a monthly fee of US $3.25 (or Q. 25.00) a month. Many children are also offered scholarships through UPAVIM. With all of this plus a healthy sense of self-esteem, UPAVIM employees hope to see their children "achieve their full potential, live in harmony, and solve many of the problems that characterize [their] lives in La Esperanza."

UPAVIM employees are hopeful. Their small impoverished community, which began as a squatter settlement on the outskirts of Guatemala City, is now realizing great improvement. Residents whose homes were initially built of cardboard and tin are now living in homes constructed of cement block. Many of their unemployed have learned skills and earn a steady income. They have a health clinic, schools, and confidence. Their secret weapon: a group of motivated women, a little opportunity, and a safe place for their children.

Carlson Companies

Family-Owned Company with Family-Focused Benefits

Carlson Companies senior training consultant, Michelle Wuollet, regularly schedules a lunch meeting with her team and a special guest: her eight-month-old son, Garrett. The meeting logistics are easy for Michelle. She simply picks Garrett up from the on-site child care center and carries him over to the cafeteria.

"My team is always asking when they get to have lunch with Garrett again," Michelle says. "Carlson is a very family-oriented organization. In this environment, bringing your son to lunch is not considered strange or inappropriate."

Just the opposite is true. Carlson Companies is a global player in the marketing, travel, and hospitality industries. Carlson brands and services employ about 190,000 people in 140 countries and include such well-known names as Radisson Hotels & Resorts, T.G.I. Friday's, and Carlson Wagonlit Travel. Still, this sizable enterprise is also a privately held, family-owned organization that puts a focus on family.

"Our vision is a great place for great people to do great work," says

Susan MacHolda, senior director of work/life diversity. "We truly value family, and we want to make sure we're helping our families balance work and life in whatever stage of life they're in. So we offer workshops on retirement planning and caring for aging parents. And we offer flexibility and support to our new mothers as they nurture and nurse their little ones."

This support begins with ErgoMOMics—a one-hour class that's designed to help expectant mothers understand how to adjust their chairs and work stations to accommodate their burgeoning bellies. For pregnant colleagues, this class is also a place to learn stretching exercises and to bond over back pain.

The next supportive gesture is a new mom or dad care package, which is sent home as soon as an employee fills out a maternity or paternity leave request. (Company policy guarantees six weeks paid maternity leave for new moms and one week for new dads.) This insulated cooler bag contains information explaining the leave-of-absence process, plus a congratulatory card and lots of new-parent goodies, including a subscription to *Working Mother* magazine, and a baby t-shirt with the Carlson company logo. The whole package is intended to let employees know that the organization is excited about "a new addition to the Carlson family."

Five years ago, Carlson Companies introduced flexible work arrangements such as job sharing, telecommuting, and compressed workweeks.

This thoughtful gesture is also a sign of the ongoing support that new mothers can expect when they return to work. Five years ago, Carlson Companies introduced flexible work arrangements such as job sharing, telecommuting, and compressed workweeks. Today, most employees take advantage of these policies, but they've proved to be a big bonus for women returning from maternity leave.

New mothers can also book time in any of the five lactation rooms, which are scattered around campus. Nicole Dombrowski, a work/life diversity rewards and recognition specialist, has been booking time in these rooms for the last six months, and she's still successfully nursing nine-month-old son Connor. "My goal is to nurse for a whole year, and the people in my department have been really supportive," Nicole says. "A month ago, we had a two-day, off-site meeting at a convention center, and I worked with the person who coordinated the event to secure a room for me to pump. I had to leave the meeting twice a day, but my colleagues were fine with the fact that I had to miss out on some things to do what I needed to do."

Carlson Companies is serious about supporting its breastfeeding mothers. The five on-site lactation rooms include soft lighting, a radio, a comfortable rocking chair, and a refrigerator to store milk. One of the rooms is located at the on-site child care center, and it was designed so mothers could go to the center and nurse their babies right there.

Michelle Wuollet took advantage of both options—pumping milk and nursing on-site. And she credits the child care center staff for making nursing possible. "They would actually call me when Garrett woke up from a nap and let me know that he was ready to eat, so I could go over there if it worked with my schedule," she says. "They were the ones who offered to call me, and they made it clear that I was welcome to come over any time."

For obvious reasons, on-site child care centers like this are a boon to breastfeeding mothers. But they're great for mothers of older children and dads, too, especially when combined with a company culture that encourages work hour visits. At Carlson, there are a lot of parents—both mothers and dads—who routinely go over to the child care center for lunch. And Carlson promotes these visits by offering lunchtime classes at the center on parenting topics.

"These programs help us retain really good people who are going through various stages of life and looking for some support and flexibility."

It's no wonder that the child care center has been immensely popular since it opened five years ago. A third-party group facilitates and manages the accredited center, with capacity for 119 children from infant to preschool age. But Carlson parents also have a voice in the process. Every other month, the center's management team meets with a group of Carlson parent representatives who have children enrolled at the center. Together, they plan events and discuss important issues.

Parents like Michelle Wuollet couldn't be more pleased. "Garrett has a busier calendar than I do," she says. "Last week was Color Week, so they dressed in a different color each day and had color-coded toys for the day. The staff also works on developmental milestones, and we hold regular conferences with Garrett's primary caregiver. Having this great arrangement is the one thing that convinced me to come back to work."

And that's a big win for Carlson Companies. Because of the organization's size, it is a challenge to try to develop progressive and aggressive programs that meet employee needs. But feedback surveys make it clear that the family-focused programs are working.

"These programs help us retain really good people who are going through various stages of life and looking for some support and flexibility," Susan MacHolda says. "We also achieve greater productivity. When a new mother comes back to work, we want to make it easy for her to visit her child in the child care center or use the lactation room to pump milk, because we know these things are important to her. It all comes down to trust. We trust our employees, and they in turn trust us."

New York

Eastman Kodak Corporation

A Picture of Health and Happiness

When Theresa Mott became pregnant, she was surprised to discover that her employer cared to know. It turns out they wanted to make sure there were no job responsibilities that would prevent her from having a healthy pregnancy. Oh, and they also wanted to give her a free breast pump. Eastman Kodak, the international corporation known for making film and cameras, is also earning a reputation for helping its breastfeeding employees. And while the support is a huge boon to Kodak employees and their babies, Kodak feels it is also helping them create a happier, healthier, and more diverse workforce.

Dr. Wayne Lednar, Medical Director for Eastman Kodak, says the company started the Nursing Mothers' Program in 1995 in order to support the American Academy of Pediatrics clear recommendations for best infant feeding practices. But there were other reasons, too. "Not only is it good nutrition, but healthier babies are also less likely to have parents take them to the pediatrician, which results, of course, in reduced parental absence time," says Dr. Lednar.

In addition to early prenatal, job-specific counseling, Kodak offers widely available private lactation rooms, a company-wide database which all nursing mothers can visit to ask questions or seek support from each other, and a free Medela Pump in Style double electric breast pump.

The pump, worth about $300, is the first valuable tool in making mothers aware of Kodak's Nursing Mothers' Program, according to Dr. Lednar. When mothers receive their new pump they are also given information on what to expect when combining breastfeeding and work. "Word has gotten around and [the complimentary pump] is something that helps in the recruitment of new moms into the program," says Dr. Lednar. Once involved in the program, new mothers soon notice other benefits.

Theresa Mott, a software engineer at Kodak, soon discovered the lactation facilities and credits the rooms as a critical tool in her breastfeeding success. "The breast pump was an extra perk. But, if I always had to search for a room, or pump in a restroom, I might have been discouraged by now and I might have given up. It would've been difficult," she says.

Kodak's company culture is one that matter-of-factly supports breastfeeding.

The lactation facilities, spaced throughout the Kodak campus, are accessible only by key or code. Though the rooms seat two, many employees enjoy a hidden benefit in the relative lack of privacy.

"Oddly enough, one of the things I find helpful is that the lactation facility is a common room. It offers the chance to talk with the other women who are also there. Amazingly, it is a great way to connect with new mothers," says Anne Bohan, a product line manager at Kodak.

Another less subtle form of peer support at Kodak can be found through the Nursing Mothers' Database. The Intranet system is an electronic bulletin board that allows women to communicate with each other using their computers at work. It was initially created at the urging of breastfeeding employees who were not comfortable using the lactation consultant that Kodak provided.

"Women were looking for advice, but often felt uncomfortable calling a stranger. When we created this bulletin board for sharing of personal experiences with each other, it really took off. It's the mother-to-mother support, but it's also that the others are also in a working environment that pertains to the pressures of the day. It tends to make the advice much more useful," says Dr. Lednar.

Of course, the pump, the rooms, and the database would all be useless in an environment where employees were discouraged from utilizing them. Kodak's company culture is one that matter-of-factly supports breastfeeding.

"I work for a woman. She absolutely knows I'm breastfeeding. I need to take off three times a day [to pump], so it is known that— 'I'm going to leave you all,' and I just get up and leave when necessary," says Bohan.

Dr. Lednar echoes that sentiment. "In ten years, I have never heard a comment about a woman who appears to be away [pumping] too often. Our supervisors are really very, very accommodating of this. They see it as a good thing for the mother and her baby." Kodak has found that employees respect and appreciate supervisors who are supportive of their personal needs. "Just being flexible about this has worked well for us," says Dr. Lednar.

And it needs to work well. As it turns out, Kodak's product line is evolving to accommodate the digital age. As they delve into health care, digital x-rays, and other electronic product lines, Kodak's need for a diverse workforce is paramount. Simply put, they need young employees—those same young employees who are often starting families. Based in Rochester, New York, Kodak does not have a geographical edge in recruiting a fresh tech-savvy workforce. They are finding, however, that caring for employees and their families helps meet their recruitment needs.

Dr. Lednar is proud of the fact that employees consistently express their appreciation for the Nursing Mothers' Program.

"As a company offers the kind of support that is relevant to the demographic that it is building a workforce around, it begins to distinguish itself. People do come, and they appreciate it," says Dr. Lednar.

While nice for recruitment, that support is priceless to a mother trying to maintain a breastfeeding relationship while working. Dr. Lednar is proud of the fact that employees consistently express their appreciation for the Nursing Mothers' Program. Further, employees report that they are able to breastfeed as long as they want.

And while it is important that Kodak's Medical Director approve of their program, the best evaluation, perhaps, is the sigh of a satisfied mother. Six months after returning to work, first-time mother Anne Bohan is pleased. "It's hard enough coming back to work. Kodak has made it a little less traumatic. You hear all of the stories about not keeping up milk supply, but I am able to keep up. I strongly encourage others to try it."

What Working Mothers Need to Know

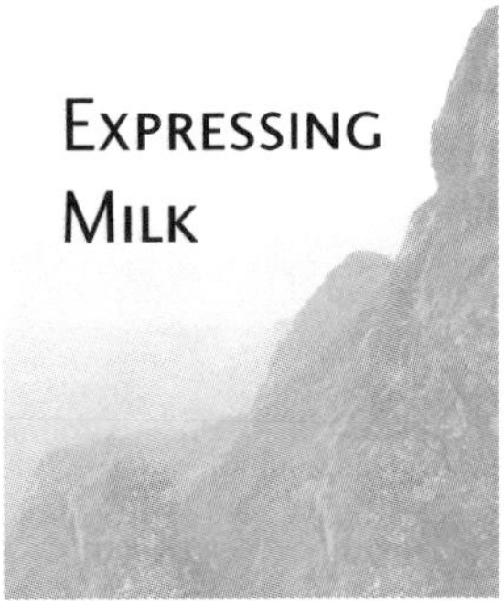

Expressing Milk

Choosing a Breast Pump

The breast pump is a tool many working mothers have a love-hate relationship with. You may tire of lugging it to and from work, cleaning it, and looking for missing parts; pumping can truly be a hassle. However, you'll probably soon learn to appreciate the efficiency with which you will be able to express milk for your baby. Despite the initial expense, pumping your milk is healthier and more economical than using formula. Below are some guidelines that will help you find the right pump for your situation.

Options

Educate yourself about the many options available. One way to gather information about what kind of pump you'll like best is to talk to experienced breastfeeding mothers about how they have handled pumping. Look for co-workers who appear to be pumping. (The discreet pump bags are a dead giveaway to those who belong to this often secret club!) Most co-workers will enjoy sharing their experiences with you. You can also meet other breastfeeding mothers at local La Leche League meetings.

The decisions you make about how to express your milk will be as individual as you and your baby are.

Factors to Consider

Some pumps require access to an electrical outlet while others use batteries or hand power. Because you'll be taking your pump to work, consider whether it is easy to transport. Many pumps have carrying cases that include cooler sections for storing milk.

Breast pumps use suction to express milk from the breasts. The most convenient pumps have adjustable levels of suction and automatically create suction and release it. Pumps that have 40 to 60 suction-and-release cycles per minute are the most effective at maintaining a full supply over an extended period of time.

Some pumps are able to pump both breasts simultaneously, which is faster and increases the amount of milk pumped. Some mothers find hand-expressing easiest and most convenient, particularly if they only express occasionally.

The chart below offers some guidelines. The decisions you make about how to express your milk will be as individual as you and your baby are, so make your decisions based on what works best for you.

Pumping Frequency	High-quality rental pumps	Personal use electric	Battery, manual cycling	Hand pumps
One to three times monthly			x	x
Two to three times weekly	x	x		
Two or more times daily	x	x		

Types of Pumps

Automatic electric piston pumps. These high-quality pumps cycle automatically, can double pump, and mimic a baby's sucking pattern most effectively. They are sometimes referred to as "hospital grade" pumps and are usually rented on a weekly or monthly basis. Occasionally corporate lactation programs will provide these pumps for use on site by their employees; each mother needs to bring her own tubing and flanges. Some examples of these are: Ameda Lact-E, Ameda SMB, Ameda Elite, Medela Classic, Medela Lactina, Medela Symphony.

Personal use automatic electric diaphragm pumps. Pumps in this category cycle automatically and most double pump. One new model in this category offers the user the option to move around while pumping because the two pump units are small enough to fit discreetly under loose clothing. Some examples of these are: Whisper Wear, Medela Pump In Style, Medela Double Ease, Ameda Purely Yours, Nurture III/Natural Choice/Double-Up.

Motor-driven pumps. These models have fewer cycles per minute and do not cycle automatically. The user must release suction during each cycle using a button or other mechanism. Women who use these pumps sometimes buy two so that they can double pump. These pumps are lightweight and may run on either batteries or with an electrical adapter. The pumps themselves are less expensive initially, but may need to be replaced if they are used frequently over a period of many months. Using batteries for power can add to the cost of these pumps as they need to be replaced often. Examples are: Medela Mini Electric, Evenflo Soft Touch Ultra, Gerber Gentle Expression.

Hand-operated pumps. These are widely available in drug stores and department stores. There are two basic kinds. Cylinder pumps have two cylinders that fit one inside the other, with a rubber gasket creating a seal between them. You generate and release suction by pulling the outer cylinder out and pushing it back in. Handle squeeze pumps create and release suction when the handle is squeezed and released. Working women who work out of the home do not usually rely on this type of pump, though they may want to have one available as a backup. Examples are: Avent Isis, Ameda Cylinder Hand Breast Pump, Lansinoh Easy Express, Medela Spring Express, Ameda One-Hand Breast Pump.

Caring For Your Pump

You do not need to clean your pump parts after each use since human milk can be kept at room temperature for 4 to 6 hours. (See milk storage guidelines later in this section.) Some working mothers purchase multiple sets of attachments for automatic pumps so they can take a clean set to work in the morning even if they did not have time to clean the parts in the evening.

Follow the manufacturer's directions as to which parts might can be washed in the dishwasher and which might need to be sterilized.

Pumps should work effectively and be comfortable to use. If your breast pump malfunctions or you have trouble learning to use it, you can call the manufacturer for help. The retailer from whom you purchased the pump may also be of help. One major manufacturer of breast pumps suggests that washing all washable parts carefully in warm, soapy water will solve most problems with pumps.

The La Leche League International catalogue offers a variety of pumps for different needs. You can view it on-line at: www.lalecheleague.org/catalog.html, or request a free copy by calling 1-800-LALECHE.

Whatever choice you make about pumping you may be surprised at how emotionally fulfilling it can be to nourish your baby with your milk. And that pump, sometimes a little cumbersome, will be a treasured tool.

Hand-Expression

Your pump just broke and you're stuck in a meeting across town with no way to release the building pressure in your breasts. What to do? Adding an additional nursing pad may buy you time from embarrassing leaks, but it won't help you feel more comfortable, nor will it provide you with much needed milk. Try hand-expression. It's a quick, cheap alternative to the electric breast pump. In fact, many women choose this low-tech option over pumping and manage to express ample milk very efficiently. Even those who don't choose hand-expression for their main method of expression will benefit from being familiar with the technique.

Many women choose hand-expression over pumping and manage to express ample milk very efficiently.

The benefits of hand-expression:

- Some women have better output with hand-expression than with a pump.
- It is convenient. There is no need to wash pump parts or worry about replacements.
- It is portable. You'll never forget your hands.
- It is natural. Skin-to-skin contact helps stimulate milk flow.

The basics of hand-expression:

- Find a warm, comfortable place to sit.
- Have a container handy if your goal is to collect milk. Express over a sink if you just need to relieve pressure.
- Massage your breasts gently to stimulate a let-down.
- Place thumb and index finger on either side of the areola, about 1 to 2 inches back from the nipple. (You will feel the enlarged portion of the milk ducts in your breasts. Feel around for a few minutes—you can't miss them.)

What's in the Pump Bag?

To help stimulate let-down:
- Picture of baby,
- Baby's pajamas or baby's blanket,
- Portable CD player, to play relaxing music,
- Magazines or books, especially related to breastfeeding or parenting.

Must Haves:
- Storage containers for milk,
- Breast flanges,
- Sterile cleaning pads, if water is not available.
- Freezer bags to store individual pump parts.

Just in case:
- Extra batteries,
- AC adapter,
- Extension cord,
- "DO NOT DISTURB" sign for door,
- Plastic door stop for non-locking rooms.

Just for you:
- Healthy snacks or lunch,
- Bottle of water,
- Work related reading material, if you are so inclined.

If you think you may have a problem with your milk supply, there are some things to consider before you become overly concerned.

- Press gently inward toward the rib cage.
- Roll fingers together toward the nipple.
- Repeat all the way around the breast. (Do not slide fingers on your skin or squeeze the nipple. This does not help milk flow and can damage sensitive tissues.)
- Continue to express from one breast until milk flow decreases from a stream to a trickle. Then change sides and express from the other breast, Most mothers express from each breast at least twice.

Most mothers become proficient at hand-expression with practice. Experiment until you find a method that is successful for you. It may feel odd at first, but it won't take long to become adept. You'll be amazed at what you and Mother Nature are able to manage!

Increasing Milk Supply When Working

Of the many fears new mothers face upon returning to work, few are as distressing as the thought of not being able to pump enough milk for their babies. Fortunately, that is rarely the case. Once lactation has been established, milk production is controlled at the breast. Simply put: the more your baby nurses (or the more you pump), the more milk you produce.

If you think you may have a problem with your milk supply, there are some things to consider before you become overly concerned:

- It is common to get very little milk when you first start pumping. Your body does not respond to the pump in the same way it responds to your baby. Your body will eventually become used to the pump, and the let-down will occur more easily.
- If you are pumping in preparation for returning to work, you are likely at home with your baby and trying to fit pumping sessions in between regular breastfeeding sessions. There simply may not be much milk to pump. When you're at work and unable to nurse your baby, it will be a different story.
- If your baby is demanding more milk at the caregiver's than you can pump, consider the possibility that he is getting enough milk but needs to suck for comfort. Try to find a bottle nipple that flows more slowly so baby has to suck more to get the milk. Ask your caregiver to see if your baby will accept a pacifier or another form of comfort.

It's better to pump for a few minutes than to skip a session entirely.

If you are sure that you are not pumping enough milk, there are lots of ways to increase production.

Change your equipment or technique

- Try a different type of pump. Review the section in this book on selecting a pump or ask your local LLL Leader about pumps that mothers find effective. You could also consider renting a hospital-quality breast pump from a local Leader or lactation consultant.
- Pump flanges come in many different sizes. A flange that is too small or too large can affect your milk output, in addition to your comfort level at the pump. Work with an LLL Leader or a lactation consultant to see that yours is the best fit possible.
- Pump thoroughly. Draining the breast completely appears to be more effective at increasing the rate of milk production than breastfeeding or expressing milk more often. Be sure to continue pumping for 2 to 5 minutes after the last drops have been expressed.

- Pump more. It can't hurt to add an additional pumping session or two to your day. Try to make time, at least until your supply increases.
- Pump in the early morning before you leave for work. Prolactin, the hormone needed for milk production, increases during the night, thus most mothers have lots of milk when they wake up in the morning.
- Try pumping both breasts at the same time. The double stimulation increases prolactin.
- Try "super switch nursing." While breastfeeding your baby or pumping with one pump flange, switch sides two or three times during each session. This increases breast stimulation and encourages more let-downs.
- Don't skip pumping sessions. It's better to pump for a few minutes than to skip a session entirely.

Babies who are away from their mothers during the day often make up for lost time by breastfeeding frequently in the evening.

Relax

- Try using relaxation techniques, deep breathing exercises, breast massage, or warm compresses for a few minutes before pumping. Stress, tension, and cool body temperature can all inhibit letdown.
- Think about your baby when you pump. Imagining your baby at your breast, smelling a piece of his clothing, looking at his picture, or calling the caregiver for an update can all help the milk flow more easily.
- Make sure you are getting good nutrition, adequate fluid, and plenty of rest.
- Keep life as simple as possible. Cut back on extra activities and ask for (or hire) help with housework and child care.

Breastfeed your baby as often as possible

Breastfeed your baby frequently when you are together. Pumping does not stimulate the breasts to produce milk as well as a nursing baby does, so don't give a bottle when you can breastfeed.

- Encourage nighttime nursing. Babies who are away from their mothers during the day often make up for lost time by breastfeeding frequently in the evening. Some babies even reverse their daily patterns by sleeping more and feeding less during the day and then clustering their feedings at night. Consider cosleeping so you can breastfeed your baby without waking up completely.

Many working mothers see this as extra bonding time.

- If your caregiver is close to your workplace, consider breastfeeding your baby during lunch and coffee breaks.
- Consider taking a "nursing vacation." Use the time off to do nothing but rest and breastfeed your baby as often as possible. The increased stimulation and extra rest will help to boost your milk supply.

Seek additional help

- Try herbs and herbal teas to increase your milk supply. Many mothers and lactation consultants believe that certain herbs such as fenugreek can stimulate your body to make more milk. Ask your physician or lactation consultant for more information.
- Get professional help. Contact your local La Leche League Leader or a board certified lactation consultant for tips on increasing your milk supply.

Breastfeeding-Friendly Child Care

Selecting a Breastfeeding-Friendly Daycare Facility

Choosing child care is one of the most difficult decisions a working mother makes. Will your baby be cared for properly? Is the facility close to your home or work? Is it clean? One crucial question you must ask of a potential caretaker is whether he or she is knowledgeable about and supportive of breastfeeding. The person or group of people you designate to care for your child will be an integral part of your breastfeeding team. Lack of support from child minders is a frustrating and unnecessary hurdle for you and your child. According to the book, *How to Pick Remarkable Quality Childcare and Education*, there are certain signs that indicate whether a child care facility will be breastfeeding-friendly.

- There is a comfortable dedicated space (e.g., not the staff office, storeroom, or the toilet facility) that is private, with comfortable armchairs, access to fresh drinking water for parents and older siblings, and good-sized cushions/pillows.
- The adults are relaxed about and happy for mothers to breastfeed in the main play area if they choose.
- The adults make a point of asking parents at the time of enroll-

ment about breastfeeding and infant nutrition and what they can do to support them and their infant. The adults continue to have ongoing communication with parents about this after enrollment.

- The adults demonstrate in their conversations and in their actions that they are non-judgmental, supportive, and knowledgeable about breastfeeding.
- The adults show they are comfortable with a mother breastfeeding an older infant or toddler and support this.
- In center-based settings there is a written breastfeeding policy for parents, staff, and management.

Reproduced with permission from pages 74-75 in Farquhar, S.E.. *How to Pick Remarkable Quality Childcare and Education.* New Zealand: Childforum Research, 2005.

Human milk provides natural immunities for a baby, which is especially important for a child who is exposed to illnesses in daycare.

Other factors to consider

Proximity. It helps to have a child care provider close to your work. Being nearby enables you to enjoy a midday nursing break. Besides providing closeness, it also helps alleviate an additional pumping session. Plus, many mothers find peace of mind in knowing they are only a few minutes away from their baby in case they are needed. Make sure your provider understands and supports your wish to "drop in" on a regular basis.

Personality. Do the care providers seem child-friendly? Do they get down at your child's level to talk and play? Do they hold him or her close when feeding? Do they light up at the things your child says and does? They should.

Experience with breastfeeding mothers/handling human milk. You'll want to discuss in advance that you will be bringing in your milk and be sure the facility is aware of proper storage and heating procedures. Also, they will need to be aware if your baby is unfamiliar with drinking from a bottle and that they may need to use another feeding method, such as a cup, spoon, or feeding syringe, until your baby is willing to take a bottle.

Amount and timing of feedings It may be important for the care providers to know that you will be coming in at certain times to breastfeed so they do not give the baby a feeding just before your expected arrival. This is also true at the end of the day if you expect to nurse the baby when you return to pick him up.

Trust your instincts. If something doesn't feel "quite right" for you and your family, it probably isn't.

Finally, don't be afraid to talk openly with your care provider about your wishes and expectations. And of course, thank them for doing a great job! Below is information that may be helpful in educating child minders, as well as opening a dialogue about your breastfed baby's needs.

Information for Daycare Providers

Importance of breastfeeding

Human milk provides natural immunities for a baby, which is especially important for a child who is exposed to illnesses in daycare. In addition, breastfeeding is a nice way for a working mother and child to bond, which is especially important because of their separation. Mothers who breastfeed and work report that continuing the breastfeeding relationship while working is crucial to them for several reasons:

- Human milk is produced by "supply and demand." The breast must receive regular stimulation (i.e., nursing or pumping) to maintain the mother's milk supply. Supplementing with formula results in less "demand" for the mother's milk. This decreases milk supply and makes it more difficult for a mother to continue producing milk.
- Mothers feel better about going to work knowing that they are providing their baby's nutrition while they are away. It is very common for mothers to say they feel they've left a small "piece of themselves" with their baby each day.
- Breastfeeding provides a warm, calming reunion for the mother and baby at the end of a day. Many working, breastfeeding mothers report that this reunion is the thing they most look forward to throughout the workday.

Guidelines on storing and handling human milk

Appearance

Human milk looks different than cow's milk or formula, but rest comfortably in knowing that it is comprised of exactly what a human baby needs to thrive. The color and consistency can vary depending on the baby's age and the mother's diet, but generally human milk looks thin and ranges in color from light yellow to blue-white. This is all normal. You will also notice that it separates in the refrigerator, leaving a layer of fat on the top, or you may see fat particles floating in the milk. This is because it is not homogenized. Shake gently to mix the fat back into the milk.

Storing Milk

Human milk is not as delicate as many think due to naturally occurring antibacterial properties. Here are some general guidelines on storage:

- At 60 degrees F (15 degrees C) human milk can be stored for up to 24 hours.
- At 66 to 72 degrees F (19 to 22 degrees C) human milk can be stored for 10 hours.
- At 79 degrees F (25 degrees C) human milk is safe from harmful bacteria for 4 to 6 hours.
- Human milk can be refrigerated for up to 8 days at 32 to 39 degrees F (0 to 4 degrees C) with no increase in harmful bacteria.
- Human milk can be frozen in a refrigerator-freezer for up to two weeks.
- Human milk can be frozen in a separate door freezer for three to four weeks.
- Human milk can be frozen in a deep freezer at 0 degrees F (-19 degrees C) for six months or longer.
- Be sure to read dates on the milk containers and use the oldest supply first.

Heating

Always wash hands and keep bottles, nipples, cups, and spoons clean. Human milk is not classified as human tissue and therefore should raise no handling concerns for providers.

Refrigerated milk

To warm refrigerated milk, hold it under running water until it reaches room temperature. Do not heat the milk directly on the stove or in a microwave. In addition to destroying valuable components in the milk, uneven heat from a microwave can cause burns.

Frozen milk

To thaw frozen milk, hold the container under cool running water and gradually add warmer water until milk is thawed and warmed to room temperature. It is also possible to immerse the container into a pan of warm water that has been heated on the stove. Do not let human milk stand at room temperature to thaw.

- If more than one container is being thawed, it is fine to combine the milk for a feeding.
- Unopened but thawed milk can be safely kept refrigerated for up to 24 hours.
- Thawed milk should not be refrozen.

Additional Tips

- Try not to heat more milk than is needed. You can always heat more if baby is still hungry.
- If baby is showing signs of hunger just before mother is to return, try to keep him satisfied with a small amount of milk as mother will likely want to nurse the baby as soon as she arrives.
- Many breastfeeding mothers find it helpful to drop in during the day to nurse, when possible. This helps to alleviate a pumping session and is a nice way for mother and baby to stay in touch during the day. Most mothers and child care providers find the minimal disruption worthwhile.
- Breastfed babies are used to being held close when they eat.

Ideally, someone other than the mother should introduce the bottle.

Introducing the Bottle

The bottle. Will your baby accept it? Will he prefer it over breastfeeding? Even tiny babies have opinions about whether it is or is not a suitable vehicle for receiving your milk. If you choose to use the bottle (rather than a dropper, spoon, cup, or feeder) it helps to keep a few tips in mind.

Getting started

Be sure breastfeeding is well established before attempting to introduce the bottle to avoid nipple confusion. Most babies are adaptable and will take a bottle if it is first offered at one month, two months, or between three and six months.

Ideally, someone other than the mother should introduce the bottle. As the mother, you will be very closely associated with breastfeeding—this is a good connection to maintain. Having the baby's father or child care provider offer the bottle may increase his cooperation while lessening the chance that he will become confused.

According to THE BREASTFEEDING ANSWER BOOK, there are some reliable ways to encourage a baby to take the bottle.

Timing. Try offering the bottle before the baby is likely to be too hungry, before his usual nursing time, when he may be more cooperative about trying something new.

Cuddle. Hold the baby lovingly while giving the bottle. Breastfed babies are used to being held close when they eat.

Mother's smell. Wrap the baby in a piece of the mother's clothing that has her smell on it while offering the bottle.

Take it slow. Instead of pushing the nipple into the baby's mouth, try laying it near his mouth and allow him to pull it in himself, or tickle the baby's mouth with the bottle nipple, as many mothers do with the breast, and wait until he opens wide to give it.

Temperature. Consider running warm water over the nipple to bring it up to body temperature, like the breast.

Nipple type. Try different types of nipples to find a shape, substance (rubber or silicone), and a hole size the baby will accept. Look for a nipple that is wide at the base, so that the baby's mouth opens wide to take the nipple.

Position. Alternate feeding positions. Some babies prefer to take a bottle in the nursing position; others like to sit propped against the caregiver's legs (like sitting in an infant seat); and others prefer not to look at the caregiver and will take the bottle if they are held facing out, with their backs against the caregiver's chest.

Movement. Try rhythmical movement that may already be calming to the baby—rocking, swaying, walking.

A few babies will be reluctant to take the bottle. Have the caregiver patiently try different ways to encourage the bottle. Do remember that there are other feeding methods that a baby may be amenable to: cup, spoon, or eyedropper. These are fine options, too.

Reverse Cycling

Now you're back at work, pumping regularly, but your baby's caregiver reports he is not interested in the daily offerings you've labored so hard for. Yet he wants to nurse continuously at home. What's going on? He may be reverse cycling. This term refers to a pattern that some babies develop when their normal routine of daytime nursing is disrupted. In short, your baby is holding out for "the real thing."

Why a baby chooses to reverse cycle

Let's face it, breastfeeding is only partly about the milk. Some babies choose to eat just enough to stave off the hunger until Mom returns. At that point, they want to nurse frequently to make up for lost calories and closeness.

Signs that your baby is reverse cycling

- Your baby takes only small amounts of expressed milk in your absence.
- He sleeps more during the day or is less active when he is with the sitter.
- He wants to nurse frequently upon your return.

If your baby has switched schedules in this way, it may be fine. In fact, some working mothers enjoy the extra closeness at night and appreciate fewer pumping sessions during the day. But there are some things to keep in mind:

How to Handle Reverse Cycling

Relax. Many (older) babies go eight hours at night without eating anything. Perhaps like those babies, yours has chosen the "less traveled" route.

Drop the schedule. Reverse cycling babies require unrestricted access to the breast in your presence.

Cosleep. Close proximity is important for babies who reverse cycle. Offer maximum nutrition and closeness by bringing your baby to bed with you and nursing often through the night.

Reminders are helpful. Encourage your baby to nurse frequently in the evening hours, even if he is cosleeping. The more he nurses before bedtime, the less likely he may be to wake you at night.

Alter quantity. Store your milk in smaller quantities to cut down on waste.

Communicate. Explain what is happening to your child care providers so they will not worry unnecessarily.

Though reverse cycling is not uncommon among breastfed babies, you do need to be alert and aware to be sure your baby continues to get enough milk. Be aware of:

Diapers. Make sure your baby is still making plenty of wet diapers and stooling regularly.

Growth. Make sure your baby is gaining weight and reaching developmental milestones.

If your baby is showing signs that he is not getting enough to eat, and is fussy or irritable, or if your milk supply is low, try increasing the number of nursing sessions when you are together and have your caregiver make an extra effort to encourage your baby to take your milk while you are gone. If you continue to have trouble, see your pediatrician or lactation consultant. If all is going well, enjoy your baby and pride yourself on having found a solution that allows your baby to be healthy, happy, and close!

Taking Baby to Work

Is it possible to work and be the primary caretaker for your child? You bet. In fact, you probably do it every day, right? You cook dinner, wash dishes, mow the lawn, make phone calls, pay bills, and paint walls. It's an ancient story. The first cave wall was probably painted by the hand that *wasn't* holding the baby. But can you do this in today's world? Would your current job allow it? It is something to think about, especially during a child's breastfeeding years. First, consider what flexibility may be available in your current job. Some common arrangements are:

Take the Baby to Work

Some women take their baby to work, with or without the help of an on-site caregiver to help out. It is not for every workplace, but can be managed (even welcomed) in some settings.

Bring Work to the Baby

Employers will often permit telecommuting and flex-time, especially on a short term basis. This allows a woman to fulfill some of her work hours from a home office. Though not always advertised, work-life balance is a growing trend in today's workforce. Don't be afraid to ask for it.

What if you get approval? Now it's time to figure out how to get some work done! Working with a small baby can be surprisingly easy. They sleep, nurse, and are contented to be held close.

As babies grow, things get trickier. Many mothers fare well, however, and find any effort it takes is worthwhile as it helps maintain the breastfeeding relationship, saves money on child care, and allows them to maintain a constant presence to their child. And, as many a working mother has been known to say, "I really miss her when we're apart!"

Here are some things to keep in mind if you are going to work at home or take your child to work

Employers will often permit telecommuting and flex-time, especially on a short term basis.

Make It Fun

- Reserve special age-appropriate toys for the hours that you work; rotate regularly.
- Swap toys with friends or visit secondhand stores from time to time to replenish the supply.
- Breastfeed often, on demand. Many working mothers report that their baby is contented to nurse a large portion of their workday. Baby stays well-fed, happy, and of course, falls asleep easily!
- Wear your baby in a sling or other type of carrier. This frees your hands while allowing your baby to feel close and connected, even when you cannot give one hundred percent of your attention.

Meeting your own needs will make you a happier, more patient mother. Eat regular nutritious meals. Read an occasional article, email a friend, take a walk.

Make It Fair

- If possible, select work hours to coincide with your child's "happier" or "nappier" times.
- Make the most of your breaks. Sit with your child, listen, talk, and play. Offering quality time reassures baby that you will be available regularly throughout a workday.
- Be finicky about using playpens, swings, etc. These can be a convenience when it is necessary to keep baby safe or you need a quick breather.
- Be willing to allow an educational program for older children from time to time. Watching an occasional TV show can be an acceptable trade-off for affording you extra time with your baby.
- Let older children know your expectations in a quiet, clear, consistent way. Let them also know the consequences of not meet-

ing your expectations.

- Have healthy snacks and drinks available, for yourself and the children, prepared in advance.

Make a Community

- If possible, create a working "co-op." Get together with another working parent whose children get along well with yours. Children can enjoy their own community while parents get some work done.
- Hire a teenage helper to play with your child for a few regular hours or during busy times. Teenagers' rates are usually affordable and children enjoy their energy.
- Consider scheduling regular "play dates" with grandparents or other family members. One working mother of twins had different sets of grandparents visit on alternate Fridays. She depended on this day to accomplish important work, and the grandparents looked forward to two special days a month when they had alone time with their grandchildren.
- Connect with other working, nursing mothers through LLLI, church, business associations, or on-line. It helps to share ideas and to know that you're not alone.

Working with your children means you will not always accomplish everything you'd like.

Your Schedule

Try to stick to a rough routine—this way you and your child know what to expect. (For example, morning means work, afternoon means play.)

That said, be willing to break from your routine if necessary.

If part-time is an option, an every other day schedule affords a little breather between workdays.

Be portable as much as possible. Laptops are handy to move around the house or take to the park; consider a wireless Internet connection. Cordless or cellular phones can help you work from the yard or on the road.

Be reasonable. Working with your baby does not have to be an "all or nothing" proposition. Some employers allow it for a percentage of an employee's work week until a baby is older. Some families schedule so that Mom and Dad telecommute and work from home on different days. Working to find a combination that suits your employer and your family is worth the effort.

Evaluate your needs. How much do you really need to work? If you can get by on less, try to do so.

Your Professional Role

Often mothers who work with their children report that they exceed an employer's expectations. This helps them maintain the privilege, proves their professionalism, and paves the way for the next mother and child seeking a flexible arrangement.

If you work with others, make sure you've politely explained why it is important that you have your baby with you. Be as courteous to colleagues as possible, being aware that even nice baby noises are…noisy. And thank those involved for their help with the arrangement.

If your present job does not lend itself to this kind of flexibility, consider what some mothers have done and start your own home-based business, allowing you to set your own hours.

Finally, know that some days will be better than others. Working with your children means you will not always accomplish everything you'd like. The trade-off is that you are with them more, they see and experience you working firsthand, and you have control of their child care. And remember, this is nothing new. The first cave-Mama undoubtedly carved her cudgel with a brood of little ones right beside her.

Cosleeping and Working Mothers

Whether you work with or away from your baby, your day will go more smoothly if you've gotten a good night's sleep. For some, that happens by cosleeping. Throughout most of human history, babies have slept next to their parents because it has been the practical thing to do for warmth and physical safety. Sharing sleep with your baby, for all or part of the night, can make both breastfeeding and parenting easier. As The Womanly Art of Breastfeeding states: "Once you can feed the baby while comfortably stretched out, you've eliminated much of the work of mothering for about eight of the 24 hours in a day."

Chances are that you have your own ideas about cosleeping and that you've heard some opinions from others, too. Here are some benefits to cosleeping, especially for working mothers.

A Protective Effect

In the ever-evolving field of research on SIDS, some studies show that breastfeeding protects against SIDS. Here are some possible reasons why:

Human milk provides protection against respiratory illnesses, including colds and flu, illnesses that increase the risk of SIDS.

Periods of apnea (times when automatic breathing stops for longer than normal) have been associated with an increased risk for SIDS. Sleep expert Dr. James McKenna, who heads a sleep lab at the University of Notre Dame, finds that babies who cosleep with their mothers have fewer periods of apnea and more small arousals, so they breathe more regularly. During cosleeping, babies' sleep cycles closely match their mothers.

Dr. McKenna also states: "Routinely bed sharing mothers tuck their bodies up and lean toward their babies to face them in ways that make overlaying of their infants difficult."

Types of Cosleeping

There are various types of cosleeping that parents have found successful. Some parents tuck baby into bed with them and sleep that way throughout the night. Others put baby to sleep in a crib or sidecar for the first few hours, then bring baby into their bed when he wakes to nurse. Others bring baby into their bed to breastfeed, but return the baby to his own bed after the feeding (if mother stays awake!). With a toddler who sleeps on a mattress or twin-size bed, mother may go to his bed when he wakes up and stay there for the rest of the night.

"Babies cry significantly less in the cosleeping environment which means that more energy can be put into growth, maintenance, and protective immune responses."

James McKenna

Benefits for the Working Mother

As a working mother, you stand to gain much from cosleeping. By sleeping close to your baby, you are able to increase the amount of skin-to-skin contact and closeness that is lost during the workday.

Babies who are apart from their mothers during the day tend to nurse more frequently at night. This can be advantageous if you are having trouble pumping enough milk during the day. Cosleeping and night nursings help your baby make up for any decrease in the amount of milk he receives during the day plus it stimulates your milk supply so you may end up being able to pump more.

Most mothers find they get more sleep if their babies are close than if they need to get up and go into another room when baby wakes at night. Why walk across a cold floor when you can snuggle close to your baby in a warm bed? Most women become proficient at sleeping while nursing and end up not waking as often when baby is cosleeping. Let's face it—you need all the sleep you can get!

If you choose to cosleep, it's important to follow these safety precautions.

- Make sure that your mattress is firm and fits tightly in the frame.
- Sheets should fit your mattress snugly.

- Loose pillows or soft blankets should be kept away from your baby's face.
- Always place your baby on his back to sleep.
- No one who shares sleep with your baby should drink alcoholic beverages, take drugs, be exceptionally obese, or be on medication that makes him or her less alert.
- Consider keeping your young baby next to his mother only, because mothers seem to be especially aware of their babies in bed.
- Keep an adult between any older child and your baby.
- Use a crib or commercially available "sidecar" next to the bed.
- Make sure the sides of the bed are either tight against the wall or far enough way from the wall that your baby can't become trapped. Or use a bed rail on the side of the adult bed.
- Keep the bed low to the ground, maybe even on the floor to minimize any falls.

Making Changes at Work

If your employer does not offer lactation facilities, consider suggesting that they start. Often all it takes is asking.

Basics of a Corporate Lactation Program:

- *Supplying a room*

  Must have:
  - ✓ Lock
  - ✓ Chair
  - ✓ Light
  - ✓ Outlet

  Nice to have:
  - ✓ Sink, for washing hands, pump parts, bottles
  - ✓ Paper towels, dish soap,
  - ✓ Small refrigerator, for storing milk
  - ✓ Reading materials

✓ Bulletin board, for sign-up sheets, photos of babies, corporate information

✓ CD player

✓ Clock

✓ Providing Pumps: These can be bought or rented by the company. They can also be supplied by the employee.

(Date here)

Dear (*Name of Employer*):

As an employee of (Company) for (XX) years, I would like to invite you to consider making a commitment to mothers who wish to continue to breastfeed their babies after returning to work by developing a Corporate Lactation Program.

Corporate Lactation Programs help promote a commitment to employee well-being and save companies thousands of dollars per year in the process. A recent study of CIGNA Corporation revealed that a corporate lactation program for employees who breastfed produced a savings of $240 annually due to a decrease in health care expenses for mothers and their children. Reduced employee absenteeism among breastfeeding mothers was also shown to save $60,000 annually. A corporate commitment to breastfeeding enables a more productive, cost-effective business.

In addition, employee loyalty is increased, which saves money and time through reduced turnover rates. Consider SAS, the international software corporation based in the eastern US. Through their health promotion efforts (of which breastfeeding support is an integral part) they have revolutionized the art of "keeping strong employees." Where normal turnover rates in the software industry range between 18 to 20 percent, SAS has turnover rates of 3 to 5 percent.

Though the term Corporate Lactation Program may sound intimidating, it can consist of a very simple set of accommodations and need not be expensive. A full Lactation Program can begin with the single step of designating one or more clean, private rooms for women to express their milk. The elaborateness of a program can vary depending on the number of breastfeeding employees and the financial resources available.

Starting a program does not have to be complicated or expensive. In fact, most nursing mothers are more than happy to help get things off the ground, and all are deeply grateful for the support. In the end, corporations find that the decreased sick leave and increased productivity and retention more than compensate for the small amount of time and money expended.

La Leche League International has packages of educational materials available to help you offer information helpful to breastfeeding mothers as part of your Corporate Lactation Program. Feel free to call 1-800-La-Leche or visit http://www.lalecheleague.org with any questions about developing a Corporate Lactation Program.

Sincerely,
(Your name

• *Measuring effectiveness*

Design a simple survey that employees are asked to fill out monthly. This can evaluate their satisfaction with the facilities provided, their intention to continue using the room, and any additional needs they may have.

• *Developing a Breastfeeding Policy*

Beyond designating a room for pumping, a written policy helps cement a business's commitment to breastfeeding mothers and creates a corporate culture of support.

Legislative Action

Contacting Legislators

In many countries such as the United States, government legislators are elected officials. They want to hear from you, the person who elects them. So don't hesitate to call, email, or write your senators or representatives about workplace-based breastfeeding legislation. Without your voice, this growing group of mothers will remain silent. Let them hear you!

So don't hesitate to call, email, or write your senators or representatives about workplace-based breastfeeding legislation.

Here are a few tips that will help when contacting your legislators by phone, fax, mail, or email:

Be well-informed. If possible, cite a specific law or bill as your focus.

Be specific and concise. Clearly state your position or concern so there is no ambiguity about what you want.

Request a specific action or response. Do you want him or her to support a bill, attend a hearing, or make you aware of his or her vote?

Be personal. Experience counts far more than statistics and facts. Your legislator probably already knows the numbers. Your job is to provide the "face." Make sure you provide your address for or reply.

Be polite. You and your argument will lose credibility if you are rude or disrespectful.

Offer yourself as a resource. Be willing to help or offer additional information that your legislator may need later. Consider phrases like, "Please consider this viewpoint," or "Please consider acting in favor of Bill XYZ," when closing.

Persist. Your representatives want to hear from you.

(Date here)

The Honorable__________________(*Full Name*) U.S. Senate (*or U.S. House of Representatives*) Washington, DC 20510 (*or 20515 for the House of Representatives*)

Dear Senator______________(*Last name of your Senator, or Dear Congressman/woman for your rep*)

Breastfeeding is a life-sustaining and cost-saving public health issue that needs more attention and support. I am urging you to learn more about breastfeeding and maternity protection for working women. Please consider supporting, The New Mothers' Breastfeeding Promotion and Protection Act, proposed by Congresswoman Carolyn Maloney (New York).

Breastfeeding and expression of human milk must have the support of Congress if we are to increase corporate and societal support for women who wish to provide optimal nutrition for their children after returning to work. Therefore, parents, employers, and policymakers must cooperate to make the benefits of breastfeeding understood as a fundamental biological right and a top health priority.

(Briefly tell your personal story related to breastfeeding and working. Relay a short, poignant illustration, if possible.)

Please respond to my letter. I am interested in providing information or answering any questions you might have. Breastfeeding protection for working women is a crucial human rights and public health issue in American society. It is time for our national legislators to focus on this issue.

I appreciate your attention.
Sincerely,

(Your name and address)

Finding your Legislators and their contact information:

If you're in the United States and are unsure of which legislator to contact, search by your zip code at the following Web addresses. You will be provided with the name of the correct representative as well as his or her contact information.

- US Government Sites
  www.house.gov/writerep/
  www.senate.gov

- US State Legislators
  www.ncsl.org/public/leglinks.cfm
- All Federal Agencies
  www.firstgov.gov/Contact.shtml
- To reach any legislator by phone, call the Capitol switchboard at 202- 224-3121.

Global Changes

Maternity Protection Worldwide

Are you aware that there is an international standard for maternity protection? It's true. The agreement by governments, employers, and workers details the rights and responsibilities in existence for all women who work and have babies. The standard, set forth by the International Labor Organization, is known as ILO Convention 183. Unfortunately, not all countries adhere to this standard. However, knowing that standards exist is an important first step in eventually seeing them implemented, if not around the world, then in your own country, office, or factory.

Sadly, many working women around the world are granted insufficient maternity leave and inadequate time for breastfeeding breaks.

Why Standards Matter

UNICEF, the World Health Assembly, and the American Academy of Pediatrics recommend exclusive breastfeeding for the first six months of a baby's life, followed by continued breastfeeding with introduction of complementary foods. The benefits of this practice include reduction of diarrhea, acute respiratory illness, and other childhood illnesses. Mothers also benefit from lower incidences of certain cancers and longer intervals between births.

Sadly, many working women around the world are granted insufficient maternity leave and inadequate time for breastfeeding breaks, leaving them little chance to put these important recommendations into practice. The International Labor Organization's standards recognize and attempt to address this problem.

What Are the Standards?

According to the ILO Convention No. 183, all working women should receive:

- 12 weeks maternity leave, with extension if necessary;
- cash benefits during leave of at least 66 percent of previous earnings;

- breastfeeding breaks totaling at least one hour per day, or a reduced workday;
- breastfeeding breaks or reduction of hours for breastfeeding compensated as working time;
- Prohibition of dismissal during maternity leave.

Who Has Ratified This Document?

The countries that have ratified ILO Convention No. 183 are: Albania, Austria, Belarus, Bulgaria, Cuba, Cyprus, Hungary, Italy, Lithuania, Romania, and Slovakia. A large block of Latin American countries did not ratify ILO 183 because it was not seen as protective enough for working women. These countries felt ratifying ILO 183 would weaken existing legislation in their countries. Other countries, such as the United States and Australia, balked at the standards, feeling they were too rigid for their countries' laws.

Your Role

What can you do if yours is not one of the countries that have ratified these standards? You can accomplish a great deal by simply being informed and aware. Chris Mulford, RN, IBCLC, Co-coordinator, Women & Work Task Force, WABA, suggests you can:

- Know whether your country has ratified the convention.
- Know what national laws, labor regulations, and/or collective bargaining agreements affect your workplace and affect you as a worker. In short, know your rights.
- Know how to report lapses if a worker's rights are not respected.
- Advocate for better laws, regulations, or collective bargaining agreements as an individual or—better yet—with other workers.
- Advocate with your government for ratification of ILO C-183, as an individual or—better yet—with other workers.

Mulford recognizes that working, breastfeeding women are a group understandably short on energy. Banding together, however, creates potential for change.

"The amount of work that has to be done is huge, and mothers don't have a lot of time and energy left over for civic work. *But* their voices definitely need to be heard. A few parents with kids showing up at a hearing or a demonstration, getting their pictures in the paper, forming a committee at a workplace to advocate for on-site child care or breastfeeding breaks...this would have power."

Learn More

To learn more about ILO Convention 183 and/or how you can affect change, visit the following Web sites:

http://www.waba.org.my/women-work/mpckit.htm

http://www.world-psi.org/

http://www.ilo.org

http://www.ibfan.org

Helpful Resources

The following Web sites include information that other mothers have found useful when combining breastfeeding with working. La Leche League International has not reviewed these resources, and is not responsible for the information or links that might be found on any Web sites besides our own: **www.lalecheleague.org**

Web Sites, in English

http://www.askdrsears.com

http://www.kellymom.com

http://www.iVillage.com/iv-ppworkpump

http://www.waba.org.my/womenwork/wwork.html

http://www.Dreamdinners.com

http://www.Worktolive.org

www.motherwear.com

www.medela.com/NewFiles/faq/coll_store.html

www.trisomy21online.com

www.breastfeeding.asn.au/bfinfo/down.html

www.mamalicious.com

http://www.breastfeedingbasics.com

http://www.PROMOM.org

http://neonatal.ama.ttuhsc.edu/lact/index.html

www.breastfeedingonline.com

www.thebirthden.com/Newman.html

http://asklenore.info/breastfeeding/abindex.html

http://www.Mothering.com

http://www.waba.org.my/womenwork/wwork.html

http://www.breastfeeding.com/workingmom.shtml

http://www.familiesandwork.org

http://breastfeeding.hypermart.net/info.html

http://www.mother-2-mother.com/

Web Sites, Non-English language

www.aleitamento.org.br (Portuguese)

http://www.tapuz.co.il/tapuzforum/main/forumpage.asp?forum=317 (Hebrew)

http://forum.bg-mamma.com/index.php. (Bulgarian)

Recommended Publications

La Leche League International is the world's largest resource for breastfeeding and related information and products. The organization distributes more than three million publications each year—all of which have been carefully evaluated to ensure that they harmonize with LLLI philosophy. Select books with confidence that they've been chosen to reflect the values of mothering through breastfeeding and attachment parenting. To place an order or request a free catalogue, visit the LLLI Web site at www.lalecheleague.org or call 800-LALECHE.

The Womanly Art of Breastfeeding

Published by La Leche League International, this comprehensive guide to breastfeeding has helped several generations of mothers provide their babies with the very best start in life. Includes a chapter on breastfeeding and working in addition to other chapters that cover breastfeeding management, benefits of breastfeeding, basic nutrition guidelines, and more!

The Balancing Act

This pamphlet addresses issues that many employed mothers face while breastfeeding. Includes information on milk expression and storage, where to find support, and features a section of resources and products.

The Breastfeeding Book
by Dr. William Sears and Martha Sears

Easy to read and thoroughly indexed, The Breastfeeding Book covers everything from the basics of breastfeeding, to how to get the baby to latch on properly, to toddler nursing and weaning. Includes informative tips and interesting facts in sidebars throughout the text.

Nursing Mother, Working Mother
by Gale Pryor

Mothers who combine breastfeeding with working will find this an immensely helpful and reassuring book. The author includes practical information on planning for and returning to employment; clear, concise tips on breastfeeding; pumping, storing, and transporting milk; and possible alternatives to full-time employment. The book suggests numerous ways mothers can build and maintain closeness with their babies in spite of separation.

Whole Foods for The Whole Family

This LLLI cookbook provides simple, easy to make food with maximum nutrition. With over 900 recipes, picky eaters, meat lovers, vegetarians, and even those with dietary restrictions will find many favorites.

New Beginnings

A bimonthly magazine filled with information on breastfeeding and mother-to-mother sharing, including a column for employed mothers, "Making It Work."

APPENDIX

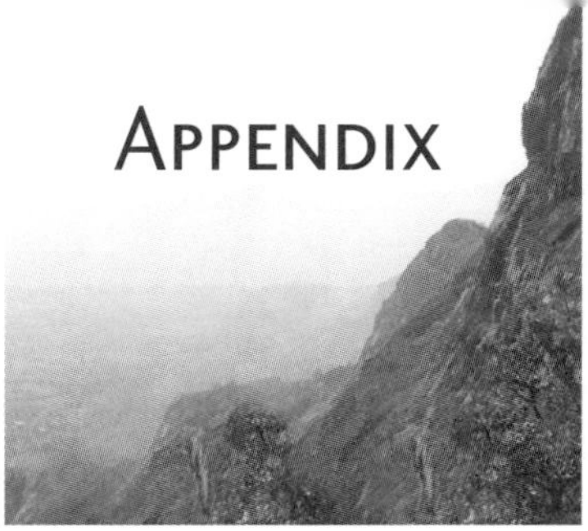

Mother-to-Mother

More mothers than we could feature enriched this book. While there was not room enough for every woman's story, we did want to share some of their sentiments, which are ripe with sincerity, honesty, humor, and love.

"There are a lot of people who can be good workers in this world, but only one who has the privilege and responsibility of being a good mom to Quinn: me."

Tamara Jackman, USA (Nurse Midwife)

"I am grateful my employer emphasizes the importance of family. I now work 22 hours a week, and my life feels more balanced. I spend lots of time with Aiden, and I still have time for myself, too. I am more productive at work because I am not stretched too thin."

Joy Jernigan, USA (Features Producer, Seattle Times)

"I decide to drive to the park right by the lakefront…and [pump] there…I manage to use a blanket, hike my dress up, get the horns attached, turn on the car, and crank up the air conditioner. (Did I mention the weather? The hottest most humid day we'd had in Milwaukee that summer.) I also decided to crank up the tunes while I'm at it.... This of course calls attention to me from the cop who's patrolling the beat, who knocks on my door and clearly thinks I'm doing something suspicious. I lift my blanket to show him what I'm doing and he quickly tips his hat down, does an about-face, and marches away."

Veronica Rusnak, USA (IT Technician Project Leader)

"I've grown to hate my pump, but I love what it stands for, and I am so proud of what I've been able to do for my baby girl."

Sandra DeBary, USA (Human Resources Recruiter)

"Being able to nurse while I work has been the most important bonding we could experience. It is hard to give up a lot of everyday mothering to someone else, even your husband, for eight hours a day. But I am the only person who can breastfeed Alex, and he knows it. Though I am not home with him all day, his first word at nine months was mama, and he says it mostly when he wants to nurse. There is nothing like coming home after a long day at work and having your little angel smile, crawl to you, say mama, and tug on your shirt."

Jennifer Villanueva-Henkle, USA (Project Coordinator)

"The biggest challenge for me hasn't been the actual pumping, but being away from my daughter. The best advice I could give anyone would be that in almost every situation, you can find a way to continue to nurse. If my job wasn't so mom-friendly I would find one that was, or I would pump in my car, or I would have my daughter brought to me during the day. There is no replacement for the nutrition and bonding that comes from nursing, and that is doubly important for a child who is away from her mother every day."

Tenille Manning Heier, USA (Writer)

"Luckily, Microsoft has a generous maternity leave policy. I was able to take five months off with my son, which allowed me the opportunity to work out the issues I was having with breastfeeding. I could not have overcome my breastfeeding challenges otherwise."

Lydia Evans Olsen, USA (Program Manager)

"I have a playpen in the corner of the office, but quite frankly, Patricia spends very little time in it. She tends to sit on my lap nursing and dozing off on my knee while I work at the computer. This does cause some problems occasionally, especially when she tries to join in the typing, banging the keyboard, or grabbing the telephone whenever she can."

Greta Holmer, Belgium (Self-Employed Translator)

"One day I was extremely tired since I was working late at home the previous evening, and Maggie was not sleeping through the night. When I went to wash out my pumping cup, one of the staff noticed that I did not button my blouse after my pumping session.... In my embarrassment to quickly button my blouse, I left the pumping cup on the counter. My assistant brought it to me a few hours later, only to inform me that a few people were a bit taken aback."

Patricia Propper, USA (Director of Academic Budgeting and Planning)

"I learned one of the cardinal rules of pumping...all pumps are not created equal! And furthermore, never purchase a breast pump manufactured by a company who also has a personal interest in the sale of infant formula! Slight conflict of interest, wouldn't you say?"

Micaela Sanchez, USA (Librarian Assistant)

"I work and breastfeed because I like to do both things. Breastfeeding makes me feel complete as a woman. I work because I want to and it makes me feel useful."

Maria del Mar Mazza, USA (Hispanic Liaison)

"I would love it if there were a cozy room where I could pump, but since I don't have access to one, I do find comfort in being surrounded by supportive co-workers while I pump at my workstation. What brings me the most satisfaction is knowing that I am giving my baby the best nutrition she can get. If you think of it that way, it's never an inconvenience."

Lilia Benjamin, USA (Social Worker)

"Knowing I have given her the best start is reassuring. Knowing our bond is strong is a blessing. Seeing her thrive is literally awesome. Would I do it all over again? Even with working? For her or another baby? In that first blessed heartbeat, you better believe it."

Kaylene Proctor, USA (Assistant Director, School of Public Affairs)

"Much to my surprise, reading the email posts about pumping gave me a lot of anxiety. I didn't realize how much of a science pumping can be turned into. There were posts regarding the daily fluctuations of ounces produced by each breast, low-milk production concerns, color changes of milk, increasing the fat content, and on and on.... I guess I just took for granted that my body produced what my son needed. I eventually stopped reading the email posts and turned to fellow pumping moms at work for support and camaraderie."

Micaela Sanchez, USA (Librarian Assistant)

"[The daycare providers] were not as knowledgeable as I thought they would be. They are used to formula and from the beginning they assumed that my child was formula-fed.... They have a preprinted sheet where they let you know how your child's day was. These sheets mentioned only formula, not human milk. It took a good month or two for them to realize how important my milk was for me and my son. Today they have that same preprinted sheet, but with an additional space for mother's milk!"

Lillyvette Cummings, USA (Clerical Position)

"My life would be so much easier if we had extended paid leaves, on-site day-care, and people who understood the importance of breastfeeding and allowed me to have a more flexible schedule! In a perfect world, I would have been able to stay home until Bridget naturally weaned, but no such world exists for me so I am a breastfeeding working mother."

Tracy McGrory, USA (Social Studies Teacher)

"One of my main motivations in trying to always find a better balance between professional goals, financial security, and mothering is to help create more options for my daughters when they become mothers. The more flexible and creative our concept of what a 'working mother' can be, the better chances our daughters will have to be professionally fulfilled, financially secure, and, most of all, the kind of mothers we all want to be."

Dana Anderson-Villamagna, USA (Journalist)

"The first boss I had when I was pumping was really irritating. I started [putting a 'Do Not Disturb' sticky note on my door] when pumping. The note on my door evolved over time to say, 'Do Not Disturb. Do Not Knock. Do Not Slide Things Under the Door. Do Not Ask When I'll Be Finished.' It was ridiculous."

Sylvia Ann Ellison, USA (Government Researcher)

"I think it's important for nursing working mothers to know that it isn't easy, it isn't convenient, and it can be very stressful. But it's such an important and brief time in the life of your baby. If you schedule your day around nursing and pumping and stick to it, I think it's a possibility to breastfeed for at least a year. It takes a great deal of dedication and perseverance, and women need to have that when they go back to work. If they go back with an attitude of 'we'll see how it goes,' it isn't going to work. It has to be a priority."

Carrie Babet, USA (Sales Manager)

"For me, pumping my milk at work is a welcome relief to the stresses of my day. It allows me to do something tangible and important for my daughter even when I am miles away. Pumping gives me a set time each day when I think only of Karis, and remember why it is that I am working so hard. The electric pump is a necessity for me. The health of my baby is a testament to the importance of breastfeeding. The close bond we share might still exist if I had not chosen to breastfeed, but there is no replacement for knowing that my body produced everything she ingested for almost seven months; that my body continued to support her even outside the womb. The fact that human milk is free is just an added benefit."

Ann Morgan Adams, USA (Technical Writer)

"One day I was breastfeeding my daughter at my mother-in-law's house, who formula-fed her children. While I was breastfeeding she said, 'You can tell you and Amber have an intimate relationship.' I thought that she was right and all the obstacles in the world couldn't take me away from the precious moments I spend breastfeeding my daughter."

Christine Joneleit, USA (Technology Staff Developer)

"I think it should be required that all state funded daycares provide formal training on how to handle human milk."

Auta Boykins, USA (Operations Analyst)

"Her face lights up when I come into her daycare [to nurse]. What an unbelievable feeling that is."

Beth Pesiri Solomita, USA (Admissions Manager)

"I think it is important to decide how important [breastfeeding] is to you before you even go back to work. It isn't easy to stay committed...I spent a lot of time in the lactation room over the past year. And, I took some grief from co-workers who didn't understand why it was so important to me.... But, as a result of my dedication, my son is 15 months old and is still nursing."

Jenika Johnson, USA (Nurse)

"I don't think I would be able to do what I do without breastfeeding. I often sit and work at my laptop while holding my child and nursing. It is just a physical impossibility to type and hold a bottle! Although I wish I could have stopped and enjoyed my babies more while they were little, I know that breastfeeding them has made us bond more and forces me to slow down at regular intervals during the day."

Sonja Becker-Boelter, USA (Michigan)

"I work a 24-hour shift. It feels as if I spend more time in the office bathroom than I do anywhere else. My supervisors, while they understand my desires for my child and my need to pump, haven't really provided me with a comfortable private area. I've adapted by leaving a chair in the corner of our bathroom."

Stephanie Purdy, USA (Emergency Medical Technician)

"My biggest challenge was finding a location for me to pump at work. I am a dance teacher at an elementary school and had been using a large walk-in closet off the dance studio, but I had not thought to clear this with the administration at the school. I had thought that if I was using my normal break time…that this would be fine. However, when they realized that I was pumping, the administration was concerned that a child could walk in on me as the closet did not lock. (This was unlikely as the children do not wander the school unsupervised.) The administration suggested that I use an office on a different floor but cautioned there would be continual traffic from workers on that floor. (In other words, there would be no privacy.) This was not acceptable to me. I ended up asking my student teacher to sit outside the door of the walk-in closet while I pumped. She graciously did so."

Elizabeth McPherson USA, (Dance Teacher)

"Nursing is for some reason not as 'normal' over here in America. I really try not to nurse in public anymore. Since Jason is older, I get a lot of angry or disgusted looks if people notice that I am nursing him. In Germany, you get a caring or a loving smile from a stranger if you sit somewhere and nurse. 'Look, how wonderful, that women is nursing her child.' "

Berit Lewis, USA (Daycare Provider)

"Sometimes I feel like I constantly have to apologize to people for their trouble as I slip away to express my milk, but the last person I would want to apologize to would be my child. So I carry on, doctoring and breastfeeding, aimed at investing as much as I can in the health of all those I can reach, from my patients at work to my baby at home."

Priti Joshi-Guske, USA (Physician, Internal Medicine)

"I am an engineer working primarily in a male dominated profession. One might think how odd it would be to be pregnant much less breastfeeding in such an environment. I am lucky to have such a great support network of peers.... Men that I work with applaud me for excusing myself to go pump and they would actually schedule meetings around my scheduled pumping sessions."

Jennifer Robino, USA (Engineer)

"My advice to women who want to make breastfeeding and working a reality is that you should be determined to breastfeed.... It is my conviction that only a breastfed individual will breastfeed or support breastfeeding. So do it for your baby and build up a healthy generation."

Ancy Dmello, India (Service Quality Manager)

"If I were to remake the US to make it easier to combine breastfeeding and work, I would:

- Have universal health care to make freelancing/consulting a more available option (many people work full-time only for the health benefits);
- Make more jobs telecommuting;
- Put daycare centers in every office building and make nursing/pumping breaks protected by law;
- Increase the Family Medical Leave Act (FMLA) to six months and find a way to subsidize that leave with some paid time off;
- Be more supportive of bringing babies into the office;
- Make breastfeeding in general, and especially in public, more accepted and encouraged."

Siobhan Green, USA (Technology Analyst)

"I returned to my job at a Washington, DC lobbying firm three days per week when my son was six weeks old. He was a voracious nurser and pumping proved to be easy for me. I knew I was producing a lot of milk but didn't realize that this was unusual. My male boss is very involved in rearing his own children and was very supportive of his wife breastfeeding. He made sure that I had the use of our small conference room to pump whenever I needed without me ever needing to ask. One day he opened the refrigerator and promptly slammed it shut. He turned to me, said, "Please don't sue me for sexual harassment, but I just can't stop myself from saying this...Oh my God! It's only noon and you have 36 ounces of milk in there! OK. That's out of my system. I'll never bring it up again if you don't sue me." He never brought it up again.

Beth Anderson, USA (Lobbyist)

"When I returned [from maternity leave], the entire office was in the middle of a major grant application submission. Since all of our jobs are paid by grants, this is of utmost importance. On the day we needed to send it out, I had to bring my three-month-old baby into the office with me. About halfway through the day, my boss and other researchers found themselves walking my baby around to soothe her while I worked. At the end, once the box was safely handed over to the shipping company, we all gathered together to toast the completion of the application. If you can imagine, I'm standing in my office, baby attached to the breast, with six or seven co-workers, including researchers and directors. At that moment, I knew we were going to be just fine."

Kerry Kokkinogenis, USA (Program Development Manager)

"I experienced some frustration with pumping until a lactation consultant suggested getting a larger flange. I have large breasts but did not know that my nipples required a flange larger than the ones that come standard with the pump. But it seemed to help and pumping has been easier."

Teresa Moser, USA (Chaplain)

"There is a delicate equation to the balance of being a working/nursing mother. In my view:

Successful working/nursing mother =Super Turbo Pump + Job you love + Supportive and helpful husband + Great Daycare Provider + Dedication to Nursing"

Kris Spazafumo, USA (Marketing Manager)

"If anyone had told me that breastfeeding my first child, Jalen, would have changed my life, I would have thought them nuts. But, after nursing her successfully for 15 months and now nursing my nine-month-old son, Luca, it is clear that breastfeeding has been truly life-changing. I can also credit my daughter and our successful nursing relationship with changing my career path. Preparing to be a mom led to countless hours of research on issues related to parenting, breastfeeding, and related topics. When faced with returning to work and not knowing where I would be pumping, I evolved into a person advocating for acceptance and real change for breastfeeding working mothers."

Gina Ciagne, USA (Public Affairs)

"Emotionally, I had such a hard time leaving him to go to work. I cried and cried—but when I got home and he snuggled up to me to nurse, he sighed and rolled his eyes closed like he was in baby heaven at last. It made me feel so much better."

Lisa Smith, USA (Oncology Nurse)

"I wore her for the few hours I was there, popping in and out of a client meeting while she nursed and snoozed. The next day my boss commented on how satisfied she had been. I had to tell him that she had been nursing all the while, and he was shocked at my ability to multi-task."

Elizabeth Selby McCarthy, USA (Paralegal)

"Most full-time working mothers have little time with children between pick up from daycare and bedtime. However, I found nature works in miraculous ways because nursing actually made me spend more time with my baby than non-breastfeeding mothers. Therefore my recommendation to all full-time working mothers is that it is essential to breastfeed. Mothers and babies are healthier, get more rest, spend necessary quality time together, develop intimate bonds and as a side bonus, save money as well."

Cheryl Louden, USA

"Being an herbalist, I was able to use some great emmenagogues (milk producing herbs). I used herbs such as fennel and fenugreek, among others to help increase my milk supply. I found goat's rue to be best at increasing my milk supply. On my days off, I let my daughter nurse as much as she wanted while carrying her in the sling."

Kaylene Proctor, USA (Multiple careers)

"I was a little nervous about flying with the baby and breastfeeding…After we took off I had to use the restroom. As I walked down the aisle, I counted five women, all different ethnicities and ages, nursing their children. In that moment I was so proud that I kept going…. It is the best thing I've ever done aside from giving birth to my son."

Tyra Harrell, USA (Head Athletic Trainer)

"When Henrique was ten months old, I returned to work in a small family company. I made less money and had fewer responsibilities than before, but on the other hand more flexibility, which allowed me to raise my two children much better than I could do when Flávia was a little baby."

Iolanda Sousa, Portugal (Electrical Engineer)

"I do believe that breastfeeding my daughter exclusively has been one of the most difficult yet rewarding things I've ever done. I have overcome dead batteries, clogged pump valves, forgotten ice packs, forgotten collection bottles and bags, not to mention no outlets and forgotten breastshields."

Jennifer Cressy, USA (Environmental Educator)

"I sincerely wish that our culture was more supportive of breastfeeding. The small part of me that is a political activist takes great pleasure in nursing in public places—my baby has the right to eat anywhere he has the right to be, and I have the right to feed him."

Julie Leith-Ross, USA (Recruitment Consultant)

"Whenever I need to go to conferences, I take my breast pump with me. I have pumped in empty classrooms, offices, in my car, dining rooms at restaurants, and even the rare breastfeeding/pumping room. At one conference at a hotel, another pumping mother and I were each given keys to private hotel rooms for the day, free of charge, so we could pump whenever needed. For me, this is what supporting breastfeeding is all about...many times I am offered the bathroom. I have had to educate people about how unacceptable an option this is. I often ask if they would like to prepare their own lunch in the bathroom, and explain how it is extremely unsanitary. Amazingly, another better, more comfortable option always comes about. I always hope the next pumping mom fares better."

Jennifer Villanueva-Henkle, USA (Project Coordinator)

"Continuing to breastfeed while returning to work has made me a stronger person and a more confident mother. I never knew I could make such a commitment and overcome some of my shyness. I had read many lists of the benefits for the babies of mothers who nurse and work, like having a happy and healthy baby and the security of nursing at the end of the day. I just never anticipated the power it would have on me as a person, as a mother, and as a woman."

Deb Marks, USA (Teacher)

"For my first day back at work, my husband wrote me a letter telling me that even though I could not be with our baby during the day, I was providing for him in a very real and meaningful way—not only financially, but as a role model and as a balanced person. I love being a mother, and I enjoy being a professional."

Tracey Whelan, USA (Communications Specialist)

"By default, working has made breastfeeding the easiest alternative for nourishing my son, Henry. Yes, handling, storing, and preparing bottles for him does take time, but knowing that he is getting the very best while I'm not able to be with him makes all the difference in the world. Leaving him every morning is the hardest thing I do each day. I have also eliminated all non-essential activities and commitments so that we spend as much time together as possible."

Sage Drake, USA (Accountant)

"I had no family around. My husband's family lives two hundred miles away…and my entire family lives on the other side of the Atlantic Ocean. By checking daycare prices, I figured out that it would be cheaper to pay a flight ticket for my youngest sister to travel and stay with me for six months to take care of my baby while I work than to pay daycare. So I did so. However, she could not stay for six months because immigration did not consider it reason enough to stay longer. So after three months, my sister had to return [to Europe]. I decided again to pay another flight ticket so she could return and stay another three months."

Olga Martin de Eugenio, USA (Program Coordinator)

"As of right now, I drive two-and-a-half hours to get to work but we will be moving soon. We selected a town that is halfway between our jobs so we can each drive equal distance, and we are bringing a nanny with us. Although I love my job, my family comes first, so sometime in the future we will extend our family further with another nursling. Until then I will continue to be the nursing mother/firefighter. I hope I can be an inspiration to other mothers who feel that separation hinders the nursing relationship. My baby and I are proof that a strong foundation built on security, attachment, and love will see its way through any obstacle."

Jennifer Crunkilton, USA (Firefighter)

"I missed so much work during my pregnancy because of hyperemesis, I could only take a four-week maternity leave. At the time I worked as a law clerk for a justice on my state's supreme court. Although he did not have leeway to extend my maternity leave, the justice I worked for was very supportive of breastfeeding. His wife was a La Leche League member and I was not the first law clerk he employed who was a nursing mother. The justice even invited me to bring my newborn daughter, Annie, to work with me. Annie came to work about half the time at first. At the court, she napped close to me tucked in a sling, wriggled around in the playpen I set up behind my desk, and was carried around the office by adoring co-workers. It was a remarkable thing to work in what has traditionally been a man's profession with my nursling at my side."

Jenny Kaleczyc, USA (Law Clerk)

"Returning to work was much more difficult for me emotionally than I had imagined. I missed the baby tremendously; I remember feeling as though someone had ripped a hole right in my heart. I made it my 'mission' to pump milk at work daily and thought of it as the next best thing to actually being the one caring for him."

Connie Young, USA (Nurse Practitioner)

"What I've learned is that there is always time for everything. There is time to work, to express, to spend time with your husband, your child, to spend time on your own. Juliane is just a baby now, but every day I see that she's growing. Before I know it, she'll be a young lady. When I feel as though breastfeeding at work is becoming too difficult, I just think, 'What's one year to spend on working and breastfeeding in Juliane's life?' She will only be a baby once, and this is one of the things I want to get right. Breastfeeding at work (and anywhere else) is just a single step that I'm making for Juliane to start her wonderful journey of a thousand miles."

Candy Co, Philippines (Marketing Director)

"I bought a container deep and wide enough to hold the milk storage bags. I also put a small cutting board into the freezer to lay the full bags on so they will freeze flat and not bulky. Before I started pumping I wrote the date and amount down on the milk storage bags. After that, I put the bags into the freezer, laying them down flat on the cutting board. I would move them into the empty container after they were frozen all the way—the freshest bag always went into the very back. It was kind of like filing away the bags. That worked well for me since I had a pretty good supply going after a while and still enough room for ice cream in the freezer."

Berit Lewis, USA (Daycare Provider)

"If my child was aware of this stage in her life, I think she would say, 'Even though my mom was always running around juggling her personal and professional life, she always found time to nurse me and was at her calmest when she did so. She would never hurry me up and would rock me gently as she nursed me.' And this is the reason I did what I did. No corner office with a big window and a huge bonus check can ever replace the look in my daughter's eyes as I would pick her up to nurse."

Sara Sangha, USA (Medical Science Liaison)

"[Breastfeeding and working] is not always easy. For example, I went to a three-day training at an airport hotel. I had nowhere to store the milk and I had to try and find a place to pump. I ended up using a bathroom stall that was not frequently visited (since I would be in there 15 to 20 minutes).... A few times while pumping, other women who heard me would ask if I was pumping and tell me how great it was and ask if I needed anything.... It may sound weird, but it made me feel like I was part of a secret club. The breastfeeding club."

Jessica Leddy, USA (Social Worker)

"He gets everything that I can possibly give him while we are away from one another. I know that he has exceptional care. He is developing physically, mentally, and socially every minute that I am away from him. Selfishly, I look at the clock in my classroom as 3:35 approaches and cannot wait to pick my child up and nurse him. Nobody else can provide him with what we share together during the time that we nurse and I love it!"

Allison Davis, USA (Special Education Teacher)

"Breastfeeding and work is hard and it takes a committed person. Milk storage and transportation to child care is a hassle. Business travel is a hassle. Lugging the pump everywhere is a hassle. Keeping on a tight pumping schedule to ensure adequate milk production is a hassle. Maintaining an appropriate diet is a hassle. The benefits have been immense though. The connection I have with my children after going back to work is priceless."

Jennifer Robino, USA (Engineer)

"When I returned to work...my department's director was incredibly helpful in lessening the impact of my return. She clearly understood the benefits to my child, but she also understood how allowing me opportunities to breastfeed my daughter made me a more productive, less stressed employee."

Karen Metivier-Carreiro, USA (Senior Policy Analyst)

"There were difficult times when I was so busy with work that I put off pumping until I had soaked through my suit, or customers were using all of the fitting rooms and I had to anxiously wait for my turn. Once I actually lost a part to my pump and my husband had to drive up to the store with Matthew so that I could nurse him. After one particularly long day, I had to pull over at a gas station to express some milk after I was delayed in rush hour traffic."

Heather Eckstein, USA (Area Sales Manager)

"I have found that having Wednesday off is important. After two days, Aidan is ready for a day together. It is also beneficial at work because I never hold up a project over a long weekend.... For so many years my career was my identity.

Getting married changed my work habits incrementally. Now, finding the right balance between my son and my work has been a much greater challenge than I anticipated."

Allison Kolar, USA (Manager, Annual Giving Programs)

"I took Eyal to work with me until he was seven months old. I kept him in his green baby buggy beside me in the little room in which I sat opposite the switchboard. I would pick him up a lot and would breastfeed him as he wanted. It was very nice. There were two reactions among the other kibbutzniks. Some reacted as…if I would single-handedly destroy the kibbutz. Then there were the others who gave me a lot of support and told me again and again what a good thing I was doing. Everyone played with Eyal and talked to him, and of course, he heard me talking on the phone all of the time. He was very precocious and developed verbally. I loved it."

Donna Ron, Israel (Kibbutz Worker)

Contributors List

La Leche League sincerely thanks the women who shared their stories with us and congratulates all mothers who have succeeded at combining breastfeeding with working.

Ada Frias de Torres, Veterinarian, Dominican Republic

Adriana Doz Verónica, Electrical Engineer, Argentina

Adrienne Custer, Soldier, US Army, US-North Carolina

Agnes Y Y Liu, Hong Kong

Alessandra Barreto Krause, Attorney, Brazil

Alicia Bartz, Writer, US-Minnesota

Alison King, Attorney, UK-England

Alla Kungar, Marketing Manager, US-Massachusetts

Allison Davis, Teacher, Special Education, US-Texas

Allison Kolar, Manager, Annual Giving Programs, US-Indiana

Amanda Alonzo, Senior Web Developer, US-California

Amber Lopez, Flight Attendant

Amy Carr, Reference Librarian, US-New York

Amy Delaney, Teacher, US-South Dakota

Ana C. Mabry, Business Analyst, US-Arkansas

Ana Novara

Ana Raquel Bueno Moraes Ribeiro, Organizational Development, Brazil

Ancy Dmello, Service Quality Manager, India

Andreia C. K. Mortensen, Postdoctoral Fellow, Neurobiology, US-Pennsylvania

Angela Bailon, Office Employee, Guatemala

Ángeles Jiménez Martínez, Nurse, Spain

Angie Armstrong, OB Nurse, US

Angie Sohler, Lactation Educator, US-Colorado

Aniele Theodore

Anita Cole, International Development, Pakistan

Anna Koh, Executive, Singapore

Anne Betting, Professor, France

Anne C. Livingston, Senior Implementation Consultant, US-Florida

Antonia Lina Ocana Jódar, School Employee, Spain

Auta Boykins Walker, Operations Analyst, US-Georgia

Avital Mulay, Computer Programmer, Israel

Azleena bt Wan Mohamad, Environmental Control Officer, Malaysia

Azrena Binti Mahmud, Malaysia

Azucena Cariazo, Spain

Beaulla Nodida, HIV and AIDS Counselor, South Africa

Berit Lewis, Child Care Provider, US-Washington

Beth Anderson, Lobbyist, US-Maryland

Beth Farrell, Information Technology Manager, US-Michigan

Beth Pesiri Solomita, Admissions Manager, US-Connecticut

Beth Stroup, Attorney, US-Illinois

Betsy Hoffmeister, Consultant, Business Owner, US-Washington

Bobbie Brown, Stocker, US-Tennessee

Brandi Wood, US

Candy Co, Marketing, Philippines

Candy Corral, ER Nurse, US-California

Caren Barth, Adjunct Instructor, US-New York

Carla Judit Arbuatti, Chemist, Argentina

Carolyn Rushworth, Pharmacist, Australia

Carrie Babet, National Sales Manager, US

Carrie McAdams, Doctoral Fellow, US-Massachusetts

Carrie Nimmo, Performer, Canada-British Columbia

Cassandra Day, Writer, US-Connecticut

Catalina Caballero Chirinos, Administrative Office Work, Peru

Catalina Legarra Pellicer, Midwife, Spain

Catherine Advocate-Ross, Teacher, US-New York

Catherine Bihet, France

Catherine Lazenby, Special Ed. Teacher, US-South Carolina

Catherine Mulholland, Technical Officer, WHO, Switzerland

Cathryn Faulring, Registered Dietician, US-New Hampshire

Cécile Cottineau, Professor, France

Cheryl Louden, Environmental Consultant, US-Michigan

Christel Germonpré, Teacher, Belgium

Christin Erwin, Dietician, Lactation Consultant, US

Christina Luebbert, Civil Engineer, US-Missouri

Christina Shouse Tourino, Professor, US-Minnesota

Christine Haviaris, Certified Public Accountant, US-New Jersey

Christine Joneleit, Technology Staff Developer, US-New York

Christy Johnson, Collateral Management Liaison, US

Clara Inés Bustamante Duque, Social Worker, Colombia

Claudia Gabriela Ocampo Montes, Office Employee, Mexico

Collette Roe, Military

Connie Young, Pediatric Nurse Practitioner, US-Florida

Crystal Hui-Man Lai, Preschool Director, Taiwan

Cynthia Matheson, School Teacher, US

Cynthia Spidell, Executive Analyst, US-Florida

Daiva Spiliauskine, Nursing Director, Lithuania

Dana Anderson-Villamagna, Journalist, US-Virginia

Danielle Drury, Clinical Coordinator, US-California

Davida Baker, US

Dawn Cockrell, Nurse Midwife, US-Texas

Deb Marks, ScienceTeacher, US-New Jersey

Denise Difallah, Biomedical Scientist, Northern Ireland

Diane Cloutier, Business Director, US

Dolly Aleya Menezes, Yoga Instructor, Pakistan

Donna Ron, Kibbutz Worker, Israel

Doris de Méndez, Marketing Assistant, Guatemala

Dorothy Watson, Statistician, US-North Carolina

Elaine Skinner, UK

Elizabeth Fisher, Assistant Professor of Social Work, US-Pennsylvania

Elizabeth Lane-Davies, Therapist/Consultant, US-Michigan

Elizabeth McPherson, Dance Teacher, US-New York

Elizabeth Parise, Business Owner, US-Massachusetts

Elizabeth Power, Foreign Service Officer, Mexico

Elizabeth Selby McCarthy, Paralegal, US-North Carolina

Ellen Kitzmiller, Attorney, US-Utah

Emily Cowan, US-New Hampshire

Emily Ethington, Software Sales, US-Nebraska

Emma Mead, General Manager in Logistics, UK

Ena du Plessis, Attorney, South Africa

Erica Anderson, US

Erica Byrne, Accounts Receivable, US-Massachusetts

Erica Hopkins, Transaction Specialist, US-Virginia

Esther Goldstein, Social Worker, Canada-Ontario

Esther Young, Sous-chef, France

Eunie Lou, Accountant, Mongolia

Fanny Hallett, France

Felicia Fogal, Marketing Director, US-Texas

Fiona Brown, European Banker, UK

Franziska Schombach, X-ray Assistant, Germany

Frédérique Renard, Teacher, France

Ghada Sayed, Pediatrician, Egypt

Gina Ciagne, Public Affairs Specialist, US-Washington, DC

Gina Hartnett, Finance Attorney, Japan-Tokyo

Greta Holmer, Translator, Belgium

Guadalupe Vega, Supplier Quality Engineer, Mexico

Haby Celestin, Executive Assistant, France

Heather Brown, Case Management Assistant, US-Florida

Heather Eckstein, Area Sales Manager, US-California

Heather Reeder, Human Resource Manager, US-Michigan

Heidi Cloutier, Social Worker, US-New Hampshire

Helen Bedford, Secretary, Personal Assistant, UK-England

Holly Lunsford, Financial Services Manager, US

Holly Robinson, Home Health Nurse, US-Missouri

Iolanda Sousa, Electrical Engineer, Portugal

Isabel Ferrari, France

Isabelle Bergeron, Flight Attendant, France

Isabelle Le Quéré, France

Jagruti Phatak, State Bank of India, India

Jane Luetchens, Psychiatric Clinical Nurse Specialist, US-Texas

Jaren Zurlo, Home Daycare Provider, US

Jeni Leaird, Peer Counselor, WIC, US,

Jenika Johnson, Nurse, US-Minnesota

Jenna McClure, Director of Retail, US-New York

Jennifer Burns, Microbiologist, US-Ohio

Jennifer Cressy, Environmental Educator, US-New York

Jennifer Crunkilton, Firefighter, US-Tennessee

Jennifer Fernandez, Paramedic, US

Jennifer Moorehead, Documentation Manager, West Bank

Jennifer Robino, Engineer, US-Arizona

Jennifer Snider, Health Coordinator, US-California

Jennifer Villanueva-Henkle, Project Coordinator, US-Ohio

Jenny Buck, Court Reporter, Hong Kong

Jenny Driscoll, Web/Publications Coordinator, US-Colorado

Jenny Kaleczyc, Attorney, US-Montana

Jessica Leddy, Social Worker, US-Illinois

Jessica Lehman, Nurse, US-Iowa

Jessica Santanella, US Air Force, US-Texas

Jill Paterson, Elementary Teacher, US-Connecticut

Jill TenBrink, Teacher's Aid, US-Michigan

Joan Cruz, Technical Support, US-New Jersey

Joy Jernigan, Features Producer, US-Washington

Judith Montgomery-Watson, Wildlife Manager, Northern Ireland

Judy Coughenour, Senior Technical Support Engineer, US-Pennsylvania

Julie Ann Joyal, Nurse, Acute Care, US-New York

Julie Hanley, ICU Nurse, US-Michigan

Julie Leith-Ross, Recruitment Consultant, US-Oregon

Julie M. Whitcher, Civil Engineer, US-Minnesota

Julie Scanell, Human Resources Manager, US

Julie Zantke, Head of Finance, Germany

Karen A. Metivier-Carreiro, Senior Policy Analyst, US-Virginia

Karen Z. Brass, Senior Sales Director, US-Colorado

Karla McGarry, Help Desk Employee, US-New York

Karmen Mlinar, Electro Technical Engineer, Slovenia

Katherine Gonzales, Maintenance Specialist, Puerto Rico

Kathy Cook, Teacher, US-Georgia

Katie Mae Isaacson, Sorter Operator, US-Georgia

Kayla Sawyer, Recreation and Fitness Specialist, US-North Carolina

Kaylene Proctor, Assistant Graduate School Director, US-Colorado

Kellie Badley, Daycare Provider, US-Oklahoma

Kerri McCabe, Attorney, US-New York

Kerry Kokkinogenis, Secretary, Personal Assistant, US-Massachusetts

Kerry Urquizo, Adult ESL Teacher, US-Illinois

Kim Johnson, Assistant Manager, Food Service, US-Missouri

Kim Lunger, Project Office Manager, US-Kentucky

Kymberlie Stefanski, Information Technology Specialist, US-Illinois

Kimberly Hunt, Administrative Assistant, US-Washington

Kris Spazafumo, Marketing Manager, US-California

Kristie Huff, Captain, US Army Nurse, US

Kristin King, Instructor, Community College, US-Washington

Laura Barbas-Rhoden, Professor, Foreign Languages, US-South Carolina

Laura Vargas Gastelum, IT Director, Mexico

Leah Bailey, Staff Sergeant, US Air Force, US-Missouri

Leslie Hershberger, Embroidery, US-Iowa

Lilia H. Benjamin, Social Worker, US-California

Liliana Yánez de Petrovich, Executive Assistant, Peru

Lilyvette Cummings, Clerical Position, US-New Jersey

Lina María Uricoechea Herrerra, Colombia

Linda Hooper, United Nations Statistician, Switzerland

Linda Steele-Thom, Marketing Assistant, US-Kansas

Lisa Garrison, Professor, US-Delaware

Lisa King, Tailoress, UK

Lisa Kopecky, Dietician, US-Nebraska

Lisa Loeppky, Flight Attendant, Canada-Alberta

Lisa Marrett, Training and Staff Development, UK-England

Lisa Smith, Oncology Nurse, US-Louisiana

Liz DeHaan, Nurse, US-Colorado

Lizette Aguilar Valer, Management Assistant, Peru

Lucy Cokes, Managing Director, UK

Lydia Evans Olsen, Program Manager, US-Washington

Lydia Requejo, Medical Assistant, US-New York

Lynn Phillips, Marketing Specialist, US-Washington, DC

Maaike Niet, Itinerant Teacher (deaf students), Canada-Nova Scotia

Margarita Santiago Ramírez, Live-in Maid, Mexico

Margot Harris, Nurse Practitioner, US-Wisconsin

Maria del Ángel Carriazo, Business Owner, Spain

Maria del Mar Mazza, Dietician, Peer Counselor, US-Illinois

Mariah Boone, Social Worker, US-Texas

Marie Hassett Spadaro, Literacy and Adult Learning, US-Massachusetts

Marie Nortier, France

Marissa Hannen, SSgt, US Air Force, US-South Carolina

Marta Marina González Pérez, Music Teacher, Spain

MaryJoan Jordan Vacarrela, Family Business, US-North Carolina

Mary Warren Bonafini, Human Resource Assistant, US-Massachusetts

Maureen Harper, Public Relations Manager, US-Ohio

Meg Gronau, Marketing Manager, US-Minnesota

Melanie Laverman, Editor, US-Iowa

Melissa Hulse, Pharmacist, US-Kansas

Melissa Reyes, University Faculty Member, Philippines

Micaela Sanchez Library Assistant, US-Colorado

Midori Fujita, District Nurse, Japan

Miosotis Rivas, Ministry of Women's Affairs, Dominican Republic

Molli Vioral, Dialysis Technician, US-Pennsylvania

Mona Nyandoro, Peace Corps Recruiter, US-California

Monica Mellado, Contraloria General de la Republica, Peru

Mònica Sabate Tornadijo, Director of Law Journal, Spain

Monika De Sanctis, Dominican Republic

Morgan Ann Adams, Technical Writer, US-California

Mrunal M. Thakekar, India

Mylea Rhynes, Kindergarten Teacher, US-Texas

Myriame Vincent, International Business Regulations, France

Nancy Hampton, Administrative Support Assistant, US-Colorado

Nancy Parsons

Natasha Hall, Artist

Natasha Hartley, Army, US-Nebraska

Neusa Ribeiros, Journalist, Brazil

Neydary Zambrano, Healthy Start Program Manager, US-Pennsylvania

Nichole Niebur, Credit Analyst, US-Nebraska

Nicola Evans, Research Scientist, US-Illinois

Nicolas Peligros

Nicole Austin Dalesio, Teacher, US-California

Nicole Tiongson, Instructor, Home Business, US-Michigan

Olga Martin de Eugenio, Program Coordinator, US-Florida

Pamela Young, Customer Training Administrator, US

Pascale Lunel, Direct Sales, France

Patricia Malley, Army Nurse, US

Patricia Propper, Academic Budgeting and Planning, US-New York

Patrícia Veloso, Quality Engineer, Brazil

Paula Gonzalez de Pichardo, Milk Bank Manager, Dominican Republic

Paula Hahn, Chemist, US-Idaho

Peggy Wilson, Retail Worker, US-Georgia

Priti Joshi-Guske, Doctor of Internal Medicine, US-Florida

Priti Mukherjee, Technical Advisor, India

Rachel Simpson, Historian, US-Colorado

Raquel Sigüenza de Micheo, Biologist, Guatemala

Rayane Abdel-Samad Khater, Lebanon

Rebecca Chin, Personal Assistant, Singapore

Rebecca Gregoire, Assistant Athletic Trainer, US-New Hampshire

Rebecca Novak Tibbitt, Senior Manager, Public Affairs, US-Connecticut

Rebecca Young, Performer, France

Renuka Bery, International Development, US-Washington, DC

Rhoda Taylor, Canada

Robyn Roche-Paull, Airplane Mechanic, US Navy, US-California

Rocio Chirinos, Water and Sanitation Dept., Peru-Lima

Roswita Dresler, Teacher, Canada-British Columbia

Ruth Gur, Physician, Israel

Ruth Tincoff, Lecturer and Research Associate, US-Massachusetts

Sage Drake, Accountant, US-Missouri

Samantha Shub, English Teacher, US-Texas

Sandra DeBary, Human Resources, US-Georgia

Sara Sangha, Medical Science Liaison, US-Louisiana

Sarah Farquhar, Child Development, New Zealand

Sarah Johnson, Labor and Delivery Nurse, US-Minnesota

Sarah Novak, Special Needs Teacher, Hong Kong

Sarah V. Olavides, Software Test Manager, UK-Wales

Shagufa Jamal, International Development, Pakistan

Shavonne Mortenson, Searcher, Title Company, US-Wisconsin

Shawn Blaesing-Thompson, Cartographer (Mapmaker), US-Washington

Shilpa Shirodkar, Steno Assistant, India

Shubhada Chaukar, Newspaper Editor, India

Silvia Valderrama Sánchez, Peru

Silviya Zaharieva Andreeva, Chief Operations Manager, Bulgaria

Siobhan Green, Technology Analyst, US-Washington, DC

Sonja Becker-Boelter, Translator, US-Michigan

Sophie Lesiège, Home Daycare Provider, Canada-Québec

Sophon Chim, Housekeeper, Cambodia

Stefany Austin, Office Manager, US-Michigan

Stephanie Pfaff, Community Health Specialist, US

Stephanie Purdy, Emergency Medical Technician, US

Sue Low, Graphic Designer, UK

Sue Prado, Lactation Consultant, US-Illinois

Susan Lundquist, Social Worker, US-Minnesota

Susan Madera, Manager, US-NY

Susan Singleton, Attorney, UK

Suzanne Brown, Account Executive, US-Virginia

Svea Maxwell, Prevention Coordinator, US-Ohio

Sylvia Ann Ellison, Government Researcher, US-Maryland

Tamar, Israel

Tamara Jackman, Nurse Midwife, US

Tamara Kaloiani , Cytologist, Republic of Georgia

Tamara Wilson, Administrative Assistant, US-North Carolina

Tammy Miner, Casino Dealer, US-Connecticut

Tanja Schülin, Physician, Netherlands

Tara Guillermo Berner, Physician, US-Louisiana

Tatiana, Interpreter, Russia

Tatiana, Accountant, Russia

Tenille Manning Heier, Writer, US-South Dakota

Teresa Millán Castillo, Government Employee

Teresa Moser, Pastoral Services Director, US-Oregon

Terri Magalhaes, Child Care Provider, US-Iowa

Thia Thomasich, Dispatcher, US-Missouri

Titia Van der Werf, Social Worker, Germany

Tracey Whelan, Communications Specialist, US-Texas

Tracy McGrory, Social Studies Teacher, US-New Jersey

Tricia Sheehan, Human Resource Manager, US-Massachusetts

Tricia Shore, Stand-up Comedian, US-California

Tricia Smith, Attorney, US

Tsviya Shir, Attorney, Israel

Tyra Harrell, Athletic Trainer, US

Tzippy, Israel

Utkarsha Naik, Actress, India

Uza, Israel

Vanessa Fucks, Nurse, France

Vedavati Habbu, Librarian, India

Veronica Aceves Navarro, Department Manager, Mexico

Veronica Garea, Nuclear Physicist, Argentina

Veronica Rusnak, IT Project Leader, US-Wisconsin

Véronique Bégin, Clinical Data Manager, France

Viana Maza Chavarría, Professor, Guatemala

Victoria Escobar, Agricultural Extensionist Worker, Bolivia

Victoria Kasanga, Home Caterer, Tanzania

Virginie Blavier, Research Institute Librarian, France

Wendy Hutchison, Science Teacher, US-Pennsylvania

Wendy Shore, Registered Nurse, Lactation Consultant, US

Yi-Chinh, Production Planner, Singapore

Yuly Medina Sanchez, Accounts Executive, Peru

Yuriko Inukai, IT Engineer, Japan

Zoe Hilton, Senior Research Scientist, Canada-Ontario

Credits

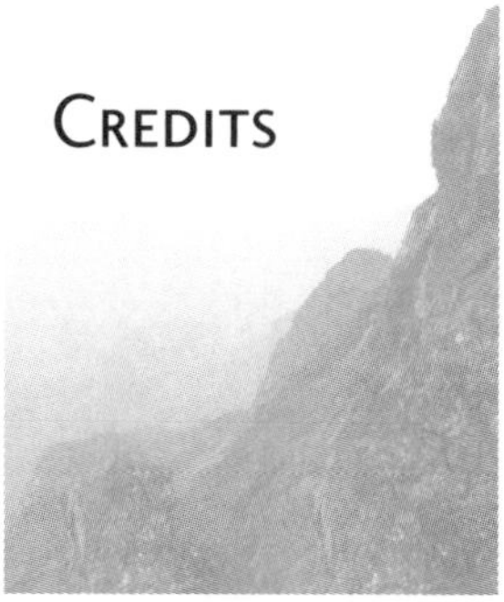

Thank you to the following translators, writers, and photographers who graciously shared their time and talent.

Translators:

Spanish:

- Natalia Smith Allen
- Jenna Nilson
- Jennifer Henkle
- Lilyvette Cummings
- Esthela Slater
- Nicole Austin
- Paulina Smith

Portuguese

- Esperança Melo
- Nicole Austin
- Andreia Mortensen
- Veronica Garea

French:

- Jo-Anne Elder
- Lynda Hicks
- Lionel Mathieu
- Nicola Evans

Hebrew:

- Hannah Katsman

Japanese

- Toshi Joliffe

Khmer

- Kim Chadwick

Georgian

- Maya Sartania

Mongolian

- Melanie Wilson

Contributing Writers:

- Alicia Bartz
- Susan Bantz-Gustafson
- Jennifer Hicks
- Melanie Laverman

Photo Credits:

- Prashant Gangal, Hirkani's Mountain
- Jennifer Fernandez, Mothering Magazine
- John Fernez, SAS
- Michelle Surkamp, Carlson Companies
- Randy Zeigler, Mayo Clinic
- Editor's Photo, Kirk Lamb

Indexer:

- Melanie Laverman

Afterword

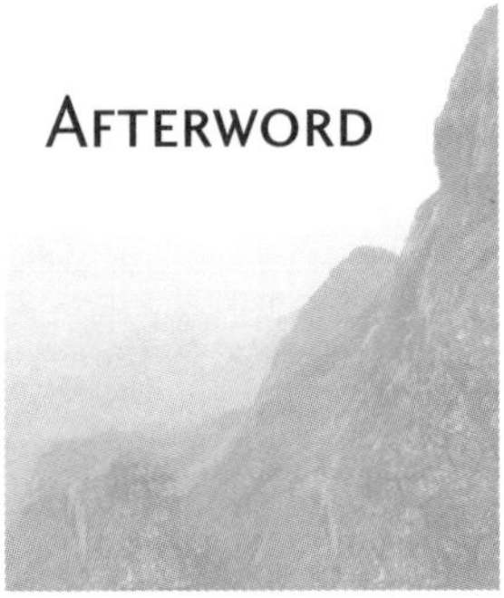

Hirkani's Daughters continues a tradition started by La Leche League in 1956, almost 50 years ago. La Leche League has succeeded through the powerful medium of women telling stories about their lives as breastfeeding mothers. By listening—validating, sharing, and learning what works—LLL helped families to re-build a breastfeeding culture in communities where breastfeeding was in danger.

These fifty years have brought huge social changes. The breastfeeding movement has been part of those changes, a quiet revolution that halted the trend of mothers and babies relying more and more on artificial feeding. In reversing that trend, we have seen breastfeeding established as a woman's human right, an international campaign to place limits on the marketing of artificial feeding products, the development of lactation consulting as a new international health care field, and the adoption of global standards for infant and young child feeding. People living in the developed world have come to realize how much there is to learn from cultures where breastfeeding is still a central element of family life.

In their stories, the women of Hirkani's Daughters show just how difficult it is to earn money while at the same time breastfeeding and mothering their children. These women needed the support of fathers, grandparents, employers/workmates, and devoted child minders. Many compromises had to be made along the way; often the arrangements had to be changed to meet new challenges.

But these stories show us how proud and satisfied these mothers are that they persevered in sustaining the breastfeeding relationship with their children in spite of needing to do their jobs.

In society's search for gender equality, isn't it time to acknowledge that men's and women's needs are not identical? Pregnancy, birth, recovery, lactation, and the care and comfort that mothers provide through breastfeeding are not things that men can do. The biological side of reproduction takes up women's time and energy. It subjects women to additional risks to life and health. Thus it is a "fact of life" that women who are mothers have different requirements from men and from women without children. Mothers have a right to maternity protection, both for their own sake and on behalf of the next generation.

In this book, some working mothers have told us about their lives. Many others are not represented here, among them subsistence farmers, market women, sweat-shop workers, and all the women who work without wages to maintain their homes, care for relatives, and do voluntary community, religious, or political work.

Every mother has a story to tell. Every story has its part to play as we work to build a world of fair and equal treatment for women— a world where breastfeeding is valued, protected, and supported.

Let us begin by listening to the stories told by Hirkani's daughters.

Chris Mulford, RN, IBCLC
Co-coordinator, Women & Work Taskforce,
World Alliance for Breastfeeding Action (WABA)

INDEX

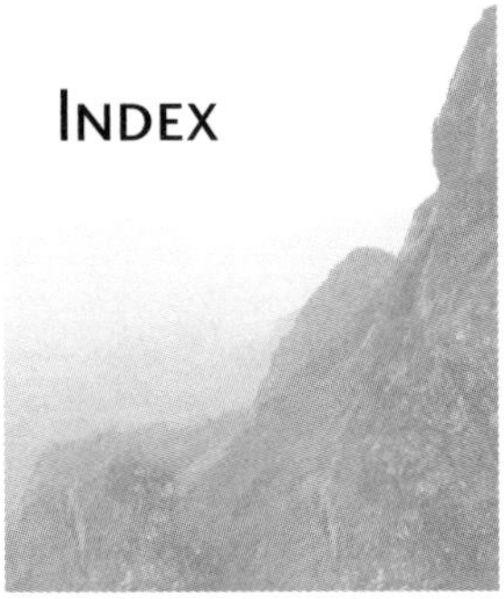

Baby carriers
back carrier, 116
front carrier, 102
sling, 13-15, 36, 72, 74, 106, 143

Bartering, 49-52

Bottles
introducing, 303-04
nipple confusion and, 70-71
refusing, 78-79, 89, 189, 204, 214, 240, 304
selecting, 24, 304

Breast milk, *See* Human milk

Breastfeeding
after breast cancer, 226-27
at daycare, 9-10, 45, 71-72, 78, 113, 143, 148-49, 159, 162-63, 240, 299-300
at home during the workday, 73, 92, 183
at work, 4, 17, 32-33, 106, 122, 140, 148, 237, 249, 284
cluster feeding, 18, 92, 182, 205, 297 *See also* Reverse cycling
cosleeping and, 79, 124, 149, 182, 185, 186, 297, 305 *See also* Cosleeping
extended, 14-15, 18, 29, 37, 65, 72, 82-87, 88-90, 104, 143, 167, 170, 182, 191, 220, 240, 247
influencing, xii, 276
information for daycare providers, 301
low milk supply and, 226-27
of twins, 18
problems establishing, 158-59
reverse cycling, 120, 304-06 *See also* Cluster feeding
tandem, 13-15, 88-90, 122, 170
when no longer pumping, 11, 17, 48, 72, 79, 91, 186, 227, 246
while pregnant, 13-14

Breast pumps
caring for, 293-94
selecting, 120, 123, 291-93

Child care
babysitter at home, 23, 44, 166, 179, 186, 189, 214-15, 233
daycare centers, 4, 7-11, 17-20, 29, 70-72, 148-49, 159, 161-63, 179, 243
family members, 95, 97, 309
fathers, 13-15, 22, 31-33, 35, 67, 78, 84, 122, 139, 168, 181, 211, 222, 248
grandmothers, 73, 85, 89, 92, 102, 105, 110, 134, 155, 183, 222, 249
in-home daycare, 36, 44, 58, 78, 143, 181, 208, 237, 240, 245
mother's helpers, 83, 116, 133, 309
nanny, 189, 213
on-site daycare, 80, 104, 112, 198, 201, 264, 280-81, 282-84
selecting, 299-301

Commuting to work, 18-19, 23-25, 107, 189, 201, 208

Contributors to this book, 339-45
Cosleeping, 79, 124, 149, 182, 185, 186, 305, 311-13

Down syndrome, 73-75

Emotions
- impact on career, 36, 227
- not working, 62-63
- returning to work, 21-27

Employers, child-friendly
- examples of, 259-88
- finding, 39-40

Expressing milk
- by hand, 170, 203, 220, 230, 250, 294-95
- discussing with co-workers, 31-33, 45-48
- ensuring privacy for, 5, 8-9, 44, 121-22, 176
- facilities for, 25-26, 31-32, 39, 58, 70, 78, 140, 155, 249
- fears about, 32
- lack of facilities for, 110, 174
- low milk volume and, 119-20, 124, 170, 227
- problems with let-down and, 8, 71, 123, 182, 227
- while traveling, 53-56
- while working, 9, 33, 47, 277
- with a hand pump, 169, 208, 293
- with an electric pump, 8-11, 19, 22-27, 31-33, 44, 54, 61, 70-72, 78, 89-90, 93, 110, 118-24, 140, 155, 169, 189, 206, 208, 226, 292-93

Father
- caring for baby, 13-15, 22, 31-33, 35, 67, 84, 139, 168, 181, 211, 222, 248
- disabled, 68-72
- ill, 82-84
- unsupportive, 90

Feeding problems
- baby in neonatal intensive care unit (NICU), 80
- baby with Down syndrome, 73
- bottle refusal, *See* Bottles, refusing
- premature baby, 93
- nipple confusion, *See* Bottles, nipple confusion and

Hand expression, 170, 203, 220, 230, 250, 294-95
Hirkani's story, xxix
Human milk
- expression of, *See* Expressing milk
- handling, guidelines for, 301-03
- information for daycare providers, 301-03
- oversupply of, 18, 120, 123
- storing, guidelines for, 302-03
- supplements for increasing supply of, 9, 19, 71, 298
- tips for increasing supply of, 8, 227, 296-98
- turning sour quickly, 16, 19, 270

Lactation programs, benefits of,
- to employees, 260-61, 275-77
- to employers, 259-60, 269, 278, 314-16

Lactation programs, features of
- basics, 314-16
- child-care referral programs, 269
- children at work, 271-74, 279-80
- classes, 264, 269, 283
- educational materials, 269, 276
- flexible schedules, 272, 283
- lactation consultants, 264, 269, 276
- lactation rooms, 264, 268-69, 276, 283, 286, 314-16
- maternity leave, paid, 272, 269, 283
- mother-to-mother support, 264, 286
- on-site health care, 265
- on-site sick child care center, 269
- paternity leave, paid, 283
- pumps and supplies, 264, 266, 268, 276, 285
- telecommuting, 272, 283

Legislation, xv-xvii, 317-319
- Argentina, 113
- Australia, 249
- Bolivia, 116
- Bulgaria, 174
- Canada, 83
- Cambodia, 223
- Dominican Republic, 102
- Egypt, 202
- France, 143
- Georgia Republic, 166
- Germany, 169
- Guatemala, 104
- India, 220
- Israel, 204
- Japan, 231
- Malaysia, 233
- Mexico, 110
- Mongolia, 236
- Netherlands, 152
- New Zealand, 253
- Northern Ireland, 186
- Pakistan, 198
- Peru, 133
- Philippines, 226
- Quebec, 29

Russia, 184
Slovenia, 154
South Africa, 214
Spain, 159
Switzerland, 148
Taiwan, 240
Tanzania, 211
United Kingdom, 140
United States
California, 4
Connecticut, 22
Department of Defense, 59
Florida, 46
Georgia, 69
Illinois, 39
Iowa, 50
Massachusetts, 17
Nebraska, 77
Texas, 8
Legislators, contacting, 316-18

Maternity protection, 318-19
Military policies, 57-59
Mothers' quotes, 325-38

Milk bank, 33

Pumping *See* Expressing milk

Resources, 317-18, 319, 320-22
Reverse cycling, 120, 186, 305-06

Single mother, 41-42, 105-08, 128-29, 165-67
Self-employed mother, 28-29, 49-52, 101-02, 178-80
Support
from co-workers, 32-33, 66-67, 70, 77-79, 89, 109-10, 114, 116-17, 176, 184, 250
from doctors, 174, 191
from employers, 38-40, 43-44, 63-65, 67, 80, 129, 176, 191,198-200, 215, 227, 236, 250
from family, 84, 90, 95, 105, 134, 163, 172, 174, 180
from husband, 4-5, 47, 102, 111, 114, 122, 134, 148, 159-60, 163, 174, 184, 191, 211
from La Leche League, 24, 37, 47, 57, 63-65, 67, 72, 74, 79, 83, 90, 103, 107, 119-21, 126, 149, 154, 185, 233, 237
requesting, 6, 31-33, 42, 45-48, 55, 67, 70-72, 81, 93-95, 121, 175, 234, 314-319
Support, lack of
from co-workers, 45-48, 57-59, 159-60, 206, 240-41, 245
from doctors, 174, 184, 240
from employer, 94, 163-64
from family, 97-98, 184
from hospital, 158-59, 174, 210

Traveling for business
delaying, 131
overnight without baby, 18, 26-27, 53-56, 166-67, 190
with baby, 36, 78, 86, 96-98, 104, 126, 132-36, 143-46, 182, 184, 190, 200

Work
changing jobs after baby, 12-15, 28, 38-40, 79-80, 112, 126, 241
flexible hours, 9, 22, 39, 63-65, 73, 81, 143, 176, 211, 227, 237, 307-08
from home, xxi, 16, 19, 63-65, 83, 113, 127, 168-70, 178-79, 190, 307-08
full-time, 3-6, 7-11, 21-27, 28-29, 30-33, 34-36, 45-48, 53-56, 57-59, 60-61, 68-72, 76-81, 153-56, 171-72, 213-16, 222, 225, 245
night shifts, 67, 152
part-time, 13-15, 37, 63-65, 83-87, 88-90, 102, 139, 156, 190, 211, 225
reasons to, 20, 34, 41, 43, 62-63, 87, 131, 132, 247
reducing hours, 47, 70, 126-27, 156, 189
taking baby to, 13-15, 16, 29, 35, 39, 41-42, 44, 63-65, 73-75, 102, 104, 116, 129, 143, 179, 189, 191, 208, 211, 220, 237, 250, 253, 307-10
transition from maternity leave, 78, 113, 181, 186, 204, 245, 249
twenty-four-hour shifts, 152

About La Leche League

La Leche League

International

La Leche League International is a nonprofit organization founded in 1956 by seven women who wanted to help other mothers learn about breastfeeding. Today La Leche League is an internationally recognized authority on breastfeeding, with a mother-to-mother network that includes La Leche League Leaders and Groups in countries all over the world. A Professional Advisory Board reviews information on medical issues.

Mothers who contact LLL find answers to their questions on breastfeeding and support from other parents who are committed to being sensitive and responsive to the needs of their babies. Local LLL Groups meet monthly to discuss breastfeeding and related issues. La Leche League Leaders are also available by telephone to offer information and encouragement when women have questions about breastfeeding.

La Leche League International is the world's largest resource for breastfeeding and related information and products. The organization distributes more than three million publications each year, including the classic how-to book, THE WOMANLY ART OF BREASTFEEDING, now in its seventh edition. Look for it in bookstores, or order from La Leche League International by calling 800-LALECHE, 847-519-9585, or 847-519-7730 weekdays between 9 am and 5 pm Central Time. Or fax your order to 847-519-0035 or order online at www.lalecheleague.org/

In Canada, call 800-665-4324, or write to LLLC, 18C Industrial Drive, Box 29, Chesterville, Ontario.